Interdisciplinary perspectives on modern history

Editors
Robert Fogel and Stephan Thernstrom

Mammon and the pursuit of Empire
ABRIDGED EDITION

Mammon and the pursuit of Empire

The economics of British imperialism

ABRIDGED EDITION

LANCE E. DAVIS
and
ROBERT A. HUTTENBACK
with the assistance of Susan Gray Davis

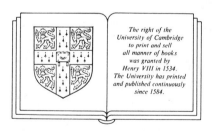

The right of the
University of Cambridge
to print and sell
all manner of books
was granted by
Henry VIII in 1534.
The University has printed
and published continuously
since 1584.

CAMBRIDGE UNIVERSITY PRESS

Cambridge
New York   New Rochelle   Melbourne   Sydney

Published by the Press Syndicate of the University of Cambridge
The Pitt Building, Trumpington Street, Cambridge CB2 1RP
32 East 57th Street, New York, NY 10022, USA
10 Stamford Road, Oakleigh, Melbourne 3166, Australia

First published 1988

Printed in the United States of America

Library of Congress Cataloging-in-Publication Data
Davis, Lance Edwin.
Mammon and the pursuit of empire.
(Interdisciplinary perspectives on modern history)
Includes index.
1. Great Britain – Colonies – Economic conditions.
2. Great Britain – Colonies – Economic policy.
I. Huttenback, Robert A.   II. Title.   III. Series.
HC259.D38   1988   330.9171'241   87–27730

British Library Cataloguing in Publication Data
Davis, Lance E.
Mammon and the pursuit of empire : the
economics of British imperialism. –
Abridged ed. – (Interdisciplinary
perspectives of modern history).
1. Economics – Great Britain – History
2. Imperialism – History   3. Great Britain
– Colonies – Economic conditions
I. Title   II. Huttenback, Robert A.
III. Series
325'.32'0941   HC255

ISBN 0 521 23612 6 hard covers
ISBN 0 521 35723 3 paperback

Contents

Preface

Hard by Westminster, the font of British power, and on the Thames Embankment, stands the statue of Boadicea – Queen of the Iceni – who died in 61 A.D., "after leading her people against the Roman Invader" as the words on the statue's base relate. On the obverse side, another inscription manifests the virtues of the dictum, "that if you can't beat them join them," for it intones in Cowper's words:

> Regions Caesar never knew
> Thy Posterity shall sway.

And indeed they did.

This book deals with an aspect of the remarkable expansion of an island nation into the far reaches of the earth. Its completion has consumed better than a decade and has taken the authors into all manner of unlikely places. Official records are by and large kept in known and accessible archives. Private papers and company records are frequently a different matter. Thus the imperatives of research required work in an abandoned meat-packing plant that was virtually without light and furniture and where even in the middle of summer the temperature numbed the extremities. In one case the relevant documents pertaining to a still-existing firm were under the floor boards of the managing director's office. Vickers provided a penthouse, and the records of Lloyds Bank were kept in the specie room under the constant gaze of television cameras.

Through it all, the authors received the support of a vast multitude of people and institutions and they are duly grateful. Cliometric research is painfully expensive, and the authors are grateful for the financial support received from the National Endowment for the Humanities (Contract No. RO–27612–77–1415), the National Science Foundation (Contract No. SOC–7809080 and BNS–8011494), the California Institute of Technology, the University of California, and the Center for Advanced Study in the Behavioral Sciences.

vii

1 The British Empire and the economics of imperialism: an introductory statement

I. Introduction

Few questions have engendered as much reappraisal, reinterpretation, and recasting as "Western Imperialism" in the late nineteenth century. At this moment, three quarters of the way through the 1980s, a majority of the countries represented in the United Nations blame imperialism for the poverty, illiteracy, and the generally unsettled condition of the Third World. In Britain, the political left still finds in the imperial past some of the explanation for slow economic growth; and Argentina continues to press irredentist land claims to an imperial relic in the South Atlantic. Nor have professional historians ignored the alleged implications of imperialism. Indeed, it is difficult to find a single economic or political historian of modern Britain who has not had something to say about the British imperial experience or the relationship between overseas finance and the climacteric in the domestic economy.

The fact that four generations of historians have been mesmerized by imperialism in theory and practice suggests that the last word may never be written. In this book, no attempt is made to reach a moral judgment on the imperial process, to differentiate between the settling of essentially unpeopled lands and the conquest of populated ones, nor to measure the social or psychic effects that the colonial experiment had on inhabitants of the imperial domain or, for that matter, on the British themselves. Rather, this is essentially a work of economic history, although at times it might better be described as political economy.

The focus is on the five decades preceding the First World War, and on the "profitability of Empire," and the identity of what might be termed the players in the imperial game. To those ends, data have been collected on the direction and volume of the portfolio finance that passed through the London capital market; the rates of return earned by firms operating at home, in the Empire, and abroad; the composition of government receipts and expenditures in those same three loci; the identities of the investors whose main concern was the Empire; and the politicians whose votes shaped the Empire.

1

As a work of economic and political history, the focus of this book is quite narrow. It has been argued that in the late nineteenth century the British Empire was a political instrument designed to increase business profits, and that incomes in the United Kingdom (at least some incomes) reflected these "exploitive" profits. At the same time, the literature argues, preoccupation with Empire diverted capital from the domestic economy, making British industry increasingly noncompetitive and, as a consequence, less profitable. It is our hope that the ensuing pages will help to determine whether or not these propositions are true.

Imperialism is a vast subject and one that touches on any number of very important issues. This work makes no attempt to be exhaustive or even to treat all the important questions that are raised by the nature of the imperial relationship. It deals only with the British Empire. Questions concerning the French or Germans in the nineteenth century or America or Russia in the twentieth are well beyond the scope of this endeavor. The primary focus is on the effect of the imperial system on Britain, not on the Empire or its residents. Dependency theories have an important place in the literature on development, but little effort is made here to assess the impact of the political economic system on indigenous populations or economies. As far as Britain is concerned, the effort is again severely limited. Economics holds the center of this stage, but even that subject is not dealt with comprehensively. No attempt, for example, is made to "explain" the growth or maintenance of an empire. Interest is limited to an examination of the role that profits may have played in motivating the political policies designed to continue and strengthen imperial ties. Once more, the examination of the effects of the Empire does not include an analysis of the long-term impact on British society and its psyche.

In the area of economics, the work examines the rate of return on Empire investment, the flows of capital that underwrote those returns, the costs inherent in maintaining or expanding that Empire, the groups that paid the costs, and those that reaped the economic benefits. The study, however, touches only briefly on the subject of trade, and addresses not at all the effects of induced changes in the terms of trade and the direction and rate of labor migration. Finally, the discussion is limited to the "formal" as opposed to "informal" Empire.

This extended caveat is not meant to minimize either the nature of this undertaking or the importance of questions that fall outside its scope. It is a statement of the limits of the present work and a recognition of the many very important questions that arise from the imperial connection that have not been examined in detail. Finally, it is an admission of the fact that, if it is not impossible, it is at least very difficult to do everything.

II. Imperial theories

Any work that claims to deal with the development of Empire cannot help but be concerned with the motives for grasping and holding an Empire; in the literature, indeed, these motives are legion. There are geopolitical explanations, the *turbulent-frontier* hypothesis, for example, for particular acts of conquest; however, attempts to generalize from these quite idiosyncratic experiences have not proved particularly enlightening. The turbulent-frontier thesis, a product of the Indian experience, conjectures that the government of an ordered area, if surrounded by a zone of disorder, must, for its own protection, conquer the "turbulent" provinces. Thus, empires would tend to advance their frontiers until they reached some great natural barrier or the borders of another stable power.[1] On the subcontinent, the argument runs, the British, through the medium of the East India Company, were willing, so long as the Mogul Empire was strong, to restrict their activities to trading stations like Surat, Bombay, and Madras. With the decline of Mogul power, however, the company was "forced" to raise military forces to quell the anarchy in the surrounding countryside; and political annexation was the inexorable next step. The final northern frontiers of British India rested along the lofty barrier of the Himalayas and the borders of the great Russian and Chinese Empires. In the West, however, less definite geographical and political limits caused constant frontier fluctuations and frequent British interference in the affairs of "turbulent" Afghanistan.

If there is a dearth of truly political theories, the same cannot be said for other conceptual frameworks. In recent years much debate has centered on the concept of *informal empire* and the influence of free trade on the establishment of British hegemony in so many parts of the world. A great deal of the discussion was vitalized by a controversial article entitled simply "Imperialism and Free Trade."[2] It is the classic statement on informal empire; it implies that formal empire or the acquisition of territory was a last resort; and that Her Majesty's Government much preferred to support British business in what were in essence client states.

Social scientists are seldom silent about any issue and also have entered the intellectual fray. They have, for example, found the motivation for imperial expansion rooted both in the precepts of social Darwinism and in the nature of society and the human animal. Joseph Schumpeter claimed that imperialism was a social atavism not prompted by economic reason or national interest, but purely by "the objectless disposition on the part of a state to unlimited forcible expansion," – a tendency encouraged, according to David Landes, by "the disparity of force between Europe and the rest of the world . . . that created the opportunity and possibility of dominion."[3] Or, as Hilaire Belloc put it: "Whatever happens we have got the maxim gun and they have not." Similarly, but at the other end of the sociological scale, humanitarianism rather than atavistic behavior has been advanced as an explanation of imperial adventures. In West and South Africa, it is argued, the British antislavery movement virtually forced the government to acquire unwanted territory in order to protect the native population – that line of analysis could be considered the "bearing of the white man's burden" in the most positive sense. More recently, a somewhat modified version, social imperialism – the marriage of social reform and aggressive expansionism – has been the focus of discussion.

Other theories have rested on individual or social psychology. Examples abound; and those that conclude that irrationality was the driving force behind the advance of empire must be given their place. How else, it is argued, is it possible to explain the strange triumphs of mindless ambition and the insane desire to "paint the map red"? Again, in an age of slow communications, the "man on the spot" could, it has been conjectured, influence events according to his own designs, unrestrained by the wishes of the home government; and empire, thus, might be considered the result of a series of idiosyncratic decisions. Cecil Rhodes in South Africa, Frederick Lugard in East Africa, and Charles Napier in India are all cited as examples of this phenomenon. In each case it is alleged the British government was presented with territory it would rather have done without. One cannot leave this particular discussion without mention of Charles "Chinese" Gordon, who, by stubbornly disobeying orders and thereby bringing about not only his own death but the massacre of the entire garrison of Khartoum, so aroused the passions of the British populace that the government was forced to acquire a province, the conquest of which it had tried studiously to avoid. But irrationality is always hard to stomach as historical explanation. Thus, Robinson and Gallagher re-entered the debate to explain the so-called "scramble for Africa" by using South Africa, Egypt, and the route to India as the necessary touchstones for implied rationality.[4]

Probably the most diverse and numerous group of imperial theorists, however, are the economic determinists. They deprecate the influence of geopolitics, of social and psychological forces, and of the "man on the spot." To them frontier turbulence might have provided opportunities, but it was the potential profits that set the rate of imperial expansion. Men might love war and strive mightily to save their fellows, but it was profit that dictated the battles to be fought and the societies to be rescued. As for the imperial proconsul, he was merely the pawn, albeit often an unwitting one, of the financiers and the bankers at home. To the economic determinists, the expansion of empire was consciously decreed by a small coterie of capitalists associated with the Stock Exchange and the great banks of England. As J. A. Hobson put it in his classic statement:

> In view of the part which the non-economic factors of patriotism, adventure, military enterprise, political ambition, and philanthropy play in imperial expansion, it may appear to impute to financiers so much power as to take a too narrowly economic view of history. And it is true that the motor-power of Imperialism is not chiefly financial: finance is rather the governor of the imperial engine directing the energy and determining its work: it does not constitute the fuel of the engine, nor does it generate the power. Finance manipulates the patriotic forces which politicians, soldiers, philanthropists, and traders generate; the enthusiasm for expansion which issues from these sources, though strong and genuine, is irregular and blind; the financial interest has those qualities of concentration and clear-sighted calculation which are needed to set Imperialism to work. An ambitious statesman, a frontier soldier, an overzealous missionary, a pushing trader, may suggest or even initiate a step of imperial expansion, may assist in educating patriotic public opinion to the urgent need of some fresh advance, but the final determination rests with the financial power.[5]

Lenin put Hobson's agents of the financial power to his own use when he wrote, " . . . all these have given birth to those distinctive characteristics of imperialism which compel us to define it as parasitic or decaying capitalism. . . . "[6]

And Bernard Shaw, probably not aware that he was an economic determinist, wrote as only an Irishman could, that an Englishman,

> . . . is never at a loss for an effective moral attitude. As the great champion of freedom and national independence, he conquers

and annexes half the world, and calls it Colonization. When he wants a new market for his adulterated Manchester goods, he sends a missionary to teach the natives the Gospel of Peace. The natives kill the missionary: he flies to arms in defence of Christianity, fights for it, conquers for it; and takes the market as a reward from heaven. . . . His watchword is always Duty; and he never forgets that the nation which lets its duty get on the opposite side of its interest is lost. . . . [7]

Even the explorer H. M. Stanley joined the ranks. He wrote:

There are forty millions of people beyond the gateway to the Congo, and the cotton spinners of Manchester are waiting to clothe them. Birmingham foundries are gleaming with the red metal that will presently be made into ironwork for them and the trinkets that shall adorn those dusky bosoms, and the ministers of Christ are zealous to bring them, the poor benighted heathen, into the Christian fold. [8]

What a happy marriage of the spiritual and the material!

Many missionaries in Africa, David Livingstone to name one, envisaged a union of commerce and Christianity – "those two pioneers of civilization" – as the salvation of Africa. In 1857, in a speech at Cambridge, Livingstone exhorted his audience "to direct your attention to Africa. I know that in a few years I shall be cut off in that country, which is now open; do not let it be shut again! I go back to Africa to try to make an open path for commerce and Christianity. . . . "[9]

Economic determinists of the Leninist persuasion find the hand of the financier everywhere; even in the acquisition of areas like the humid and inhospitable lands of West Africa that were marginal at best. To them, imperialism was a symptom of the final crisis of capitalism, the time when the competition for protected markets that were needed to absorb the increasing domestic production was at its height. Consequently, they argued, the control of markets, even those that would have been considered worthless in previous decades, became necessary for survival.

Of all the explanations of Empire, none is more compelling than the one concerned with economic gain. Regardless of the weight given to the importance of the various motives for imperial expansion, few doubted that once hegemony was established, economics (if not economic determinism) emerged as an important force in questions of imperial governance and continuity. British authorities were constantly worried about the costs of Empire. As early as 1828 one of the directors of the East India Company wrote the governor-general:

> The expenses of [the Indian establishment] are now under consideration and I trust that they may be greatly reduced without injury to the public interest – and I would fain hope and believe that under your Lordship's administration, if Peace and Tranquillity be preserved in India, the embarrassments in which the Company's affairs are now involved will be removed and that we shall be able to render a good account of our government of India both as respects our Financial and Political administration.[10]

And for the years under study, almost every colonial governor, whether in India, Canada, or West Africa, received similar instructions. Whitehall consistently opposed the assumption of any new responsibilities – at least when they threatened to become a drain on the exchequer. Yet, this attitude does not appear to have prevented lands that were clearly unprofitable, at least in the public sense, from coming under the British flag.

While it would be perfectly appropriate to analyze any or all the political, economic, social, or psychological factors associated with imperialism, this work centers on the economic ones. That choice is dictated not only by the place they hold in the rhetoric on imperialism but by the kind of quantitative data that are available. That type of information is less readily available for questions of politics, society, and psychology. Our question is straightforward: To what degree was Britain's prosperity in the late nineteenth century dependent on its economic and political relations with its Empire?

III. The growth and development of the Empire

While the search for profits may have underlain the growth of Empire, the mechanism that is supposed to have connected the cause with the effect is sometimes obscure. It has been said, with at least the spirit of truth, that the British Empire was founded in a fit of absence of mind, and that the largely *ad hoc* development of the overseas extensions of Britain herself owed more to traditional British pragmatism than to any master plan emanating from the corridors of Whitehall. In 1926, Lord Balfour defined the lengthy imperial experience by contending that the Empire "considered as a whole ... defies classification and bears no resemblance to any other political organization which now exists or has ever yet been tried."[11]

These descriptions do not sit well with the assumption of an underlying economic rationale.

The unique hybrid termed "the Empire" enjoyed at least two incarnations. The so-called first empire was limited largely to North America and the Caribbean. There the desire to rid the home islands of religious and political dissidents combined with a mercantilist doctrine of state to allow settlers to plant the British flag on the Eastern Seaboard of the continent and on the sugar islands of the West Indies. It was an empire of settlement – of colonies peopled by British immigrants – and it died to all intents and purposes with the American Revolution.

The "Second British Empire," whose birth coincided with the death throes of the first, was founded, if for any rational reason, on ambitions for increased foreign trade. Ideally, it was to have been a chain of trading posts protected by strategically placed naval bases. The attainment of wealth through commerce was to have been its purpose, but the profits were not to have been diminished by the expense of colonization and the costs of warfare that had proved so frustrating in North America. Constitutional developments in the Second Empire spawned the "Empire–Commonwealth." From the 1850s onward, both laws and policies led to a dichotomy between the increasingly autonomous colonies of the white settlement and the dependent possessions.

A policy designed to generate revenues without costs may have been rational, but the pattern of development failed to follow the anticipated path. As economists are so fond of arguing: "There is no such thing as a free lunch." The West Indian sugar islands remained of major economic significance; however, profits proved unattainable without administrative expense. An imperial connection with North America was unavoidable because Canada – ironically acquired to protect the lands further south, now gone – was still part of the Empire. In the Southern Hemisphere, Australia and New Zealand were rediscovered and occupied, and the population explosion of the nineteenth century peopled these new possessions with British immigrants. In India, the stable structure of the Mogul Empire, under whose aegis the East India Company had once securely conducted business, had collapsed, and that development created a vacuum into which the British felt themselves forced to move. Thus, the second Empire was no less free of cost than the first – the administration and protection of Canada, Australia, New Zealand, and the other lands all demanded the expenditure of resources.

Once committed, however reluctantly and unwillingly, questions of communication and access could not be avoided by the home authorities and their servants in the field. Consequently, the British ship of state set sail on a whole new troubled sea when the Cape of Good Hope was wrested from the Dutch in 1814. The conquest was designed to facilitate the journey to India; and similar considerations, this time to protect the Suez Canal route to the east, led to the establishment of British control in Egypt. Nor, as it turned out, was British hegemony in Africa limited to the Cape and Egypt. Over the course of the nineteenth century, a variety of factors prompted continued expansion throughout the continent – into East, West, and Central Africa and into the Sudan. Inadvertence, greed, humanitarianism, personal ambition, missionary zeal, fear of foreign intervention, and that curious phenomenon, "prestige imperialism," which whetted the British appetite for expansion toward the end of the century – all may have played their part. In addition to new possessions in Africa, the nineteenth century saw Northwest India; Burma; the Malayan archipelago; Brunei, Sarawak, and Hong Kong; Cyprus; Fiji, Tonga, and the islands of the Western Pacific Group; Mauritius, the Seychelles, and, to all intents and purposes, Egypt coming under the Crown (see Appendixes 1.1, 1.2, and 1.3).

Commercial companies, religious dissidents, planters, and adventurers were at least as important in extending the bounds of Empire as the soldiers and sailors of the monarch and all were probably more important than the politicians who served Her Majesty. Indeed until the third quarter of the nineteenth century the whole enterprise prompted either ennui or outright hostility in Britain itself. As late as 1865 Sir Charles Adderley, the British colonial reformer and Parliament's most eloquent anti-imperial spokesman, had asserted in the House that the four British possessions on the West Coast of Africa wasted a million pounds a year. The attempt to create a "civilized" Negro community in Sierra Leone, he claimed, had failed; the Gold Coast had involved the British government in several unjustifiable wars; and the trade of Gambia and Lagos was at best negligible.[12] The Committee on West African Affairs, a Parliamentary select committee, created in response to Adderley's protest, recommended:

> All further extension of territory or assumption of government, or new treaties offering protection to native tribes, would be inexpedient. . . . The object of our policy should be to encourage in the natives the exercise of those qualities which may render it possible for us more and more to transfer to them the adminis-

tration of all the governments, with a view to our ultimate withdrawal from all, except probably Sierra Leone.[13]

By 1866, the Colonial Secretary, Edward Cardwell, was able to report
that the West African establishments had been drastically reduced.[14]

It was only six years later that Disraeli rose in London's Great
Crystal Palace to attack the anti-imperial bias of Gladstone's Liberal
Party. He urged his listeners to take pride in an Empire "which may
become the source of incalculable strength and happiness to this
land." And he issued a stentorian challenge to his audience.

> Will [you], [he asked] be content to be a comfortable England,
> modeled and moulded upon Continental principles and meeting
> in due course an inevitable fate, or . . . will [you] be a great coun-
> try, an Imperial country, a country where your sons, when they
> rise, rise to paramount positions, and obtain not merely the es-
> teem of their countrymen, but the respect of the world.[15]

Disraeli's words did not fall on deaf ears. The Conservative Party
consciously used empire as an election issue and was swept into
power on a wave of votes from the newly enfranchised urban working class to whom the vicarious pleasure of ruling an Empire upon
which the sun never set appeared to offset a more logical loyalty to
the Liberals.

Even then, however, public enthusiasm was usually not matched
by official elation. The Treasury continued to rail against the costs
of Empire, and debates on imperial, and particularly Indian, issues
were calculated to empty the halls of Parliament. The growth of
colonial responsibilities somehow ran counter to the burgeoning of
liberalism and humanitarianism in Britain, and a solution to that
dilemma required the development of a philosophical foundation
and an administrative doctrine in keeping with the prevailing climate
of public opinion – no easy matter.

The period of high imperialism lasted hardly more than two and
a half decades. It began at the Crystal Palace and ended at Mafeking.
The Boer War, fought against a gallant and badly outnumbered foe
and for gold rather than virtue, seemed to many to strip away whatever aura of moral rectitude had become attached to the concept of
Empire. Even worse, the costs of imperial glory rose. During this
brief span of years the nation entered into an intense colonial rivalry
with both the French and the Germans, and more than once a major
war was only narrowly averted. It is a testimony to the degree to
which imperialism had developed a mindless drive of its own that
far more territory was added to the British Empire during the administration of the anti-imperialist Gladstone than during the govern-

ment of the expansionist Disraeli.[16] The Liberals added territory at the rate of 87,000 square miles per year in contrast to the Conservatives' paltry 5,300.

The new Empire was far from homogeneous. On the one hand there were the colonies of white settlement: Canada, the Australian colonies, New Zealand, and, in some sense, South Africa. On the other, there were India and the colonies of the "dependent empire"; predominantly nonwhite, centered in Asia, but including, by the end of the century, large tracts of Africa as well.[17] The latter group could in addition to India again be divided into colonies, protectorates, and protected states. India, of course, fell under the administrative cognizance of the India Office, with its employees in both London and the subcontinent. In India the Governor General, the direct representative of Her Majesty and her government, held sway; but his decisions were often tempered by pressure from his department heads and their supporting bureaucracies as well as from any number of special interest groups who acted through the India Council. Colonies, or Crown Colonies, as they came to be known, developed a form of government with a powerful governor advised by an appointed executive council and working with, but not responsible to, a legislative council. The proportion of elected to "official" members on that council varied. In most colonies, the council gradually developed into a representative legislative assembly that acted either unicamerally or as the lower house in a bicameral legislature. In the latter case the executive council acted as the upper body.

That the dependent Empire, and particularly India, should remain under the close scrutiny of Whitehall was never questioned – at least in Britain – until well into the twentieth century. Indeed it had been the intention of the authorities to pursue the same philosophy in those lands largely peopled by whites as well. It was assumed that the loss of the American colonies had been due to the "benign neglect" that had allowed the colonists to believe they possessed rights and privileges that were actually vested in the Crown and Parliament. Consequently, most policy makers agreed with William Knox, a former undersecretary in the Colonial Department, when he argued, "It was better to have no colonies at all than not to have them subservient to the maritime strength and commercial interests of Great Britain."[18] On the basis of this premise, Canada, the only remaining "white" colony of significance, was kept under a tight rein in the years following the American Revolution.

The revolts that broke out in that colony in 1837 caused a shock wave to run through the British body politic. Inattention had brought on one revolution; and, now, close control had, seemingly, produced the same result. This dilemma was solved by an estimably pragmatic strategem: *responsible government*. As propounded by Lord Durham in his report of 1839, it was simplicity itself.

> Every purpose of popular control might be combined with every advantage of vesting the immediate choice of advisers in the Crown were the Colonial Governor to be instructed to secure the cooperation of the Assembly in his policy, by entrusting its administration to such men as could command a majority; and if he were given to understand that he need count on no aid from home in any difference with the Assembly, that should not directly involve the relations between the mother country and the Colony. . . . [19]

Essentially, the formula implied colonial self-government; and, although Durham attempted to reserve British control over the sale of public lands, tariffs, and foreign affairs, the first two limitations went by the boards immediately and the last as soon as the colony found it in its best interests.

Responsible government was established in Canada in 1847, and the institution quickly spread to the other colonies of white settlement. If the goal of the British Government was colonial self-sufficiency, responsible government would seem to have been the ideal solution. Increased autonomy, however, allowed colonial legislatures to reject British requests for financial support in what London assumed was a shared responsibility – the administration and defense of the Empire. The more affluent parts of the dependent Empire were in a somewhat less happy position; but, ultimately, it was the British taxpayers, and to a lesser extent those of India, Ceylon, Singapore, and Hong Kong, who shouldered most of the burden.

The reluctance of Britain to develop the administrative mechanisms needed to preside over an Empire is perhaps best captured by the history of the physical premises from whence imperial authority flowed. Until the third quarter of the nineteenth century, the Colonial Office was located at 14 Downing Street and a single house further west. The buildings were gloomy and so damp that the basements where many of the staff worked had to be pumped out daily. To help prevent the buildings from collapsing, records were packed into the walls and foundations; and fires had to be kept burning twenty-four hours a day to stop even the current files from dissolving. Sound passed unimpeded through the walls, and by the

1860s ominous groanings and frequent tremors led to the fear that despite all efforts the edifices would soon be reduced to heaps of rubble.

The administrative structure of the Colonial Office matched its architectural history. In 1801 the position of Secretary of State for War and Colonies was created, and responsibility for imperial affairs was transferred from the home office. The concerns of the secretary of state were dominated by military matters and the marriage of war and colonies was not a happy one. The situation was, however, somewhat improved in 1806 when an extra undersecretary for military affairs was appointed; and the original appointee was left free to devote his energies to colonial matters. Six years later the Colonial Office was recognized as a distinct unit, although technically certain responsibilities associated with military operations remained with it until 1854.

From 1825, the table of organization of the Colonial Office called for, in addition to the secretary of state and the Parliamentary undersecretary, a permanent undersecretary, a chief clerk, 17 clerks, a counsel, a librarian and his assistant, a registrar and his assistant, a private secretary for the secretary of state, a précis writer, 2 office keepers, 2 porters, and a housekeeper – for a total of 31. As late as 1849, however, the staff actually numbered but 23, and even as late as 1907, the total was only 125. Reforms in 1850 and 1870 altered the staffing schedule; but the division of work into a general and four geographical departments – the North American, the West Indian, the Australian, and the African and Mediterranean – remained essentially unaltered. The first decade of the twentieth century saw one further refinement: the bifurcation of the Colonial Office into a Crown Colonies and a Dominions Division.[20]

Ancillary administrative agencies associated with the Colonial Office included the Land and Emigration Board and the Crown Agents. Between 1840 and 1878 the former agency was charged with administering the sale of Crown lands and assisting in the administration of emigration policies. The latter office grew out of an 1858 decision that the numerous and largely independent Agents General of the Crown Colonies, who as Colonial Office appointees represented individual colonies in business, finance, and purchasing, were to be reconstituted as a joint body known as the Crown Agents for the Colonies. With the rise of the self-governing colonies, and as the more autonomous entities were encouraged to appoint their own representatives, the Crown Agents' central concern became the Crown Colonies.

In the field the governor was the executive arm of the Colonial Office. In the colonies of the dependent Empire, though often assisted by advisory and protolegislative councils, his powers were at times close to absolute; however, the degree of his primacy varied from colony to colony. In those colonies with responsible government, the governor represented his imperial masters in London and acted as a ceremonial head of state, but he was subject to the policies developed by his ministers.

In terms of numbers, the British Empire was run by very few people. It was hardly the great system of outdoor relief for the upper classes suggested by George Cornwall Lewis. For example, the Colonial Office list for 1892 numbers about 2,400; and the total thirty years previously had been less than 1,000. Included were not only the mighty but second clerks, second class inspectors, cashiers, cadets, a subdistributer of stamps, a compiler of labor ordinances, the interpreter to the resident magistrate in Durban, a "landing waiter" in Antigua, bishops, minor prelates, some military officers, and a considerable number of retired personnel. In addition, virtually all elected and appointed indigenous officials of the colonial governments were included – the mayors of small towns and functionaries of provincial county halls – as well as living persons who had at some time been associated with the colonial service but who no longer were. The India Office list for 1896 included some 3,000 persons (up from 2,000 a decade earlier). They were roughly comparable in status to those on the Colonial Office list, and many of them were Indian. Thus, the British Empire at the apogee of its existence was managed by less than 6,000 souls! Nor is the story of the effect of the Empire on employment much altered if the 75,000 odd troops stationed in India and the 45,000 serving in the colonies are added to the total. Whatever can be said about the financial burden of Empire, that institution would seem to have provided a great deal of ego enhancement with few major additions to the civil list.

India was the single most visible jewel in the imperial crown. It was an empire in itself and far too massive and complex an undertaking ever to fall under the aegis of the Colonial Office. Until 1858, the British dominions in India were governed through the fiat of the East India Company, its directors, and "secret committee," although the real power lay with the Board of Control for India, an organ of the British government. The company's chief administrative officer in India was the governor-general. At the end of the Mutiny, the East India Company's charter was revoked; and the subcontinent came directly under the Crown. The India Office became the new governing agency in Britain; and through the governor-general, soon to be also a viceroy, it administered British India directly and the Princely States indirectly. The Secretary of State for India assumed the duties previously carried out by the chairman of the board of control; and, because of the importance of the position, the secretary was added to the cabinet. He was advised by a Council, and certain of his decisions had to be made "in Council."

The organization of the India Office was similar to that of the Colonial Office. The secretary was assisted by a permanent and a parliamentary undersecretary and by an assistant secretary who also served also as clerk of the Council. Most of the India Office's departments corresponded to committees of the original Company's Council (finance, political, military, revenue and statistics, judicial, and public works and stores); and each was staffed by a secretary, an assistant-secretary, and several clerks. There was also a director-general of the stores department, an accountant general, a registrar, superintendent of records, director of funds, legal advisor, librarian, and several others. An auditor was attached to the office, and his appointment had to be countersigned by the Chancellor of the Exchequer.

India was the Treasury's ideal. It conducted its affairs as that agency thought a British dependency should. Since the subcontinent had no effective form of self-government, it was legally at the mercy of whatever policies its British governors and the authorities in Whitehall might devise. India underwrote all of its own administrative costs. There were no occasions, as in other dependent possessions, when a bare treasure chamber necessitated a British subsidy. So sui generis was India's position within the British Empire that even the heart of the devoutest "Little Englander" – that dedicated opponent of virtually all things imperial – was inclined to beat a little faster at the thought of the Union Jack flying over the battlements of Fort St. George, Fort St. David, or one of the subcontinent's other bastions of Empire.

India's unique structure afforded both the government of India and the India Office considerable independence from the Treasury. The Colonial Office was not so fortunate but, once established, its functionaries, like bureaucrats everywhere, moved to capture what they judged to be their rightful domain. The result was a series of administrative wars fought not only with the Treasury but also with Customs, the Post Office, and the Board of Ordinance – offices that in 1858 still maintained their own officials in the colonies. Eventually, most of these jurisdictional problems were solved. The Treasury, most ancient and powerful of government agencies, however, proved a stubborn exception. Organized into a finance and four "control" divisions, it exerted in theory virtually absolute power over British expenditures both foreign and domestic. It was this claim to omnipotence in the financial sphere that led to conflict with many government offices, but particularly with the Colonial Office. In fact, Treasury control was less all-encompassing than that agency tried to assume, and the Colonial Office was in time able to establish some degree of independence from its Argus-eyed rival.

As Gladstone pointed out when he was first Lord of the Treasury and Chancellor of the Exchequer: "We are only one department side by side with others, with very limited powers; it is more after all by moral suasion . . . that our influence is exercised, than by any large power we have."[21] The Treasury was not empowered to question departmental policy, only the financial arrangements supporting that policy; but it would be illusory to think that ensuring the most efficient and economical method of implementing a policy decision did not affect policy itself.

When all was said and done, the Treasury's chief power lay in obstruction. One minister and certainly a combination of several could usually frustrate the exchequer, but success required both energy and coordination. Robert Kubicek, a student of the British bureaucracy, explained the Treasury's real source of power as follows:

> The Treasury's role in control of expenditure was presumably subsidiary to that of Parliament. Yet, departmental estimates could not be submitted to the political arena until approved by one of the Treasury's control divisions. The spending departments had to accept the Treasury's decisions on proposed new expenditures, subject only to reversal by the cabinet. An auxiliary branch, the comptroller and auditor-general's department, examined the manner in which the funds allocated were spent.[22]

Imperial expenditures were less easily controlled by the Treasury than domestic ones. Colonies could not be allowed to go bankrupt, and the financial status of most Crown Colonies was usually precarious. They were dependent on an uncertain local revenue that was frequently not only insufficient to pay the governor's salary but also allowed no contingency for emergencies. As a result, British support was often required. In case of financial distress, the usual instrument of imperial assistance was the grant-in-aid. This subvention was awarded either to supplement a colony's general revenue or for some specific purpose. Grants-in-aid were an exception to the general rule that imperial funds could only be spent on items enumerated in Parliamentary votes and that all accounts had to be balanced by year's end.

For colonies with responsible government, imperially guaranteed loans rather than grants-in-aid were the key to development. The Cabinet and Parliament alone held the power to undertake an imperial guarantee, and the Treasury's role was largely a supervisory one limited to overseeing colonial compliance with the regulations regarding the establishment of a sinking fund and the rules for repayment.

Until the last third of the nineteenth century, the Treasury theoretically controlled the revenue and expenditure of Crown Colonies. Annual estimates were prepared by departmental officers in the colony and were approved successively by the colonial financial officers, the governor (with the advice of the Executive and Legislative Councils), and the Treasury. Only then was the estimate reported to Parliament. In theory no expenditure was to be incurred without prior Treasury approval.

As the power of the Colonial Office increased, fewer Parliamentary returns were demanded from the colonies; and Treasury control decreased. By 1868, while the Treasury supervised the accounts of eighteen Crown Colonies, eighteen others fell under the gaze of the Colonial Office alone. Whether a colony came under Treasury or Colonial Office control was largely a matter of historical accident. The audit of the accounts of all colonies was left by law to the discretion of the Treasury, but that agency in turn agreed, so long as no imperial (i.e., British) monies were involved, to delegate the authority to the Colonial Office. Treasury audit of Crown Colony accounts was thus confined to those colonies receiving grants-in-aid. Even then, however, colonies with grants designated for specific purposes – governor's salary, colonial steamers, mail service, or what have you – needed only to forward a yearly abstract for purpose of examination.[23] Treasury control, after March 1870, was limited to matters of imperial concern. No subject dealing with Crown Colonies was to be referred to the Treasury "except such as would be equally referred in Colonies of equal importance which possess representative institutions."[24]

At the same time, however, the Treasury was still charged with supervising the annual estimates, particularly any increases in the civil establishment, of Crown Colonies receiving grants-in-aid in support of their general revenues. In the case of those colonies that had not received grants in support of general revenues but that owed money to the Home Government, had received aid in the form of a guaranteed loan, or had been awarded a specific grant-in-aid, the Colonial Office had only to furnish the Treasury with an annual statement of revenue, expenditure, and public debt.

Despite the increased colonial and Colonial Office independence, no item seemed too minute to escape the Treasury's gimlet-eyed functionaries, whether in the estimates, later requests for augmentations, or in the actual record of expenditures. It took some eight years for the Treasury to accept an accommodation regarding the accounts of Sir Theophilus Shepstone, who had led an expedition into the Transvaal in 1877. Shepstone had had the temerity to charge his official account for presents given to native chiefs: "My Lords can only express their astonishment," an aroused Treasury wrote to the Colonial Office, "that any officer should have imagined that coats, hairbrushes and fishing guards, and the like would be passed without explanation, nor can they admit the explanation now offered to be satisfactory."[25] When in 1885 the Transvaal duly paid the British government £7,546–17–6 due on a loan, the Treasury promptly complained (and in error) that the payment was four pence short!! "My Lords request," the Treasury archly wrote the Colonial Office, "that the High Commissioner in South Africa might be instructed to call upon the Transvaal Government to apply this additional sum of 4d on the next occasion of payment."[26]

Although the engraving of a public seal for the government of British Guiana was in time sanctioned, the Treasury still wished to determine why the estimates for the screw press, copper counters, and box were £5–5 more than had previously been paid by St. Kitts and Nevis. With estimable moral rectitude, the Treasury concluded: " . . . My Lords are not prepared to sanction new items which cannot be warranted by recent precedent, and would ask an explanation for the increase of charges to which they refer."[27] Nor, despite the history of British humanitarianism, did the Treasury ever sanction the payment of fifteen shillings and two pence to Gambia " . . . on account of the maintenance of a liberated African woman."[28] But the Treasury was not always small-minded. In 1893, for example, it agreed to the appropriation of an additional £5 per month to hire an extra night guard for the Mafeking jail:

> The description given in the enclosure to your letter of the escape from a cell in which five men were confined of two prisoners, one of whom had two wooden legs, by making a hole through

or under a 14 inch brick cell wall, with the handle of a bucket, convinces My Lords that a single Gaoler cannot keep the prisoners under proper supervision at night without assistance.[29]

Perhaps the Treasury's obdurate determination to emerge triumphant on matters of minutiae was rooted in the almost constant frustration it encountered on questions of greater moment. The appropriate level of a colony's military contribution was a source of continuous dispute, and it all too often produced a conflict between the Treasury and the Colonial Office at home and between Her Majesty's government and the colony abroad. In the Treasury's eyes, colonial contributions were always too low. When hostilities – whether local, and hence exclusively a colonial responsibility, or partly of imperial significance – erupted, the colonies seemed never to pay their appropriate share. In the end the Treasury was nearly always forced to acquiesce in settlements with which it was totally out of sympathy. "... Colonies are under a natural temptation," the Lords of the Treasury averred, "to prefer that the pacification of their native neighbours should be accomplished by means of an armed expedition at the cost of the mother country, rather than by measures of conciliation at the expense of the colony...."[30]

Nor was colonial (not to mention Colonial Office) recalcitrance in the Treasury's eyes limited to the military sphere. The same violations of "accepted imperial financial dogma" occurred on the civil stage as well. In January 1888, for example, the Treasury wrote the Colonial Office:

> Their Lordships will view with regret the refusal of the Colony of Vancouver Island to pay back advances made in 1859–65 for lighthouses on the shore of the Straits of Juan de Fuca. They are willing to write off the debt in actuality but they want to keep it on record as a warning to the Treasury that actual security must be taken from the government of dependencies for the repayment of a loan, since the instance now under consideration shows that a promise to pay may not be observed.[31]

If the Treasury rarely carried the day on arguments involving military or civil expenditures, it also received little support in its attempts to reduce the salaries of colonial officials in times of economic depression. At one point, however, Fiji at least acted in the recommended manner, and the Treasury was able to write approvingly:

> The financial history of Fiji affords a striking illustration, on the one hand, of the danger of increasing establishments on the faith

of continuing prosperity, and, on the other, as my Lords are happy to add, of the success with which circumstances of great depression can be met by resolute self-denial and a spirit of independence.

Furthermore, when and if it became possible to restore the former salary levels, the Treasury recommended it should be made clear that the continuance of the higher rate was

> ... dependent on the prosperity of the colony, and no restoration should be permitted until the whole of the floating debt has been redeemed and a scheme has been set on foot for repaying the imperial loan.[32]

To its credit the Treasury did manage to keep Indian and colonial administrative expenses below those of comparable entities throughout the world. As Chart 1.1 indicates, while the responsibly governed colonies, over which the Treasury exercised almost no control, spent on administration at about the same rate as a typical foreign developed country or of Great Britain itself, the dependent colonies spent at only four-fifths the level of a typical underdeveloped country; and the level of those expenditures in India stood in about that same proportion in relation to the administrative expenditures of the Princely States.

To assume that the Colonial Office judged the Treasury to be nothing more than an unattractive nuisance would be a mistake. It was rarely averse to using supposed Treasury opposition as the pretext for disallowing certain items in the colonial estimates. In 1891, Charles Lucas, then private secretary to the permanent undersecretary in the Colonial Office, wrote on the question of the Ceylon military contribution:

> Of late, as far as I can judge, the leading people in the colony have been more and more regarding [the Colonial Office] as their friend, and it is very important to maintain such a feeling. I incline to think less harm would be done in the long run if a larger increase were exacted, after it had been made patent that the Colonial Office had made its stand and been overborne. ...[33]

Interagency rivalry in Britain itself was only one of the complexities underlying imperial governance. Of greater importance was the relationship between the mother country and her often unruly offspring. Although most of the colonies of the dependent Empire enjoyed legislative institutions, they tended to be advisory; and the governor and the Colonial Office remained very much in control.

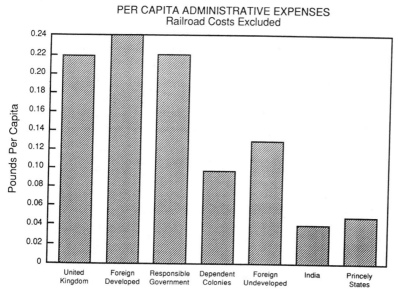

PER CAPITA ADMINISTRATIVE EXPENSES
Railroad Costs Excluded

Chart 1.1

In those possessions blessed with responsible government, however, the governor was at best a constitutional monarch. Technically, he enjoyed a veto over colonial legislation or the power to refer it to London "for the signification of Her Majesty's pleasure"; however, these rights were invoked but rarely and then usually with disastrous results. For all intents and purposes the colonies with responsible government acted without regard to British strictures or sensibilities on matters of economic interest. Despite their de facto independence, or perhaps because of it, the knowledge that the British government retained some hypothetical de jure powers over colonial legislation caused considerable resentment and a sense of some subservience in the dominions. Considering the reality of the situation, however, one might wonder how much of those expressed feelings should be put down to political posturing.

To prevent the development of stress and to relieve these feelings of frustration and inferiority, the British in 1887 established a new institution. As a part of the celebration of Queen Victoria's Golden Jubilee, the British government invited delegates from the Crown Colonies and Dominions to London for a political conference. This assemblage was the first of the Colonial (later Imperial) Conferences. Those conferences (soon limited to the Dominions alone) provided an institutional mechanism for introducing structural change into the political matrix and became in many ways the key to the survival of the Empire. Of all the areas of common concern, foreign affairs remained most directly under the control of the British government. To a large extent this situation was not the product of British policy but of the assumption in the Dominions that, since they shouldered virtually none of the costs of defense, nonconsultation meant noninvolvement. World War I was to prove how very wrong they had been, and that war brought an end to the British "monopoly."

This sketch then, in brief, captures the development of the administrative structure that supported the British Empire as it evolved in the nineteenth century, and it outlines the institutions that shaped both economic and political behavior. They established the context of Empire and the environment in which the business and political communities met, competed, and cooperated to produce what can be termed the "British Imperial Experience."

IV. The profitability of Empire

This study of the economics of Empire begins with an examination of the long-term finance that flowed through the London capital market. Those estimates are to be used to assess the importance of the Empire to British savers and investors and to locate areas and industries of British financial penetration. With the levels of investment in hand, the private profits earned on this investment are the next subject of investigation. That analysis focuses not only on the overall rate of return but attempts also to specify the particular industries that proved most profitable.

Since profits are not unrelated to government expenditures, the level of such expenditures that can be viewed as business supporting becomes the next subject of concern. A general note: Since nothing can be successfully examined in isolation, throughout this study business and fiscal behavior in the United Kingdom and in the colonies with responsible government is analyzed against the background of a set of foreign developed countries; behavior of the dependent colonies, against the record of a group of foreign underdeveloped countries; and Indian activities against both that latter set of countries and against that of the Indian Princely States.

Following the examination of government spending, the study turns to the question of the cost of Empire. Both the defense and the financial and administrative components of the imperial subsidy are examined in detail. Private profits and social costs are two of the five major pieces of the puzzle. The third is put in place with an examination of the ownership of imperial enterprise; those owners were, after all, the winners in the imperial game. The fourth – a study of the losers – rests on an examination of the incidence of the taxes on the British taxpayers that paid the imperial bills. Finally, an attempt is made to uncover the mechanism of the possible swindle through an examination of British political institutions in the late nineteenth century.

APPENDIX 1.1

THE GROWTH OF EMPIRE

Colony Name	Date Added*	In Empire 1860	Change 1860-69	Change 1870-79	Change 1880-89	Change 1890-99	Change 1900-09	Dates for Which Financial Records Are Included From	To
		(1,000s of Square Miles)							
A. Responsible Government									
1. Australia	1901	(2,974.6)							
a. New South Wales(1)		310.4						1860	1902
b. Queensland(1)		670.5						1860	1902
c. South Australia(1)		380.1						1860	1902
d. South Australia(2)		523.6						1887	1902
(Northern Territory)									
e. Tasmania(1)		26.2						1860	1902
f. Victoria(1)		87.9						1860	1902
g. Western Australia(1)		975.9						1860	1902
2. Canada	1867	(3,894.7)						1867	1913
a. Nova Scotia(3)		21.4							
b. New Brunswick(3)		28.0							
c. Ontario(3)		260.9							
d. Quebec(3)		351.9							
e. Manitoba(5)		238.7							
f. British Columbia(6)		357.6							
g. Prince Edward Island(7)		2.2							
h. Alberta(8)		253.5							
i. Saskatchewan(8)		250.7							
j. Yukon		207.1							
k. Northwest Territory(4)		1,922.7							
3. Newfoundland		(162.7)							
a. Newfoundland		42.7							
b. Labrador		120.0							
4. New Zealand		103.3							
5. Union of South Africa	1910	(473.2)						1911	1912
a. Cape Colony		277.0						1860	1910
b. Natal		35.4						1860	1910
c. Orange River	1900						50.4	1902	1910
d. Transvaal	1902						110.4	1903	1910

(1,000's of Square Miles)

Colony Name	Date Added	In Empire 1860	Change 1860-69	Change 1870-79	Change 1880-89	Change 1890-99	Change 1900-09	Dates for Which Financial Records Are Included From	To
B. India									
a. British India (including Burma)		1,097.8		53.8	87.4		38.7	1860	1913
b. Princely States		675.3		78.0	68.7			1860	1913
C. Dependent Colonies									
1. Asia									
a. Ceylon		25.3						1860	1912
b. Straits Settlements		1.6						1864	1912
c. Labuan		0.0						1860	1906
d. Hong Kong		0.4						1860	1912
e. Federated Malay States									
(1) Perak	1896			7.9				1895	1912
(2) Selangor	1874			3.2				1882	1894
(3) Sungei-Ujong	1874			2.6				1883	1894
(4) Pahang	1875-76				14.0			1891	1895
(5) Negri-Sembilan	1887							1891	1894
f. North Borneo	1874-89				31.1			1883	1894
g. Brunei	1881				2.6			1891	1912
h. Sarawak	1888				42.0			1896	1912
i. Unfederated Malay States	1888								
(1) Kelantan	1909						5.0		
(2) Trenggam	1909						6.0		
(3) Kedah	1909						3.2		
(4) Perlis	1909						.3		
(5) Johore	1885								
j. Weihei	1898					.3			
2. Pacific									
a. Fiji	1874			7.4				1876	1912
b. British New Guinea	1884				90.5			1889	1912
c. British Solomon Islands	1893					14.6		1898	1913
d. Gilbert & Ellice Isle	1896-99					.2		1896	1913
e. Tonga	1900						.4	1905	1912

25

Colony Name	Date Added	In Empire 1860	Change 1860-69	Change 1870-79	Change 1880-89	Change 1890-99	Change 1900-09	Dates for Which Financial Records Are Included From	To
3. Africa									
a. Ascension & St. Helena		.1						1860	1912
b. Gambia		4.0						1860	1912
c. Sierra Leone		30.0						1860	1912
d. Gold Coast		91.7						1860	1912
e. Lagos	1861		28.6					1868	1906
f. Basutoland	1868		11.7					1877	1913
g. Egypt	1882				400.0			1882	1913
h. Somali Coast Protect.	1884				68.0			1898	1913
i. Bechuanaland	1885				275.0			1897	1913
j. Niger Coast & So.Nigeria	1885				91.9			1868	1912
k. Northern Nigeria	1885				276.0			1901	1913
l. Zanzibar	1890					1.0		1892	1912
m. Southern Rhodesia	1890					37.9		1905	1912
n. Nyasaland	1891					291.0		1904	1912
o. Northern Rhodesia	1893					148.6		1895	1913
p. Uganda	1893					110.3		1896	1913
q. Kenya (Br. East Africa)	1895					245.1			
r. Sudan	1898					1,014.6	6.7	1905	1913
s. Swaziland	1903								
4. Indian Ocean									
a. Aden (inc Perim & Socotra)		10.4						1860	1912
b. Mauritius		.8						1886	1912
c. Seychelles		.2							
5. Europe									
a. Gibralter		.0						1860	1913
b. Malta		.1						1860	1913
c. Ionian Islands		.7	-.7					1860	1863
d. Cyprus	1878			3.6				1879	1913

26

		(1,000's of Square Miles)						Dates for Which Financial Records Are Included	
Colony Name	Date Added	In Empire 1860	Change 1860–69	Change 1870–79	Change 1880–89	Change 1890–99	Change 1900–09	From	To
6. Caribbean and South America									
a. Antigua		.2						1867	1913
b. Bahamas		4.4						1860	1913
c. Barbados		.2						1860	1912
d. Bermuda		.0						1860	1912
e. British Guinea		89.5						1860	1912
f. British Honduras		8.6						1860	1913
g. British Virgin Islands		.1						1860	1913
h. Dominica		.3						1860	1913
i. Falkland Islands		4.6						1860	1913
j. Grenada		.1						1860	1913
k. Jamaica		4.5						1860	1913
l. Montserrat		.0						1860	1913
m. St. Kitts-Nevis-Anguilla		.2						1860	1913
n. St. Lucia		.2						1860	1913
o. St. Vincent		.2						1860	1913
p. Tabago		.1						1860	1913
q. Trinidad		1.9						1860	1913
r. Turks Island		.2						1860	1912
s. Virgin Islands		.1						1860	1913

	In Empire 1860	Change 1860–69	Change 1870–79	Change 1880–89	Change 1890–99	Change 1900–09	From
Total Responsible Government	7,447.1					160.4	7,608.1
Total India	1,773.1		131.8	156.1		38.7	2,099.7
Total Dependent Colonies	280.7	39.6	24.7	940.1	1,863.6	21.6	3,170.3
Total	9,501.5	39.6	156.5	1,096.2	1,863.6	220.7	12,878.1
% Change		0.4	1.6	11.3	16.6	1.7	35.5

*In the case of colonies with responsible government, the date when this status was attained.

(1) a+b+c+e+f+g into Commonwealth 1901
(2) Into Commonwealth 1911
(3) Into Dominion of Canada 1867
(4) Into Dominion of Canada 1869
(5) Into Dominion of Canada 1870
(6) Into Dominion of Canada 1871
(7) Into Dominion of Canada 1873
(8) Into Dominion of Canada 1905

27

APPENDIX 1.2

EMPIRE POPULATION BY STATUS

	UK	RG	DC	India	Dependent Colonies	Overseas Empire	Total	UK	RG	DC	India	Dependent Empire
	(in 1,000s)							(Percents)				
1862	29,245	5,434	3,647	139,360	143,007	148,441	177,686	16.5	3.1	2.1	78.4	80.5
67	30,409	5,961	4,319	148,674	152,993	188,954	189,363	16.1	3.1	2.3	78.5	80.8
1872	31,874	7,018	5,399	160,788	166,187	173,205	205,079	15.5	3.4	2.6	78.4	81.0
77	33,576	7,834	6,167	177,702	183,869	191,703	225,279	14.9	3.5	2.7	78.9	81.6
1882	35,206	8,801	13,800	209,017	222,822	231,623	266,824	13.2	3.3	5.2	78.3	83.5
87	36,598	9,795	15,342	260,741	276,083	285,878	322,476	11.3	3.0	4.8	80.9	85.6
1892	38,134	10,876	18,337	288,683	307,020	317,896	356,030	10.7	3.1	5.2	81.1	86.2
97	39,937	12,258	25,993	292,207	318,200	330,458	370,395	10.8	3.3	7.0	78.9	85.9
1902	41,483	14,331	39,405	296,453	335,858	350,189	391,672	10.6	3.7	10.1	75.7	85.7
07	43,737	21,877	46,258	301,795	348,043	369,930	413,667	10.6	5.3	11.2	73.0	84.1
1912	45,436	24,186	51,852	322,441	374,293	398,479	443,915	10.2	5.4	11.7	72.6	84.3

UK: United Kingdom
RG: Responsible Government
DG: Dependent Colonies

NOTE: Anglo Egyptian Sudan is not included. If it were the 1902 Dependent Empire figure would be
increased to about 2,000,000; the 1907 figure by about 2,500,000; and the 1912 by about 3,000,000.

APPENDIX 1.3

Foreign Countries and Indian Princely States
Data From Which for the Years Indicated are Used in this Study

COUNTRIES	YEARS
Foreign Developed	
Austria-Hungary	1860-1912
Belgium	1860-1914
Denmark	1860-1913
France	1860-1912
Germany	1871-1912
Italy	1864-1913
Japan	1900-1913
Netherlands	1860-1868; 1881-1905
Norway	1890-1913
Portugal	1861-1914
Prussia	1860-1868
Russia	1860-1912
Spain	1860-1913
Sweden	1860-1913
Switzerland	1860-1868; 1896-1899
United States of America	1860-1913
Foreign Undeveloped	
Argentina	1863-1913
Brazil	1860-1912
Bulgaria	1905-1912
Colombia	1873-1913
Costa Rica	1868-1913
Ecuador	1885-1904
Egypt	1880; 1881
El Salvador	1900-1913
Guatemala	1869-1913
Haiti	1892; 1893
Honduras	1888-1913
Japan	1868-1899
Liberia	1892-1912
Mexico	1869-1913
Nicaragua	1895-1912
Paraguay	1887-1914
Peru	1860-1872; 1885-1913
Romania	1883-1890
Santo Domingo	1884; 1891; 1901-1912
Serbia	1907-1911
Siam	1894-1912
Tunisia	1896-1912
Turkey	1860-1913
Uruguay	1880-1913
Venezuela	1884-1913

```
Indian Princely States
        Ali-Rajpur              1888-1897; 1909-1913
        Baroda                  1880-1912
        Barwani                 1888-1897
        Cochin                  1889-1913
        Dhar                    1888-1897; 1912-1913
        Hyderabad               1884-1912
        Jamkhandi               1889-1913
        Jhabua                  1888-1897
        Jobat                   1888-1897; 1912-1913
        Kapurthala              1874-1889
        Kolhapur                1874-1913
        Manipur                 1893-1913
        Mysore                  1861-1912
        Pudukkottai             1879-1913
        Rampur                  1892-1898; 1909-1913
        Savantvadi              1870-1912
        Teri                    1893-1913
        Travancore              1865-1913
```

2   The export of British finance: 1865–1914

I. Introduction

I. Introduction

In the late nineteenth century a tourist might take the Crystal Palace or the Tower Bridge as evidence of Britain's development. If that tourist were a businessman from the American Midwest or the German Ruhr he would be likely to equate power and development with sparks from the forges of Cleveland or the sound of riveting from the shipyards of the Clyde. It was, however, the City that drew the attention of the foreign "men of money," be they J. P. Morgan, the American financier, or Gustav von Meuissen, the president of the Darmstadler Bank. Christened the Eighth Wonder of the modern world, the City provided the link that bound the vast accumulations of Victorian savings to investments in locations as disparate as the Midlands, the Midwest, and the Mid-Pacific. It was to the City that Andrew Carnegie had turned to finance his first steel enterprise; and it was there, too, that the Nizam of Hyderabad had gone for funds to finance his railway in the hills of South Central India. Nor was the market limited to overseas investment; it also continued to fuel the engines of domestic growth. Vickers, for example, drew extensively on the City to finance its growth from a small specialty steel producer on the River Don to the armament giant of the early twentieth century.

Perhaps even more important, the interest and profits generated by these investments flowed back into London, and were a major source of the prosperity that characterized the British economy. Joseph Schumpeter, Austrian banker and Harvard economist, in discussing the "third Kondratieff" – a fifty-year-long economic swing, attributed in most of the world to the innovation of electricity and electrical equipment – noted that "the English case presents a striking contrast." So striking were its features, that he labeled the period the "neomercantilist" Kondratieff.[1]

> The strong increase in capital exports . . . complements this. Foreign and particularly colonial enterprise and lending was the dominant feature of the period. Rubber, oil, South African gold and diamonds, Egyptian cotton, sugar, irrigation, South Ameri-

30

can (Argentinian) land developments, the financing of Japan and colonial communities (municipalities, particularly Canadian) afford examples of the way in which England, more than through domestic development, took part in the industrial process which carried the Kondratieff prosperity. The London money market concerned itself mainly with foreign and colonial issues to an extent never equaled in England or in any other country. The great issuing houses in particular, almost exclusively cultivated this business, managing, sometimes rigging, the market for it.[2]

Schumpeter wrote just before the outbreak of the Second World War, but the importance of the London market was well understood by contemporaries as well. Among the classical economists both John Stewart Mill and Karl Marx had worried about the effects of overseas capital transfers. To the former the flow provided a means to increase the supply of cheap food, establish markets for British manufacturers, and arrest the decline in the rate of profit in England:

> Thus the exportation of capital is an agent of great efficiency in extending the field for that which remains and it may be said truly that up to a certain point the more capital that we send away the more we shall possess and be able to retain at home.[3]

Marx too noted the flow and, surprisingly, not only was his analysis similar to Mill's, but so were his conclusions.

> If capital is sent to foreign countries, it is not done because there is absolutely no employment at home. It is done because it can be employed at a higher rate in the foreign country. . . . These higher rates of profits . . . sent home . . . enter into the equalization of the general rate of profit and keep it up to that extent.[4]

Nor did Marx argue that the increased foreign rate was necessarily dependent on exploitation. While such exploitation was one possible cause, there was also, he argued, a substantial probability that the difference was due merely to the transitory monopoly profits attributed to the innovation of new production techniques in the underdeveloped country, "in the same way a manufacturer who exploits a new invention before it becomes general undersells his competitors and yet sells his commodities above their individual value."[5]

Although Alfred Marshall shared Mill's and Marx's view that foreign investment contributed positively to domestic welfare, he admitted that there were numerous advantages to domestic commitments. On balance, however, Marshall felt that overseas investment, in particular investment in the colonies, was very attractive, since, "Capital is abundant in England; and she has few openings in which it can be made to yield a very high return."[6] Like

Marx, Marshall saw the high overseas rates as a temporary phenomenon resting on rents attached to new lands and new processes.

As the relative position of the British economy shifted, so economists' views on the utility of capital exports also changed. Few, however, doubted that the exports redounded to the benefit of the overseas recipients; their concerns were with the impact on the domestic economy. It was not until the present century that such investments came to be viewed by some as an unmitigated evil, injuring both the lender and the borrower.

Hardly had the Boer War ended than J. A. Hobson launched an attack on all things imperial. Beginning with the oft-quoted remark, "Although the new Imperialism has been bad business for the nation, it has been good business for certain classes and certain trades within the nation,"[7] Hobson's conclusions have provided the basis for three-quarters of a century of neo-Marxist rhetoric. Engels wrote: " . . . colonization today is merely a subsidiary of the stock exchange"; Rosa Luxemburg argued that: "Imperialism is the political expression of the accumulation of capital"; but it was Lenin whose definition of imperialism included, " . . . the merging of bank capital with industrial capital, and the creation on the basis of this 'financial capital' of a financial oligarchy, [and] the export of capital which has been extremely important as distinguished from the export of commodities. . . . "[8] It was also Lenin who focused his attention on the concentration of British overseas finance in the Empire. He argued: "The principal sphere of investment of British capital are the British colonies," and he put their share at almost 50 percent.[9]

Recognition of the importance of capital outflows was not limited to academic economists or critics of the system. Contemporary politicians took note of the phenomenon and speculated about its impact on the British economy. Joseph Chamberlain was convinced that capital transfers were the sinews of Empire, and that prosperity both overseas and at home rested on a continuation of those flows. Lenin may have gone too far, when he concluded that, "leading British bourgeois politicians fully appreciated the connection between what might be called purely economic and the political–social roots of imperialism."[10] Chamberlain, however, certainly espoused the principle that the Empire should be a source of monetary profit to the mother country; and he believed that those profits should be supported by substantial capital transfers, even if those transfers had to be subsidized. In a famous Birmingham address he laid the basis for the policy of that "creative imperialism" that he attempted

to effect during his tenure at the Colonial Office. To Chamberlain it
was

> ... not enough to occupy certain great spaces of the world's sur-
> face unless you can make the best of them, unless you are willing
> to develop them. We are the landlords of a great estate; it is the
> duty of the landlord to develop his estate. . . . In my opinion, it
> would be the wisest course for the government of this country
> to use British capital and British credit in order to create an in-
> strument of trade in all . . . new important countries.[11]

Of course, Treasury objections severely constrained official actions,
but the issue was important and it did yield a plethora of policy
recommendations and at least a few monetary subsidies.[12]

Neither Chamberlain nor Hobson could easily reach for a statistical
compendium of overseas finance; and, if Lenin had such a source
available, he chose not to use it. Thus, while all three were strong
on rhetoric, and more than one on polemics as well, none was able
to provide an accurate assessment of the role of the London capital
market in the development of the international economy in the late
nineteenth century. In 1914, C. K. Hobson (no relation of J. A.) made
the first academic foray into the statistical bramble of government
and business finance; and since that time a parade of distinguished
scholars have joined in the attempt to systematize and analyze the
reports of the financial press of the period.[13] This discussion is based
on those same sources; and while it provides some substantive re-
visions, it (more importantly) extends that earlier work in several
new directions.

There is no straightforward relationship between financial issues
and capital transfers; and, as it became possible to estimate those
transfers directly, academic interest turned away from the scrutiny
of financial issues. The shift in attention from finance to capital is
not surprising; for the great majority of economic questions, it is the
net flows of resources that are important. From the point of view
of certain questions in economic history, however, and from the
point of view of questions concerning the political economy of imperialism in particular, it is the volume and composition of the sales
of stocks and bonds that are relevant.

The nexus of "Finance Capitalism" as outlined by Hobson and
Lenin was the financial relationship between Britain and the overseas areas that were the recipients of her "fiscal largess." That relationship is better captured by the financial than by the real capital
movements. If, for example, a British firm invested half a million

pounds in Assam tea plantations and half a million pounds in domestic distribution facilities, it had a £1-million interest in maintaining an empire connection; but a measure based on real capital flows would indicate a level of commitment of only half that amount. Again, if a British firm were to invest in a Colorado cattle ranch, and then, at a later day, to sell out to American interests and reinvest in a similar enterprise in the Canadian prairies, the real capital index would pick up the first, but not the second, of those transactions. From the point of view of the political economy of empire, however, it is only the latter that is relevant. It appears, therefore, that a new issue series based on the contemporary financial press provides an imperfect but superior index of imperial economic activity and clearly a better measure of the financial connection between Britain and its empire.

The figures cited in this study do not include the finance transferred by nonpublic companies, by some public companies floating issues on provincial exchanges, and by direct investment. It is possible that inclusion of those omitted transfers might have changed the results; but subsidiary evidence indicates that the provincial exchanges were inclined to specialize in domestic securities and that the bulk of private offerings were domestic. Taken together, these factors suggest that the estimates of the proportion of foreign and Empire securities can be viewed as providing a maximum evaluation of their actual importance to the British market. Thus, it appears unlikely that the general conclusions would have been much altered if allowance for the omitted transfers had been made. Still, the caveat remains: This chapter is entitled "The Export of British Finance," not "The Export of Capital." It focuses on the spatial and industrial distribution of finance, not on the amount raised by the British savers, nor on the level of the accumulated total of overseas finance.

While the data differ in some ways from the general outlines first proposed by C. K. Hobson and later revised by Segal and Simon, the primary purpose of this exercise is not to replace one set of estimates with another – but to expand the coverage and make it possible to provide a quantitative estimate of the extent and character of "finance imperialism." A number of alternative series were constructed; but there were only relatively small differences among them, and, in an attempt to *maximize* the estimate of the importance of imperial finance, the series reported are the "minimum" estimates. That is, no attempt has been made to add issues whose existence can be inferred from, but whose presence was not reported by, the financial press. Moreover, issues reported as partly "taken up" abroad (almost all foreign as opposed to domestic or Empire issues) have also been excluded.

In addition to estimates of the magnitude of the aggregate financial flows, the industrial composition of those flows, and a continent-by-continent breakdown of those flows, the data provide, first, a measure of the industrial distribution of the flows to each continent, and second, within each continent, an allocation of those latter transfers between domestic, foreign, and empire recipients. Both of the last are necessary prerequisites for any accurate assessment of the political economy of British imperialism in the fifty years leading up to World War I.

II. The data: gross flows

Annual flows averaged something less than £40 million per year in the late 1860s, rose to about £55 million in the early 1870s, and to more than £90 million between 1875 and 1884. From then until the end of the century the annual total fluctuated between £70 and £85 million, but thereafter they increased steadily. It was more than £130 million in 1900–4, £145 million in 1905–9 and £175 million in 1910–14. In "real" pounds of 1913 (that is, adjusted for changes in the price level), those total flows averaged £40 million over the decade 1865–74; £75 million in 1875–84; £98 million in 1885–94; £130 million in 1895–1904; and £173 million over the last pre-war decade.[14]

Clearly, the British market directed a vast quantity of finance into a myriad of activities throughout the world. To put these aggregate figures into perspective, during the peak years the market handled about £4.5 each year for every man, woman, and child in England, Scotland, and Wales; and, even in the periods of low activity, the average was in excess of £1.5. Since national income amounted on average to less than £40 per person per year, it is easy to see why Lenin spoke of "Finance Capitalism."

Europe may well have been the world's banker, but Britain was the majority stockholder in that enterprise. For capital, as opposed to finance, it is estimated that Britain accounted for 75 percent of all international movements in 1900, and although its share declined thereafter, it was still in excess of 40 percent in 1913.[15] In the case of foreign investment in the United States, for example, the United Kingdom's share of total foreign investment is estimated to have been 80 percent in 1880, 72 percent in 1900, and 59 percent in 1913.[16] Despite these figures, it is necessary to examine the spatial and industrial composition of the financial flows before it is possible to

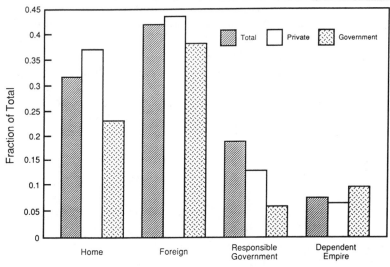

Chart 2.1

conclude that *Empire* finance either played an important role in underwriting British prosperity or served to drain funds away from the domestic enterprise, or that it provided the foundation of finance imperialism in the Hobson–Lenin–Chamberlain sense of the word (see Charts 2.1 and 2.2).

Over the entire fifty-year period, about 42 percent of the "minimum" total went to the foreign sector, somewhat less than a third remained at home, and the remaining quarter supported Empire activities. The overall averages, while providing some feeling for magnitudes, mask important facets of the transfer process. Traditional historiography asserts that, as the nation's capital streamed abroad, late Victorian industry was starved for lack of new investment. These figures provide no evidence that would indicate that the domestic economy suffered financial deprivation. From 1880 to 1904 it received more than 35 percent of the total available finance, and for the last decade the fraction was almost one-half. Moreover, in the private sector (private industry is, after all, the subject of the conventional interpretation), the result is even clearer: The domestic average for the entire period is nearly 40 percent. The variety of

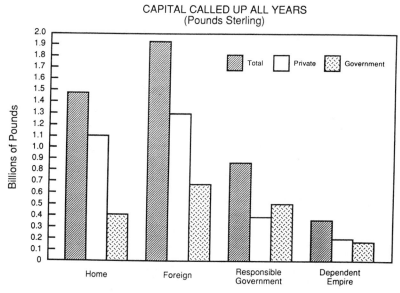

Chart 2.2

enterprises funded suggests that the market was at least as willing to finance the new growth industries as the traditional iron and textile firms; and an examination of the loan component of that financial stream indicates that domestic firms were able to borrow at rates only slightly above the consol rate – rates that were much below the charges levied on overseas or Empire firms.

The rhetoric on finance imperialism, however, concentrates on the fraction of British finance that went into the Empire (see Chart 2.3). Over the fifty years from 1865 to 1914, that proportion is about 25 percent of the total, but it is biased upwards by the transfers made during the last decade. For the period before 1900, about which Hobson wrote and which Lenin paraphrased, the proportion is only about one in five. Furthermore, of either fraction, only one-third went to the dependent Empire, the rest to the colonies with responsible government. In terms of private finance, while foreign firms received almost 45 percent and domestic, 40, *all* Empire firms absorbed less than one-fifth of the total; and the dependent governments received only about a third of that. The domestic share, on the other hand, was above 40 percent in every decade until the

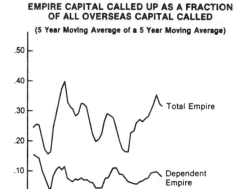

**EMPIRE CAPITAL CALLED UP AS A FRACTION
OF ALL OVERSEAS CAPITAL CALLED**

(5 Year Moving Average of a 5 Year Moving Average)

Chart 2.3

1890s, when it declined in response to a wave of finance directed toward the foreign sector and the self-governing colonies. In the case of government finance, the story is different. The foreign sector received something less than 40 percent; the Empire's share ballooned to about the same level; but that of the domestic economy fell to less than a quarter. Of the governmental total, however, only about one pound in eleven went to India and the dependent colonies.

The picture is clear. Britain was indeed a major supplier of the world's finance; but the Empire was not its major customer. Despite the Empire's somewhat more significant role in the market for government finance, there is little evidence that at any time, at least before 1905, it provided a significant alternative for private funds pushed out of Britain by low domestic returns, or a fertile ground for investment at high "exploitative monopolistic" rates.

These observations are confirmed by a closer examination of the funds that did move into the Empire. Of that total, the regions with responsible government received over 70 percent. Of the remaining fraction, India received about two-thirds and the dependent colonies the remainder. As a fraction of all (home, foreign, and Empire) finance, the colonies with responsible government garnered about 20 percent, India, 5 percent, and the other dependent possessions, a little more than 2 percent. Limiting observation to private finance reduces further the role of the Empire in general, and of the dependent Empire in particular. The share of the colonies with re-

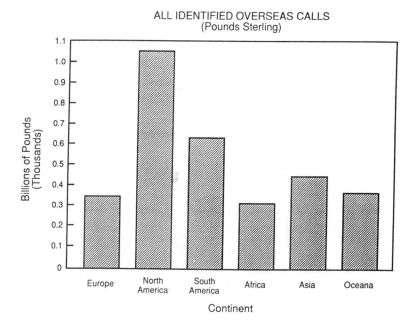

ALL IDENTIFIED OVERSEAS CALLS
(Pounds Sterling)

Chart 2.4

sponsible government falls from 19 to 13 percent, and the dependent Empire, from 7.5 to 6.5 percent.

III. The data: geographic distribution (See Charts 2.4 and 2.5)

If Europe is defined without the United Kingdom, the North American continent was the most important recipient of British finance; it attracted a quarter of all British finance, and slightly more than a third of the overseas total. It was, however, the foreign sector (largely the United States) that early drew the bulk of the funds, although that domination all but disappeared in the present century. The United States and Mexico accounted for more than three-quarters of the total before 1905, but only about half thereafter.

Of the Empire total, almost all went to what is now Canada. The increase in the Empire's share during the late 1880s and again in the last decade was largely associated with increased investment in Canadian railroads. In the 1880s, the Canadian Pacific and the Grand Trunk of Canada were the major recipients of London funds, but a number of smaller lines, including the Atlantic and Northwestern;

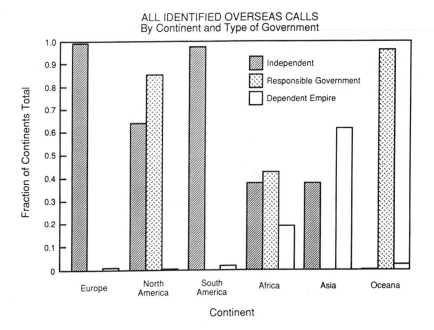

Chart 2.5

the Midland of Canada; the Ontario and Quebec; the Que' Appelle, Long Lake, and Saskatchewan; the Quebec Central; the Quebec and St. John; and the Western Countries (Nova Scotia) also floated substantial issues. Railroads were somewhat less important in the second surge of Canadian finance, but they still made up the bulk of the issues. Once more, a few roads (the Canadian Pacific, the Grand Trunk, and the Canadian Northern) were the major recipients, but again access to the capital market was not limited to those firms. Railroads such as the Edmonton, Dunvegan and British Columbia, the Pacific Great Eastern, the Terminal Cities, and the Atlantic, Quebec, and Western also received substantial transfusions.

The history of Canadian development, and the major role played by international capital movements in that development, is well known. At the time of confederation one-half of domestic capital formation was financed from abroad; and, although that fraction declined somewhat in the late nineteenth century, it was over the 50-percent threshold again at the outbreak of the First World War. That late surge was triggered by the opening of commercial wheat production on the prairies, but it was reinforced by a wave of industrial investment resting on Canadian tariff and patent policy and by investment in the second and third transcontinental railroads. These two railroads alone absorbed almost 8 percent of Canadian GNP.[17] The financial data mirror and enhance these results. They identify the railroad finance that underwrote the links that tied the prairies to Eastern and European markets in the late 1870s and 1880s and the outpouring of railroad and industrial issues that flooded the London market after 1902.

South of the forty-ninth parallel, the development of a domestic capital market reduced American dependence on British finance. The North American total had reached £18 million a year between 1880 and 1889, but it had fallen to less than half that amount by the end of the century. In the immediate pre-war period, however, the flows again increased. Between 1905 and 1914, the United States and Mexico received £272 million, and the Canadians tapped the British market for an additional £257 million.[18]

In terms of the total volume of overseas finance, Central and South America ranked second. As late as the 1870s, British companies controlled almost three-quarters of Argentine railways and that interest is reflected in the financial data. Over the full fifty-year period the southern continent received about one-fifth of the overseas total.[19] That proportion was, however, subject to wide variation. After absorbing almost a third of the overseas flow in the last half of the 1880s, for example, the continent's borrowers received less than half that much during the next decade. During both surges and recessions, however, the formal Empire received only a tiny fraction (about 1 percent). The Western Hemisphere thus absorbed nearly two-fifths of all London-based finance and more than half of the overseas total. Of that total, the foreign sector received more than three-quarters and Canada almost an additional fourth. The dependent colonies together drew only about half of 1 percent.

"Europe" stood fifth, on the list of continents: It drew about £1 in 9 of overseas finance. Of that £350 million total, only £1.3 million went to Britain's European colonies (Gibraltar, Cyprus, and Malta). Thus, of the three "western" continents (continents that accounted for almost two-thirds of overseas finance), the foreign sector received almost four-fifths of the total, and Canada (and the colonies that went to make up Canada) drew an additional 20 percent. The dependent Empire drew far less than 1 percent.

On the three remaining continents, regions that absorbed about a third of the overseas total, there may have been some opportunity for economic imperialism. Of the three, Asia received the largest share (about one-seventh), and although the foreign sector could hardly be termed insignificant, more than three-fifths went to the Empire. India was the major beneficiary, but the subcontinent's share declined from almost the entire Empire total to less than £3 in 4 as the tin and rubber industries on the Malay peninsula began to tap the London market.

As time passed, the development of Japan and the increasing attractiveness of China as an area for foreign investment reduced the Empire's dominance. Between 1865 and 1885, the foreign sector accounted for only about £1 in 8 of the Asian total, but it represented almost four times that proportion in the last pre-war decade. In that later period, government borrowing involved the national governments of Japan, China, and Siam; and the local governments of cities like Tokyo, Nagoya, Osaka, and Yokohama. In the private sector there were railroad issues of the Imperial China, the Manila, and the Philippine railroads; financial issues from the Industrial Bank of Japan and the National Bank of China; and agriculture and extractive issues of firms like the Anglo-Dutch plantations of Java, the Chinese Engineering and Mining Company, the Hayeop (Dutch Borneo) Rubber Estates, the Mendaris (Sumatra) Rubber and Produce Estates, and the Royal Dutch Company for the Working of Petroleum Wells in the Netherlands Indies.

Of all the continents, none was more clearly a British financial preserve than Oceania (Australia, New Zealand, and the Pacific Islands). Although only sparsely populated (fewer than 6 million inhabitants at the beginning of the twentieth century compared with some 7 million in greater London alone), it received almost as much of Britain's overseas financial transfers as all of Europe. From the 1860s to the 1890s, investment boomed; and a large portion of that new capital (a fraction that ranged from about a quarter, in the 1870s and 1890s, to almost a half, in the 1860s and 1880s) was financed by the United Kingdom. In the peak decade (the 1880s) the continent accounted for almost one-fifth of all Britain's overseas finance. On any measure that takes account of population, Britain contributed more to Oceania than to any other continent; and almost all went to the Empire.

Unlike Canada, in Australasia the majority of the transfers were public. In the Dominion, about one-third of the total was governmental; in the Commonwealth, the figure was more than three-fourths and in the peak decade it was over four-fifths. Given the independent attitude of the Australasian governments and the horror with which the British government greeted each new financial issue, it can hardly be argued that it was the British who were forcing their savings on an unwilling set of colonists. In 1875 Lord Carnarvon, Secretary of State for the Colonies, wrote: "I am not surprised that you are rather startled at the Treasury at the financial speed at which New Zealand is travelling. At the same time the crisis may not come yet. . . . "[20] Australia and New Zealand had voracious financial appetites. The dependent colonies, however, received very little of the Empire total; 98 percent went either to colonies with responsible government, or to those (like Western Australia) about to achieve that status.

Finally there is Africa – the region that, along with India, has been the target for most of the anti-imperial rhetoric. Imperialism there may well have been, but it does not appear to have been finance imperialism. The continent ranks last among the overseas recipients, and the figure is as large as it is (about 10 percent) only because of the heavy flows during the period of the South African "difficulties." Nor were the bulk of those flows directed toward the dependent Empire. While the reshuffling of allegiances that followed the Boer War blurs the distinctions between foreign, responsible, and dependent regions, some trends can be distinguished. Over the entire fifty years, the foreign sector received almost 40 percent of African finance – a total that would have been even higher had the Transvaal and the Orange Free State not been absorbed into the Empire in 1902.[21] The Empire's share was divided between responsible and dependent governments in a ratio of about two to one, if the two newly acquired colonies are classified as responsibly governed in the years from 1902 to 1906. In no year before 1895 did the dependent Empire in Africa absorb as much as £1 million; and the average for the entire period was only about a third of that figure.

Europe, the Western Hemisphere, and Australasia provide little comfort to the prophets of finance imperialism, if that term is understood to imply major financial transfers to parts of the dependent Empire. Only Lenin, even among the neo-Marxists, argued that Britain had substantial exploitative control over the self-governing colonies.[22] Certainly the British were under no illusion about their ability to affect governmental policy in those colonies, even when those policies directly affected the mother country. As early as 1871 Kimberley lamented that "the effect of the New Zealand [tariff] Bill would undoubtedly be that New Zealand might admit Sydney made shoes free and charge any duty she pleased on shoes from Northhampton," but he admitted nothing could be done.[23] Such comments, not only on tariff issues but on issues as widely diverse as loan repayments, provision for the common defense, and attempts by colonial governments to expand their economic and political power into neighboring territories, were common.

If any evidence is to be found to support the concept of financial imperialism, it must come from either Asia or Africa. Yet, less than one-quarter of all overseas finance was transferred to these two continents and only half of that amount to India and the dependent colonies. Even in the twentieth century, when these latter flows peaked, they accounted for only one-tenth of all finance passing through the British capital market. If, as Hobson argued, "final determination rests with the financial power," or, as Lenin concluded, "British bourgeois politicians fully appreciated the connection between what might be called the purely economic and the political–social roots of imperialism," it is unclear why the Empire developed as it did.

IV. The data: industrial composition (See Charts 2.6 and 2.7)

About two-thirds of all issues were private; more than half of private finance went into transport; and transport meant railroads (over 95 percent of the sector's total).[24] The industry's share was even higher during the first two decades as the British financed not only European and American railroads but domestic lines as well. A list of all the railways that turned to the London market would be very long. Between 1865 and 1880, for example, it included, among others, such famous names as the Caledonian, the three Greats (Eastern, Northern, and Western), the Midlands, the North British, and the South Eastern in the United Kingdom; the B&O, the Erie, the Milwaukee, the New York Central, the Katy, the Pennsy, the Reading, the Southern Pacific, and the Union Pacific in the United States; and the Charkof-Azoff, the Dutch Rhenish, the Orel-Vitebsk, the Roumanian, the Southern Austria, and the Orleans and Chalons in Europe. The market also provided substantial funds for railways whose names were never household words and that have long since faded into history; the Cuxhaven, the Des Moines Valley, the Dunaburk and Witepsk, the Edinburgh and Bathgate, the Keokuk and Kansas City, the Plymouth, the Kankakee and Pacific, and the Taff Vale.

The fraction of total finance accounted for by transportation declined somewhat as the networks in Britain, Europe, and the United States neared completion, but it rose once again as construction boomed in the parts of the Empire with responsible government. That later surge was largely concentrated in Canada, but there were

ALL IDENTIFIED CALLS
By Industry

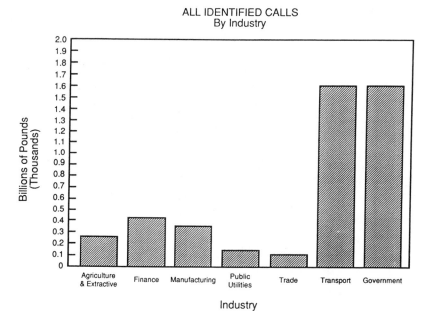

Chart 2.6

major issues from Australia – the Midlands and Western Australia – and from South Africa – the New Cape Central and the Vryheid (Natal). Over the fifty-year period hardly less than £1.6 billion were directed toward the transport sector, and of that total almost all went to railways.

No other industrial sector attracted nearly as much private capital as the railways, although finance did command about one-fourth as much. Manufacturing ranked third. Relatively unimportant until the mid-1880s, it represented a substantial draw on the total thereafter; and in the late 1890s it drew an average of £16 million a year – just less than a fifth of all finance. The sector's importance declined in the first decade of the present century, but rose again just before the assassination of the Archduke. Of the other three private industrial sectors, agriculture and extractive absorbed approximately 8 percent, public utilities some 5 percent, and trade and services about 4 percent of the private total.

Although the government absorbed only one-fourth of domestic finance, the average for the foreign sector was about one-third, and in the Empire it was well above half. The explanation for the com-

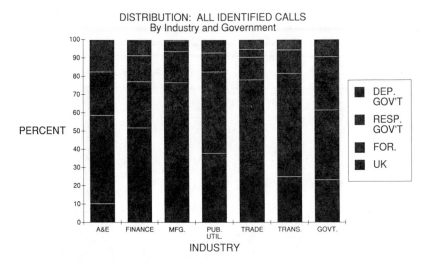

Chart 2.7

paratively high proportion of government in overseas finance reflects in part the relative difficulty of marketing foreign private issues, and, in part, marked differences in the composition of demand. The former consideration must have had implications for the public–private mix in both countries and colonies far removed from the London financial center.

There are sharp contrasts between the composition of the total financial flows and the streams received by the domestic, foreign, and Empire sectors; and these differences are important for any understanding of the financial roots of imperialism. Chart 2.8 shows the relative importance of finance flowing into the six private industrial sectors in the home, foreign, and Empire markets as compared with the averages of those flows in the total. Any figure larger than 100 indicates a flow relatively greater than the average of all transfers; any figure less than 100, a smaller-than-typical proportion. For example, the Empire transport figure of 144 indicates that, as a proportion of all flows, transport in the Empire was almost one and a half times as important as that industry was in the world market. Similarly, the UK figure of 68 indicates that in Britain transport issues

RELATIVE IMPORTANCE OF THE INDUSTRIAL SECTORS
(Proportion of the Sector in Total Flow Equals 100)

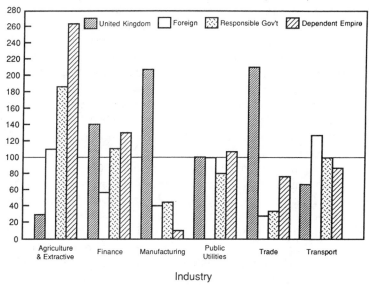

Chart 2.8

were less than 70 percent as important as they were in the London market's total.

At home, the agriculture and extractive sector was only about one-fourth as important as it was in the world total; and, over time, the index fell. Similarly, transport's share of the home market was substantially below that industry's share in the all-finance total; and it is marked by a steady decline as the domestic railway network was completed. Before 1890 domestic public utilities issues appeared less frequently than the average, but over the succeeding two decades they became much more prominent. Much of domestic gas and water investment antedates 1865; however, the diffusion of electricity, slow by U.S. and German but fast by world standards, raised the domestic sector's share in the first decade of the twentieth century. In the United Kingdom the other three industries all reflect proportions well above 100: finance almost half again as much, and trade and services and manufacturing more than twice that average level.

In the foreign sector, the indexes for finance, manufacturing, and trade and services are well below the average, and none appear to have been increasing. Public utilities stand almost at the all-finance average. The agriculture and extractive industry, however, is slightly above. Given the British investors' experience with American mining securities, the latter figure is somewhat surprising; but it seems to reflect popular perceptions of the sector's profit potential even if that potential was sometimes not realized. In the years immediately after the American Civil War, British investors, it is alleged, proved particularly susceptible to the lure of the American West. Any Englishman interested in Western mining – so the story goes – was considered a sitting duck by native sharpshooters. After one particularly shady transaction, a noted London financial journal wrote that the British investors involved had fallen victim to "gold extracting with a vengeance."[25] The *Statist* of July 18, 1885, noted that, "When novices meddle with foreign or colonial mines, they play to lose. American mines," the journal continued, "were not very remunerative. They are got up exclusively for export."[26] American cattle ranching, too, seemed to have fired the British investor's imagination. Profitable in the late 1870s and early 1880s, British-owned cattle companies had by the end of the century suffered major financial reverses. The loss to British investors between 1884 and 1900 has been placed at about $18,000,000.[27]

In the case of transport, the foreign sector received more than what could be termed its "fair" share. Over time, the index rose from 1880 to the mid-1890s, but declined somewhat after 1905. Again, as in the case of the agricultural and extractive sector, American railways exerted an almost hypnotic effect on the British investor. As late as 1865 there had not been an American railway stock or bond on the British market, but twenty years later British involvement was so great that a collapse in American railway securities resulted in a depression throughout Britain.[28]

Railway investment in South America, particularly in Argentina and Peru, was also heavy.[29] The Peruvian Corporation, a British firm, for example, counted among its holdings no less than eight of that nation's railways. As in the United States, investment patterns were often more enthusiastic than wise. In reference to the Chimbote Railway, the corporation's records point out:

> In the early days of the Corporation hope was always held out
> that as soon as various coal deposits were reached there would
> be immediate traffic for the railway. In practice, however, the
> first coal deposit reached . . . proved quite worthless and the
> same was found to be the case with the coal deposits at
> Huallancana. . . .[30]

Again, the Central Railway was conceived in part to serve the Cerro de Pasco silver mines; but because of wrongheaded intransigence the corporation lost that concession even before the line was completed. As the company records admit:

> It is evident that the Corporation had abundant opportunity and power to retain this concession to construct the railway and open up the mines but all this was allowed to fall in other hands. [To add insult to injury copper was discovered]... the existence of which the original concessionaries had no idea....[31]

In the Empire, manufacturing and trade and services both received substantially smaller fractions of total finance than "world" levels. Empire transport, however, received funds in proportions that were more or less "typical"; and the sector's share of finance stood above the general average. That latter figure reflects in large part the issues of the financial, land, and investment companies that inflated the sector total, particularly in the last three decades of the century. Those firms were closely tied to land and depended for their profits on well-defined property rights. Similarly, Empire agricultural and extractive firms received much more than their proportionate shares; and the sector's share was particularly large in the decade from 1896 to 1905. That late-century surge was associated not with agriculture but with mining (particularly gold mining). Although the list of firms included those as familiar as De Beers, it was dominated by names with a get-rich-quick aura, including, for example, the Ivanhoe, the World's Treasure, and the Corsair.

While the empire played third fiddle to the home and foreign sectors in terms of total resources drawn from the Victorian financial markets, it displayed a greater than average affinity for finance and for agriculture and extractive issues. In the colonies with responsible government the agriculture and extractive industries drew substantially above-average proportions of finance, but even those inflated indexes were well below those displayed by the dependent colonies. In the case of finance, the self-governing colonies received somewhat more than average amounts; however, that figure largely reflects the boom in land and development companies in Australasia in the decade and a half after 1875, and in South Africa during the 1890s.

In transport, the self-governing colonies received about "typical" proportions; and while they were somewhat above all-Empire averages in manufacturing, they were below that figure for trade and commerce. For public utilities, on the other hand, the fractions received were below the all-world, the all-Empire, and the foreign sector's averages. In summary, it appears that in the areas of the Empire with responsible government (and they were the parts of the Empire that attracted the greatest absolute levels of finance), the stream of private finance tended to be directed toward the agriculture and extractive industries, toward finance, and, to a lesser degree, toward transport.

Although the dependent colonies received less than 3 percent of all private finance, the industrial composition of that flow was quite different from the patterns prevailing in the self-governing colonies or in India, the other part of the dependent empire. In manufacturing, trade and services, and transport, the dependent colonies received substantially less-than-normal proportions; and there is no evidence of an upward trend in any of the three series. In the agriculture and extractive sector, in finance, and in the public utilities, the dependent colonies drew proportions of financial issues that were well above both Empire and all-world levels. For the agriculture and extractive sector it was more than four times all-world levels; for finance the ratio was about two and a half times; and in the case of the public utilities the relative flow was about 25 percent above the "standard." Moreover, these levels were almost as high at the end of the period as they had been at the beginning. Mines, farms, gas companies, and waterworks do not require further explanations; but within the financial sector it was the land and development companies that produced the bloated sectoral estimate. The economic performance of these firms depended upon the capital gains accruing to the landed property in their portfolios. Thus, it appears that in the dependent colonies, finance imperialism, to the degree that it existed, was intimately connected to the possession of land and a legal structure that gave British investors the right to relatively unfettered exercise of their ownership privileges.

In India, transport and the agriculture and extractive sectors drew relative shares of finance almost 50 percent above the world average. In the case of the latter, major transfusions were received between 1880 and 1905; but, both earlier and later, the subcontinent drew less than normal proportions. While tea, rubber, and even oil companies contributed to that midperiod rise, the greatest impetus came from the financial demands of the Indian gold fields. Firms like the Assam Oil Company, the Consolidated Tea and Lands Company, the Imperial Tea Company, and the India Rubber Estates all managed to market issues with values in excess of £100,000, but the Gold Fields of Mysore drew £691,000, the Mysore Reef Gold £500,000, the Kempinkote Gold Field £275,000, and even mines with names like Coromandel, Dharwai, and Jibutil floated issues worth more than £100,000.

The market for transport issues remained vital throughout the period; and railroads were almost as important a component of private finance in India, as they were in the foreign sector. On the subcontinent, railroad finance was bolstered immeasurably by the government's guarantee of interest payments. From 1859 to 1869 the guarantee stood at 5 percent; and even the modified scheme, initiated in 1879, left the figure at 4 percent – given the current rate on government bonds (3.1 percent), even the smaller figure was no mean inducement to a potential investor.

To summarize: The concept of finance imperialism, insofar as it has any substance, must have been linked to the agricultural and extractive sector throughout the dependent Empire, to the financial, land, and development component of the finance industry in the dependent colonies, and to railroads in India.

Relative measures suggest something about tendencies, and perhaps about relative profit rates; however, the Hobson–Lenin argument does not hinge on such tendencies but on the magnitude of finance directed toward the Empire. From the relative measures it is possible to infer that some Empire activities were more profitable than others; and those inferences suggest something about the nature of imperialism; but if the proposition to be examined concludes that exploitative profits drove the imperial engine, it is total magnitude of the transfers that must be examined. Total profits, not the rate of profit, are relevant to the argument; and here the evidence is much more ambiguous.

In the case of the agriculture and extractive sector, almost one-half of the total flow went into the foreign sector; and the Empire's share was just above 40 percent. Of that figure, about two-fifths went to the dependent Empire (the dependent colonies and India) and the proportion shows some tendency to increase over time, although those gains were concentrated in the dependent colonies. Still, the amount of agriculture and extractive finance channeled to colonies with responsible government was substantial (about a quarter of the total), and the foreign sector's share was larger than the entire amount received by the Empire. Thus, although the dependent Empire may well have been a lucrative area for agricultural and extractive investment, political dominance, although perhaps useful, was clearly not a necessary prerequisite.

In the case of finance, the home market received more than one-half the total funds, the foreign sector about one-quarter, and the Empire the remainder. The self-governing colonies took about two-fifths of the Empire's share and the dependent Empire about 60 percent.

For manufacturing, the Empire was unimportant, and the dependent portion insignificant. The entire Empire drew hardly more than 5 percent, although that fraction tripled in the last pre-war decade. Of that total, nine-tenths went to the colonies with responsible government, leaving hardly more than one-half of 1 percent for both India and the dependent colonies. Even in the final decade, when the Empire's fraction was almost one-fifth of the industry total, it was Canada, growing behind substantial tariff barriers, that drew the major share. While both the Australian Smelting Company and Ohlssons' Cape Brewery appear on the list of Empire firms issuing large blocks of securities (i.e., more than £100,000) in the years after 1905, thirty-six of those thirty-eight firms were located in the North American Dominion. The Imperial Tobacco Company of Canada itself attracted £2,635,000; and, although no other firm received as much, a greater total was received by the Dominion's embryonic steel industry (Algoma Steel, Canada Iron, Dominion Iron and Steel, and the Steel Company of Canada).

The Empire's share of all trade and service finance was less than 10 percent; but, of that sum, the dependent Empire drew more than half. The dependent colonies received only a tiny fraction, but India alone attracted more than all colonies with responsible government. That latter (and somewhat surprising) result was the product of the last five years covered by the study, when the subcontinent drew over £3,000,000 in trade finance. In that late surge Shell Oil was particularly important.

The home market absorbed about two-fifths of the funds destined for the public utilities, and the foreign sector somewhat more. Of the remainder, the self-governing colonies received about 60 percent and the dependent regions, 40 percent. If, however, the years 1910–14 are excluded – a quinquennium that saw the colonies with responsible government absorbing an eighth of all public utility finance – the "dependent" Empire outdrew the self-governing sector.[32]

For transport, foreign sector demand was by far the most important. It accounted for about a third of the total before 1880, and over 60 percent thereafter. Firms in the United Kingdom drew another 25 percent, but those in the Empire received almost one-fifth, and that share increased substantially during the present century. While the bulk of the flow went to colonies with responsible government, something less than a third went to the dependent Empire. India was the recipient of almost all of those funds.

The Empire received almost 40 percent of all government finance, but more than three-quarters was accounted for by the issues of the responsible governments – about £1 in 10 of the total figure was taken by the dependent Empire. Of that sum, India received four-fifths, and the dependent colonies the remainder. As it was with the agricultural and extractive industries, transport, and the public utilities in the private portion of the dependent economies, it appears that a continued supply of financial instruments issued by the governments of dependent Empire may have been an important consideration for the few, if not the many, among British investors.

V. The data: industrial composition of regional finance

The industrial and geographic composition of the flows of finance provide evidence that at some times, in some places, and in some industries, the dependent Empire might have exerted noticeable pressure on British investors and the London financial community. A further breakdown of the "financial flows" makes it possible to isolate those "times and places" where arguments about the exploitative nature of finance imperialism cannot be dismissed as patently false.

The economic needs of an area, and therefore its demand for finance, are not the same in all places. Thus, instead of an all-world standard, the flows of funds to the dependent Empire may better be measured against continentwide standards. Thus Charts 2.9 and 2.10 should be read like Chart 2.8, except the standard is the behavior of borrowers in Africa and Asia, not the entire world.

An examination of the geographic distribution of flows strongly indicates that "those places" (where finance imperialism might have reigned) could only be in Africa or Asia. The dependent colonies in Europe, North and South America, and Australasia drew less than one-half of 1 percent of all London-based finance; and, no matter how profitable those investments were, it is inconceivable that they could have had any noticeable impact on the British economy. The dependent Empire in Africa and Asia absorbed a little more than 7 percent of the total. Expropriation or dramatic changes in the yields of those issues might well have had an impact on Britain; and certainly they would have been felt in the financial centers.

Although the total level of African finance amounted to no more than 10 percent of the overseas total, there were important differences between the flows destined for the dependent colonies and those that went to the other political regions on the African continent. Despite the lure of King Solomon's mines and later agricultural expansion in east Africa, the decade 1865–74 aside, the relative proportions of finance received by the dependent colonies (60) was well

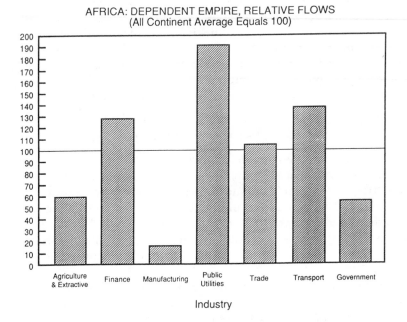

AFRICA: DEPENDENT EMPIRE, RELATIVE FLOWS
(All Continent Average Equals 100)

Industry

Chart 2.9

below the continentwide average and even further below the proportions received by the colonies with responsible government. Although the totals were not large, the shares of public utilities (193), transport (138), and finance (129) received by those dependent colonies were well above the all-continent figure, and the share of trade and services, slightly above it. The finance totals in Africa, as elsewhere, are inflated by receipts of the financial, land, and development firms.

In Asia, the dependent colonies and India developed differently. For the former, the proportion of agriculture and extractive finance was high, almost three times the continent average; and it accounted for almost half of all the finance received by those colonies. Finance, too, was well above continent averages and accounted for about a fifth of the total transfers to those colonies. Again, it was companies in the land and the land-related industries that inflated the total. For no other industry did the dependent colonies approach the continent average.

The flows to the agriculture and extractive sector were a much smaller proportion of the total finance in India than elsewhere in the Asian dependent Empire (only £1 in 5). Although India's total

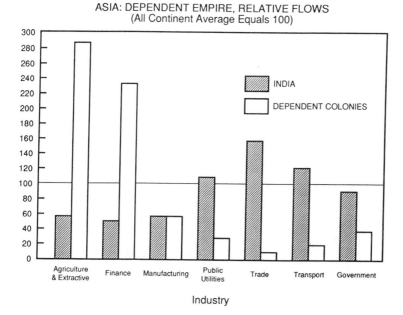

Chart 2.10

private financial receipts were five times those of the continent's dependent colonies, the total amount of agriculture and extractive finance was only about three-fourths that received by those colonial possessions. The trade and services proportion was, however, more than one and a half times the Asian average; and, perhaps most important, the fraction flowing to transport finance was one and a quarter times the foreign and almost six times the share in the dependent colonies. In India public utilities too drew somewhat more than typical proportions. Lastly, the share of government issues in total Indian finance was almost twice the level that prevailed in the dependent colonies of Asia and Africa, although, due to foreign borrowing, it fell somewhat below the continent average.

VI. Conclusion

If the "old" Empire attracted traders and planters who left Britain to earn their fortunes in the far-flung corners of the imperial domain, its later incarnation is alleged to have appealed to investors who supported entrepreneurs in their attempts to open new markets for the products of British industry, and who organized new sources of raw materials for the factories at home. No doubt the romance of Empire and the lure of distant places played their part; and it is not possible to deny that to many the City, with its satchel of Empire securities, appeared far more dynamic and exciting than the bicycle factories of the Midlands. With few exceptions, however, the dependent Empire did not draw large quantities of British finance.

By almost any standards, the London securities market was remarkable for the scale of its activity. The sales of new issues alone amounted to £34 million in 1865 and £192 million in 1914. To put it another way, the sales came to one pound ten shillings in 1865 and four pounds ten shillings in 1914 for every man, woman, and child in the United Kingdom. Over that fifty-year period, the British markets directed close to £5 billion of new finance to government and businesses across the entire globe. While Britain was the recipient of almost one-third of the total, the remainder poured across the seas. The question, however, still remains: Granted that finance was important both to the British economic process and to the psychological well-being of the middle and upper classes, how important was the Empire to the British economy and body politic? To answer this question, attention should be directed to those flows that might have been affected by the imperial connection and should exclude the foreign and domestic finance. The British domestic share was about 30 percent of the total, and the foreign sector accounts for at least another 45 percent.

Nevertheless, the £1.2 billion that did go to the Empire was no small sum. It is, however, a figure that cannot be taken at face value. Given the ability of the colonies with responsible government to bend the political process to their own ends, there was little chance for British capitalists to garner more than competitive returns in those places. The responsibly governed colonies consistently refused to pay for even their share of imperial expenditures. They failed to favor British imports, and they continually pressed the British government to engage in political adventures where the economic profits, if they existed at all, redounded to the benefit of the colonies. The self-governing colonies accounted for 17 percent of all new issues. Thus, taken together, the domestic economy, foreign governments, and colonies with responsible government accounted for more than 90 percent of the new funds that passed through the British capital markets. Less than 10 percent went to the dependent Empire. That sum was not, however, distributed evenly throughout the world. Of £355 million, Asia drew more than three-quarters and

Africa an additional sixth. Oceania absorbed only about 2 percent, if Western Australia and the Northern Territories are included among colonies with responsible government. The dependent colonies in North, Central, and South America, the Caribbean, and Europe together received about the same share. In aggregate terms, it appears that the dependent Empire received such a small share of the capital flows that, under any reasonable set of assumptions, a redirection of those resources to other parts of the world would only trivially have affected the realized rate of return. Moreover, if recent history provides any clue, even had those dependent areas been independent, they would have continued to attract some British finance.

If the dependent Empire was alluring to British financiers and savers, the attraction was clearly limited. To the degree that it existed at all, it seems to have been connected in India with transport and, to a lesser degree, with trade and public utilities. In the dependent colonies, the appeal appears to have been associated with investments in the agriculture and extractive industries, with finance and government of lesser importance. Again it is useful to reiterate the importance of the political connection in most of the sectors that drew heavily on Britain's financial resources. There are, however, no grounds for thinking that, in terms of the volume of finance alone, the dependent Empire could have played an important role in shaping the British economy. For the occasional investor, it might well have been important, but the few investments involved would have had to yield spectacular profits to have provided the engine to drive either the domestic economy or the British political machine.

3 British business and the profits from Empire

I. The setting

" . . . Protection is quite gone," Queen Victoria wrote her uncle the King of Belgium in 1852, and to all intents and purposes it was.[1] The nation was embarking on a new course that connoted a change in the British economy – an economy that was just approaching the apogee of its relative power. Before 1850, the economic progress had been largely domestic; but thereafter the area of expansion was much broader, encompassing not only the United Kingdom, but the Empire and most of the rest of the world.

Textiles, the extractive industries, and iron lay at the heart of Britain's midcentury predominance; and these same industries led the shift from domestic to world markets. In 1839, the country had produced just over half a million tons of pig iron; by 1913 that figure had risen tenfold. Of more direct relevance, in the first year only one-sixth of the total had been directed toward the export market; but, by the end of the period, exports absorbed almost one-half.

In the case of coal, output quadrupled in the sixty years after 1854; and exports, which had amounted to barely 5 percent at the beginning, accounted for more than 25 percent in 1913. Over the same period, cotton textile production did not quite triple; but exports more than quadrupled. It is not that the domestic market was dormant, but rather that in the overseas market, British business had found a new source of strength. Dominance in iron and, later, steel led to similar pre-eminence in shipbuilding and weaponry; and the economic infrastructure that supported manufacturing superiority led also to leadership in world commerce and banking.

The great burgeoning of commercial, industrial, and manufacturing activity in Victorian Britain demanded that increased attention be paid to questions of business organization, in general; and the redirection of activity from Britain to the lands overseas called for more scrutiny of the question of limited liability, in particular. For an economy expanding on the basis of new technologies that were often characterized by decreasing costs, the private or family firm frequently lacked the access to finance sufficient to permit the suc-

58

cessful exploitation of those technical opportunities. Moreover, as the focus of business moved abroad it became increasingly difficult to convince investors to make commitments that had no limits on liability. Legislation in 1844 was less than perfect. The Act of 1856 established "effective general Limited Liability," but it was the Companies Act of 1862 that was, in fact, the necessary and vital vehicle. Under that law any seven or more associates, provided their objects were lawful, might constitute themselves a company with limited liability by simply subscribing to a memorandum of association.

British entrepreneurs took advantage of the new statutes, but perhaps not as rapidly as might have been predicted. Between 1856 and 1862 an average of 380 corporate charters were granted each year; in the following decade the number rose to 700. Over the next ten years the annual figure was 1,125; for the period 1883–92, 2,150; followed by 4,000 in the 1890s; and almost 5,400 in the decade 1903 through 1912. The delay in adopting the new institutional framework was less marked among recently formed concerns than among the old family enterprises; and it was much more prevalent among firms doing business in the foreign and Empire sectors than those operating in Scotland or the Midlands. Even when old family-held firms did take corporate charters, control tended to remain under the control of a few. The Cunard Line, for example, became a limited company in 1878; but 60 percent of the equity remained in the hands of three families.[2]

As late as the mid-1880s, while limited liability had gained great favor among firms concerned with coal, iron, and engineering, the vast majority of manufacturing companies were still family businesses.[3] This same bias is also apparent in the classification scheme used by the London Stock Exchange – that agency, after all, limited its dealings in the private sector to the issues of corporations. As late as 1900, although iron, coal, and steel firms were listed in one category and brewing and distilling in another, all the other industries that make up the manufacturing and commercial sector were combined into a single classification. Wool, cotton, linen, silk, lace, hosiery, cutlery, pottery, bicycle manufacture, retail and wholesale trade were still in the main privately controlled enterprises; and even brewing did not become truly public until the end of the 1880s.

II. The problem

Such was the business environment in the third decade of Victorian reign as British entrepreneurs began to turn with increasing frequency to overseas activities. The contribution made by British capital to the development of the overseas economy in the late nineteenth and early twentieth centuries has been assessed. Over the half century that preceded the outbreak of the First World War, capital exports from Britain amounted to more than 5 percent of that nation's gross national product; and by the end of the period those exports accounted for about £3 in every 4 of the national savings.[4] The outflow may well represent the largest absolute voluntary capital transfer in the history of the world; and it certainly represents the greatest relative effort. Had the British saver chosen to invest these accumulations in a different manner, the course of development both in England and abroad would have been very different.

Most of the capital flow was directed not toward the Empire but to the United States and Latin America; and of the one-fourth that was Empire-bound, the vast majority of the resources went to the colonies of white settlement, not to the dependent Empire. Thus, it is still not clear what part British capitalism played in the development of the Empire or, conversely, what role the Empire played in the development of British capitalism. The latter question is the concern of this chapter. At the same time that capital exports surged, despite the attraction of Empire, the lure of exotic markets, and the task of financing the world's railroad network, the domestic economy continued to attract a very significant portion of the finance that passed through the nation's formal capital markets and almost all of the funds that bypassed those markets.

The statistical portrait seems very clear, but it does not appear to be the picture painted by Hobson and Lenin, nor, for that matter, the one drawn by Shaw and Stanley.[5] To Hobson and Lenin, resource exhaustion, a poor distribution of the gains of economic growth, and a decline in opportunities at home drove profits lower; and the business community in an attempt to recover those lost profits in protected markets used its political influence to promote imperial development. The Shaw–Stanley scenario is slightly different, but the last act is much the same. "Those dusky bosoms" represented new markets with a potential demand for British products that, if captured, could yield profits far in excess of the ones available at home or in the parts of the world not controlled by Whitehall. To effect this result, say Shaw and Stanley, business used its influence to develop and perhaps extend the area under British control. The first scenario might be viewed as hegemony by push and the second as Empire by pull; but both attribute the development and persistence of the British Empire to a rational economic calculation; a calculation that indicated investment in the political structure of Empire would be profitable.

Both, in short, rested on the assumption that profits in Empire were higher than those available elsewhere or, to state the maxim somewhat differently, that the resources to be tapped in the colonized areas were so valuable that their exploitation would raise the world profit rate substantially. The fact that the capital directed toward the dependent Empire was such a small fraction of the total casts some doubt on the Shaw–Stanley scenario; and the apparent vitality of the domestic economy carries a similar message for the Hobson–Lenin argument. Still, at the beginning of the twentieth century there were only 46 million residents of the British Isles; and it may have been that the Empire, while employing only a tiny fraction of the total available finance, yielded very high returns on that small commitment. Such returns would, of course, have had to have been very high. If, as appears likely, long-term investment in the dependent Empire in 1914 was about £480 million, and a reasonable rate of return in the United Kingdom was around 4.4 percent (the consol rate plus 1 percent), the returns on those investments in the colonies and India would have had to have been nearly 30 percent to raise Britain's per capita income by 5 percent.[6] It is thus possible that the high income levels observed in the United Kingdom could have been maintained by Empire profits; and the finance that flowed into the domestic and foreign economies was merely the surplus that could not be absorbed at the "monopolistic and exploitative rates" that prevailed within the Empire. Of course, it is not necessary that national income increased substantially for some individuals to have become very much better off because of their Empire investments.

A careful examination of either of these arguments requires more than the estimate of the capital flows. It is necessary to compare the profits that could have been earned in the Empire with those that would have been available in the domestic and foreign sectors had the Empire not existed. The questions then become: (1) Was it rational for the British to invest in the legal and political structure required to maintain an Empire, and, (2) if it was, to whom did the benefits accrue?

Arguments based on ex ante beliefs are always difficult to answer, since most historical evidence is, by definition, ex post; and it is possible to argue that any decision was rational, given a set of expectations that could have been, but were not, realized. Consequently, "facts," no matter how compelling, do not constitute proof;

however, circumstances sometimes permit inferences to be made about ex ante expectations from ex post evidence. The political and economic decisions that affected the Empire were made over more than half a century, and while British financial history is replete with speculative "bubbles," none lasted forever. Businessmen and investors did learn. Hence, the realized returns on home, Empire, and foreign investments, although providing direct evidence only on actual profits, also provide indirect evidence on the *expected* long-run returns from these ventures.

Such relative returns provide indirect evidence on two questions. First, were returns sufficient to make the average British citizen better off than he or she would have been had the Empire not existed? Second, were they great enough to make at least some more affluent, even if the average Briton did not benefit and may, in fact, have been made poorer? If the answer to either question is yes, then one cannot deny the possibility that it was the search for economic profits that underwrote the Empire. Moreover, if the answer to the first question is no but the answer to the second, yes, then the scope of the inquiry must be expanded to include the British political arena, if the nature of the imperial enterprise is to be understood.

To answer either question, it is first necessary to test the strictly economic argument that profits in the Empire were higher than those at home. A second step involves the comparison of Empire and domestic returns with those available abroad, outside the Empire. Any repatriation of Empire investments would certainly have driven domestic rates down, and it is possible to argue that the Empire was important not because rates were higher than those available at home, but because the flow of capital to the Empire kept domestic profits high. The threat of a repatriation disaster could be greatly mitigated if a third alternative (the foreign sector) could have provided a close substitute for Empire investment. Moreover, investments in the foreign sector did not impose financial exactions on the British taxpayer, although parallel levies in the Empire may have appeared as costs to British investors; and, more importantly, opportunities in that third sector were readily available to the potential British investor in the nineteenth century. Finally, that "third margin," encompassing as it did most of the rest of the world, was very large in relation to the amount of investment in the dependent Empire. The estimates of the flows of portfolio investment indicate that over the entire fifty-year period that culminated in the First World War, the dependent Empire (India and the Colonies without representative government) absorbed less than 8 percent of all of the City's overseas issues; while the foreign sector received more than five times as much.

If Empire returns were higher than domestic or foreign, some individuals almost certainly benefited from the nation's investment in Empire. If the profits were sufficient to allow the empire to remain the investment of choice even after the social costs (defense, for example) had been deducted, then the average Briton could have benefited; and all that is left to be done is to account for the fact that the returns were not distributed more equitably. If returns were not sufficient to make Empire investment profitable after all costs are charged, questions of political mechanism become important. How large, then, were the profits that accrued to the businessman who chose to employ his capital in India, Australia, Canada, or Lagos; and how do they compare with those gleaned by contemporaries who chose to direct their energies toward the Midlands, the United States, or Argentina?

Although the word profit is a part of every child's vocabulary, it is often used by both children and adults with little thought as to its meaning; and efforts to provide a more precise definition often generate more heat than light. Any serious attempt to discuss the rate of return on investment, let alone on the difference between rates on imperial, home, and foreign investment, however, requires such a definition. Most studies of imperial profitability have defined *profits* as the market rate of return earned on stocks and bonds bought or sold in the securities market. Economists, as well as anyone who has ever purchased a share of stock, have come to understand that security prices adjust to equalize the rate of return on investment in all similar securities. Thus, the market rate of return on any of a group of home, foreign, and Empire securities would differ from the others only by the risk premium; and a comparison provides no clues as to the underlying economic profitability of the assets in which the funds were invested. To finesse the problem introduced by rapid market adjustment, attention here has been refocused away from the securities market toward the accounting records of individual firms. The rate of return estimates generated from these antique accounts are the ratios of a firm's profits (its revenues less its costs) to the value of its actual physical assets.[7] This measure, because the denominator contains "all" assets, not just invested capital, is almost always less than the rate of return on equity, the more usual measure of the rate of return on "capital."

III. Rate of return by industry

The analysis in this chapter is based on the records of just less than 500 firms operating at home, in the Empire, or in the foreign sector. All were British owned or British chartered; and they therefore represented a viable set of investment alternatives to the potential British investor. The information on their operations was drawn from three sources. Of the total, almost 250 were chosen from a random sample of corporations whose shares were traded on the London Stock Exchange some time between 1883 and 1912.[8] For these firms the financial data are drawn from the reports filed "annually" with the Exchange.[9] Most often, they were the annual statements presented to their stockholders.

The second group, slightly fewer in number, includes partnerships and sole proprietorships as well as corporations; and their records provide some coverage of the years 1860–82 as well as 1883–1912.[10] Selection of these concerns, however, was based on no systematic sampling, unless choice on the basis of existence and availability of records can be believed to provide a random sample of the firms that existed in the past. The specific companies were included only because some portion of their original records, as opposed to statements designed for public consumption, exist and are available for analysis.[11] Finally, a third group includes a handful of British domestic railways.[12] Their financial records were taken from the annual reports to the British government, and they were chosen only because they provided a modicum of regional representation.

Because some firms borrowed heavily, others sold stock, and still others depended on the retention of earnings, this accounting measure – the ratio of profits to assets – of the rate of return is not appropriate for an analysis of all-industry profitability. It does, however, provide a very powerful tool for comparing firms in the same industry since those firms tended to have similar financial habits. Charts 3.1 and 3.2 display estimates of the relative rates of return for similar time periods for firms operating at home, abroad, and in the Empire for each of twelve industries. For simplicity, home returns have been set equal to 100, and "profits" from the foreign and Empire sectors are expressed as percentages of that figure. A number larger than 100 indicates that the foreign or Empire firms earned more than domestic, a number smaller than 100, that domestic firms were more profitable.

Two caveats: The sector totals are merely unweighted averages of the constituent industries, and the data cover only those years for

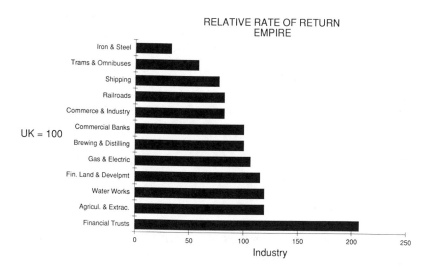

Chart 3.1

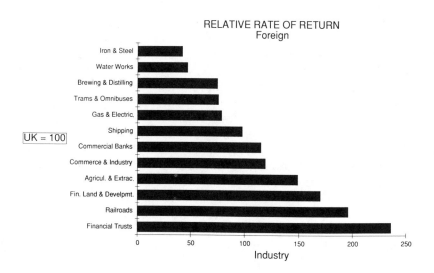

Chart 3.2

which there are observations on domestic, foreign, *and* Empire firms. Even with these restrictions, the figures appear to capture the overall flavor of British investment experience in the years between the 1860s and the First World War. For simplicity's sake, the twelve industries can be combined into five sectors: agriculture and extractive, financial (a combination of commercial banks, financial land and development, and financial trusts), public utilities (gas and electric plus waterworks), and transport (trams and omnibuses, shipping, and railroads).

In three sectors (agricultural and extractive, financial, and public utilities) Empire returns exceeded those available at home; but only in the last were they higher than those earned by firms in overseas areas not under British hegemony. In the other two sectors, commercial and manufacturing and transport, returns were lower. The trusts held investment portfolios; but in the Empire, the great bulk of the private securities held by those trusts were in the land-related industries, public utilities and transport. Those were, after all, almost the only Empire securities. To the extent that Empire firms were more profitable than domestic, it was largely because of profits earned in either the agricultural and extractive or the public utility industries: industries whose success depended upon the ability of their managers to exercise some property right. Those industries depended on friendly courts to reaffirm their ownership of mines or farms or on an administration willing to grant and maintain the charters that gave them control over a natural monopoly. In short, industries in need of a government cognizant of, and sympathetic to, their needs. The owners of those industries appear to have benefited from the Empire connection to the extent of a profit inflation of more than a third; but, even then, it is only the public utilities that earned more than the foreign alternatives.

In terms of the numbers of firms, the commercial and industrial industry was by far the largest. Equally importantly, the sample for that industry contains observations on firms in every sector (domestic, foreign, and Empire) in every year from 1860 to 1912. Thus, for commercial and industrial, more than any other industry, earnings provide a clue to the relative changes in the domestic and Empire sectors over the years. If, in an attempt to discover something about the potential for growth or the "spirit of the economy," interest is focused on the total number and variety of firms, as opposed to the size of individual enterprises, the commercial and industrial sector is certainly the most significant.

Perhaps the single most important conclusion to be drawn from the fiscal history of these firms does not concern the Empire but, rather, the much maligned British domestic economy. Industrial and commercial enterprises performed far better than conventional wisdom has indicated; and while there is evidence of a long-run decline in profits, it is no more rapid than the fall in foreign, and less so than the decline in Empire, returns. For the entire period, domestic returns in the commercial and industrial sector averaged 12 percent. While the figure was almost 14 percent from 1865 to 1890, it remained above 10 percent from then until the turn of the century. It was only in the years from 1900 to 1912 that the rate fell below that level, and even then it was more than 7 percent.

For the entire period, there is little to choose between the performance of the commercial and industrial firms in the foreign and the domestic sectors; the average return was about 12 percent for both. In the Empire, the picture was substantially different. Although the average was almost 11 percent, profits were very high over the first two and one-half decades (nearly 15 percent) but much lower thereafter. From 1885 onwards, they averaged less than 7 percent – a sharp contrast to the 10 percent returned by domestic and the 13 percent earned in the foreign sector.

A history of the firms suggests an explanation for the remarkably buoyant domestic earnings – the rise of a set of businesses serving the mass consumer market. It was a phenomenon that, with the exception of a few firms like Liebig's Extract of Meat, did not seem to exist (at least for the British investor) in the Empire and foreign sectors. The Maypole Dairy, for example, served the London metropolitan area. From 1895 to 1909 the company returned 23 percent on an asset base that grew from a quarter of a million pounds to three times that amount. Between 1890 and 1894, eleven out of thirty-three domestic commercial and industrial firms averaged returns of more than 9 percent (the high was 43 percent); and in the next quinquennium there were eighteen, of forty-nine. In contrast to the performance of other industries, while overall profits did fall, returns to some firms at least remained high. The years 1900–5 saw sixteen (out of fifty-eight) firms earn more than 9 percent, and one managed almost 60.

Far from stagnating, the domestic economy gives every evidence of robust growth. That effervescence is nowhere better captured than in the variety of the enterprises that were launched. Some firms succeeded and some did not, but the range of activities would surprise a modern visitor from Route 128 or the Silicon Valley; and it must have absolutely amazed a nineteenth-century traveler from Boston or Berlin. The De La Rue Company printed postage stamps and, in an eighteen-month period (November 1879 to July 1881), produced almost one and a half billion, although hard times lay not far ahead. Thus, vitality did not always imply profitability – a conclusion that is supported by the history of the Metropolitan Tower Construction Company. The firm was chartered to erect an exact replica of the Eiffel Tower in the London suburb of Wembley. (Another tower was planned for Chicago.) Although construction never proceeded further than the second stage, that much *was* completed. There, high in the air, a dance floor was erected and a public bar opened. The half-finished structure, the noise, and the bibulous crowd so annoyed the neighbors that the authorities withdrew the company's liquor license. That step doomed the faltering enterprise and in August 1906, the directors ordered that their dream, now deemed a "public eyesore," be dismantled.[13]

Glasgow-based Alley Maclellan was incorporated in the first years of the twentieth century and provides yet another example of the diversity, but not necessarily the success, of British industry. Although the corporate charter gave the managers permission to act as engineers, iron founders, brass founders, shipbuilders, marine engineers, electrical engineers, smiths, boilermakers, galvanizers, pattern makers, merchants, and metallurgists, the company's actual purpose was to manufacture a "steam waggon."

At the more mundane end of the spectrum was Peek Frean and Company, the pioneer biscuit manufacturer. Founded in 1857, the firm soon became a leader in the mass distribution of bakery products. Early growth was based on the innovation of aerated bread (bread that, since it became stale only slowly, could be packaged). In 1889 the company produced the first chocolate biscuit, the "Chocolate Table"; but, as often happens, while early innovation led to profits, imitation was swift. For five years returns averaged more than 30 percent, but thereafter they fell rapidly. The firm celebrated its fiftieth anniversary with a great jubilee extravaganza; and, in an attempt to regain leadership in the biscuit field, introduced a new product, the "Tilia." Unfortunately the innovation was never well received. By 1911 the company's management reported that business was still reasonably lucrative but that the high profits of the 1890s were a thing of the past.[14]

In the early decades of the study, Empire profits, particularly those earned by the diversified trading firms in the dependent Empire, were very high, although individual investments were not large. Between 1860 and 1865, Cox Brothers earned over 20 percent per year, and both Leon and Sons and F&A Swanzy, more than three-quarters of that amount; but the assets of the three West African trading companies together totaled little more than a quarter of a million pounds. With increased competition, profits declined; and it was the mid-1890s before there were signs of Empire revival. In that second surge the leaders were again firms based in the dependent Empire. In the last five years of the nineteenth century, the Royal Niger Company returned almost 18 percent, Leon and Sons about 14 percent, and the Falkland Islands Meat Company about 10 percent. Such returns were certainly good, but they provide little evidence of lucrative exploitative manipulation, even if the standard is the domestic, let alone the foreign sector.

The Tarkwa Trading Company did business on the Gold Coast; and it provides a more typical example of a fairly successful colonial enterprise after competition had begun to erode the "first entrant" returns. In 1908, management reviewed the company's achievements. "It is only five years since we started this business in Tarkwa with very small capital of £2,500 cash, of which upwards to £1,000 was expended in preliminary expenses and buildings at Tarkwa."[15] The business proved to be a success from the start and in spite of the great disadvantage "of insufficient capital and considerable competition, our most formidable competition has ceased to exist, and nearly all the European trade is in our hands. We have now upwards to £30,000 invested in our business."[16] In the quinquennium 1905–9, the company earned 6 percent, and in the years between 1910 and 1912 it averaged almost 10 percent on its assets that now totaled £61,000. Even in the period of initial penetration, not all firms did well. Less successful, for example was Lintott, Spink, and Co., whose agent in the 1870s sat disconsolately on McCarthy Island off the coast of Gambia surrounded by peanuts and without bags in which to ship them!

Some domestic and Empire firms were successful as were some that operated in the foreign sector. Liebig Extract of Meat was organized in 1867 with an initial capitalization of half a million pounds to manufacture the pure and genuine "extractum" which had been developed by Baron Liebig and Professor Pettenkoffer. "... One pound of meat extract," the prospectus asserted, "contained the soluable part of thirty pounds of the finest meat, free from fat and gelatine." The makers claimed that less than one-half a teaspoon of extract dissolved in half a pint of hot water "makes at once strong beef tea or mutton broth." Furthermore, one pound of extract together with some bread and potatoes could provide a hearty soup for 130 men at only a penny a serving.[17]

At first the undertaking was extremely profitable. Before the advent of refrigerator ships, South American cattle were valued for their hides alone; and the meat was left on the pampas to rot. With the discovery of the extract, those heretofore waste products could be put to valuable use. Although the spread of refrigerator ships made it possible to export chilled beef to Europe and raised the price of the firm's major input, sales of extract were still profitable; and, as demand increased, Liebig turned to cattle ranching. By the turn of the century the company owned herds of cattle in South America and was beginning to invest in Africa as well.

Profits induce imitation and rivals appeared on the scene. Liebig's annual report for 1886 lamented the decline in profits and reported the increase in the number of "fake" extracts. Despite continual attempts to improve the product (in 1897, for example, the firm retained the services of Sir Henry E. Roscoe, Fellow of the Royal Society), rivals did not disappear. In 1900, the managers plaintively reported that: "All these competitors wish to profit from the enormous amount we have spent on advertising. . . . They generally imitate our package as nearly as possible. In order to protect the public as much as possible, we have been obliged to adopt an additional trademark for our jars, making conspicuous the word LEMCO, the initials of Liebig's Extract of Meat Company. Being an easy word to remember, we hope that it will in large correct the evil of substitution."[18]

Some competitors posed even greater threats. Dr. E. Kemmerich ran a successful meat extract business for several years before Liebig bought him out. More threatening was Dr. George L. Johnston who, in 1877, introduced "Johnston's Fluid Beef." Because of technical difficulties, Liebig had been capable of selling its product only in bulk, but Johnston was able to package "Fluid Beef" in small bottles. The new competitor thus gained direct access to the mass consumer market – a market that was denied Liebig. Moreover, Johnston's product had yet another asset: its name, Bovril. The public found that appellation particularly seductive, combining, as it did, connotations of bovine and virile. Liebig admitted that "the invention of the weird word must now be considered as a stroke of brilliant inspiration."[19] In 1901, Liebig countered with a new name of its own, OXO, but it never attained the same level of public appeal as its competitor; and Liebig, while strong in Britain itself, found it difficult to sell either LEMCO or OXO on the Continent. Finally, in 1911 Liebig developed the OXO (bouillon) cube. The extract, now packaged in dry form, gave the firm access to the entire market. Cubes could be sold in quantities small enough to cost only a penny; and in this form OXO was accessible to working-class budgets. Parity was achieved, and to this day OXO with its little cube and Bovril with its happy name both appear on the supermarket shelves.

Antony Gibbs's South American venture is a second example of a British enterprise in a foreign environment, and its history underscores the dependence of such undertakings on the good offices of the local government. A substantial fraction of the firm's operations involved the guano and nitrate trades; and the resulting connection with the land and, therefore, property rights involved the company in both the internal politics and the international disputes of Chile. In 1902, after arbitration had settled a boundary dispute between that country and Argentina, direct pressure by those governments involved Gibbs in attempts to sell four battleships that the nations had bought in anticipation of major hostilities. Two were easily sold to the Japanese; but it took time, tact, and pressure to convince the British Admiralty that it really needed the remaining two built, as they were, to South American specifications and unlike anything the Royal Navy had ever used or was likely to ever want.

Again, in 1911, Chile determined to add a battleship of the dreadnaught class to its navy. Once more the government sought the good offices of Antony Gibbs and Company; but this time the company was less successful. The firm wrote the Japanese ambassador in London: "We should be greatly obliged if your Excellency would kindly let us know whether the Japanese government were in a position to offer us a Battleship such as would be likely to meet the requirements of our friends and we beg that your Excellency will favour us with an early reply."[20] Not surprisingly, the Japanese answered in the negative, and there the matter rested.[21]

Iron and steel, be it on the Clyde, in Cleveland, or in Wales, so the tale goes, performed poorly in the late Victorian period. The causes of that performance, if stylized facts are to be believed, lay, at least in part, in the resistance shown by iron- and steelmakers to the innovation of modern technological practices. Recent work has cast substantial doubt on the traditional version of the story, and the rate-of-return data tend to reinforce the reinterpretation.[22] Although domestic returns in iron and steel were lower than those displayed by the other industries in the manufacturing and commercial sector, the differences were not great; moreover, during the Edwardian period, the subject of most criticism, the comparison is quite favorable. From 1860 to 1912, the industry averaged over a 10-percent return (compared with about the same level in brewing, and 12 in the commercial and industrial complex); but in the twentieth century the figures were 8, 5, and 7. The fiscal history of individual concerns underscores the financial success of at least some British firms. The Anderston foundry, for example, returned almost 30 percent in the last half of both the 1860s and in the 1870s; and that colossus of the future, Vickers, recorded a profit of more than 12 percent. The name Vickers had initially made its appearance in 1829 with the organization of Naylor, Hutchinson, and Vickers; a firm that soon became Naylor, Vickers, and Company. The company's origins lay in steel, but its future depended on diversification: into specialty steel, armaments, armor plating, and naval construction. In 1867, the partnership was turned into a limited company under the name Vickers, Sons, and Company, Ltd.; and its first acquisition, the Naval Construction and Armaments Company, bringing with it the Barrow Shipbuilding Company, established these new directions. The new subsidiaries were important for the firm's growth over the last quarter of the century, but of even greater significance was the acquisition of the Maxim, Rodenfelt Guns and Ammunition Company. With that takeover, Vickers and its salesmen reached into the far corners of the globe. In 1860, Vickers's assets were less than half a million pounds, but by the turn of the century they were four times that large.

In the years between 1890 and 1894, fifteen domestic iron and steel firms (out of a total of forty-two) earned more than 10 percent; and between then and the end of the century, fourteen (out of forty-two) surpassed that threshold. A similar number earned more than 10 percent in the succeeding quinquennium, and eleven in the three years ending in 1912. While there were profitable domestic firms there were also, of course, some that were far less successful. James and George Thompson lost, on average, 1 percent per year over the last half of the 1880s, but that was an improvement on the average 3-percent losses recorded in the previous decade.

Abroad, the record stands in stark contrast. In the thirty-three years after 1880, domestic firms averaged 9 percent, but foreign ones only 4; and even that figure rests on the very strong performance of the foreign industry in the last three years. Admittedly, it appears that the British made peculiar choices in their foreign investment decisions. The firms whose earnings are reported were located in countries like Spain and Russia rather than, as would appear more reasonable, in the United States or Germany. Still, it was the Spanish and Russian firms that turned to the London capital markets, and it was their shares that the British purchased.

Despite the relatively lackluster performance of foreign iron and steel companies, their record looks good if the basis of comparison is Empire firms. Although the latter's performance improved after the turn of the century, the entire industry – an industry populated by firms like the Bengal Iron and Steel Company – showed, on average, a net loss for the years between 1880 and 1912. That figure is, however, something of a statistical artifact provided by the very high losses of a small number of firms in the first quinquennium; but even if those years are excised, the average return is still only one-third of the domestic and four-fifths of the foreign average. In the twentieth century, however, when domestic earnings were 8 percent and foreign 3 percent, the Empire firms, although still not matching the domestic performance, returned 6 percent.

Breweries and distilleries are the third industry in the manufacturing and commercial sector. Breweries had been small firms producing for local markets until the 1880s, when improvements in quality control made it economic to greatly increase the scale of production. At the same time, however, the Liberals – a party committed to at least some limited form of prohibition – pushed through a series of legislative acts designed to reduce the number of public houses. Political and technical pressure combined to force breweries to integrate retailing with their traditionally manufacturing activities to gain a firm hold on some number of the still licensed pubs that were now needed to market their much expanded output. Integration required capital; and this demand for finance forced many brewers to turn to the formal capital markets. The subsequent outpouring of shares made breweries one of the most actively traded stocks on the exchange.

Until that time returns in domestic brewing differed little from the other manufacturing and trading enterprises (13 percent as compared with 14 in commercial and industrial, and 12 in iron and steel). Over the ensuing quarter-century, and despite substantial technical development, the industry's relative position eroded (7 percent, compared with 11 and 10) as firms suffered capital losses when licenses were canceled and as the cost of acquiring additional licensed outlets rose. A few breweries remained quite profitable. Gray and Sons of Maldon returned 13 percent in the 1890s and two-thirds as much in the next century. On the other hand, the much larger Flower and Sons incurred an average loss of almost 3 percent in the years after 1909.

While average returns in the foreign brewing and distilling sector were not high (only 3 percent between 1890 and 1904) the statistic is somewhat misleading. The record indicates that in the 1890s British promoters bought what appears to have been almost every foreign brewery that came on the market. That frenzy saw a long list of foreign breweries (including such household names as the Antwerp Tivoli, the St. Pauli, and Goebel's) reincorporated in London and sold to British investors. The spirited bidding pushed prices for those brewing properties above their cost of replacement. Over time, as those inflated assets were depreciated, the investments appeared moderately profitable. Goebel's, for example, after returning less than 5 percent in its first fifteen years under British control, earned three times that much in the next eight. Over the last three years of the study the entire group averaged 10 percent – twice the domestic and five times the Empire average.

Empire breweries entered the stock exchange as part of the same speculative boom. While the colonies with responsible government were well represented (from Canada came the Dominion, from South Africa Ohlssons Cape Brewery, and from Australia the Melbourne Brewery and Distillery, to cite only three) there were few, if any, from the dependent Empire. Despite the fact that the same motivation appears to have underlain the Empire promotions, the pattern of returns is quite different than that of their foreign counterparts. More profitable than domestic until 1905, profits fell sharply over the last eight years.

Of the three industries in the transport sector (railroads, shipping, and trams and omnibuses), the first was by any measure the most important. Deemed by historians both "the leading sector" and "the nation's first big business," the spread of the rail network to every continent on the globe was heavily underwritten, and the process much accelerated, by British capital. Those flows first financed railroads at home and were then redirected to most of the rest of the world. The British were almost solely responsible for the South American network and initial construction in Asia and the Middle East. The same accumulations provided, in addition, finance for a not insignificant fraction of the North American and European networks as well. In the Empire Indian railroad policy has come in for considerable criticism, but the subcontinent had, by the turn of the century, a better developed rail complex than any other underdeveloped region. Indian rails were, however, only a part of Empire activities supported by British finance. Without those financial infusions, developments in the self-governing colonies would have been very much slower, and they were totally responsible for what rail lines there were in Africa.

At home the skeleton of the system was in place before 1860. In that year, Britain boasted 9,100 miles of railroad track, a figure that is almost one-half the mileage the nation boasted in 1926 – the apogee of railroad development. By 1860 domestic railroads could hardly have been called pioneer enterprises. In fact, the government had begun to regulate railroad rates as early at the 1850s. Profits reflected both the development of competition and the growth of regulation. Returns averaged something more than 3 percent over the entire period and there is little to choose between the early and late decades.

Foreign railroads, at least those outside of western Europe and the eastern United States, could well be viewed as pioneer projects, and their returns appear to bear out this classification. Over the entire period foreign rails returned almost twice as much as the domestic lines, and that ratio was maintained for the years after 1885. It has been argued, and only partly in jest, that the British paid for the American railroad network three times in the nineteenth century; and periodic financial eruptions, like the Baring crises of the early 1890s, suggest that investments in South America were also not without their problems. Overall, however, the markets in North, South, and Central America opened by British finance were profitable; and the railroads captured a part of those profits. In the last half of the 1880s, for example, the São Paulo Brazilian Railroad returned 12 percent; and in the last three years of the study, the Tehuantapec National Railroad yielded almost as much.

In the Empire railroad investment was in large measure directed toward India and the colonies with responsible government, although roads like the Mashonaland and the Natal and Zululand must have come close to treading the line between self-governing and dependent colonies. Among the colonies with responsible government, Canada was the chief beneficiary; and while the transcontinental routes were the largest recipients, there were funds for roads like the Que' Appelle, Long Lake, and Saskatchawan and the White Pass and Yukon. The Australian colonial governments were direct participants in much of the island continent's railroad construction, but the London exchange listed roads like the Midlands and Western Australia. In New Zealand and in South Africa, as well, British investors aided the construction of the transport network.

In the dependent Empire it was India that dominated transport investment. Like Canada and Australia, the pattern was one of very mixed private and public enterprise. The first railroads were private, but they were supported by very strong government guarantees of invested capital. Later, in the 1880s, after a decade-long experiment with government ownership, the pattern of construction under government guarantee (although a slightly more modest one) re-emerged.

Despite, or perhaps because of, government involvement, profits on Empire railroads were not high, if the standard is foreign, or even domestic, enterprise. Over the years from 1885 until 1912 the average return on those empire roads was only two-fifths that of their foreign and four-fifths that of their domestic confreres; and only in the last three years did returns exceed those available at home.

If there were large profits flowing from Empire railroads, they were captured by shippers or consumers (or perhaps managers and workers). Despite their "quasimonopolistic" position, there is no evidence to suggest that the Empire roads garnered higher returns than those in Britain, where routes were competitive and regulation relatively stringent; and they appear also to have been much below those returned by railroads in the foreign sector in general, and Central and South American in particular.

Unlike railroads or steel mills, it is very easy to move a ship from the Liverpool–New York to the London–Capetown run, and it is only slightly more difficult to return it from serving Empire coaling stations in the Indian ocean to hauling coals from Newcastle to Hull. Not surprisingly, therefore, there is little to choose between earnings in domestic and foreign shipping; and probably between those two sectors and the Empire as well. For the years after 1895 both domestic and foreign returns averaged about 6.5 percent; and Empire earnings, inflated by the profits garnered in supporting the military during the Boer War, were about 1 percent higher. The weight of these wartime earnings was, of course, borne in large part by the British taxpayer rather than the Empire consumer.

While real and threatened competition prevented any long-run imperial "exploitation," the superstructure of Empire did influence the rate of return on both foreign and Empire and (probably) domestic shipping. Industry profits were inflated by a steady stream of government subsidies: subsidies sufficient to guarantee a steady flow of investment into an economic activity that was obviously of vital concern to an island nation with outposts scattered throughout the world.

Cunard provides an excellent example of the kind of government subsidization of private business that, while rare in nineteenth-century Britain, was common in the shipping industry. In 1902 the company concluded a contract with Her Majesty's government that committed it to build two ships for the Atlantic trade (the *Mauritania* and the *Lusitania*), and to make its entire fleet available for government charter in case of a national emergency.[23] Cunard, in turn, was to receive a construction loan at 2.5 percent (the rate on government bonds was 2.9 percent) and an annual subvention, once the ships were in service, of £150,000.[24] The offer was seductive enough that the company was prepared to accept a number of additional strictures on its behavior. Management agreed that all masters, engineers, and officers of the watch, as well as three-fourths of the crew, would be British subjects; that all officers would hold commissions in the naval reserve; and that the firm would remain a purely British enterprise for twenty years.[25] The government was clearly concerned both about military threats to its far-flung Empire and the need to maintain the islands' supplies should war break out.

Historically, commercialization has been linked with urbanization; and the world's most commercialized nation was also its most urbanized. At midcentury more than one-half of Great Britain's population lived in cities, a level of urban concentration not reached in the United States until 1920. As cities grow so does the demand for urban transport; and by the ascension of Edward VII a London resident could choose to travel to work on almost any combination of four very different transport technologies. The journey from home to office could have been made on a horse-drawn tram (the precursor of the streetcar), or by way of the Underground (the still-used District, Metropolitan, and Circle Lines began to operate in the 1860s – the latter, although nominally restricted to engines using smokeless coal, was known by its customers as the "Sewer" Line). Another alternative was the motorbus, first introduced to London streets in 1900 (seven years before the Model T Ford). Finally, there were the "Tubes," the electrified subways that had begun to operate at the end of the nineteenth century.

Abroad and in the Empire urbanization was slower and demand for urban transport grew less rapidly. Still, by the turn of the century, although only New York had gotten into the electrified subway business (the shares of the IRT traded on the London exchange) and no one had ventured into the steam underground technology, there were electric tramways in places like Aukland, Colombo, and Mexico City, and at least horsedrawn ones in Bombay, Calcutta, and on Ascension Island.

On average, domestic rates of return in the urban transport business were greater than foreign, and those, in turn, higher than Empire, but the pattern changed after the turn of the century. British returns were very high in the later decades of the nineteenth century, but between 1900 and 1912, as the Tubes and motorized omnibuses provided more and more competition, the domestic industry reported lower profits than its foreign and Empire counterparts. The figures for that period were 2 percent, compared with half again that much in the foreign, and more than twice as much in the Empire sectors.

Higher returns were associated with the newly electrified tramways operating as government-granted monopolies in the cities of Canada, Australia, South Africa, and later India. There was substantially less intertechnological competition in both the foreign and Empire sectors; and, while regulation and competition kept profits at home down, in the foreign sector political decisions appeared to favor domestic consumers over foreign investors. These forces seem, however, to have operated with less force in the Empire. Slow urban growth may have dampened the incentives for external competition, and the political structure was possibly favorably biased toward "foreign" investors, at least those from the mother country.

The story that emerges from the study of trams and omnibuses after the turn of the century, when foreign and Empire activities shifted to modes of urban transport that operated under the protection of natural or chartered monopolies, is a tale that is repeated in both of the two industries that make up the public utility sector: gas and electricity and waterworks. Because of the indivisibilities in distribution, both were classic natural monopolies.

Regulation, first local and then national, came early to the British domestic gas industry – early enough that it had not yet become the gas and electric industry. Although data going back into the 1830s and 1840s – data required for an accurate comparison – are not a part of this study, the returns for the years after 1860 indicate that the regulatory authorities do not appear to have overly constrained profits before the turn of the century. Sample firms averaged returns of almost 9 percent, and the highest averages were observed in the last decade of the century. The pattern changed in the present century; and over the last twelve years of the study, even though the industry had by this time expanded to include both gas and electric firms, in only 7 of 107 firm-years did a company earn more than 7 percent (and none earned 8). Even those averages are inflated by the new electric companies; the record for the gas companies alone was even worse. There, average profit was only 4 percent.

In the United Kingdom the manufacture of gas was technically very advanced, but the firms that manufactured it were also very powerful politically. High technology meant relatively low costs, and the price of gas was cheaper in Britain than in Germany or the

United States. Political entrenchment, however, meant that the firms were well placed to resist the encroachment of alternative technologies. In 1890, one-third of the American urban lighting market was served by electricity; in Britain, there was, for all intents and purposes, no electricity. Ten years later when the new product had captured three-fifths of the American market, the British figure was barely one home in ten.[26]

Of the companies whose records were examined in detail, most expended some resources attempting to block the charters of electric companies. Only the Barnett Gas Company sought a charter that would permit it to expand into electric service.

Overseas the story had similar overtones, but its conclusion was somewhat different. Taking gas and electrical firms together and focusing only on those years after 1900 when competition began to erode the profits of domestic gas companies and when government regulation of both gas and electric companies appears to have become more effective, firms in foreign countries earned on average slightly less than 6 percent, while those in the Empire returned more than 8 percent. In comparison, the domestic rate, although substantially below the 10 percent returned during the heady 1890s, was just less than 7.

In the foreign sector, firms depended on the good will of the local government to maintain their charters, and were as a result subject to intense political pressure. British-owned utilities in Rosario, Argentina, provide a well-documented example. The end of the war with Paraguay had produced an acute xenophobia, and the rise of Buenos Aires as a rival port had led to lagging economic growth in the city. The British-owned utilities provided a handy scapegoat, and politicians competed to press rates down. As a consequence, profits, when they existed at all, were sporadic and elusive.[27]

If there was one sector where exploitative returns could have been earned in the Empire, it was the public utilities. In the colonies of white settlement and in the dependent Empire, "honest government" protected the utilities from both "venal" rate manipulation and the need to pay political bribes. In both, regulation, to the extent that it existed at all, was apparently even less effective than in the home country; and electricity was slower in becoming an effective competitor. Moreover, in the dependent Empire it is possible that the chartering process was biased in favor of British firms (the colonies with responsible government had a long history of favoring their own citizens). The Bombay Gas Company, for example, in the years from 1901 to 1911 returned almost 7 percent per year. The British domestic average for gas companies was 4 percent, and the most profitable firm in the sample returned barely more than 5.

Electricity was an excellent substitute for gas, and omnibuses a reasonable alternative to trams, but there weren't, and still aren't, any viable substitutes for water. At home the pattern of returns from waterworks mirrored those displayed by the gas and electric industry. High throughout the nineteenth century, they were particularly high in the 1890s; however, after the turn of the century they were in the 6–7-percent range that characterized gas and electric profits.

Abroad, in the foreign sector, politics clearly outweighed monopoly; and returns from such disparate cities as Beyrouth, Seville, Montevideo, and Shanghai were only about one-half of those garnered in Barnet, Bridgend, Sutherland, and South Shields. In the Empire, however, returns were very high. Over the entire period firms in cities like Alexandria, Colombo, Bulawayo, and Kimberly earned about one-third more than those in the United Kingdom (and about three times as much as those in the foreign sector). And while domestic returns fell dramatically after the turn of the century, there is no evidence of any decline in Empire profits.

The British and colonial governments had the power to grant monopoly charters; but gas, light, and water were of relatively limited importance. In heavily urbanized Great Britain, for example, as late as the 1920s, the capital of the gas, light, and water industries together constituted less than 5 percent of the nation's capital stock. In the Empire the figures were almost certainly smaller. A review of the financial flows suggests that the public utilities received about 2 percent of all finance bound for the Empire, and while the figure for the dependent colonies and India is slightly higher, it barely exceeds 3 percent.

The colonial governments did, however, have another and very important economic function: They defined, assigned, and maintained a system of property rights. In India the British were careful to preserve the structure that they thought existed before the subcontinent came under the Crown, but even there, when property was sold, those transfers were affirmed by the judges appointed and paid by a British administration. Elsewhere in the Empire, particularly in those regions without established systems of individual property rights, the role of the colonial government was even more important. In the colonies of white settlement, British émigrés quickly took over most of the productive resources (although in New Zealand the Maoris did not give up without a struggle); and in some of the dependent colonies a similar pattern emerged. In some areas, like the Caribbean, it was British plantation owners who exercised those rights. In other regions, West Africa, for example, it was the managers of British firms who, while perhaps only assuming temporary residence, still exercized control of some agricultural and mineral rights.

Early penetration – penetration effected under the sympathetic eye of the government in London – gave British settlers and businessmen an opportunity to gain control of potentially valuable lands; and the imperial government validated those rights. To any American familiar with the saga of western expansion, the story is a familiar one; and it is one that had its counterparts in colonies like Jamaica during the first Empire and in Canada, Australia, and Africa during the second. Thus the fiscal success of British firms operating in the land-related sector are an important component of any analysis of the profitability of Empire.

The extractive and agricultural industry is an amalgam of the stock exchange's mining and tea and coffee industries, combined with the coal firms from the iron, coal, and steel classification, and the agricultural and extractive enterprises (particularly nitrate) from the commercial and industrial list. The history of these firms lends substance to the belief that profits, particularly those to first entrants, were not unrelated to the ability to exercise a protected property right. Although Empire returns to the land-related industries were lower than foreign, they were almost 20 percent higher than domestic in the years where comparable data are available.

At home, although returns were highly volatile, there is no evidence of any long-term erosion; and these returns were inflated by the performance of the much-maligned coal industry. At some point resource exhaustion must have become an important factor; but during the period in question, collieries proved relatively prosperous (helped in part, no doubt, by the naval arms race); and they were particularly profitable during the Boer War.

It was the foreign sector that reported the highest earnings, and to a large extent it was the profits of the South American nitrate fields that accounted for them. The Liverpool Nitrate Company, for example, although by no means typical, returned on average 23 percent in the years from 1885 to 1912. Good profit performance was not, however, limited to nitrates. Firms like the Consett Spanish Iron Company continually reported earnings in excess of 15 percent.

It is worthy of note that the records of the agricultural and extractive firms indicate that in the foreign sector property rights were not perfectly secure. Time and time again firms reported that they had been forced to incur heavy expenses contesting those rights in the Chilean or Ecuadorian courts; and on occasion they noted that some costs were involved in convincing the local political authorities to recognize their claim at all. In the case of this industry, however, profits were sufficient to underwrite relatively high returns in spite of the political costs. It would be interesting to see what fate befell the nitrate companies when the Treaty of Versailles reduced the demand for munitions and armor.

In the Empire it was, in the early years, the tea and coffee companies operating in India and Ceylon – firms like the Assam Tea Company – that contributed most heavily to the stockholders pocketbooks. Later it was the South African gold fields that were the source of those profits. In both cases firms that entered the industry early and were able to take control of good land and valuable mineral deposits did very well. Those that came later and had to settle for less fertile land or low-yield seams fared, on average, much less so. The story of Cecil Rhodes is well known, but for every Rhodes there was at least one Ashanti Goldfields. That firm was launched to develop gold-mining properties in the Gold Coast, and it led such a beleaguered existence that its directors were at one time besieged by American miners demanding their pay.

Still, on average, the Empire firms outperformed their domestic counterparts; and, to the extent that the structure of Empire made it possible to acquire and maintain the property rights that underlay those profits, the Empire contributed to at least some Britons' well being. The experience of the foreign firms, however, suggests that stability, although certainly helpful, was not a necessary condition for success.

Since land and development companies held portfolios of property, it is hardly surprising that their relative returns reflect closely the performance of the agriculture and extractive enterprises. They were, in fact, the growth industry of the late nineteenth century; and that growth was almost certainly based on their earning experience in the 1860s and 1870s. In that period, returns in both the Empire and the foreign sector were about twice the level of the later decades. Empire investments in those prosperous years were concentrated in Canada, Australia, and New Zealand; while the majority of the foreign investment was in North and South America. By 1884 the New Zealand and Australian Land Company, a firm that had operated since 1867, owned 1,047,680 acres, and bred 224,785 new lambs annually. The owners of the San Jacinto Land Company, for example, recognized early the future profitability of southern California agriculture.

Success, as it is wont to do, attracted imitators who not only invested in the dependent Empire, as well as the self-governing colonies, but began to turn their attention to land speculation in the United Kingdom as well. Thus, while the stock exchange continued to report on firms such as the Manitoba Mortgage and Investment Company, names like the Anibiri Wassau Exploration Company and The Combined Rhodesian Syndicate appear with increasing frequency. At home, the most lucrative investments were in commercial and residential property in the rapidly growing cities; and, of these, London was the recipient of more than its share. The Leicester Real Property Company and the City and West End Properties are just two of the firms whose shares began to trade on the exchange.

Entry added new firms and undercut the industry's profits. Both Empire and foreign returns fell by about half; and domestic returns were never high to begin with. Still, although average returns were down, the Empire continued to return more than its domestic counterparts. At the same time, foreign development companies, although subject to much more variance, continued to earn more than those in the Empire.

IV. Interindustry comparison

The discussion of relative rates of return has revolved around a measure of the rate of profit on total assets. To the extent that firms in the same industry faced similar technologies and competed in the same capital markets, it provides a reasonably consistent and fairly unambiguous measure of the underlying productivity of economic resources committed to a particular activity, be it brewing, banking, or batique making. As attention was directed away from the "industry" to some higher form of aggregation, the assumption of similar capital structures becomes less tenable, and the measure less reliable.

The debate over imperialism has not been directed toward industry profits, but rather to "the rate of return." The industry-by-industry analysis has shown quite clearly that, in most cases, Empire investment was not particularly profitable; but that, in some industries (those related to land ownership and the public utilities), it was. If the latter were important enough, overall returns might have been sufficiently high to make the imperial adventure, on net, a profitable enterprise. Despite both theoretical and empirical problems, some

Chart 3.3

measure of the average rate of return is obviously required both to respond to the rhetoric and to assess that profitability. It should, however, be recognized that any such measure is flawed and raises at least as many questions as it answers. It may be possible to examine "the" rate of return; but the reader should tread warily: Caveat emptor.

Charts 3.3, 3.4, and 3.5 display three measures of that general rate. The first (the rate of return on all capital claims – equity, bonds, loans, and open-book credit) can be interpreted as "the" rate only on the assumptions that all activities are equally risky and that the total return to all capital claims is independent of industry. The second (the rate of return on the value of contributed equity) has meaning if somehow this peculiar measure captures what investors would have "earned" had some gains (or losses) not already been garnered (or absorbed) as capital gains (or losses) by previous owners. The third (the rate of return on assets of firms in the goods-producing sector – commercial and industrial, iron and steel, and brewing and distilling – were merged because they have somewhat similar capital structures and were chosen because they are both diverse and well represented in the sample) may be appropriate if the experience of these firms reflect economic trends in the general economies of home, foreign, and Empire sectors as a whole. [Chart 3.6 displays the returns to Empire firms relative to domestic earnings for the each of the three measures]. A final warning: None of the

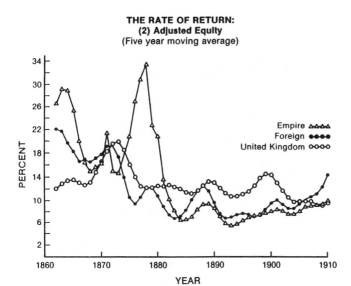

Chart 3.4

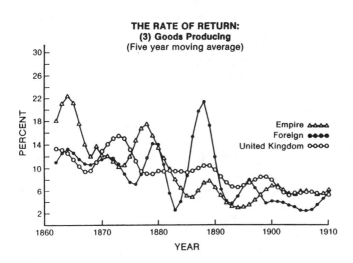

Chart 3.5

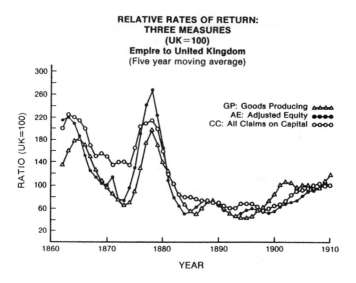

RELATIVE RATES OF RETURN:
THREE MEASURES
(UK=100)
Empire to United Kingdom
(Five year moving average)

GP: Goods Producing △△△△
AE: Adjusted Equity ●●●●
CC: All Claims on Capital ○○○○

Chart 3.6

averages are weighted; and at best they capture only the experience of firms in the sample with no adjustment for the actual structures of economic activity and investment in the domestic, foreign, and Empire sectors.[28] Again, proceed with caution.

Not surprisingly, given the basis on which the three measures were constructed, there are differences in level; but in addition, at times the three diverge sharply. The surge of foreign earnings in the late 1870s and early 1880s affected the goods-producing sector more than the "economy"; and the late-1890s rise in domestic profits is reduced when coal mining is excluded. It is apparent that certain events affected some firms or sectors more than they did others; however, the overall patterns displayed by the three measures are very similar. That latter fact may add some credence to the analysis of "the" rate of return, especially as the conclusions appear suscep-tible to a wide variety of specifications of the rate. The trend in all three measures is downward; and the rate of that decline is greater for the foreign than for the domestic sector and greater for Empire than for foreign.

Most importantly from the point of view of this analysis, the return on investment in Great Britain, however measured, was certainly not below and was probably substantially above the Empire return from the middle of the 1880s until the turn of the century. Any comparison is sensitive to the measure chosen but, in general, it appears that Empire returns were about two-thirds of domestic and four-fifths of foreign over that two-decade span.

For the earlier and later periods the results are different. By all three measures profits in Empire were much above domestic and foreign returns through at least the first twenty years of the study. A part of that difference may be merely a statistical artifact. There were a relatively small number of Empire firms in the sample in those early years (they accounted for only about 10 percent of the total sample); and an inordinately high fraction of these Empire firms were "pioneer" enterprises (i.e., firms operating in newly opened regions). In contrast the domestic and foreign measures were less likely to be affected by the performance of a few "outliers"; and most of those firms operated in developed areas. Thus, sample bias may have magnified Empire profits.

Despite the possibility of some distortion, the evidence appears conclusive: British business found the Empire a "good place to do business" until the early 1880s; and that conclusion holds whether the yardstick chosen is foreign or domestic profits. Although the result is somewhat sensitive to the measure used, it would seem that in those halcyon days the Englishman who put his savings to work in Canada, Australia, or India received a third again as much as he would have had he chosen the more familiar alternatives in Clydeside, Tyneside, or even "Thamesside," and about half again as much as he would have earned in France, the United States, or Argentina.

Finally, while the comparisons for the first and second periods seem fairly conclusive, those for the first decades of the twentieth century are more in doubt. Returns in all three sectors are very similar; but it appears that as World War I approached, Empire returns edged ahead of domestic. As between Empire and foreign, there appears to have been little to choose.

In terms of the rhetoric on imperialism, one conclusion stands out. No matter how profitable the Empire was in the early decades, as the "crisis of capitalism" approached (the domestic rate of profit was declining – albeit slowly) and as Britain rushed into the "age of high imperialism," the Empire did not offer a better, and perhaps not even as good an alternative as the foreign sector; and neither Empire nor foreign sectors appear to have been as attractive as the domestic economy. In the earlier years the Empire connection may have made a difference; but for the potential British investor in the years after 1880, the Empire was economically a snare and a delusion – a flame not worth the candle.

4 Government expenditure in support of business

I. Introduction

While investments in the dependent Empire never loomed large in the total British portfolio, they were almost certainly a sizeable fraction of some individuals' holdings; and investments in those parts of the Empire with responsible government were important to a significantly larger number of British citizens. In the later decades those Empire investments (while, on average, yielding less than returns available at home) may have been slightly more profitable than other overseas alternatives, and they were certainly not substantially less so. Moreover, at some times and in some places and for some industries, imperial investments were relatively profitable regardless of the measures chosen. Moreover, even those investments that appear relatively unprofitable shared with their more lucrative counterparts the fruits of government expenditures in support of business.

Aerospace engineers in El Segundo, California, and dairy farmers in Grundy Center, Iowa, will recognize that business profits are not unrelated to government policy, and there is no evidence to suggest that in the nineteenth-century British businessmen were any less astute. If a California engineer or an Iowa farmer were asked about such government policies he or she would most likely respond in terms of the impact of the B-1 bomber on aircraft sales or of price supports on butter prices. Today, however, government policies are far more pervasive, and their influence on all aspects of economic life is taken for granted. In an earlier age the "responsibilities of government" were less clearly recognized, and the costs of some services devolved on the business community when the government chose not to provide them. The evidence indicates that nineteenth-century businessmen realized that, if the government could be made to assume "its responsibilities," any number of "free" services could be produced that would drastically reduce the costs of doing business.

A smoothly functioning legal system makes it possible to enforce contracts cheaply and to effect transactions that would otherwise have proved prohibitively expensive. Governmentally underwritten military and police forces mean that business does not have to carry the cost of private armies and guards to protect property. The East India Company, for example, had among its costs of operation not only a very large army but a naval force as well. If the government built roads and maintained postal and telegraph services, private transaction and marketing costs were much reduced, and so the story goes. The British Empire was a political system, and it should, in principle, have been possible to arrange affairs to produce a pattern of expenditures that would provide support to private business and at the same time charge costs to others.

In the foreign sector, the British investor had little influence over the amount government chose to spend in support of business nor was there any easy way to shift the burden imposed by those expenditures. In the Empire, however, it may have been possible to increase the level of support and transfer the costs to either the colonial taxpayer or his British cousin. To the degree that British business could influence colonial governments to adopt such policies, the level of private profits in the Empire was higher than it would otherwise have been, and the level of losses, when they occurred, lower.

Investment in "business" overhead capital includes not only the traditional additions to the real capital stock but a number of items not always included in the standard social accounts. The real capital inventory involves roads, bridges, buildings, railroads, gas and waterworks, sewage systems, lighthouses, harbors, rabbit fences, and a host of other kinds of physical capital. In the nontraditional category are counted the expenditures made to increase the productivity of labor (education, public health, and the support of immigration), and those that maintained and enforced property rights (police, the courts, and probably a portion of military expenditures). In addition to overhead capital the business sector benefited from a myriad of other policies that substituted government expenditure for private cost. Such policies included, for example, production subsidies and governmental funding for institutions such as agricultural marketing boards and immigration services.

To say that the political structure of Empire could have been used to manipulate expenditures for the benefit of British business is not to argue that it did. To answer *that* question it is necessary to examine the level and composition of Empire expenditures. It should be obvious, however, that no figure on road expenditures in Ceylon has much significance when examined in isolation; and it can contribute to an answer to the underlying question only if analyzed in the context of the fiscal behavior of other governments. The data on the functional distribution of expenditures presented in this chapter encompass, therefore, the United Kingdom, India, fifteen colonies with responsible government, fifty-nine colonies and protectorates in some form of dependent status, eighteen Indian Princely States, sixteen foreign countries classed as developed, and twenty-five categorized as underdeveloped. To compensate for wide variations in size, all figures are reported in per capita terms.

One important caveat should be borne in mind. These are data from "national" (or "colonial") units, and do not include the expenditures at all political levels. In the case of the United States, for example, the data are for federal expenditures and exclude those of states, counties, and cities. The smaller or less developed the political unit, the more likely it is that expenditures will be centralized. Thus, comparisons between units of very different size or state of development tend to be distorted.

In the following pages, the total and four subclasses (law and justice, public works, science and human capital, and direct business support) of expenditures are examined in detail: The total because it provides an index of the role of government in the economy; the others because they include most of the "business-supporting" activities.[1] *Law and justice* reflect the expenses incurred in maintaining property rights and enforcing contracts. *Public works* are, of course, the real capital component of social-overhead investment. Railroads were certainly an important part of that category of investment, and they would have to be included in any enumeration of a nation's infrastructure. In a comparison of government policies, however, their inclusion raises serious problems. They were sometimes government owned, on other occasions privately held, or, yet again, occasionally financed jointly by the public and private sectors. Their inclusion in the totals for some countries or colonies (those where railroads were public charges) and their omission from others distorts intercountry comparisons. Still, government expenditure on railroad construction was often large; therefore, public works are examined both with and without the capital expenditures on railroads.[2] *Science and human capital* picks up the nontraditional capital components of the infrastructure. The category includes expenditures on education, science, medicine, charity, relief, immigration, and even religion.[3] Expenditures in *direct support of business* include not only such administrative departments as labor and commerce,

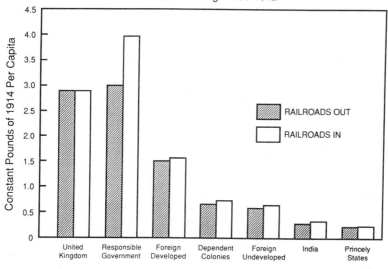

Chart 4.1

but subsidies or any other expenditures made in support of agriculture, manufacturing, commerce, or mining.

II. The pattern of expenditure

In the late nineteenth and early twentieth centuries, total per capita expenditures in Great Britain were high, if the standard is other developed countries (Chart 4.1). Excluding railroads, U.K. national expenditures averaged £2–18–5 over the period covered by this study, and they reached £5–0–7 in the period 1900–4. Comparable figures for Germany were £1–5–7, for France, £2–17–5, and for the United States, £1–7–2. The United Kingdom level is almost twice that of the average developed country, although France spent nearly as much.

In the Empire, however, the colonies with responsible government spent at rates slightly above the British. For all such colonies, the annual average was £3–0–10; however, the propensity for ''Big Government'' was not equally strong throughout the Empire. The expenditures averaged £6–7–7 in the six Australian colonies, £6–8–10 in New Zealand, but only £2–8–7 in South Africa, and a mere 11 shillings in North America.

If per capita expenditure is any measure of the role of the government in the economy, the Australasian pattern is unmatched anywhere in the world. Even in Tasmania, the colony with the lowest levels of spending, the rate was almost one and one-half times that in the United Kingdom. Given the fact that the per capita Australian gross national product averaged less than £50 annually, these colonies maintained government structures of nearly contemporary proportions.[4]

In the dependent Empire, the story is mixed. Among the dependent colonies the figure was more than 13 shillings. This number is low when compared with the United Kingdom, but it is about 10 percent higher than the comparable measure for the underdeveloped countries. In the case of India the average was much lower, 6 shillings, but while well below that of the underdeveloped countries, it was 30 percent higher than the levels observed in the Princely States. That average is, however, somewhat misleading since, in the years after 1885, expenditures were actually higher in those states. Throughout the non–Indian Empire at least, governments (regardless of level of constitutional development) tended to spend at levels higher than those independent countries in comparable stages of development.

a. Law and justice (see Chart 4.2)

A casual inspection of the budgets of the dependent colonies could lead to the conclusion that British imperialism should be viewed not as a political but as a moral institution designed to bring temperance to the "uncivilized" masses of the underdeveloped world. For many colonies the liquor tax was a significant source of revenue; and police, jails, and courts were among the major items of expenditure. Moreover, a surprisingly large fraction of the legal effort was devoted to the arrest, conviction, and incarceration of inebriates. Levity aside, the Empire was marked by relatively high levels of expenditure on law and justice, and some substantial fraction of those expenditures provided the legal sinews that tied a decentralized economy together.

A system of law and justice that provides for the definition and enforcement of a set of property rights and that allows for both civil and criminal enforcement of these rights is an almost necessary

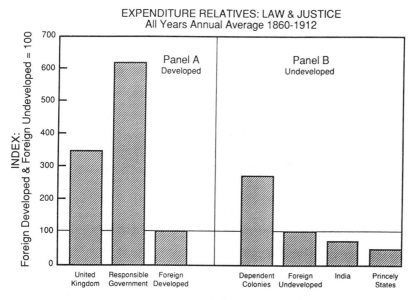

EXPENDITURE RELATIVES: LAW & JUSTICE
All Years Annual Average 1860-1912

Chart 4.2

precondition for an operating free-enterprise economy. When British businessmen ventured into foreign markets, they were at times required to make substantial "side payments" to assure that the local authorities enforced their (the businessmen's) alleged property rights; and even these payments were frequently insufficient to keep those rights from being "redefined," not infrequently in the middle of a business transaction. When the costs of the resources required to establish and enforce property rights are transferred to society as a whole, the private rate of return is increased. In the Empire rights were both well defined and enforced – at society's expense – and the external evidence indicates that the benefits were substantial. While they accrued in part to local citizens, they also worked to the benefit of British businessmen who, unlike their native counterparts, paid few of the costs.

In the United Kingdom expenditures on law and justice averaged almost 3 shillings per person per year – a figure that represented about 5 percent of all expenditures. These figures were substantially higher than the 10 pence that characterized the expenditures of an average developed country; and of those countries only Belgium spent more, and Portugal, Denmark, and the Netherlands, as much as three-fifths, of the United Kingdom figure. Even the United Kingdom expenditures appear small when compared with those of the colonies with responsible government. There the average annual expenditure was 5 shillings. While the Australasian average was high, that region was not alone in diverting resources into the area of law and justice. Although there was substantial colony-to-colony variation, the six original Australian colonies averaged 12 shillings, but New Zealand spent only a little more than 8. Moreover, while expenditures in Western Australia (£1–2–5) were the highest in the world, the 15 shillings and 5 pence spent in the Transvaal was second. The four self-governing colonies in Africa averaged about 8 shillings, and only in North America was the average below the level in the United Kingdom. Even there, Newfoundland spent almost as much, and Canada – despite the absence of provincial expenditures in these calculations – was slightly above the average for the world's developed nations.

In the dependent Empire the scenario was repeated, but the emphasis was perhaps even stronger. In the underdeveloped countries of the world there appears to have been growing concern for law and order (if not justice). Expenditures in support of these ends were hardly below the level in the developed nations, and as a fraction of total expenditures they were substantially higher. In the dependent colonies, the average figure was more than 2 shillings, and while that number is biased upward by a few colonies that spent at very high levels (the Falkland Islands spent more than 11 shillings; Gibraltar, in excess of 10; British Honduras, almost 10; and Hong Kong, 8 shillings), it was also held down by the most underdeveloped colonies, where the army served as the police force (in East and Central Africa, the average was less than 7 pence). In West Africa and the Caribbean, where British rule had been long in place and where distinct military forces existed, the expenditures tended to be compressed between 2 and 5 shillings. Among the nations in the underdeveloped category, only three spent more than 2 shillings, and, of those three, the figure for one was 2 shillings and 2 pence, and for a second, 2 shillings and 5 pence. In the dependent Empire the arm of justice was certainly both long and strong.

The Indian data might lead one to quite different conclusions. If the standard is the Princely States, then India's per capita figure of 7 pence is about half again their average, but the proportion of the Indian budget directed toward those activities is only slightly higher than the share of expenditures that law and justice commanded in

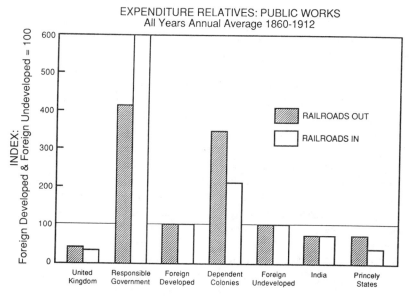

EXPENDITURE RELATIVES: PUBLIC WORKS
All Years Annual Average 1860-1912

Chart 4.3

those states. Moreover, when the measure is the average under-developed country, the Indian percentage figure is somewhat higher, but the per capita figure is lower. In fact, India exceeded only five of the twenty-five countries (Colombia, Costa Rica, Japan, Liberia, and Venezuela) in its level of expenditure for law and justice. While there may have been economies of scale in the provision of justice and, perhaps, the local courts were more important on the subcontinent, expenditure levels were low, and the explanation of that situation unclear. The qualitative evidence indicates that the legal system operated well and that property rights were defined and protected.

b. Public works (see Chart 4.3)

Institutional overhead can increase private profits, but so can investment in real capital. When the costs of all physical improvements are assessed directly against the business sector, private profits plummet – a lesson learned at some cost by investors in the chartered companies. When the services of the capital are available at less than full cost, business firms capture a part of those savings and profits respond accordingly. The infrastructure that supported the railroads and telegraphs was at least partly charged to users, but there was little direct connection between use and the incidence of the costs of the roads, bridges, and canals that constituted a more than substantial fraction of total expenditures on public works. How well did the Empire supply its citizens (and perhaps the British businessman as well) with the services of the stock of physical capital?

In the United Kingdom the contribution appears quite low when compared with the foreign developed countries. In part, this is because the data on which the study is based were drawn from national budgets. On the other hand, it should be borne in mind that there were no government expenditures on railroads in the United Kingdom – something that was not true in many of the other developed countries. In the 1860s, when government support for the railroads had been suggested, it was rejected not only because it would "depress the price of government securities" but because it would "tend to give us [the government] by degrees a control over the proceedings of the companies, and throw upon us a considerable but ill defined and imperfect responsibility for the management of the Railway," a responsibility that the British government was unwilling to assume.[5] Other nations were less hesitant.

In Britain private enterprise (although often regulated) continued to operate most public utilities considerably longer than in many other developed countries, but times were changing. While railroads were still beyond reach, the government was in the process of nationalizing the telegraphs. As Sir Stafford Northcote, the President of the Board of Trade (later, the Secretary of State for India and, still later, Lord Iddesleigh), said in writing to Disraeli,

> As a general rule one looks doubtfully at proposals that the government should carry on business on its own account but . . . the telegraph is treading on the heels of the post office and it is quite possible that a few improvements of detail might make it a possible rival. . . .[6]

In 1878 the government did take over the telegraphs; and within the span of only a few years government management transformed what had been a profitable enterprise into a perpetual drain on the Treasury. Given that enviable record, it was perhaps just as well that the government did not accept responsibility for the railroads. Whatever the case, if railroads are excluded from the public works calculation, the United Kingdom spent 1 shilling and 2 pence per capita, compared to 2 shillings and 10 pence for the developed countries (a ratio of 1:2.5). If railroads are included, the ratio is one to three.

In those parts of the Empire with responsible government, there was far less hesitation to turn to government to complete the social overhead infrastructure. A typical developed country spent less than 3 shillings per person per year on all public works, excluding railroads, but the colonies with responsible government were spending almost 12. If railroads are added, the average for developed countries rises to about 4 shillings. The responsibly governed colony figure, however, reaches more than £1. Even without the railroads, while a typical developed country spent less than 10 percent of its budget on public works, the average self-governing colony committed almost twice that figure.

In the case of expenditure on public works the Australasian colonies were again the most profligate. Even if railroads are excluded, the six Australian colonies averaged £1.12 and New Zealand, £1–0–2. Elsewhere, the South African colonies spent more than 8 shillings, Newfoundland, more than 7, and Canada, 5. When railroads are added, all numbers increase but particularly the Australasian, to almost £3, and New Zealand to almost 2. The South African average rises to more than 12 1/2 shillings, and the Canadian to 7 1/2. The level attained in Oceania – a level that was almost seven times that spent in an average developed country, even if railroads are not considered – is particularly striking. The nearest foreign rival to those colonies was Belgium, a country with a centralized public works administration, and Belgium spent less than 12 shillings.

There is considerable question as to the motivation that underlay the expenditure patterns in the colonies with responsible government. Those colonies were growing rapidly, their population was young, and they had had a much shorter history over which they could have accumulated a stock of social overhead capital. Thus, form of government or Empire status aside, they could be expected to devote a greater fraction of their current resources to such investment than older, long-settled areas. Still, the levels are so very much higher than those observed elsewhere that it appears unlikely that age alone can account for the difference. For example, over the years 1870 to 1900 in the Pacific region of the United States – a young and rapidly developing area – the federal government spent 2 shillings and the states an additional 1 shilling and 5 pence per capita per year on social overhead investment.[7] It appears reasonable to conclude that the colonies with responsible government, and particularly those in Oceania, displayed a strong inclination to devote funds to public investment; and, while a desire to increase business profits may not have been the reason for their behavior, it should be clear that the business community benefited.

In the dependent Empire there was again a marked difference between the colonies and India. Overall the colonies spent almost 3 shillings (increased by a fifth with the addition of railroads) – 20 percent of all expenditures. These figures, while paling in comparison to Australia and New Zealand, still stand out when compared to the 10 pence (6 percent of total expenditures) that was typical of the underdeveloped countries, and they compare more than favorably with the just less than 3 shillings, and 9 percent, of the developed ones. Inclusion of the railroads, however, makes the contrast somewhat less dramatic; but, even then, colonial expenditures were very much higher than those of the underdeveloped countries, and almost equal to those observed in the developed sector. The foreign countries, both developed and undeveloped, do, however, display a more rapid rate of increase. In the Empire, there appears to have been no single official policy on public works. The differences in expenditure levels among the dependent colonies were very wide. While the average expenditure was just less than 3 shillings, eighteen dependent colonies spent less than 10 pence, and twelve others, less than 2 shillings.

In any given colony, it appears that the level of expenditure depended in large measure on the policies of the particular colonial government, although these policies were at times modified by Whitehall. Certainly Milner, while in South Africa, viewed public works as a necessary investment. In a letter to Viscount Churchill he wrote:

> It is essential that we should start with the recognition of two fundamental principles: the first is a liberal expenditure on the development of the new colonies as a condition precedent to that great expansion of revenue to which we must look if they are, besides providing for their own growth needs, to share the burden of the British war debt. No great growth of revenue is possible without such expenditures.[8]

But it is not clear how much support he received from London. Similarly, the attempt by the British government to push particular development plans often brought howls of protest even from the British businessmen who were supposed to benefit. For example, the West African trader, John Holt, when speaking of government policies toward the West African Railways, referred to, "These vampires of our colonies who are in Downing Street and ... care not what becomes of them."[9] Still, between the local governors and their advisors and the central administration in London, the dependent colonies structured their public sector expenditures to yield a substantial block of real capital.

In India, few subjects attracted more official attention than the public works department. From the 1860s until the turn of the century, two debates raged: Should public works be undertaken by the public or by the private sector, and within the public sector, what was the appropriate level and composition of public investment? Of the two, the former occupied more of the policy makers' attention. As early as 1865 John Lawrence, the Governor General, wrote:

> I am strongly under the opinion that the government should undertake such work itself. For social, financial, and even political reasons, I consider this to be the right course. With all its shortcomings I believe it could be shown that the Public Works Department can – and does – work cheaper than private companies. I consider that with all precaution, private companies by the pressure they can bring to bear on government, both at home and in India, will force us into an arrangement and engagement injurious to the state and the people.[10]

In a subsequent letter to Northcote, Lawrence reiterated, "There is nothing which a company can do, which the state cannot do better and cheaper."[11]

However, financial problems soon tempered these strong convictions. Lawrence came to realize that, despite his preference for state enterprise, he would accept private initiatives "rather than have no more canals ... ," and he recognized that private funding "is the only mode of raising additional revenue to which there will be no murmur."[12] Nor were the concerns all financial and political. Questions were frequently raised about the efficiency of the public sector. In 1868 Northcote worried, "whether anything can be devised to supply the loss of the keen stimulus of self interest, which makes the private adventurer direct all his energies. ... "[13] But the old policies persisted. Ten years later Lord Lytton, the viceroy, wrote: " ... The public works department of the government of India has always been, when left to itself, the most extravagant, the worst managed, and altogether the least satisfactory branch of our administration."[14]

Despite the strong commitment of some Englishmen, such as Lawrence, to a socialized public works system, that "ideal" eroded in the face of political, financial, and efficiency arguments. In 1881 Devonshire at the India Office wrote to the viceroy, Lord Ripon:

> I see a considerable disinclination to the admission of private enterprise in India Railways in the council here, and probably the same feeling exists more strongly in India. There is sure to be soon a strong protest and reaction against the restruction of expenditure on useful public works, and it seems to me the only ground on which we should be able to take our stand will be that by restructuring our own operations we will be giving a fair field to private enterprise.[15]

And Ripon himself averred,

> There are two possible modes of doing so [financing railroads to prevent famines]. We may either devote to this purpose a much larger annual sum of money, raised either by taxation or borrowing, or we may once again appeal to private enterprise to do the work for us. Which of these two methods shall we adopt? I am strongly of the opinion that it is to the latter that we should turn.[16]

But established bureaucracies have lives of their own, and policy changes are effected at best slowly. In 1899, Lord Curzon, now in the viceregal chair, wrote Northcote at the India Office,

> ... I find a perfect chorus of dissatisfaction as to the manner in which the [public works] department reviews and treats offers of railway construction that come from responsible quarters in England and India. I saw yesterday a small private deputation of merchants who gave me specific cases. ... The outcry in the papers is unanimous, bitter and strong. ... [17]

The Indian expenditure data reflect the ebbs and flows of policy concerning public works, and the role of the private, as opposed to the public, sector in building them. The first railway in India was opened on April 15, 1853, and for a number of years most construction was carried out by British joint-stock companies that were guaranteed a 5-percent return on their capital outlay, as well as one-half of the surplus profits. In 1870 the government of India, in a shift that reflected Lawrence's views, changed its transportation policy. Thereafter new railway lines were to be built by the state. The government's resources, however, proved inadequate, and in 1880 the Raj again turned to the private sector. Three different types of contracts were signed, but all provided that the guaranteed interest not exceed 4 percent, and gave the shareholders less than half the surplus profits. In addition, any line built under these new contracts was to become the property of the government in twenty years.

When all is said and done, India spent on public works at a lower rate than the underdeveloped countries, and at a level similar to the Princely States. Moreover, unlike the other sectors, where expenditures rose over time, in India they peaked in the early 1880s and declined thereafter. As a percentage of the government's budget, the Indian average was one-quarter higher than the figure for the underdeveloped countries, but only two-thirds of the average of the Princely States. Inclusion of railroads raises the Indian levels substantially. The same adjustment, however, pushes the foreign underdeveloped indices upward as well, and India's relative position changes but little. If railways are included, expenditures are boosted above those that are reported by the Princely States.[18] Even the inclusion of the railroads does not do full justice to public works expenditures in India. The figures still omit the investment bound up in the state subsidy to "private" railroad investment.

In comparison with the level of expenditures in the underdeveloped countries, if public but not subsidized private railroads are included, India spent more than eight of the underdeveloped countries and ten of the Princely States. Even without railroads, Indian expenditures were greater than those in several Caribbean, Central, and South American countries – El Salvador and Peru, for example– and some large but not budgetarily centralized countries (Japan and Turkey, to cite two). In India government policy changed in the 1880s, and thereafter the government's contribution to the "nation's" capital stock declined dramatically. Although that change was in part a response to political pressure from business groups in Britain, it was in large measure dictated by financial exigencies.

The physical capital component of the infrastructure was heavily socialized in the colonies with responsible government and, by a different yardstick, in the dependent colonies as well. In India the levels were lower. Even there, however, per capita investment exceeded the figures for the poorest underdeveloped nations. The imperial businessman was advantageously placed to draw on the investments of society, and that conclusion holds before consideration is given to the subsidy provided by government guarantees to the "private" Indian railroads.

c. Human capital (see Chart 4.4)

Investment can take a variety of forms and not all yield physical capital. Among the nontraditional components of the capital stock are the resources devoted to investment in human capital. The term human capital is a broad one, encompassing expenditures on

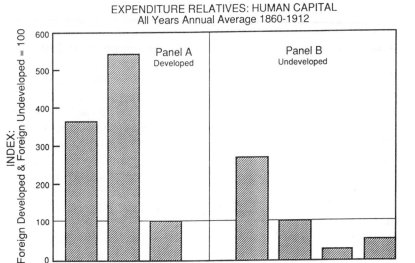

Chart 4.4

food, clothing, and housing for children in the years before they can become productive, on public health and medicine that permit people to work longer and harder, on formal education and on-the-job training, and on distribution schemes that prevent or mitigate famines and pestilence. While a part of these costs are always borne by the worker or the worker's family, economic development has been linked with some movement toward partial socialization. In the absence of slavery, generalized investment in human capital by private firms is seldom profitable; and, for a complex series of reasons, even individuals tend to invest in themselves at less than optimum levels. Failing some form of government subsidy, the level of investment in human capital is almost always less than the optimal amount, and the productivity of the economy suffers accordingly.

In the United Kingdom expenditures at the national level in the early years were very low in absolute terms, but about equal to expenditures elsewhere in the developed world. Beginning in the mid-1870s, however, expenditures on human capital rose rapidly, and by 1912 they averaged more than 13 shillings per person. Overall, the fifty-two-year average was about 4 1/2 shillings – something in excess of 6 percent of all expenditures. In the 1860s, expenditures in the developed countries were about equal to those in Britain, and spending in the underdeveloped sector was about half that level. As in the United Kingdom, both levels rose over time; but the rates of growth of expenditures in the foreign sectors were much slower. Overall, foreign developed countries averaged just over 1 shilling, and underdeveloped ones, about 7 pence. In terms of their total budgets, the underdeveloped countries spent slightly less than the British (a larger fraction early, a smaller one later), and the developed countries a little less than that (more than the British early, much less later).

Because of the differences in the levels of government-assigned responsibility for education, the human capital comparisons are probably the least reliable among the various estimates of resources devoted to supporting business activities. Among the developed countries only France and Sweden spent at levels about equal to the United Kingdom. The German and U.S. figures were low, at least in part because almost all educational expenditures were made by state and local authorities. State and local expenditures on education were, for example, about 15 shillings in the United States in 1902, and about the same in Prussia a decade later.[19] Compare those figures with the U.K. national average of 4 shillings and 5 pence for all expenditures on human capital.

In the Empire outside of India the levels of expenditure on human capital were surprisingly high. In the colonies with responsible government, the all-years average was more than 6 1/2 shillings, about one and one-half times the British national figure. Among those colonies, New Zealand averaged almost 17, and the six Australian colonies followed, with just over 15 shillings. The South African average was over 6 shillings, but in North America, although Newfoundland spent somewhat more, Canada expended only 1 shilling and 2 pence.

Although the colonies with responsible government devoted more than twice as much of their budget to human capital as did the countries in the foreign developed sector, the relationship between the dependent colonies and the underdeveloped nations was even more extreme. In those colonies expenditures were more than 2 shillings, a figure that appears small in comparison with the responsibly governed colonies, but very high if the standard is the 10 pence that was the average of the world's underdeveloped countries (or the 1 shilling, 2 pence of the developed ones, for that matter). Again, the wide colony-to-colony variation in expenditures suggests that the actual policies tended to reflect the views of individual governors and their advisors rather than any coherent centralized scheme. While twenty-six of the dependent colonies spent less than 1 shilling, twenty-two spent more than 4 shillings. That latter group included Mauritius, Malta, British Guiana, and almost all of the Caribbean Islands.

If Britain committed some resources to human capital, and the colonies in the Empire relatively more, the same cannot be said for India. Overall, the Indian government spent only 2 pence (about 4 percent of all expenditures), while even the Princely States were spending 5 pence, and more than 10 percent of their budgets. Among the twenty-five independent underdeveloped countries, only one spent less than India; and neighboring Siam spent more than 2 shillings, and 6 percent of its budget. Moreover, although the trend almost everywhere in the world was upward, there is little evidence of movement in the Indian series.

Nor were the British unaware of the low level of expenditures on human capital in India.[20] In 1871 Lord Mayo wrote to Argyll at the India Office, concerning education,

> I know that millions have been spent and will be spent which might have been and could be spent in . . . elevating the children of the soil. We have done much but we could do a great deal more – it is, however, impossible unless we spend less on the interests and more on the people.[21]

Ten years later the dissatisfactions were similar. At that time Ripon wrote to Gladstone:

> . . . I am also engaged in what can be done to extend and improve our system of primary education. A good deal has been done to encourage higher education here, but elementary education has been too much neglected. . . .[22]

And soon thereafter a memorandum from Randolph Churchill lamented:

> . . . everyday brings to our notice fresh objects for which public education is most desirable – take the development of primary education alone, in which much has been done for an Asiatic country, the educational means are still significantly deficient as compared with any civilized standard.[23]

But despite the concerns that both the political rhetoric and the data uniquely manifest, policy did not change. Rather, Hardinge wrote in 1911:

Our educational policy in this country has yet to be formed. At the present moment we are anxious to spend money on technical education at the same time Gokhale and some of his followers advocate very strongly free primary education which they would like to make compulsory. . . . I cannot help but feel that, apart from their desire for educational advantages for the people, they have the idea at the back of their heads that education will create unrest among a class without whom they feel that no movement in the country can acquire any serious force. . . . [24]

In India it appears that political concerns and a general disinclination to spend money combined to warp the structure of social overhead investment in a way that could well have redounded against profits and productivity.

d. Direct government support for business: manufacturing, agriculture, and natural resources (see Chart 4.5)

Today no one is surprised when even those governments most committed to private enterprise devote a significant block of their resources to providing direct support to business. That commitment, however, grew up rather slowly over the course of the late nineteenth century. In the United Kingdom, for example, trade and industry did not emerge as a separately reported category of expenditures until 1928, although of course there were expenditures toward those ends much earlier. In other nations the activities were officially acknowledged sooner, but similar caveats apply. For these reasons, the reader should view these figures as a minimum estimate of the levels of government support. In the United Kingdom the identified undertakings absorbed an average of 1 1/2 shillings per year, but 2 1/2 shillings over the last twelve years. In the developed countries the comparable figures were 1 and almost 2 shillings; and among the underdeveloped countries, just less than 1 and 1 1/2 shillings. In both the developed and undeveloped countries, the fraction of budget devoted to direct support was about 5 percent.

In the Empire, the colonies with responsible government seem to have discovered the value of business-supporting expenditures long before anyone else was more than dimly aware of their possible advantages. Over the entire fifty-two-year period they absorbed almost 7 percent of these colonies' budgets, even when the budget totals are inflated by the inclusion of funds spent on railway construction. That percentage translates into an annual per capita ex-

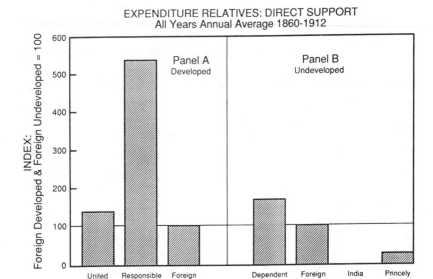

Chart 4.5

penditure level of 5 1/2 shillings. Among the colonies with responsible government, New Zealand spent, on average, 19 shillings; the six Australian colonies, more than 10; the South African colonies, almost 5 shillings; Newfoundland, over 3 shillings; and Canada, more than 2 shillings.

Even the dependent colonies, while spending at a much lower level than their more autonomous fellows, still spent, on average, at least as much as either the industrialized or the underdeveloped countries, although at the end of the period they were probably spending somewhat less. In these colonies the government felt little compunction about expenditures directed toward improving business. For example in 1908, Walter Davidson, the Governor of the Seychelles reported:

> The Agricultural Board sent in a series of unanimous resolutions
> asking that the surplus revenues of the colony be invested in
> loans to planters. They have my hearty sympathy, as long as the
> Loan Board is the Governor and the Executive Council, so there
> can be no hanky panky or bad debts. I hold that investments

locally to develop land bearing interest at 6 percent are better value than 3 percent gilt edged securities at home. . . . [25]

The highest levels of these direct business-supporting activities were in the Falklands, Trinidad, and Bermuda, but twenty-eight dependent colonies spent more than 1 shilling. At the other end of the spectrum, thirteen dependent colonies spent 2 pence or less. The explanation of the colony-to-colony variation in expenditures is difficult to discover; however, there does appear to be some loose correlation between the average level of direct business support and the state of the colony's development. Most of the larger Caribbean islands, Hong Kong, the Straits, and similar settlements are in the top half of the list, while the African colonies and the small Caribbean islands make up the bulk of the bottom.

While government support in the dependent colonies was substantial by the standards of the underdeveloped world, the same was not true for India. On the subcontinent few resources except those budgeted for transport appear to have been committed directly to the support of any business. In the early years there were some expenditures in support of private irrigation schemes, but they were never large. In 1882 the government moved briefly and tentatively into the business sector:

> The government of India have for some time past had under special consideration the importance of developing the iron industry in India. The Bengal Iron Works have consequently been purchased for the sum Rs 4, 30, 761 (£43,000). His excellency the Governor General in Council is now pleased that they will be retransferred for that sum together with any indespensible outlays to any parties who may establish satisfactorily that they are in possession of sufficient skill and resources and bona fide prepared to carry on the manufacture of iron and steel. . . . [26]

It was, however, a step from which there was almost immediate withdrawal. Later, when a scheme for an agricultural bank was proposed, all Minto could write was:

> . . . I very much wish we could induce the people of India to invest more money in undertakings in their own country. . . . On the face of it there is much in its [the Agricultural Bank's] favour. The intention of relieving the agriculturist from debt and enabling him to borrow at a lower rate than at present is excellent, but one is thrown back on the fact that this is to be done by English speculators counting on a rate of interest – a very high one ac-

cording to English ideas – to be gleaned from India and safe-
guarded by guarantees from the government of India. . . .[27]

The contrast with Davidson's letter is instructive. Even the governments of the Princely States expended more on direct business
support than the Indian government. Those principalities spent at
a rate that, although below most of the dependent Empire, was still
well above those that prevailed in the part of the subcontinent under
direct British control. In India the government may have been committed to laissez faire (if so, it is a strange contrast with the early
attitudes toward public works), or perhaps only to not spending
money; and periodic famines made it nearly impossible to carry out
any systematic program, no matter how the politicians felt. Whatever the reason, there is no evidence that the government of India
or the India Office ever skewed the budget in a way that would
have made British investment particularly profitable.

III. Conclusion

Chart 4.6 summarizes all the expenditures made in support of business. It is possible to conclude that the evidence supports the con-
tention that governments in the Empire biased their expenditures
in the direction of providing substantial support for the British business community; however, the results are not quite those that the
critics of Empire might have expected.

In the United Kingdom, the national annual per capita expenditure
in support of business averaged 8 shillings and 5 pence. That figure
is higher than the average for foreign developed countries; however,
given the relative development of the United Kingdom, a substantial
portion of the difference almost certainly reflects that position rather
than a major difference in "taste." The British and the foreign developed series display similar trends, and, as a fraction of total expenditure, those foreign countries appear to have devoted even
more "effort" to business-supporting activities than did the government in Whitehall.

In the Empire, at least in those parts with responsible government,
there is evidence of such a difference in "tastes." Even if railroads
are excluded, the average level of spending on business-supporting
activities is over three times the level at home; and, if railways are
included, the ratio rises to more than four. A part of the difference
can, of course, be traced to the allocation of functions between governmental levels. If the total (national plus local) expenditure figure

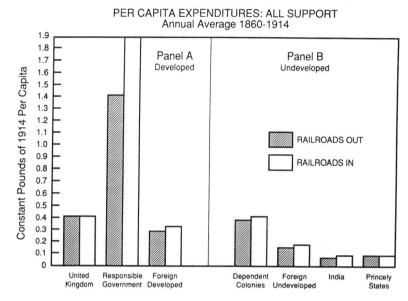

PER CAPITA EXPENDITURES: ALL SUPPORT
Annual Average 1860-1914

Chart 4.6

for the United Kingdom is used, the ratio falls to less than one when railroads are excluded. That comparison is, of course, overdrawn since expenditures by cities and subcolonial units are not included in the figures for the self-governing colonies. The colonies with responsible government do appear to have displayed considerable inclination to support their own (and, in the process, even British) business.

In the dependent colonies the evidence of a "taste" difference appears almost equally strong. Levels of spending were less than in colonies with responsible government, but close to being as high as the national totals in the United Kingdom. Moreover, the almost 8 shillings per person represented more than one-half of the total budgets of those colonies. That proportion is very much above levels in the United Kingdom or either foreign sector, and somewhat above the typical proportions in the profligate colonies with responsible government.

In India, the evidence runs in the other direction. The average level of expenditures is much below that of the foreign underdeveloped sector, but, as a fraction of the total, the "effort" is not dissimilar. More compelling, in both absolute and relative terms, if railroads are excluded, India spent less on public works, human capital, the legal structure, and direct business support than did the Princely States. Those comparisons, when coupled with the qualitative evidence on government decision making, indicate that the relevant governmental policies were less the product of pressure from British business than the result of the government of India's perception of local needs.

In the responsibly governed Empire, where Britain had almost no voice in policy, expenditures were by far the highest. In those dependent colonies where local citizens had at least some access to the political process the expenditure levels were next highest, but in the colonial possessions where that access was minimal (even though they may well have been potentially the most productive from the British businessman's viewpoint) expenditures were lowest. Of the fifteen dependent colonies with average expenditures of more than 18 shillings, five were in the Caribbean, seven were other island colonies (Falklands, St. Helena, Gibraltar, Hong Kong, Malta, Tonga, and Mauritius), and the other three were on the Malay peninsula (the Federated Malay States, Selangor, and Perak). Only in Hong Kong, the Federated Malay States, and Tonga does it appear that these expenditures primarily served a foreign business community, and in the last instance the European community was not British but Australasian. Conversely, of the twenty colonies that spent less than 5 shillings, thirteen were in West, Central, or East Africa – areas of alleged economic imperialism. Finally, on the Indian subcontinent (where the voice of British business should have been easily heard) per capita expenditures fell at the thirtieth percentile of the dependent-colony list (forty-four above, one equal, and nineteen below); and over time Indian expenditures did not increase. Little more was spent in the twentieth century than in the 1860s. On the other hand, in the United Kingdom the ratio of last- to first-decade expenditures was almost four to one, in the foreign developed sector it was almost that high; in the foreign underdeveloped sector it was more than six to one; and, even in the Princely States, it was two to one. To the extent that the British business community had any political interest or influence, it does not appear to have used it effectively; and that influence seems to have been particularly ineffective in India.

The analysis of expenditure patterns cannot deny the allegation that the British warped the political process to bolster the profits of their business community. On the other hand, it does not confirm the charge. If the British government had set out to effect such a policy, the political mechanism should have produced quite different results. Political control was great in India and least effective in the colonies with responsible government. Therefore the evidence of manipulation (some measure of the level of expenditures in support of business) should have been strongest in India and weakest in the colonies of white settlement. The actual facts are just the reverse. Evidence of government influence on behalf of business is weakest in India where political control was almost absolute. Next come the dependent colonies where there was often at least some local consultation. Finally, government involvement is the most significant in those colonies where British political control was the least evident. Thus, an alternative explanation clearly appears in order. Yes, government may well have warped the political process to aid business, but it could have been the local not the British business community that manipulated the political system. British businessmen did, of course, benefit; but it appears that the British government was a less effective instrument of business control than that provided by the local politicians.

5 The costs of defending an empire: the British and colonial taxpayer

I. The struggle for colonial involvement

The Empire was an attractive alternative to British investors in part because of the subsidy supplied by the British taxpayers. Guaranteed loans, grants-in-aid of official salaries, public works, and disaster relief all served to reduce the financial burden on the colonies and hence increased the potential return to the investor. Of all the subsidies enjoyed by the colonies, and by the British investors in those colonies, however, none was more lucrative than the subsidy for defense.

In the early history of the Empire there was a certain air of official indifference associated with questions of the cost of the military. It was only when the drain on the British exchequer engendered by the colonial phases of the Anglo–French wars became apparent that British officials began seriously considering the financial burdens of imperial defense. Eighteenth-century attempts at transferring those costs to the Empire were both clumsy and ineffectual. At the end of the French and Indian War, British taxes were the highest in the Western world. They averaged about 6 percent of net national product, and more than four-fifths of those revenues were devoted either to military expenditures or to service charges on the national debt – a debt that can be traced, in large part, to military operations on the North American continent. At the same time, taxes in the thirteen colonies were the lowest among the countries for whom records exist – lower even than those in Poland.[1]

The history of the British attempt to transfer a portion of the defense burden to those colonies is well known. It was met first with rhetoric:

> Why in the name of wonder, could not Great Britain protect us
> . . . for the sake of their trade, which you say the British merchants
> are very fond of and which raised Great Britain to a pitch of glory
> beyond every other nation.[2]

Then, with Indian feathers and tomahawks, and finally, with Concord, Bunker Hill, and Yorktown. All for a policy that, even if completely successful, would have done nothing more than edge

American levies up past Poland to the position of the "country" with the second-lowest taxes in the Western world. Even that emaciated policy was a failure; and an empire was lost.

Constitutional developments in the next century complicated matters still further, if indeed additional complication was possible. In the mid-nineteenth century most of the colonies of white settlement were granted responsible government – a status that implied a paradox. Responsible government loosened the bands that tied the colonies to Great Britain and lifted the hand of Whitehall from most areas of government. Colonial legislatures were required to underwrite the costs of purely domestic services, but they could not be forced to share the burden of imperial – that is, empirewide – expenses. The self-governing colonies saw little advantage in supporting an imperial defense establishment. They were convinced the British taxpayer would assume that responsibility if they did not, and in large measure they were correct.

The struggle over the defense burden was fought in two arenas: overseas, between the colonies and the British government, and domestically, between the Treasury – guardian of the public purse – and the Colonial Office. Neither the British government nor the Treasury seemed to understand that the preservation of the British Empire was intimately linked with the happiness of white British subjects and that attempts to coerce that group would quite likely produce other Lexingtons and Concords, not to mention Yorktowns. The Colonial Office, however, was very aware of this danger.

Once the nature of the problem was understood, Parliament was usually more concerned with the costs of the Empire than with any glories it might impart to the British Crown. In a debate of March 30, 1860, for instance, Sir Charles Adderley – a frequent and vocal Empire critic – rose in the Commons to complain of the high cost of imperial defense. He asserted Great Britain contributed £4,000,000 to the maintenance of security while the colonies contributed less than £40,000. "Why," he asked, "should the colonies be exempted from paying for their own defense?" Parliamentary emotions on the question of defense expenditures ran surprisingly high. Again, it was Adderley who captured the prevailing spirit when he averred that "it was absolutely unparalleled in the history of the world that any portion of an empire – colonial, provincial or otherwise – should be so exempted in purse and person from the cost of its own defences" as was a British colony.[3]

Reflecting the Commons's concern, in 1860 a Colonial Office committee urged that the colonies be deemed militarily self-sufficient and should, therefore, not expect to draw on domestic resources. Words alone, however, did not satisfy Parliament. On March 5, 1861, Arthur Mills moved the creation of a select committee on colonial military expenditure. The only sure way of retaining the colonies, he contended, was to enable them both to govern and defend themselves. The committee was duly appointed, with Mills as chairman, and it grappled with the issues in detail. Evidence before the body indicated that there were more than 44,000 troops (over a third of the total British armed forces) stationed in colonial garrisons. Slightly more than half of these were in Malta, Gibraltar, Bermuda, Halifax, St. Helena, and Mauritius, stations that were considered particularly vital for defense purposes and designated "imperial fortresses." The rest of the "imperial" army was scattered throughout the Empire, with heaviest concentrations in New Zealand, beset with Maori problems, and South Africa, involved in incessant wars with the indigenous African tribes. At the time of the investigation, the British exchequer contributed almost £1.75 million toward the cost of those forces, and the colonies, only one-fifth as much.[4] The committee's final report was filed on March 4, 1862. It accepted the British government's responsibility for military expenses arising from imperial policy; but for internal order, the report placed that "main responsibility" on the colonies.[5] Reports are, however, one thing, effective policies quite another.

With the advent of responsible government, the self-governing colonies lost British subsidies for internal administration, but they were, in return, able to refuse aid on matters of "imperial" as opposed to local concern. It was a case of point–counterpoint as to what constituted an imperial as opposed to a purely local concern, and the colonies were never loath to exploit that ambiguity. In 1900, for instance, New Zealand appealed for British assistance in the construction of harbor defenses, contending that the defense of its harbors was a matter of imperial consequence. The prime minister, Richard Seddon, wrote:

> ... the chief drawback has been the finding of the capital required for the completion of our harbor defences, the equipment of the defence forces, the purchase of great and small arms and ammunition. ... I therefore, with much reason, urge that it would be of advantage to the Mother Country ... if the monies required ... were raised by the Imperial authorities and advanced to the colony. ... There would ... be the direct advantages to the Imperial authorities and the Empire in having a reserve force established ready for any contingency that might arise. ...[6]

In general, Her Majesty's government took the position that land defenses were the sole responsibility of the local government and that Empire-wide expenses, such as the navy, should be shared; but it was a stance with which the self-governing colonies took strenuous and effective issue.

The controversy over the definition of "imperial" responsibility spilled over to the offices in Whitehall. In 1886, when the Colonial Office favored the expenditure of British funds for the defenses of Table Bay, Simonstown, and Cape Town, the Treasury stood stoutly in opposition and urged the abandonment of all work, if Cape Colony did not agree to pay the costs.[7] Robert Meade, one of the assistant undersecretaries at the Colonial Office, reached close to the heart of the matter when he contended,

> Defence is an ambiguous word in relation to a colony like the Cape with 1) a large native population, and 2) a seaboard liable to attack by enemies in war. If we claim in general terms that the Imperial troops are there for 'defence,' and that the colony ought to pay their cost, the colony might in turn claim to make use of them in native wars, which would be a losing bargain for the home government in the end, and might lead to incalculable expenses.[8]

Whatever ambivalence may have been aroused vis-à-vis the responsibilities of the self-governing colonies, the same ought not be said for the rest of the Empire – at least as far as official opinion in London was concerned. The absence of viable representative institutions, institutions that in the self-governing colonies provided a protective shield against even what must be considered reasonable demands from Whitehall, should have made it easy to draw funds for imperial defense from colonial revenues. Moreover, the fact that these colonies often depended on parliamentary subsidies and non-repayable grants-in-aid should have made them particularly vulnerable to British demands. Actually, the British government was able to exact at least some contributions from a few of the dependencies: India, Ceylon, Mauritius, Hong Kong, and the Straits Settlements all made not insubstantial payments; but the colonies of white settlement and many of the dependent colonies as well remained largely immune. As Edward Cardwell, the Secretary of State for War, wrote George Granville at the Colonial Office in 1869:

> ... It is not, I think satisfactory to Parliament ... that the Australian colonies and the Cape ... shall contribute at a much lower rate than is required from Ceylon, a Crown Colony, or that the

Dominion of Canada, the most powerful and not the least prosperous of Her Majesty's possessions shall . . . be an exception to
the rule which requires contributions from the colonies.[9]

Because of the recognized unfairness of the allocation, Parliament
and the Colonial Office moved to redress the balance, but not, perhaps, in the manner that the Treasury would have preferred. Both
politicians and Colonial Office bureaucrats realized that Mauritius
had defense costs only because it was a "fortress" in an Empire it
never chose to join and whose shipping it had been elected to protect. When the Treasury, in 1889, attempted to increase the military
charge upon Hong Kong, the Colonial Office resisted. The guardians
of the dependent colonies pointed out that the island was endangered only because it was a coaling station and naval depot from
which vessels bound for China and Japan were protected in a

> . . . trade which is mainly independent of H. Kong and which is
> carried on for the benefit of the mother country and the British
> taxpayer. . . . The 'British taxpayer' who plays so large a part in
> the Treasury position, is probably the only person who is strongly
> interested in the defence of Hong Kong. The Island produces
> nothing, and the defence of it is the defence of British trade. . . ."[10]

Similarly, Sir W. H. Gregory, a former governor of Ceylon, wrote
the Colonial Office in 1891, "The defence of Ceylon, is the defence
of English supremacy against the substitution of some other European power's; it is not the defence of an independent state."[11]

The Treasury for its part persisted in equating the responsibilities
of British and colonial taxpayers. As a consequence conflicts between
it and the Colonial Office were common and not infrequently had
to be decided at the Cabinet level. Correspondence between the two
offices could be vituperous. At one point the Colonial Office petu-
lantly wrote the Treasury "to express his Lordship's regret that the
unusual language employed respecting himself and a former Secretary of State as well as officers of this department" precluded any
action of a nature desired by the Treasury from being taken.[12] When
the Treasury, in its turn, accused the Colonial Office of placing
excessive and unjustifiable burdens on the British taxpayer, the Colonial Office remarked, "This is a serious charge for one public office to make against another. . . . It is without foundation . . . and
scurrilous."[13]

Regardless of the Treasury or of their state of constitutional development, all colonies were advantageously positioned when it
came to avoiding imperial impost to cover the costs of actual hos-

tilities. Wars were not infrequent along the imperial borders, and the initial expenses were almost always paid by the local governor from the treasury chest – a fund of several hundred thousand pounds financed by the Colonial Office and held in the colonies for public services and emergencies.[14] Once the imperial monies had been expended, the Treasury usually enjoyed but small success in recouping its monetary advances.

Sierra Leone, for instance, was singularly reluctant to pay the expenses of military operations conducted in the colony during 1898 and 1899. The total sum advanced exceeded £45,000, and the colony was expected to pay an initial installment of £10,000, to be followed by an annual payment of £5,000 until the debt was discharged. At the end of 1900, the War Office wrote the Treasury: "It will be seen . . . that no remittance can at present be expected, even in respect of the first installment. I am to add that it is not clear why additional expenditure has been incurred on other services within the colony."[15] As an indication of the difficulties Whitehall encountered with even the least redoubtable of colonies, it is to be noted that Sierra Leone did not disgorge any monies until 1905, and even then it remitted only two-thirds of the sum demanded.[16] A few years later, despite the absence of strong representative institutions, Sierra Leone was again able to resist War Office pressure to contribute a yearly sum toward its own defense, although the colony regularly accrued a budgetary surplus of more than £20,000 a year.

At another level, and as a surprise to some, the cooperation of that archimperialist Sir George Goldie and his Royal Niger Company was equally hard to enlist. Salisbury complained that "the company's troops will take their orders from him [Goldie] and not from us. . . . What we want is not his assistance but his men to act as Queen's troops and take their orders like any other. . . ."[17] To make matters worse, Goldie assumed that it was the British government's responsibility to protect the company's territory. Lord Sanderson, at the Foreign Office, wrote, "I do not know where Goldie finds his doctrine that the Charter implies that Her Majesty's government will undertake to defend the Company's territory against all European powers."[18]

Even the smallest victory was hard to gain. During the 1862 war in Gambia, the Treasury wrote the Colonial Office: "Milords are of opinion that no sufficient case has been made for our relieving the Government of Gambia from colonial expenses incurred in connection with the war against the king of Badiboo."[19] The amounts in question were hardly large. The fine of £2,400 that had been imposed on the offending monarch would have effectively paid for the war, but the governor had already remitted three-fourths of the mulct to the king to induce him to sign a treaty guaranteeing free trade within this territory. In this case the Treasury eventually recouped its losses, but not quickly or easily.[20]

But "success" was the exception rather than the rule. Thus, despite vigorous official protest, the British taxpayer bore the entire £900,000 cost of the Ashanti War of 1873. In 1878, Sir Michael Hicks-Beach, the Secretary of the State for the colonies, wrote Sir Bartle Frere in South Africa:

> There is . . . one reason in favour of keeping the peace to which I do not think I have much adverted and that is the question of cost. . . . We shall make Natal bear some of the cost already incurred on account of Zulu affairs and if there is a war, she must bear more. I hope you will impress this clearly on the people there at once.[21]

Nevertheless, the Zulu War broke out in 1879, and, as a temporary expedient, the expenses were defrayed by the British government. Peace came, but not repayment. Only one-fourth of the £1 million that the hostilities had cost was ever squeezed from a reluctant Natal. Sir Garnett Wolseley in frustration wrote to Hicks-Beach:

> This little puffed up council has command of the purse strings as fully as the House of Commons has at home, and its members are more puffed up with an idea of importance even than your English country member is. . . . If you want any money from them for imperial purposes, you can only get it as a bargain by giving them something in return. . . .[22]

Similarly, the Treasury was never able to gain full recompense from Cape Colony for its share of the £1.75 million spent on the Ninth Frontier or Border War.[23] The governor, Sir Bartle Frere, had anticipated difficulty. He urged the Colonial Office merely to send him a dispatch containing the amount due, and the monies would then be forthcoming. He cautioned Whitehall that, "in doing this, please remember how very sensitive colonists are and have the dispatch worded as little as possible in the imperative mood. . . ."[24] But London was clearly not sympathetic enough. Six months, later the governor wrote, ". . . the colonists here are incensed at the want of appreciation of the efforts they have made . . . to provide for their own defence. . . ."[25] As late as January 1882, the Treasury was still trying to collect some portion of the debt, but the lowered demand of £216,363 was still considered excessive by the colonists. As a consequence the Treasury, in defeat, wrote the Colonial Office: "My Lords will consent to accept £150,000 in full discharge of the debt. . . ."[26]

When the Cape ceased to make its annual contribution of £10,000 toward the upkeep of the imperial garrison in the colony, the Treasury could only reserve the right to reopen the subject and lament, "My Lords cannot, however leave unnoticed the implication . . . that a colony should not be called upon to contribute towards the cost of a force maintained as an imperial garrison within its territory, with this opinion Milords cannot agree."[27] Even a colony as insignificant as Bermuda was able to successfully refuse a Treasury request for a military contribution.[28]

The costs of the Anglo–Boer War charged to the imperial exchequer totaled £217,166,000. Most of that sum was paid by the British taxpayer; but, for years, the colonies and the home country continued to wrangle over the apportionment of those expenses. In 1908 the Treasury claimed that the Cape still owed His Majesty's government £182,978–12–4 for the refund of war-related customs duties; but as usual it again found itself weaponless and finally surrendered. "With regard to the outstanding balance . . . due from the Cape Government in respect of supplies," the guardians of the public purse tiredly wrote the Colonial Office, "my Lords do not propose to press for further payment of this sum."[29] Colonial intransigence was not new. A generation earlier Robert Lowe (later Lord Sherbrooke), Gladstone's first Chancellor of the Exchequer, had written, "Instead of taxing them as our forefathers claimed to do, we, in the matter of this military expenditure, permit them in a great degree to tax us. . . ."[30]

While it might be argued that the Anglo–Boer War was of sufficient magnitude to be judged an imperial responsibility, no such justification can be found in the case of New Zealand's Maori War or in that of the threat of internal strife in Canada prompted by Louis Reals's uprising on the Red River. New Zealand, at least, spent more on defense than any other self-governing colony; however, while the colonists happily accepted British support against the Maoris, they ended hostilities as soon as the aid was withdrawn. As Lord Lyttleton, the colonial reformer, wrote to his brother-in-law Gladstone: " . . . The colonists have been so long carried in nurses arms they cannot stand on their own feet. My belief is that this war against some 2,000 aborigines has cost John Bull the best part of £3,000,000. There's a perfect caricature of political relations. . . ."[31] Similarly, the

British tried for years without success to collect some repayment of the funds they had spent to put down the Red River rebellion.

Canada proved particularly difficult. In 1863 with an American army poised on their border, the best response the Canadians could muster to the British appeal for support was the assertion that "the best defense for Canada is no defense at all."[32] At that time the British were spending almost £900,000 per year on Canadian defense, a level that was maintained until 1868.[33] Nor were those attitudes tempered by the passage of time, as the later discussion of the immediate pre–World War I period will attest.

Not only did the self-governing colonies refuse to pay for their own defense, but they also importuned the British government to underwrite military operations designed solely to expand the Empire in directions that the colonists thought profitable. In the 1880s, for example, the Australians were interested in increasing their sphere of influence in the South Pacific. Lord Derby, in discussing the Australian attitudes, invoked a comparison to the Monroe Doctrine. " . . . but there is one essential difference," he wrote Gladstone, "the colonists expect us to do their fighting for them." More generally, he felt: " . . . colonists are always willing to help us and stand by us provided we will pay all the money and take all the risks."[34]

Whitehall was not, however, totally without recourse. It somehow forced the Straits Settlements to bear all costs of the Perak War of 1875, and British troops were ultimately recalled from most of the self-governing colonies. The "withdrawal of the legions," initiated in New Zealand in the 1860s, culminated in 1871 when the last British troops marched out of the Quebec Citadel, while the band played "Good-bye, Sweetheart," and "Auld Lang Syne."[35]

The "withdrawal," however, did not imply that British forces no longer continued to serve in "imperial fortresses" or that they did not later appear in beleaguered parts of the self-governing Empire; nor was withdrawal costless. The political support of the white settlers was important to preservation of the Empire, and ways had to be found to sweeten an otherwise bitter pill. Thus, at the same time that British troops were leaving the some 250,000 settlers in New Zealand to face some 50,000 Maoris alone, Edward Cardwell, now the secretary of state for the colonies, urged Parliament to grant the colony an imperially guaranteed loan of £1,000,000.[36]

Attempts to shift the defense burden to the colonists continued, and financial pressure was sometimes employed to encourage the recalcitrant. In 1880, for example, the Treasury wrote the Colonial

Office that it was its understanding that Lord Kimberley, the secretary of state for the colonies, had authorized Natal to raise a loan
only on condition that it recognized its pecuniary responsibilities
regarding the Zulu War.[37] Natal got the loan, but the manner in
which the colony recognized its responsibilities may not have been
what Kimberley had in mind. The colony remained obdurately opposed to paying what the home government thought was Natal's
just share of the costs of the Zulu War.

In general, the stronger the representative institutions of a colony,
the better it was able to resist the Treasury; but a colony as small
and basically insignificant as Mauritius was, like Bermuda, able to
reduce, if not totally repulse, a British demand for a military contribution. In 1891 the Legislative Council voted only £20,000 of the
£25,000 requested by Whitehall. Impotent, the Treasury informed
the Colonial Office, that "Her Majesty's Government remonstrated
vainly."[38]

One thing is certain: In case of doubt, the imperial authorities (that
is, the British) paid. Discussing the impending assumption of control
over the Transvaal in 1878, Sir Garnett Wolseley, the commanding
general, wrote:

> ... we must make up our mind to rule over a country in which
> at present the majority and for a long time hereafter a large pro-
> portion of the people, are and will be discontented ... to enable
> us to hold our own we must be prepared to maintain a large
> garrison of British troops here, the expense of which must be
> defrayed by the Imperial exchequer.[39]

To which Sir Michael Hicks-Beach, the Secretary of State for the
Colonies, roared in frustration, "Now I confess this seems to be a
position that can hardly be maintained. I feel pretty confident that
if the next general election placed the Liberal party in power, they
would not maintain it. . . ."[40]

In many ways, Great Britain seemed a helpless giant as it faced
its self-confident and often arrogant offspring. When Queensland
threatened to intervene in the affairs of New Guinea, Lord Sel-
bourne, in writing to Gladstone, expressed himself as strongly opposed to any annexation: " . . . I am, at present, unable to conceive
of any necessity, or justification, for taking the whole of this immense
country that can be made and I should consider such an act impolitic
in a very high degree, and also morally unjustifiable. . . . " But his
Lordship conceded that "if New Guinea must come under the British

flag, colonial sovereignty would be unacceptable and the British would have to act themselves."[41] Three years later, Edward Stanhope at the Foreign Office wrote Randolph Churchill:

> I am sorry to have to trouble you about New Guinea . . . I am afraid that the English Government is so far committed that it will be already compelled to make a considerable Imperial contribution . . . toward starting New Guinea. I hate . . . [this] as much as you . . . but the obligations of this country will force it upon us.[42]

Fiji, too, came under British jurisdiction, largely as a consequence of Australasian pressure. Yet, when the secretary of state, Lord Carnarvon, had the temerity to ask for a financial contribution from Australia and New Zealand to help defray the costs, the request was unhesitatingly rejected. Lord Normanby, the governor of New Zealand, explained the views of his prime minister, Julius Vogel, to Carnarvon:

> He believes that underlying the replies of all the colonies there have been two feelings: first, that the Mother Country was drifting into an entirely new colonial, or rather anti-colonial policy, that in times past she did not hesitate to incur colonial expenditures, that assuming possession of Fiji was analogous to many previous cases; that to ask contributions from the colonies was a novel proceeding connected only with the presumed policy of casting off the colonies, and that to acquiesce in it would argue an acceptance by the colonies of the new position it was desired to assign to them.[43]

In 1885, Lord Derby, the Conservative leader, wrote Gladstone about the designs of Natal on Zululand: "All the world waits for us to take Zululand, only because it is next door. . . . This passion for annexation and consequent contempt for the economy is not more to my taste than yours. . . . "[44] But the world's perception was correct and Zululand was annexed.

Whatever controversy prevailed over the appropriate role for the self-governing and dependent colonies, most critics of Empire smiled on India, though some with more insight continued to question its contribution to the public weal. It was pointed out that India did not draw directly on the British exchequer, and the expenses not only of the Indian army but of British regiments stationed on the subcontinent were drawn from the Indian revenues. Indian regiments were also used in hostilities conducted beyond the bounds of the subcontinent in campaigns that were clearly imperial rather than purely Indian responsibilities. Indian troops served in Persia, 1856–7 and twice in China, first in 1857–60, and again during the Boxer Rebellion of 1900, when they helped relieve Peking. They participated in the Abyssinian campaign of 1864, the Afghan War of 1878–80, the operations in Egypt during 1882–5, and they fought in East and Central Africa in 1897–8. Further service in Africa occurred during the Anglo–Boer War, and in the East African and Somaliland campaigns of 1902–4. The Indian Army mounted the invasion of Tibet in 1903–4. And during World War I, India provided the largest volunteer army in history in aid of the Allied cause – notably in Mesopotamia and on the Western Front.

When the Indian Army was used in imperial wars, the British exchequer sometimes defrayed the costs, but often it did not. India bore both the ordinary and extraordinary costs of the Persian campaign; and the heavy expense of the second Afghan War, despite its imperial implications, fell exclusively on the Indian budget. More surprisingly, in the Abyssinian campaign of 1864, the pay of troops and the charges for vessels employed in the expedition "which would have been charged under the Revenues of India if such troops or vessels had remained in that Country or Seas adjacent," Parliament declared, "shall continue to be so charged. . . ."[45]

To a succession of British viceroys and liberal politicians the evidence was incontrovertible. London, they argued, had successfully transferred a significant portion of the home defense burden to the Indians. Lawrence's response to the 1864 decision was one of outrage, and nothing that occurred later changed his mind.[46] A few years later he argued:

> India is . . . required to pay all the expenses of every British soldier required in India, and even to supply a sum which will cover the cost of keeping up this force; and yet when a portion of these troops leaves the country, they are still charged to India.[47]

Further, he pointed out:

> India is treated differently from the colonies. No one would think of asking any of the latter to pay a portion of the expenses of Afghanistan, no statesman would charge Canada or Australia. . . .[48]

It was the start of a debate that was to span the rest of the century. An attempt by Parliament to saddle India with the imperial costs of the Egyptian campaign prompted Lord Ripon to vent his spleen:

> I think if you will try to realise what the condition of a human
> being must be who has to live on £2–14–0 a year, you will not be
> surprised that I feel it my bounden duty to resist to the utmost
> of my power the imposition of any fresh burden upon him on
> account of the objects in which he is not directly interested.[49]

To these men the case was clear. India was a poor country and it
was being asked to subsidize imperial defense out of all proportion
to its position. Not only was it being forced to bear a substantial
portion of the costs that should have fallen on the other parts of the
Empire, but it was being asked to shoulder a portion of the British
burden as well. India paid the direct costs of both Indian and British
troops in India, as well as some fraction of the costs of Indian troops
used in largely imperial adventures. The subcontinent thus supported a military reserve for the entire British Empire. A popular
piece of contemporary doggerel seemed to support the government
of India's view:

> We don't want to fight
> But by Jingo if we do
> We'll stay at home and mind the store
> And leave it to the mild Hindoo

Nevertheless, there were Britons who thought the evidence less
than conclusive; and as the quantitative evidence indicates, they
were correct. Gladstone, for example, failed to see India as a great
asset to imperial defense:

> I am one of those who think that to the actual, as distinguished
> from the reputed, strength of the empire, India adds nothing.
> She immensely adds to the responsibilities of Government and I
> am rather moving toward the belief that by our army arrange-
> ments we [at home] have made her . . . [the basis for expenditures]
> which might have been avoided.[50]

And even Kimberley averred: "But for India, I feel certain that no
Egyptian expedition would ever have taken place. . . ."[51] The rulers
of India both in the East and in London continued to press for
reductions in the "unjust" Indian military contribution. However,
as Lord George Hamilton, the Secretary of State for India, recognized, ". . . I am not unlikely for the future to find myself in a
minority of one in the Cabinet as regards India's contribution."[52]

Queen Victoria's Golden Jubilee was the occasion for the calling
of the first of the Colonial (later Imperial) Conferences that were to
become a regular consultative mechanism for the British community.
Defense and particularly the naval situation in Australasian waters

was at the top on the agenda of the first such conference. The discussions were long and on the whole barren. The Australasian colonies, and for that matter all the self- governing parts of the British Empire, were reluctant to contribute to a military establishment over which they had no control. Finally an agreement was reached. The Australian Squadron of the Royal Navy would be increased by the addition of five fast cruisers and two torpedo gunboats to protect "the floating trade in Australian waters."[53]

The decision, however, was not a complete triumph for British diplomacy. Even though two of the cruisers and one of the torpedo boats were to be held in reserve, the colonies refused to fund the enterprise in its entirety. The imperial government agreed to advance £850,000 toward the initial costs of the vessels and to pay the capital expenses of commissioning the reserve squadron in time of war. The colonies were to see to general maintenance and pay interest on the capital cost up to a limit of £35,000 annually. This naval agreement was one of the few concrete achievements of the conference, and it appears that the Australasian colonies had achieved a remarkably good bargain. For a very modest price they were guaranteed that four ships would remain in the vicinity of Australia in times of peace and seven in times of war; and, in addition, the British also agreed to keep two British warships in New Zealand waters on all occasions.

A decade later, the conference once more devoted much of its energy to imperial defense. The Australian colonies and New Zealand undertook to contribute £226,000 a year toward the maintenance of a Royal Navy Squadron in the Pacific; and that contribution was later increased by £14,000.[54] Although the actual cost of the squadron was probably three times their contribution, Australia was far from satisfied. Alfred Deaken, the prime minister, wrote:

> While fully recognising the paramount importance of 'unity of control' for all the naval forces of the Empire, the people regard the present contribution of £200,000 to the cost of the Imperial Navy as being somewhat in the nature of a tribute, and it is therefore desirable, if possible, to find some means by which Australia can assist the Admiralty in the naval defence of the Empire without offence to the constitutional doctrine that the Government levies taxation and should be responsible for the expenditures and management.[55]

Outside of Australasia, the conference proved even less productive from the British point of view. The other self-governing colonies offered no contributions during the nineteenth century, but they made some small concessions in the twentieth. In 1902, Newfoundland agreed to pay a capital sum of £1,800 plus £3,000 a year for inaugurating and maintaining a branch of the Royal Naval Reserve. Cape Colony pledged the price of a battleship but later commuted this undertaking into a yearly subsidy of £50,000, and Natal agreed to contribute £35,000 annually.[56] The annual cost of the South African squadron was, however, more than £1 million a year, and more than 2 million had been spent out of the Naval Works Loan Account on harbor works at Simonstown alone.[57] All in all, colonial contributions toward imperial defense were very small. As Sir William Jervois, who during his years of service was governor of both South Australia and New Zealand, wrote to the Colonial Office,

> It is with these governments as with popular governments elsewhere; if war appears likely they are for the time being very energetic, but as the probability of hostility wanes, their ardour decreases . . . they do not much care to expend money on objects from which they derive no popularity.[58]

Lord Minto, the former Governor-General of Canada, wrote Sir Wilfrid Laurier asking for Canadian assistance in the impending war in South Africa to which Laurier stonily replied:

> . . . the present case does not seem to be one, in which England if there is war, ought to ask us, or even expect us to take part, nor do I believe that it would add to the strength of the imperial sentiment to assent at this juncture that the colonies should assume the burden of military expenditures.[59]

It was the old story repeated again. British politicians were harsh in their judgment of the senior Dominion. " . . . Canada," Chamberlain wrote, "claims to be part of the Empire and shares in all its privileges. . . . She asks for control of Imperial negotiations when her interests are concerned, full preference in Imperial contracts, and for special consideration in Imperial negotiation. On the other hand, she repudiates her share of Imperial defence. . . ."[60] Hicks-Beach now Chancellor of the Exchequer, found it "especially intolerable that Canada, which calls herself a nation, should do absolutely nothing to defend her coast."[61] In writing to Salisbury he took his reasoning one step further. "I think both Canada and Australia should be warned that in the event of our being engaged in a naval war, our navy will have other things to do than provide for their defence."[62] The rhetoric was, however, merely empty bluster – there was nothing the British government could do – there were no sanctions that they could employ – that did not threaten costs well above any potential revenues.

By 1907 the troubles in South Africa were over, but permanent peace appeared farther away than ever. For the first time the British delegates to the Imperial Conference were able to convey a sense of alarm to the Dominion leaders; and, building on the limited progress achieved at the preceding gatherings, a plan to increase the Pacific fleet was adopted. That newly enlarged fleet was to have three squadrons – East Indies, Australia, and China – and each would include one battle cruiser, three light cruisers, six destroyers, and three submarines. The total capital expenditure needed to underwrite the expansion was estimated at more than £11 million.

The Australian government agreed to maintain the Australian squadron and to pay more of the capital cost of the squadron's battle cruiser. The New Zealand delegates affirmed a willingness to finance the battle cruiser for the China squadron and to increase the colony's annual contribution to naval maintenance from £40,000 to £100,000. As a result, three years later the keels for two battle cruisers, the *Australia* and *New Zealand*, and for two of the nine light cruisers were laid down in the shipyards of Great Britain. Moreover, in a totally uncharacteristic display of intergovernmental cooperation, the colonial delegates agreed that, while the Dominion-financed warships would remain under their control in peacetime, those vessels could be deployed at the Admiralty's discretion in time of war.

The 1907 conference could be deemed a success, since it did manage to achieve a marginal redistribution of the defense burden from Britain to the self-governing colonies in Australasia. Canada was, however, a quite different matter. That Dominion refused to contribute either financially or in kind to any naval force, and its delegates limited themselves to noting the potential defense benefits that flowed from their Fisheries Protection Service. That service, the Canadian delegates argued, cost over £50,000 a year, maintained an *armed* gunboat on the Great Lakes – a vessel soon to be joined by one operating off the Pacific coast – and "all at no cost to the British taxpayer."[63] In 1906, however, Canada did assume fiscal responsibility for the naval base at Halifax and, three years later, for Esquimalt as well. The annual cost of operating the Halifax station was £31,600 and the Esquimalt transfer added an additional £27,300 to the Dominion's budget.[64]

If 1907 was a success, the same cannot be said for the next meeting in 1911. Sir Edward Grey, the foreign secretary, addressed the prime ministers of Australia, Canada, New Zealand, and South Africa; and informed them, in no uncertain terms, that war was imminent. The announcement, however, had little effect on the self-governing recalcitrants. On the other hand, the government of the Federated Malay states did present a capital ship, the *H.M.S. Malaya* to the Royal Navy.[65]

The British government had, by 1911, determined that gaining voluntary defense contributions from the self-governing Dominions was an almost impossible task. They also, however, discovered that extracting either voluntary or coerced contributions from the dependent colonies was only marginally easier. Before 1895 the government had attempted to conclude agreements with each dependent colony covering the contribution that both Britain and the colony would make to the colony's defense. The negotiations can be described as, at best, an unedifying process, filled with mutual recriminations, petty accounting controversies, and endless financial bickering. How much could a colony afford to pay? What items should be excluded from the calculation of the revenue "defense base"? What was the appropriate rate of exchange to transform Straits or Canadian dollars or Indian rupees into British pounds? Who had the responsibility to pay for repairs to military buildings and equipment?

At the end of the century, in an attempt to restore some sanity and order to the process, the interminable individual negotiations were replaced by a new general policy. Each colony, the Colonial Office decreed, would contribute a flat percentage of its gross governmental revenues. The figure for the Straits and Hong Kong was set at 17.5 percent (later raised to 20); that of Ceylon, at 7.5 (raised to 9); and Mauritius, at 5 percent.[66] Over the previous decades the Straits had actually contributed 19 percent; Hong Kong, 15; Ceylon, 6; and Mauritius, 3 percent of their gross revenues. While the new policy produced some small increase in the military contribution of the four colonies, no percentage was set for fifty-six of the sixty dependent colonies.

Harold Cox, in a House of Commons debate of February 15, 1907, placed the military expenses of the United Kingdom at £66,000,000 and those of the colonies at £887,000. Figures quoted by the Treasury in 1912 indicated that in terms of actual cash, the Straits contributed £190,000; Hong Kong, £118,000; Ceylon, £138,000; and Mauritius, £25,000. These four colonies, together with Egypt's £150,000, provided more than three-quarters of the total Empire defense contribution.[67] As for the other dependent colonies, no orderly process was ever devised; and the vagaries of constitutional development,

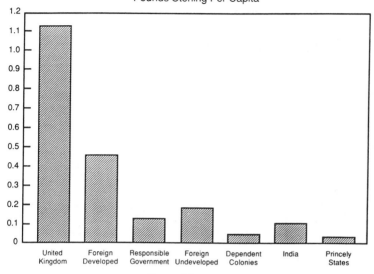

DEFENSE EXPENDITURE: ALL YEARS AVERAGE
Pounds Sterling Per Capita

Type of Government

Chart 5.1 (a)

income, and administrative policy produced a very diffuse pattern
of contributions. Thus, at the beginning of the century, the military
garrison in Jamaica cost £200,000 a year, but the colony contributed
nothing!

II. Defense expenditure patterns

How did diplomatic and political policy translate into expenditures?
The data indicate that in the late nineteenth and early twentieth
centuries, Great Britain maintained the highest levels of per capita
defense expenditures in the world. The fifty-three-year average of
£1.14 reflects levels that rose from £.74 in the 1860s to £1.58 in the
last pre-war decade, and the average for the first thirteen years of
the present century stood at £2.04 – almost 4 percent of national
income. By comparison, the German average was two-thirds, and
the French, three-quarters, of the British figure. Defense represented
37 percent of governmental expenditures in the United Kingdom,
while the figure for the rest of the developed world was under 30.
See Charts 5.1(a), 5.1(b), and 5.2.

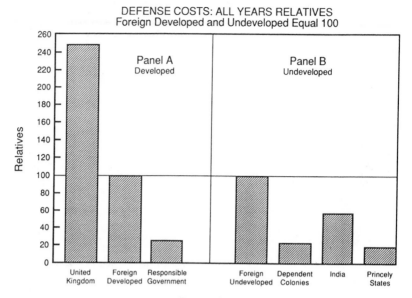

DEFENSE COSTS: ALL YEARS RELATIVES
Foreign Developed and Undeveloped Equal 100

Chart 5.1 (b)

That Britain shouldered a disproportionately large share of the defense of the Empire was clear to many in Parliament and Whitehall; but even the initiated were often unaware of the dimensions of the defense subsidy. The government of India (and hence the Indian taxpayer) underwrote the direct costs of military expenditures actually incurred on the subcontinent and, in addition, contributed armies, in part supported to these same Indian revenues, to the defense of the Empire as a whole. Casual perusal of this evidence would seem to indicate that, from the point of view of defense, India was totally self-supporting; and, indeed, it came closer to achieving this desirable – from the British point of view – state, than any other colony or dominion. It is, however, important to emphasize that, even in the case of India, local contributions fell short of what may be assumed to have been the "true" costs of Indian defense. Indian defense expenditures were significantly less than those of comparable independent nations – although higher than the Princely States – and the gap was growing. Karl Marx, for example, a keen observer but hardly a professional politician, was well aware of the problem. He wrote:

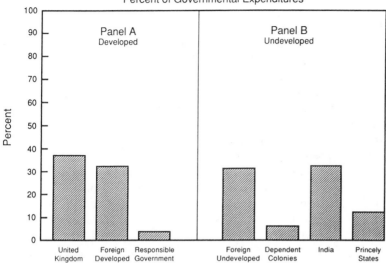

DEFENSE EXPENDITURES: ALL YEARS PERCENT
Percent of Governmental Expenditures

Chart 5.2

It is evident that individuals gain largely by the English connection with India, and of course their gain goes to increase the sum of national wealth. But against this a very large offset is made. The military and naval expenses paid out of the pocket of the people of England on Indian account . . . and it may be doubted whether, on the whole, this dominion does not threaten to cost quite as much as it can ever be expected to come to.[68]

Marx's comments show that he had a political scientist's sense of the late 1850s, but they also suggest that he was truly prophetic about the future of the Anglo–Indian relationship. By 1912, the Indian military commitment had fallen to about half what it had been when Marx wrote. Moreover, although by Empire standards the Indian contribution remained high (below that of the self-governing colonies, but twice that of the dependent colonies and the Princely States), it was very low if the appropriate standard is the countries that made up the underdeveloped foreign sector.[69] Over the last half of the period, per capita Indian military expenditures were about half the average level of those countries. Among the twenty-five nations in that group, only four (Colombia, Tunisia, Costa Rica, and

Liberia) spent less, and Tunisia was not exactly independent. For comparable periods, neighboring Siam, for example, spent about a third again as much.

While the evidence indicates that, in absolute terms, India was not the paragon that some officers of the Treasury suggested, if the Empire is examined relatively, the subcontinent should still be viewed as a "model" dependency. Among the colonies with self-government the trend in military expenditures was upward; but over the entire period, defense cost a colonial taxpayer less than 1 shilling and 9 pence a year; and, even in the last decade before World War I, it took the taxes of nine residents of those self-governing colonies to make up what a single British taxpayer was forced to contribute to the Empire's defense. Overall those colonies committed less than one-twenty-fifth of their budgets to defense. In contrast, residents of a foreign developed country paid, on average, four times as much; and even in the last decade before the War, that proportion held. While the Canadians, Australians, and Afrikaners directed £1 in 25 of governmental expenditures toward defense, the figure in the rest of the developed world was almost 1 in 3.

Of all those Dominions, only New Zealand spent at a rate even vaguely commensurate with its constitutional or developmental status. Every New Zealander contributed more than 5 shillings per annum to the defense establishment; and, although that figure was only three-fifths the level of a citizen of a typical developed country, it was half again that of a resident of an underdeveloped one. While New Zealand may not have provided an ideal, elsewhere the picture was even bleaker. The Australian colonies spent much less than half as much as their South Pacific cousins, the Canadians and South Africans about a third as much, and expenditures in Newfoundland were only about 2 pence a person a year. The Australian propensity to spend heavily on administration, capital improvement, business, and almost everything else, while depending in part on a willingness to tax and borrow, rested also on the colonies' ability to avoid committing resources to the military.

In the dependent colonies, despite their near-monopoly of political control, the British government's attempts to shift the defense burden appear to have come closer to approximating the Australian–Canadian experience than the New Zealand–Indian one: that is, policies that were close to total failure. Those dependent colonies, on average, spent no more than 7 pence a year, a mere 6 percent of their budgets on defense. Of the sixty-four such colonies, only thirteen spent as much as 1 shilling, and only six (Pehang, the Falkland Islands, the Straits Settlements,

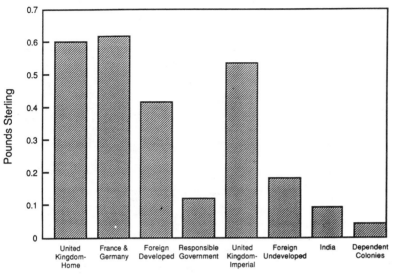

DEFENSE EXPENDITURES: ALL YEARS PER CAPITA

Chart 5.3

Hong Kong, Southern Rhodesia, and the Somali Coast Protectorate) more than three. A tiny handful, five, spent more than the typical underdeveloped country (2 shillings and 3 pence); but two-thirds of the dependent colonies spent less than the average of the three least-prepared underdeveloped countries.

The facts strongly suggest that, unlike the other developed powers of the late nineteenth century, Britain maintained not a single but two military and naval establishments: one for domestic defense and another for protection of the Empire. Compare, for example, the average British expenditures of £1–2–10 with the French and German average of about one half that amount (12 shillings and 5 pence). It is possible to gain some insight into the relative magnitudes of the two British enterprises by roughly allocating military and naval expenditures between home and imperial defense.[70] Such an exercise (see Chart 5.3) indicates that expenditures for home defense, while above the average for all developed countries, was about equal to those of France and Germany. The second military and naval establishment – the one designed to protect the Empire – cost somewhat less, but the charges were still substantially higher than the amount that a typical developed nation spent for its defense. On average, Britain spent about £20 million a year on that second establishment – £20 million that, had the world been different, might have been raised in the colonies.

An indication of the fiscal effects of the British subsidy can be gained by examining the world as it might have appeared had the colonies been responsible for their own defense. Although any particular allocation is arbitrary, the absence of the £20-million subsidy provided by the British taxpayer would likely have forced the colonies with responsible government to increase their expenditures to a level commensurate with the average defense expenditure of the developed countries, to raise the level in the dependent colonies to equal those of a typical underdeveloped nation, and to push Indian expenditures – given the apparent economies of scale – to almost three-quarters of that amount. Thus, it appears that Britain came very close to making up the total "shortfall" in colonial defense expenditures. As an earlier generation of British politicians had learned from their experience in dealing with the American colonists in the eighteenth century, and as their twentieth-century peers in Moscow and Washington, D.C., have discovered in the four decades since Hiroshima, "It costs a lot of money to maintain an empire."

Some idea of the financial sacrifice the British taxpayer was asked to make for defense of the Empire can be gained from Charts 5.4(a) and 5.4(b). This exercise in speculative history compares actual British defense expenditures and those of a typical developed country with those that would have prevailed had: (a) citizens of the colonies with responsible government paid the taxes necessary to maintain a level of defense expenditures equal to those prevailing in the developed world; (b) residents of the dependent colonies been forced to maintain a defense establishment equivalent to that of an average underdeveloped nation, and (c) Indians paid for a level of defense equal to an underdeveloped country.

A shift in the defense burden to the responsible and self-governing colonies would have eased the tax load on the average Britain somewhat (by about four shillings a year); but a policy that would have increased Indian military expenditures to a level equivalent to that maintained by a typical "underdeveloped" country would have reduced his tax burden by 15 shillings and 10 pence. Moreover, if the British government had been able to effect all three changes, instead of paying two and a half times as much as a resident of a typical developed country, the British taxpayer would have had to reach into his pocket for only a third of that sum.

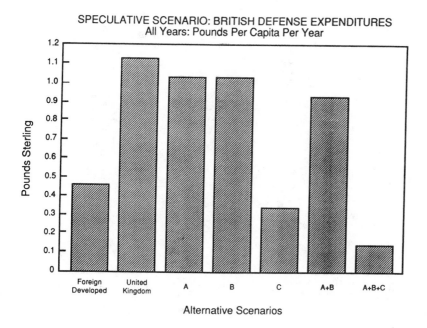

SPECULATIVE SCENARIO: BRITISH DEFENSE EXPENDITURES
All Years: Pounds Per Capita Per Year

Chart 5.4 (a)

These figures are, of course, the averages for the entire period; however, the evidence does not indicate that, as time passed, the government in Whitehall became more proficient in effecting a transfer of the defense burden to the colonies. Instead, it appears that the British subsidy to the Empire increased as the period wore on. Each year, during the first thirteen of the twentieth century, for example, every resident of the home islands contributed 4 shillings to the "shortfall" in the defense budgets of the colonies with responsible government, the same amount as a subsidy to the dependent colonies, and 19 shillings and 5 pence to the Indian "deficit." Altogether in that period, the share of the total defense subsidy falling on each Briton was an impressive £1–7–5 per year.

Although precise prediction is impossible, it can be conjectured that, in the absence of Empire, tax loads on the British taxpayer could have been greatly reduced, or resources made available for more productive investment with no decline in the level of consumption. If, for example, all British possessions had assumed levels of defense expenditures equal to those borne by countries at similar stages of development, the tax burden on the average Briton could

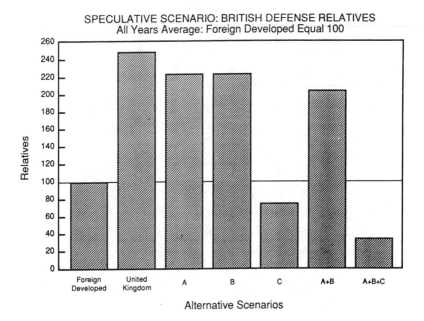

SPECULATIVE SCENARIO: BRITISH DEFENSE RELATIVES
All Years Average: Foreign Developed Equal 100

Chart 5.4 (b)

have been reduced by an amount equal to about one-fifth of national savings. If Britain had possessed no Empire and had spent at the level of France and Germany on the military establishment, the savings would have been 12 shillings and 7 pence per capita per year or about one-eighth of national savings.

While the British taxpayer paid, his colonial confreres prospered – at least those in the colonies of white settlement. It is almost certainly no coincidence that Canada, New Zealand, and Australia were among the "nations" that devoted the highest proportion of their incomes to education and social overhead investment.[71] For the dependent Empire the benefits are more obscure. They contributed less than independent countries at similar stages of development; but it is not obvious what the weight of their defense burden would have been had there been no expansionist European powers to threaten their survival.

6 British subsidies to the Empire: the nondefense component

Although the defense umbrella raised by the Queen and Parliament over the far reaches of the Empire was the most costly component of the imperial subsidy, it was not the only part of that complex political–economic machine. In addition, British borrowers bore a substantial fraction of the indirect costs engendered by their government's sometimes tacit, at times formal, decisions to underwrite colonial loans. British taxpayers shouldered the financial burden of a steady stream of direct subsidies to the dependent Empire; and British business and labor absorbed the majority of the costs imposed by the monopsonistic practices of the Crown Agents for the Colonies. As with the defense subsidy, the prime beneficiaries were the residents of the Empire; but a secondary recipient of the imperial largess were the owners of colonially based enterprise whose firms would otherwise have had to bear substantially higher local tax burdens.

I. Loans and interest

Colonial loans, underwritten by either formal or informal parliamentary guarantees, provided a substantial block of funds that was used to enhance the colonial economies. From the point of view of the British government, a Parliamentary guarantee was a particularly useful policy instrument since it did not involve the disbursement of tax monies and, therefore, did not raise the ire of the British voter. At the same time, however, it did provide a very significant subsidy. With a guarantee a colony could gain access to funds at rates of interest substantially below those it would have had to pay had it been forced to compete directly with the United States, Argentina, Greece, or Japan. There is, however, no such thing as a free lunch, to coin a phrase. President Lyndon Johnson managed to finance the Viet Nam war without a tax increase, but American citizens discovered that the particular policy did not change the total cost of the war – it merely appeared in a different guise. In the same way that Americans found their pocketbooks shrinking as inflation took its

137

toll, British borrowers found themselves obliged to pay more for loans; British consumers found themselves paying more for goods and services; and the rate of growth of the domestic capital stock (both public and private) slackened.

Since the investing public appeared to believe (and probably correctly) that its government would not let the loans to any colonial government (Dominion, colony, city, or rabbit district) go into default, the "informal" guarantee covered loans issued for a multitude of purposes; but the official guarantees were most often given for particular projects that the Colonial Office felt were not a part of the regular process of government. The British government, for example, considered making loans to Jamaica because of hurricane damage, to Barbados to counteract the threat of political disturbance, to Newfoundland to purchase French fishing rights, and to the Sudan for development of the cotton-growing industry.[1] Such loans were not normal and it was not only the Treasury that tended to object. In the case of the Barbados loan, for example, Northcote wrote:

> ...I feel I cannot encourage you in this matter. We must not make the P.W. [public works] loan fund the resource of everyone who is in distress, otherwise we shall soon be in trouble. There are many meritorious classes in England who are suffering from the complaint of a temporary impecuniosity, and whom it would be very tempting to assist by loans of public money at low interest, but where could we stop? I am sure that a loan to the Barbadians would be a very dangerous precedent. ...[2]

Nor was Parliament always blind to the differential advantage afforded by imperial guarantees. Bonar Law in opposing the Transvaal loan guarantee bill of 1907 averred that:

> ...it was generosity at the expense of other people, not only at the expense of Great Britain but of the self-governing colonies which desired to borrow money but which had not the inestimable advantage of being the particular pet of His Majesty's Government.[3]

In terms of magnitude, the second-largest component of the imperial subsidy was almost certainly the savings in interest costs on these "guaranteed" loans. In the late nineteenth century the British capital market was the largest and most sophisticated in the world, and most of the finance that passed through it came from the savings of British subjects. Those savers reflected the characteristics of the market itself. They were willing to finance gold mines in Africa, cattle ranches in Colorado, and gasworks in Bombay at a time when

that those policies would be continued were sufficient to convince the British investor that, even if colonial issues were not quite as safe as consols, they were much closer to that ideal than the issues of foreign governments in Asia or South America or, at times, even across the Channel. Thus, the loans issued on behalf of the dependent colonies rose from a total of almost £7.5 million in the last decade of the nineteenth century to about £20 million in the next.[8]

The colonies with responsible government enjoyed greater independence from scrutiny than their dependent confreres but, through the first two-thirds of the nineteenth century, they continued to depend on imperial guarantees. As the century progressed the guarantee became less important; and by the late 1870s, most of the self-governing colonies found that they could borrow on the open market without direct British governmental support. Indirect assistance was nonetheless still needed; and it came in the form of the Colonial Stock Act of 1877. That act allowed colonies to replace debentures chargeable to a particular source of revenue with stock "inscribed" in London and thus easily traded on the Stock Exchange. Subsequently, the trustee status accorded most colonial issues made them even more marketable.

It may well have been that the recognition of continuing governmental scrutiny helped make the issues of the dependent colonies attractive to investors; however, it is not so clear why those investors maintained confidence in Dominion issues. Yet, the figures indicate they did. In 1890, for example, the governments of Australia owed £143 million pounds; Canada, 59; New Zealand, 39; the Cape, 24; and Natal, £5 million – a total of £270 million or £25.17 for every resident of those parts of the Empire. In contrast, in that same year, while India's outstanding debt reached £193 million, the total for the rest of the dependent Empire was a mere £6 million (the West Indies had borrowed 2.8; Ceylon, 2.5; and Mauritius, .7).[9]

Julius Vogel, prime minister of New Zealand, discovered the joys of painless growth through borrowing, and he launched that colony on a public works spree that was to last through most of the century. There is seldom a shortage of politicians willing to imitate successful new ideas, and Vogel's spread rapidly across the Tasman Sea and somewhat more slowly into Canada and South Africa. Between 1870 and 1900 annual per capita borrowing rose from £30–12 to £65–10 in New Zealand, and from £17–2 to £53 in Australia; moreover, these figures do not include the issues of the local authorities in those colonies. Of all the government issues, U.K. local, foreign, and Empire, included in a detailed study of selected years between 1885

and 1912, just less than £1 out of 7 went to Australia and a not
greatly dissimilar fraction to New Zealand.

Given the number and size of these offerings it may be surprising
that the British investor appears to have examined them with a less
jaundiced eye than he used to examine the prospectus of an Argentine offering in support of the railroads or a Greek government
loan based on the revenues of the tobacco monopoly. The British
government certainly expressed doubt about the quality and quantity of those Empire issues. In 1875, for example, Lord Northcote,
Chancellor of the Exchequer, wrote: "Herbert has told me of Vogel's
request for a guarantee to a £4,000,000 loan and I write one line of
precaution, as I know of Vogel's character, to say that in my opinion
the proposal is simply inadmissable. . . . "[10]

Despite these concerns, the colonies with responsible government
borrowed on terms that, although perhaps not quite as favorable as
those received by India and the dependent colonies, were still far
below the rates charged even the most advanced nations.[11] The
ability of these colonies to raise large blocks of capital at very low
rates came as something of a surprise to the British government
during the heady days of Vogel's spending and borrowing extravaganza when most officials were making dire predictions about the
long-run outcome of this massive violation of fiscal orthodoxy. In
1875, for example, the then Secretary of State for the Colonies, Lord
Carnarvon, wrote:

> I am not surprised that you are rather startled at the Treasury at
> the financial speed at which New Zealand is traveling. At the
> same time the crisis may not come yet – it may even be indefi-
> nitely postponed – and you have probably observed the last loan
> has been obtained by the Colony on very favorable terms. . . . [12]

Nor does the distance of a century make the explanation of the
British investor's willingness to underwrite these activities any more
apparent. One can never be certain what it was that motivated the
investors to act as they did, but the explanation cannot lie in legal
guarantees nor in effective Treasury control. The Treasury prevented
the dependent colonies from diverting loan funds to unauthorized
uses, but for the colonies with responsible government that check
was lacking even when the loans carried British guarantees. As
Carnarvon observed:

> . . . The point to which I am anxious to look is this: Parliament
> guarantees a loan for a certain purpose, and charges the Treasury
> with the duty of seeing that the money raised under the guarantee

is applied to the purpose for which the guarantee was given. If it should, in whole or in part, be diverted to other purposes, Parliament should be justly angry with the Treasury. Some years ago, I think, Canada raised a loan under imperial guarantees for a railroad and proceeded to apply a portion to fortifications . . . and there was a row about it in the House of Commons.[13]

A row, perhaps, but the guarantee was not rescinded. Two facts are certain. First, even in the absence of legal guarantees the colonies with responsible government were able to borrow and borrow heavily at rates only slightly above those available at home. Second, except for a single New Zealand Harbour Board Loan, no Empire issue appeared on the Council of Foreign Bondholders list of bonds in default from the formation of that organization in the early 1870s until the outbreak of World War I. Perhaps the typical investor believed that the British government would step in if default threatened; certainly there were few chances to test that assumption. On the other hand, possibly the risk class to which he assigned those Empire issues correctly reflected economic reality. Still, if the latter inference is correct, one is left to wonder why the bonds of Queensland and Natal appeared less risky than the offerings of a stable government in western Europe.

That the Empire received favorable treatment in the capital market has been well recognized. Thus far, however, there have been few attempts to determine the size of the imperial interest subsidy. How exactly did the system of guarantees, control, and investor faith affect the prices that India, the colonies, and the Dominions had to pay? Each year, the *Stock Exchange Official Yearbook* reported the new issues that had been added to the Stock Exchange's Official List and these can provide some evidence on the question.[14] Within the Empire, India consistently paid less for capital than either the dependent colonies or those with responsible government. Between the dependent colonies and those with responsible government there is little to choose, although it appears that in the years before 1901 the former may have paid slightly less and in the later years somewhat more.[15] The data encompass all government loans marketed in London in eighteen of the thirty-one years between 1882 and 1912 for which information on the size of the issue, its maturity, the price at which it sold, and the stated interest rate were reported. All in all there were 944 such loans included: 308 from the United Kingdom, 339 from the Empire, and 297 from the rest of the world. Regression analysis, a statistical technique, made it possible to relate the interest

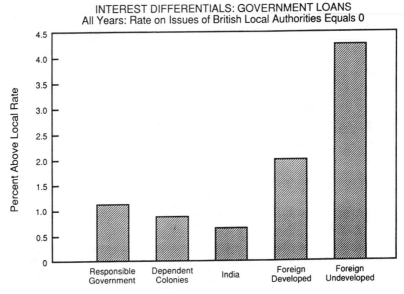

INTEREST DIFFERENTIALS: GOVERNMENT LOANS
All Years: Rate on Issues of British Local Authorities Equals 0

Chart 6.1

charges on those loans to the current rate on British consols, the size of the issue, the duration of the loans (all factors that might be thought to effect the charge), and, most importantly, the type of government that issued the bond.[16] After "adjustment" for the issue-specific factors, the effect of the type of government on the rate charged is quite revealing.[17]

Chart 6.1 shows the differential between the interest charges on the issues of local authorities in the United Kingdom and those imposed on borrowers from other governments.

Within the Empire, India consistently paid less for capital than either the dependent colonies or those with responsible government. Between the dependent colonies and those with responsible government there is little to choose. India paid less than 1 percent and the colonies, about 1 percent, more than the domestic Local Authorities.

Foreign developed countries, on the other hand, paid in excess of 2 percent more than did British local authorities, but for the governments of underdeveloped countries the differential was more than 4 percent. It appears, therefore, that if India and the dependent colonies are comparable to the underdeveloped nations included in the sample and if the colonies with responsible government can be compared with the developed countries, membership in the Empire seems to have meant that on average loans were about 3.5 percent cheaper for India and the dependent colonies and just less than 1 percent less expensive for the colonies with responsible government. Empire status made colonial loans appear less risky to the potential lender. Under other political arrangements the government of India might have found itself in competition with the governments of Liberia, Argentina, or China, but it actually found itself competing instead with London, Manchester, and Yorkshire, to say nothing of Vickers, Peek-Frean, and the London Tower Construction Company.

This shift in Empire demand from the "risky" to the "safe" market was not without cost to the British whether they were taxpayers, consumers, or businessmen. The new demand for funds caused the interest rates on "safe" bonds to rise and thus increased the costs of borrowing to the British central government and local authorities (to say nothing of domestic business firms); and the increase made some projects, both public and private, appear too expensive. That increase and its effects are not the product of some twentieth-century economists' imagination; they were well recognized by contemporary observers. In the words of the foreign correspondent for the *New York Daily Tribune*:

> It is true that successive loans by the Indian Company in the London market would . . . prevent . . . the further fall in the rate of interest; but such a fall is exactly required for the revival of British industry and commerce. Any artificial check put upon the downward movement of the rate of discount is equivalent to an enhancement in the cost of production and the terms of credit, which in its present weak state, English trade feels itself unable to bear. Hence the general distress of the announcement of the British loan.[18]

Since it is not possible to determine by how much interest rates increased, and since a significant fraction of the recipients of the higher rate were British, it is very difficult to estimate the costs to Britain of that transfer. With some very strong assumptions, however, it is possible to estimate the magnitude of the benefits that accrued to the Empire (see Chart 6.2). If the estimates of the "interest differential" are taken as indicative, the volume of finance set at the level of the estimates in Chapter 2, and the maturity of loans set equal to the average values of the 339 examined, then the total gain

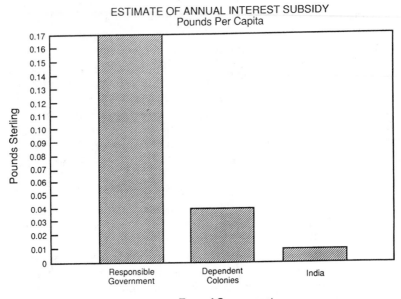

ESTIMATE OF ANNUAL INTEREST SUBSIDY
Pounds Per Capita

Chart 6.2

was about £216,000,000 or about 5 pence per capita per year. Those gains were not, however, distributed equally across the Empire.[19]

Although the level of savings per pound borrowed was not high, the colonies with responsible government received the most (3 shillings and 5 pence). (If the basis for comparison had been foreign underdeveloped rather than foreign developed countries per capita the savings would have been more than 10 shillings.) The dependent colonies benefited to the extent of about 10 pence a year, or approximately 5 percent of their tax bill. The explanation of the relatively small level of savings rests not with the price component of the subsidy (3.4 percent) but with the dependent colonies' hesitancy – a hesitancy that reflected at least in part the policy of the Colonial Office – to use the London market before the turn of the century. The Indian subsidy, although the largest of the three in terms of value, was distributed across a very large population; and savings amounted to only about 2 pence per person per year. Even that figure, however, was the equivalent of about 6 percent of the annual taxes paid by a resident of the subcontinent. Moreover, the reader should bear in mind these are minimum estimates: All benefits from loans to railroads and short-term borrowing have been excluded. All in all, it appears that the imperial connection again proved quite remunerative, although it was certainly more profitable for members with voting privileges.

Interest payments can be viewed as the ghost of Christmas past. They are not a burden passed from one generation to another, but they do represent real claims that some members of society must pay to others. In a world where balanced budgets were the order of the day and where commitment to the gold standard made any long-term deviation from the position difficult, interest payments represented a real claim on present tax resources and they limited the governments' expenditure options. In India, for example, the need to pay interest – even on loans made for such worthy purposes as famine relief – played a major role in dictating the functional profile of the government's budget.

Compared to the underdeveloped world the total interest payments charged to the budget of the colonies of the dependent Empire were very low. In the foreign underdeveloped sector, the funds raised by loans were often used to support military adventures, to prevent civil revolution, or merely to cover administrative deficits. In the dependent Empire, the loans that were approved provided funds to build highways or railroads; repair hurricane destruction; put in gas, water, or sewage plants; or, perhaps, to underwrite immigration. These activities were at times profitable in their own right but, whether that was true or not, they almost always raised the level of private profits for those businessmen who did not bear all the interest costs.

Empire residents and the owners of firms that operated in the Empire were clear beneficiaries of the interest subsidy; as to the identities of the other players and the magnitudes of their gains and losses there are no estimates, only speculations. Foreign borrowers probably were somewhat better off since they no longer were faced by Empire competition in the market for "risky" finance. Given the higher interest rates, the Empire's draw on that market would probably have been less than the £13.5 million that the colonies actually absorbed; but even a figure one-half or one-third that high would certainly have raised the rates faced by countries like Argentina, Mexico, and China.

Within the United Kingdom interest rates (both public and private) must have been higher than they otherwise would have been; but just how much higher is impossible to say. In the years from 1865 to 1914 almost two-thirds of the "safe" government loans passing through the London market were made to Empire borrowers. Some domestic projects must have been priced out of the market, and to the extent that the total benefits from these undertakings were not captured in the interest charges, there would have been some social loss. In addition, to the extent that some of the Empire lenders lived outside the United Kingdom (like the American defense umbrella, the British loan–guarantee umbrella spread its protection beyond the nation's borders), the loss in interest charges was a loss to Britain. There were, however, offsets. To the extent that some British-owned firms operated in the foreign sector and competed for "risky" funds, their gains from lower charges must be counted again the higher rates paid by domestic borrowers.

As for the residents of the United Kingdom, the greater interest payments were not a total loss but in part merely a transfer. Taxpayers paid more, but that extra income was received by the bondholders. The best estimates indicate that the majority of the tax bill was paid by the middle and working classes and that a large fraction of the bonds were held by the upper classes. To the extent that the two groups – bondholders and taxpayers – differed, the costs of the interest subsidy was borne by one and a part of that cost received as income by the other.

The home country was a heavy borrower; and its taxpayers paid the cost. While the level of interest charges declined somewhat over time, they averaged more than 14 shillings per capita – a quarter of all government expenditures. Among the other developed nations, borrowing also gradually became a habit; and interest payments rose. Still, such charges averaged only 5 shillings – about a fifth of those countries' total budgets. In the Empire, some of the colonies with responsible government had proved themselves profligate borrowers but, across all, the average interest charge (11 shillings and 10 pence), while more than twice that of the foreign developed sector, was still only two-thirds of the home country's total (see Charts 6.3 and 6.4).

Julius Vogel notwithstanding, it was Australia that paid the largest amounts of interest to its bondholders. The six colonies averaged more than £1.5 per capita per year, although the figures declined somewhat with the formation of the Commonwealth. New Zealand was a substantial contributor, but its annual charges were less than those in the United Kingdom. In South Africa only the Cape proved a significant borrower, but even there annual interest charges were a mere three shillings. That figure was duplicated in Newfoundland, but Canada paid more than seven shillings. Australia was a clear

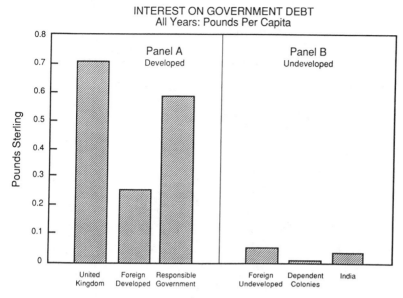

Chart 6.3

winner in the interest sweepstakes, but Canada paid 40 percent more than a typical developed country, and New Zealand two and a half times as much.

The self-governing colonies borrowed heavily and were subject to substantial debt charges. Government supervision meant that the dependent colonies did not and were not. If the standard is foreign underdeveloped countries (1 shilling and 2 pence – one-tenth of expenditures), they can be said to have borrowed hardly at all. In the dependent colonies the average per capita interest payment was only 2 pence per annum – a budget share of about 1 percent. Moreover, of the sixty-four dependent colonies, thirty-three spent no money at all on interest.

In India the absolute level was higher, and interest absorbed about 12 percent of the budget; however, the average was only 10 pence per capita, still less than the levels prevailing in the underdeveloped countries. Moreover, while both per capita expenditure and budget share were doubling in the latter countries, in India they were falling. They averaged 1 shilling 7 pence, and 20 percent in

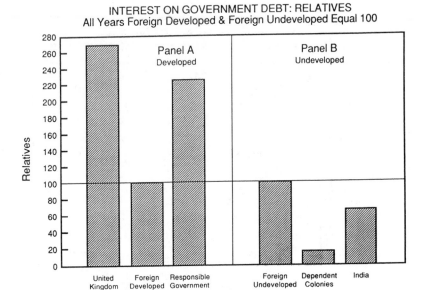

INTEREST ON GOVERNMENT DEBT: RELATIVES
All Years Foreign Developed & Foreign Undeveloped Equal 100

Chart 6.4

the 1860s, but by 1910 those figures had decreased to 5 pence, and 8 percent.

Britain has long had a history of dependence on the capital market; but in those parts of the Empire over which it exercised some substantial control, the Treasury remained firm in its resolve that they should not follow the home precedent. For better or worse and despite the subsidized rates, the burden of debt rested lightly. It seems possible to conclude that as far as public borrowing was concerned, being a British colony, whether self-governing or dependent, provided a privileged entree to the London capital market. In addition, it involved a hidden subsidy paid in part by the British taxpayer. On the other hand, both the dependent colonies and India were constrained from exercising that privilege too frequently; and it is possible, although not likely, that, to the extent that the weakening of controls would have permitted those colonies to borrow more at the "safe" rate, both the interest rate and the colonies' development might have been constrained by the Empire connection.

II. Direct assistance

Parliament with the usually grudging acquiescence and recommendation of the Treasury was prepared from time to time to come to the financial assistance of British colonies and not require repayment. Although the individual grants were usually not large, the amount rose steadily. It had totaled £1.5 million in the 1880s, and that figure had risen almost ninefold by the last decade before the war. For the period 1880 to 1914 the total amount of direct and unrepaid assistance was more than £25 million – a figure that works out to a per capita contribution by every man, woman, and child in the British Isles of almost 5 pence per year.[20] A disbursement might be voted in support of the budget of a colony whose resources were insufficient to support the normal functions of government, or the vote might be specifically directed toward the salary of the governor and his staff. Most frequently, however, grants-in-aid were designed to attack specific problems: a public works project, disaster relief, or native education, to cite only three examples.

Often the Colonial Office saw the need for a grant-in-aid to a colony, but found itself opposed by the Treasury. In 1882, for instance, Kimberley at the Colonial Office wrote Gladstone:

> I wish to make an appeal for mercy from the Treasury in the case of Malta. The Maltese complain bitterly (1) of the governor's salary, (2) the expensive drainage works which they say are only required for the garrison and ought not be paid from local funds, (3) the drawbacks on stores for the troops. . . . It must I think be a matter of interest to us that the Maltese should be well affected by this country. The safety of the fortress in times of war would be seriously endangered if they were hostile. I am sorry to say there is amongst them a chronic and growing discontent.[21]

The funds disbursed by the British government in direct support of the dependent colonies increased over the years. In 1879, the figure amounted to less than £100,000, but by 1900, it was ten times that amount. Of this latter sum, £414,635 went to the Gold Coast, whose budget had fallen into deficit because of the colony's new responsibilities in its northern territories and hostilities against the Ashanti.

At times direct aid constituted a significant fraction of a colony's total revenue. In Nigeria, between 1900 and 1912, the figures ranged between 12 and 44 percent; and in 1901 direct aid constituted 88 percent of the Gold Coast's revenue. Usually, however, the ratio was less than £1 in 20.[22]

Direct grants were also frequently made for matters of general imperial concern rather than for the benefit of a particular colony. As a means of improving communication within an Empire in which defense was a major concern, the British government provided subsidies for shipping lines that carried the mail, and for "All-British" cable services. The colonies occasionally played a subordinate but financially supportive role in these endeavors. British-financed shipping subsidies totaled almost £1 million annually as early as the 1860s. At that time, close to £900,000 went to three lines: P and O, Royal Mail, and Cunard.[23] Later a great expansion both in service and subsidy resulted from the passage of the Imperial Penny Postage Act of 1899. The law was designed to provide an increased volume of mail and better imperial communication as a concomitant of lower postage rates; and this indeed was the result. The implementation of the act, however, required increased government subsidies.[24]

The process of financing, to say nothing of constructing, transoceanic cables was often tortuous. The great Pacific cable designed to link Australia with Canada was first proposed at the Colonial Conference of 1887, but negotiations leading to its construction were not completed until 1900, and it did not come into operation until 1903. For much of the time the Treasury, concerned with limiting British liability, constituted the chief obstacle. Finally, an acceptable formula was agreed upon; Parliament would advance £2,000,000 to a consortium consisting of Australia, New Zealand, and Canada. Those Dominions pledged, in turn, to raise a loan on the open market and to use the proceeds to repay the British government. It was hoped that the revenues generated by the line would pay for the sinking fund, interest, and operating costs. Any deficits or surpluses were to be shared by the three contracting parties and Britain itself. After a long, complex negotiation the shares were set at: Australia, 6; Canada, 5; New Zealand, 2; and Britain, 5.[25] The line opened in 1903, and the first year's operating deficit of £87,500 was divided according to the agreed formula, and the same was true for the next several years. In time, however, the cable did become self-supporting. The total cost to Britain of this one venture – including interest charges on capital during construction, of about £116,000, and an operating subsidy that had totaled £130,000 by 1914 – was in excess of £250,000. Nor was the Pacific cable the only such enterprise to receive operating and construction subsidies. In 1904, for example, eight companies received direct British support totaling almost £100,000. The greatest award was £25,000 to the Pacific Cable Company and the smallest, £3,500 to the Eastern and South African Telegraph Company.[26] The largest single contribution was, however, to the Uganda Railway.[27] The construction of that railroad was begun in 1895 and completed in 1902. Construction costs constituted an imperial expense of £5,550,000. The line did not even begin to pay its running costs until 1906, and earnings certainly never covered expenditures. Between 1895 and 1914, the British taxpayers' contribution to the interest costs and sinking fund of the railroad amounted to an additional £3,351,000 – a figure, like the shipping and telegraph subsidies – not included in the estimate of miscellaneous administrative subsides previously discussed; and, of that total, more than £2,000,000 was incurred after the line was completed!

The star-crossed railway was one of the most controversial undertakings ever sponsored by Whitehall.[28] The meter-gauge line which ran from Mombasa to Kisumu on Lake Victoria covered 587 miles and traversed a mountain escarpment 7,000 feet high. Built largely by Indian labor, not the least of its troubles was the campaign waged against the construction gangs by a pride of man-eating lions. Henry Labouchere, the "Little England" Radical, was probably more right than wrong when he satirically declaimed:

> What will it cost no words can express;
> What is its object no brain can suppose;
> Where it will start from no one can guess;
> Where it goes nobody knows.
> What is the use of it none can conjecture;
> What it will carry there's none can define;
> And in spite of George Curzon's superior lecture,
> It clearly is naught but a lunatic line.[29]

III. The Crown Agents

The indispensable agency for the marketing of colonial securities and much else besides was the Crown Agents Department. The roots of that institution lay in the eighteenth century, when the colonies began to retain agents in London to pursue their commercial, political, and financial interests. At the same time, the government in Whitehall appointed officials to supervise colonial expenditures under Parliamentary grants. In time the situation became sufficiently confusing to require administrative reform, and in 1833 the Colonial Office and the Treasury agreed to a new policy. There were to be just two Crown Agents, and they were not to act as a direct adjunct of either of the two departments. They were not housed in the Colonial Office, but were given a separate establishment. The Agents were also given a surprising degree of independence, albeit they were under the general supervision, first, of the Treasury, and then, after 1880, of the Colonial Office, with the Treasury prepared to consult on "extraordinary occasions."[30]

By 1880, the Crown Agents had become the purchasing agents and loan negotiators for the dependent colonies. In 1874, the Colonial Office decreed that all goods imported for the public service of the crown colonies had to be purchased through the Crown Agents. At first they represented all colonies; however, in 1880, the Crown Agents were deprived of the right to represent self-governing colonies in most dealings. These increasingly autonomous entities were to maintain individual agents in London, but this official change had only a limited effect.[31] In the year 1908, for example, the Crown Agents acted on behalf of twenty-four colonies, eleven protectorates, and Zanzibar; and they still continued to conduct certain financial undertakings for Cape Colony, Natal, New Zealand, Western Australia, the Orange River Colony, and the Transvaal.[32]

Although there were only two Crown Agents, the support they were accorded was not insignificant. In 1900, the staff of well over 200 included a secretary, 8 department heads, 11 deputy department heads, 23 section heads, 65 clerks, 52 copyists, 20 typists, and a dozen miscellaneous functionaries.[33] The entire Colonial Office, in contrast, had an establishment of only 125. The areas of Crown Agents' concern were seemingly endless. They took a major role in the construction of colonial public works and particularly railroads. They drew up all contracts, placed all orders for plants and stores, supervised the execution of contracts and inspections, arranged for the shipment of goods, recruited engineers for colonial construction projects, and saw to the design of colonial currencies and stamps. They provided their clients with pistols, saddles, tropical headgear, perambulators, fezzes, "artic footwarmers," money clips, zouave jackets, sewing machines, gin, and so on, almost ad infinitum. The office, in 1908 alone, processed 9,000 orders requiring 24,000 separate contracts.[34] Railway equipment was always a major responsibility for the Crown Agents. In the year 1904, for example, they oversaw purchase of railway locomotives valued at £139,825.[35] In that same year, the total of commercial, railway, and general business stores purchased and shipped amounted to £2,541,936; while financial transactions, loans, and miscellaneous business conducted on behalf of the colonies came to another £22,903,901.[36]

There are few remaining records of the actual purchases made by the Crown Agents, but over the first years of the present century the annual total appears to have ranged from £2 million to £2.6 million.[37] If the ratio between those figures and the total expenditures of the dependent colonies provides a reasonable index, it appears that the purchases made by the Agents for the colonies totaled almost £125 million between 1860 and 1912. That figure is not huge, but even if the Agents' bargaining ability netted only a conjectured 10-percent price reduction (many of the purchases were for railroad and other specialized equipment and those markets were probably not competitive), the colonial savings would have averaged a quarter of a million pounds a year.

It is remarkable that all this activity was generated by an office whose employees, "... have no formal Constitution and who are not part of the United Kingdom Civil Service or of the United Kingdom Government machine.... Their functions are not anywhere laid down except inferentially by reference to certain Colonial Regulations.... In general their position rests entirely on useage...."[38] In his study of the Crown Agents, A. W. Abbott, former Senior Crown Agent, placed their importance in perspective when he pointed out that "over a total period of 140 years the Crown Agents have bought or sold £2,000 million worth of equipment, invested over £3,000 million worth of funds, and issued and managed £300 million of market loans...."[39]

How did the Crown Agents go about their business? When it came to purchasing, the list of firms qualified to bid for contracts was determined by the Agents. In 1904, for example, thirty-five firms including some foreign ones were invited to bid on £135,549 worth of rail contracts. On the other hand, only nine companies were given the opportunity to tender bids for the £139,825 in locomotive contracts. For a small contract involving £4,664 for telegraph insulators, the Crown Agents felt two competing bids would be sufficient.[40] While concerns about bias were surprisingly rare, in at least one instance a colonial client was worried that British companies were being favored over local firms. The evidence, however, was not compelling.[41]

In the case of loan flotations the borrowing colony established the highest permissible rate of interest, fixed the amount desired, and set what other conditions it saw fit. The secretary of state then authorized the Crown Agents to seek the loan on the best terms possible. At first (circa 1860) advertisements were filed for tenders for debentures carrying a stated rate of interest. Offers were subject to a minimum price – one that was as a rule not disclosed until the tenders were opened. Later, bonds were offered at a fixed price and "success" was assured by having the issues underwritten by private agencies who could comply with the regulations contained in the Colonial Stocks Acts of 1877 and 1900. Underwriting arrangements were placed in the hands of a regular group of brokers on whom the Crown Agents felt they could rely. The brokers were expected not only to place the underwriting in "substantial hands" but also to confine it, insofar as possible, to institutions that could be relied upon to hold the bonds until the market could absorb them without breaking. Underwriters normally received a commission of 1 percent on colonial stock, and the brokers, .25 percent.[42]

Between 1860 and 1914 the Crown Agents, acting through one of several private brokers (most often Scrimegour & Co.), successfully marketed almost £85 million in long-term government securities. That total does not, of course, include the short-term loans the Agents made directly to the colonies. Slightly over half of the £85 million represented issues of six colonies that either had or were soon to be granted responsible government. However, some £40 million were issued by twenty-five dependent colonies; the largest was a loan of £8.1 million to Southern Rhodesia, the smallest £3,000 to Montserrat.[43] The colonies with responsible government often preferred to utilize the services of the Crown Agents because of their low cost, but Colonial Office policy gradually forced them to employ their own agents.[44]

It is difficult to estimate the savings in flotation costs generated by the Agents, but the reluctance displayed by colonies like New Zealand to abandon the agency's good offices suggests that they were substantial. What is certain is that the dependent colonies paid brokerage and other flotation fees that were no higher than those charged by firms who underwrote the issues of the world's most developed nations. In commenting on the role of the Crown Agents, the chronicler of the early twentieth-century capital market wrote:

> It would, perhaps, be more exact to say that he [the broker] *allots* the underwriting, for it seems probable that the parties with whom he places it, would usually accept their quotas even though such a commitment happened at the moment to be particularly unwelcome.[45]

It was not only the colonies with responsible government that displayed an inclination to continue to employ the Crown Agents. Even today the Agents continue to act for several countries that, while dependent colonies in the nineteenth century, are now independent. Writing in 1921, F. Lavington shows why this may be true:

> It seems tolerably certain that Colonial and Indian securities are sold to the public at a fair price and a modest cost . . . [and] that there is little scope for abuse in the marketing of highly reputable stocks.[46]

That the Crown Agents had immense power in their capacity as agents to choose brokers for loans and to assign contracts for the purchase of equipment is too evident to need elaboration. Charges against them were frequent and as a consequence a major Parliamentary enquiry was completed in 1909. After an extensive investigation, the report suggested only minor organizational changes; and the Crown Agents' conduct was found to be, in general, above reproach. Given the amounts of money with which the Crown Agents dealt, it is not surprising that accusations of such alleged offenses as "accepting return commissions" were levied against them.[47] Cases of dishonesty were, however, remarkably rare.

The Agents' colonial customers were, of course, not always satisfied. For instance, in 1902 the manner in which a Ceylon 3-percent loan was handled came under severe criticism. The payment of what was deemed an extra dividend and the fact that the issue fetched only 91.2 percent lay at the heart of the dissatisfaction.[48] Again, when in 1910 the Crown Agents negotiated a second installment of an authorized £7,861,457 3.5-percent loan on behalf of the Straits Settlements for 95.5 percent, the governor, Sir John Anderson, was furious. He accused the Crown Agents of having failed to consult with his government and as a consequence of having negotiated too small a loan at an inappropriate rate.[49] R. C. Antrobus, one of the Agents, denied the allegations and defended his office's position: "We claim . . . that the Colony has been well served by us in this matter and we cannot help feeling disappointed that our success in the conduct of this very important and responsible business should . . . have failed to obtain for us any expression of approval. . . ."[50]

Aside from their direct economic function, at times the Crown Agents were able to assist the British government in effecting its foreign policy. Money raised by the Crown Agents for Hong Kong in 1906 was then loaned by Hong Kong to Hukuan and Lianghuang in China.[51] Previously, in 1905, a direct loan had been made to the viceroy of Wu Chang, who was apparently considered more reliable

than the Chinese government, to make it possible for him to re-
purchase the concession for the Kowloon–Canton Railway from the
King of Belgium. In a letter of September 22, 1905, the Colonial
Office thanked the Crown Agents for their "valuable assistance."[52]

The Crown Agents' files provide evidence of the diversity of their
financial endeavors. In 1891, for instance, they were involved in
raising a loan for the tiny Caribbean Island of St. Kitts. The funds
were designed to cover a new water supply for the windward side
of the island, completion of the public library, the construction of
new treasury buildings, renovation of the medical baths, construction of a leper asylum, the opening of new cemeteries, improvements
of public roads, hospital refurbishment, and enlargement of the
prison of Besseterre – and all of that for only £23,500.[53] Even this
loan was far from the smallest marketed by the Agents. In 1879,
they raised a 5-percent waterworks-construction loan of £3,000 for
the Montserrat government. As an aside, it might be mentioned that
the second installment of that loan was only £300![54] At the other
extreme, the Crown Agents managed a £35,000,000 loan designed to cover a number of post–Boer War exigencies, including
£19,000,000 for railway construction in the Transvaal.[55]

The Crown Agents' services were not provided free to the colonies;
the Agents demanded and received recompense for their activities.
Colonies were charged a flat 1-percent commission for stores purchased on their behalf by the Crown Agents. In addition, an annual
contribution (in 1908, for example, it ranged from £30 and £650) was
assessed against colonies conducting over £100,000 worth of nonloan
business through the office.[56] A .5-percent commission was also
charged on the issue and repayment of loans, and .25-percent on
the payment of interest. Overdrafts had to be settled at bank rates
but never at less than 3 percent. From this income, which amounted
to as much as £100,000 per annum, the Crown Agents paid all office
expenses including their own salaries. Surpluses were invested to
cover possible future deficits.[57] The records indicate no instance of
colonial complaint at these charges. The benefits provided by the
Office of the Crown Agents for the colonies in the vital areas of
purchasing and loan management were too evident to bear more
than petty carping.

It appears almost impossible to quantify with any precision the
contribution of the Crown Agents' to the colonial subsidy, but it
does appear possible to speculate about its magnitude. In comparison to defense and interest subsidies it was probably not great; but
if the Agents' monopsony power yielded as little as 10 percent on

the purchases of the dependent colonies, and their monopoly power, 1 percent on the flotation costs of security issues, the subsidy would have totaled £136 million, an average of £2.5 million a year. Even cutting that figure in half suggests a subsidy of well over £1 million per annum or about 10 pence for each resident of England, Wales, and Scotland to whom otherwise the bulk of these rents would almost certainly have accrued.

IV. Trade

Although a discussion of trade is not within the purview of this book, some mention of it should be made in the context of British subsidies to the Empire. All colonies had easier access to the British market than they would have, had there been no financially assisted railroads or subsidized steamship lines. Australia and New Zealand, for example, particularly benefited when the British government provided cold-storage facilities on mail vessels. In an era of free trade, British markets were largely unencumbered by tariff restrictions. On the other hand, the so-called Dominions were, for their part, free to erect barriers against the importation of British goods; and many did so with a vengence. Alexander Galt's Canadian tariff act of 1859, the initial protective tariff in the Empire, was only the first of a long list of such laws.

Whatever the case, it must have been a comfort to the imperial community to have the British market as a first and last resort. While few colonies were as completely dependent on the home market as South Africa, it can be said with considerable assurance that the availability of a free British market and a subsidized communications network were vital to the health and welfare of possessions such as Australia and New Zealand. For other colonies the imperial connection was less important. To Britain the Empire was significant but not crucial.

A more detailed scrutiny of these trade flows is instructive.[58] The heavy dependence of some colonies on the British market is reflected in their trade statistics: 66 percent of South African exports went to the United Kingdom in 1860–2, 92 percent in 1885–7, and 91 percent in 1910–12. In the case of New Zealand, the totals were 38 percent, 68 percent, and 83 percent. Comparable figures for Canada were 41, 49, and 43; and for Newfoundland, 31, 24, and 26. Thus, 48 percent of all exports from the colonies with responsible government found their destination in Great Britain in 1860–2, 53 percent in 1885–7, and 60 percent in 1910–12.

Surprisingly, particularly for those who accept Lenin's arguments, the figures for the dependent Empire are much smaller – 43 percent in the first triennium, 26 percent the second, and 43 percent in the third. Nor was the total for India substantially different: 44, 40, and 30. In contrast, only 11 percent of British exports went to the colonies with responsible government in 1860–2, and no more than 15 percent in 1885–7 and 1910–12. For India, the comparable figures were 11, 17, and 12, and for the dependent Empire, 4, 3, and 5 percent. The vast majority of British exports went to other independent countries: 75 percent in 1860–2, 65 percent in 1885–7, and 68 percent in 1910–12.

While exports to the Empire were relatively small from Britain's point of view, these goods were of much greater importance to the Empire itself, although the British share of the market was falling in India and the responsibly governed colonies during the third triennium. India received 62 percent of its imports from Britain in the first period, 71 in the second, and 55 in the third. The figures for the self-governing Dominions were 52, 48, and 38 percent. For the dependent colonies, on the other hand, dependency was apparently increasing. The figure for 1910–12 was 38 percent, where in 1885–7 it had totaled a mere 19.

Overall, with the exception of India, Great Britain maintained a fair balance between its Empire exports and imports. Among its main Empire trading partners were Canada, New Zealand, and Australia. For Canada the average annual balance of trade, while a substantial negative £1.2 million in the years 1860–2, had become slightly positive (£29,000) in the second triennium, and by 1910–12 the account showed a considerable surplus of £2,576,000. For New Zealand the figures were not dissimilar: £630,000, £113,000, and £981,000. Nor does the Australian case differ substantially – the deficits were large through the 1880s, −£2,473,000 and −£5,636,000, but the account had also gone surplus by the end of the first decade of the present century (+£4,492,000). India, however, continued to run massive trade deficits. The averages for the three periods were: −£8,377,000, −£16,101,000, and −£24,336,000. It appears reasonable to conclude that access to the British market was of great importance to most colonies; that India depended heavily on Britain for its imports; but that this was less true for the Dominions and dependent colonies. As for Great Britain itself, trade with the Empire was not of overwhelming significance and, from the most independent of its colonies, the unencumbered welcome of their products into the United Kingdom earned not reciprocity but considerable tariff barriers.

Interimperial trade was largely insignificant. As late as the triennium 1910–12, India sent less than 3 percent of its exports to the colonies with responsible government and only 8 percent to the rest of the dependent Empire. At the same time, imports from these sources amounted to only 5 and 4 percent of the Indian total. In those years, the colonies with responsible government directed 3 percent of their exports to India, 5 percent to other responsibly governed colonies, and only 1 percent to the dependent colonies. The comparable import figures were 5, 4, and 3 percent. The dependent colonies sent 6 percent of their exports and received 17 percent of their imports from India. The figures for their trade with the colonies with responsible government were 5 and 3 percent; and for trade with other dependent colonies, some 4 percent. Again, analysis of the figures for 1910–12 indicates that of all Empire trade, 33 percent originated in Britain; 9 percent in India, 5 percent in Australia; 3 percent in Canada and South Africa; 1 percent in New Zealand (a total of 12 percent in the responsibly governed colonies); and 5 percent in the dependent colonies. A very substantial 41 percent originated in the foreign sector.

In summation, Great Britain provided both visible and invisible subsidies to the Empire. In the former category are grants-in-aid and subsidies for steamship and telegraph communication; in the latter, defense, trade advantages, and subsidized interest rates. From a strictly economic point of view the imperial connection was profitable – or more correctly the British taxpayer paid and the colonies benefited. The value of those benefits was high for the colonists in the regions of white settlements; although a part of the subsidy did accrue to those British residents who invested in the overseas Empire. For the remainder of the Empire, the returns are less obvious. Given the behavior of the independent underdeveloped countries, there is no reason to believe that the inhabitants of the dependent Empire, had they possessed similar liberties, would, even at the subsidized prices, have selected the particular market basket of public goods that the Colonial and India Office chose on their behalf. For India and the dependent colonies one cannot rule out the conclusion that everyone (Britons and natives alike) lost – a true Pareto pessimum.

7   The shareholders in imperial
enterprises

I. Introduction

The empire was profitable for some, and, even when it was not, losses were lower than they would have been had the British not shouldered the burden of the Empire subsidy. If the Empire investors were not the same people who paid the taxes, imperialism, at least in part, can be viewed as a process of income transfer from British taxpayers to imperial investors. To determine if, in fact, this hypothesis is correct, both imperial investors and British taxpayers must be identified.

The Company Acts of 1856 and 1862 required corporations to report the names of their stockholders each year. That report usually included not only names, but addresses and occupations as well; and it is these annual reports that provide the basis for this study. The three samples (of domestic, of foreign, and of Empire firms) were drawn from among the corporations listed in the *Stock Exchange Official Yearbook*.[1] It was often the case that a firm was listed before it had offered its shares for public sales, and in those instances the annual report listed only the original promoters. In an attempt to capture the "public" imperialists, the reports used were those submitted three to five years after initial incorporation. There were in total 260 firms with 79,994 shareholders. Of the total, 59 (with 15,220 shareholders) were classified as domestic, 75 (with 25,044 registered owners) as foreign, and 126 (with 39,680 shareholders) as Empire firms.[2]

The occupational categories are largely self-explanatory, but there were some (less than 2 percent) multiple occupations. One additional caveat. There are some problems with nominee holders.[3] They did exist, and they are difficult to identify. In addition, it is clear that stocks were often held in the name of a banker, a stockbroker, a solicitor, an employee, a wife, or a relative; and these present a more difficult dilemma. Subsidiary studies indicate that the problem may not be too serious, but for Empire and foreign firms there may be some overstatement of the proportion held by brokers, women, clerks, and bankers, and an underenumeration of the holdings of

Peers and Gents.[4] The taxonomy was designed to minimize the holdings of the elites and to maximize those of the business community. Thus any conclusions about elite participation can be viewed as reflecting the "worst case" (i.e., it is a minimum estimate of their investment). On the other hand, statements concerning business participation may overstate the contributions of that group.

For the analysis of the geographic distribution of stockholders, England has been divided into nine regions (the North, Yorkshire, Lancashire, Midlands Industrial, West, East, South and Southwest, Home Counties and London). Within London, addresses in "EC" (East Center, or the City) present a problem. Not only was it the most common location of nominee holders but, more importantly, shareholders often used their banks and brokers as convenience addresses. Therefore, London averages have been calculated both with and without that district. The former probably overstates the importance of the metropolis but, since there were many shareholders who lived or worked in the City, the latter certainly understates it.

The basic index utilized in this analysis is the fraction of the total value of a firm's capital stock that is owned by a particular occupational group or by the residents of some specific region.[5] Clearly, since a focus of this study is on the relationship between stock ownership and economic and political behavior, this index is not ideal. A measure that reflected either the relative or absolute importance of a class of investments (i.e., home, foreign, or Empire) to a group of holders might, to cite only two of many possible alternatives, provide a better measure.[6] Unfortunately, since those data are not available, the measure actually employed should be viewed as, at best, a proxy for the ideal measure. As such, however, it has at least one desirable characteristic. Members of the middle class were far more numerous than their counterparts in the upper class. One estimate, for example, indicates that only 3 out of 100 Britons, not in the working class, were actually in the upper class; and no one is likely to believe that the ratio was any lower than 5 or 10 to 1.[7] Thus, if the upper class held a larger fraction of the equities of Empire business, it is almost certain that the income arising from those shares must have been on average greater for each member of that class than it was on average for members of the middle class.

In the late nineteenth century the concentration of major wealth shifted from the traditional upper class, most of whose investments were in land, to businessmen. In Britain these businessmen were generally assumed to have been engaged in commerce and finance rather than manufacturing and industry, but, at least for the period under study, that assumption may be somewhat misplaced. Of the almost 200 nonlanded millionaires enumerated between 1860 and 1919, half earned their fortunes in trade and commerce and half in the industrial sectors.[8]

II. The occupational distribution of shareholders

The All-Firms enumeration provides some general insight into the types of persons who held shares in domestic, foreign, and Empire firms. The average investment was £1,908; domestic investments were smaller than foreign, and foreign smaller than Empire. Moreover, while there was some difference in level, that ordering holds for both Elites and Others; but not for businessmen. Their foreign investments were on average larger than their Empire ones.

Within the business community, all groups except merchants had a much greater affinity for domestic than foreign or Empire shares. On average, Business held about 50 percent of domestic, but only 30 percent of overseas, shares. Among businessmen, only merchants held as high a proportion of overseas as domestic shares; for the professions and for businessmen engaged in agriculture, maritime pursuits, transportation, communication, and mining the ratio was about one to two, and for manufacturers, one to three. Given the importance of overseas commerce in the British economic matrix and the proclivity of Business to invest in "what they know," it is hardly surprising that the merchants seem to have behaved somewhat differently than their confreres from other business activities.

The second group, the Elites, pursued a markedly different investment strategy. They held less than 30 percent of domestic, but almost 40 percent of foreign and Empire, shares. Peers and Gents, the most numerous group, held about a fifth of the value of domestic, but a quarter of foreign and Empire, securities. Smaller but still substantial proportions were held by the financial community – 4 percent of domestic, 8 percent of foreign and Empire. The other subgroups were much less important, but it is interesting to note that the military displayed a slightly greater preference for foreign than for Empire investment.

The third general group, Others, is very diverse and generalizations have little meaning. However, the pattern displayed by some of its constituent elements appears worthy of note. The tiny holdings of Laborers indicate that "people's capitalism" had made very little headway in the late nineteenth century, but it is interesting that workers held any shares at all. Other Firms held 4 percent of domestic, 8 percent of foreign, and 14 percent of Empire shares. While at times these represented interfirm holdings of nascent multinationals, such was not usually the case. Instead, they were most often blocks of shares held by commercial and private banks, land and development companies, and financial trusts. Together these financial firms accounted for more than one-half of interfirm holdings. Lastly, women held almost 8 percent of domestic, 5 percent of foreign, and 6 percent of Empire shares.

What can be inferred about the contrasting record of Business and Elites *vis-à-vis* the investments they did make in the Empire? There are at least two possible measures of the demonstrated industrial "taste" of the two groups. On the one hand it is possible to compare holdings in a single industry in the Empire with average holdings in that industry across all sectors; on the other, by focusing on a single industry it is possible to contrast Empire with domestic investors. To the extent that both measures lead to similar results, and in this case they do, it should be possible to conclude something about the investment choices of the two groups, and therefore, perhaps, learn something about their interest in the Empire. Table 7.1 displays the results of the All-Investments comparisons for the empire when the focus is narrowed to just Business and the Elites. For each industry the figures in the Business and Elite columns show the ratio of the proportion of the value of a typical firm's shares that Business or the Elites held in the Empire firms in that industry, to that same proportion, calculated for their holdings of all firms in that industry. Consequently, the figure of 180 for Business in shipping indicates that businessmen were 1.8 times as likely to own Empire shipping shares as they were to own the equities of shipping lines in general; and the figure of 38 for the Elites indicates that they were only .38 as likely to hold those shares. Thus, while the figures say nothing about absolute holdings, a comparison of the two numbers indicates that, relative to all investment in shipping, a businessman was almost five times as likely to have selected an Empire shipping line as was a member of the elite.

In the case of the Business sector, it is quite clear that, to the degree that businessmen invested in the Empire at all, their proclivities ran strongly to shipping, to commercial and industrial firms, to canal and dock companies, to mines, and to tea and coffee plantations. Mines and mealtime beverages aside, it appears that when businessmen turned their attention to the Empire, they tended to

Table 7.1. *Relative attractiveness of Empire investments (businessmen and elites only)*
Occupations' holdings in all locations, industry total = 100

Industry	Business	Elites	Business/elites
Shipping	180	38	4.76
Commercial & industrial	151	61	2.48
Canals & docks	135	72	1.87
Tea & coffee	132	75	1.76
Mines	129	78	1.65
Breweries & distilleries	99	101	0.98
Financial trusts	96	103	0.93
Waterworks	89	108	0.82
Iron, coal, & steel	87	110	0.80
Gas & light	85	111	0.77
Telephones & telegraphs	72	122	0.59
Trams & omnibuses	71	123	0.58
Commercial banks	67	126	0.53
Financial, land, & development	56	134	0.42
Railroads	56	134	0.41

place their resources in activities related to their businesses at home. Concomitantly, it would seem that the butchers, bakers, and candlestickmakers showed a strong disinclination to invest in commercial banks, financial, land and investment companies, railroads, telephone and telegraph companies, and firms operating trams and omnibuses. The unifying principle is less clear, but there seems to have been a hesitancy to invest in financial enterprises and transportation.

It is possible to extend the argument by examining the relationship between Business and Elite investment in these "outlying" industries in the Empire and their investments in the foreign sector (compare Table 7.1 with Table 7.2). Given the demonstrated inclination to invest in some and not in other activities, were these tendencies a reflection of Empire-related factors or just of overseas investment in general? The evidence indicates that the two groups did not consider all overseas investment in the same light. A comparison of the Business/Elite indexes for the fourteen industries with both foreign and Empire firms (there were only Empire tea and coffee firms) indicates that there is some similarity, but probably less than might have been supposed. The rank order correlation between the two

Table 7.2. *Relative attractiveness of foreign investments (businessmen and elites only)*
Occupations' holdings in all locations, industry total = 100

Industry	Business	Elites	Business/elites
Shipping	153	58	2.64
Commercial & industrial	122	83	1.46
Canals & docks	114	89	1.28
Mines	103	98	1.05
Breweries & distilleries	84	113	0.74
Financial trusts	88	109	0.81
Waterworks	111	91	1.22
Iron, coal, & steel	98	102	.96
Gas & light	146	64	2.30
Telephones & telegraphs	20	163	0.12
Trams & omnibuses	66	127	0.52
Commercial banks	109	93	1.18
Financial, land, & development	88	109	0.80
Rairoads	115	88	1.46

lists is only about a third. (1.0 would indicate that the two were identical, 0.0 that they were completely unrelated.)

For Business, a group that displayed no particular affinity for Empire as opposed to overseas investment in general, of the four comparable industries that attracted strong interest in the Empire, two emerge at the head of the foreign list, and the others remain in the upper half. Of the five at the bottom of the Empire list, three retain that rating in the foreign array; however, railroads move from last to fourth, gas and light companies from ninth to second, and commercial banks from twelfth to seventh.

The Elites showed a strong preference for Empire investment in railroads, financial, land and investment companies, commercial banks, trams and omnibus companies, and telephone and telegraph undertakings. At the same time, they appear to have been much less willing to invest in shipping lines, canal and dock companies, tea and coffee plantations, and mines. In the case of the commercial and industrial sector, their behavior changes with the yardstick employed. If the measure chosen is their domestic habits, they appear to have been attracted to commercial and industrial enterprises in the Empire; but if the standard is "typical Elite behavior," their commitment to trade, commerce, and manufacturing was very low.

One conclusion is obvious; the Elites actively shunned domestic commercial and industrial activities.

As in the case of the business community, elite investments in the foreign sector did not precisely reflect their behavior in the Empire. Of the five most-favored Empire industries, three remain on the foreign most desired list; but railroads fall from first to eleventh and commercial banks from third to eighth. Among those industries where Elite inclinations in the foreign sector were less strong than in the Empire, the index of gas and light companies falls from 111 to 64 and that of waterworks from 108 to 91. At the other end of the spectrum of taste, shipping, commercial and industrial firms, and canals and docks remain very low, but mining rises from eleventh to seventh. In general, it appears that the Empire attracted investment of the Elites in railroads, public utilities, and banking, but that if they were interested in directly supporting the production and distribution of commodities they looked elsewhere.

A word might be in order about the stockholders whose shareholdings were of considerable value. Nineteen investors held shares in a single company valued at between £25,000 and £50,000; twenty-two had holdings between £50,000 and £100,000, and thirty-five held securities worth more than £100,000. Of this last group, twenty-two were Peers and Gents, ten were merchants, and three were bankers. The single largest investment was £804,000 in Dalgety and Company, and not surprisingly it was held by Frederick G. Dalgety. The most popular security for the large investors was, however, the Bengal Nagpur Railroad. No less than eighteen of thirty-five investors who reported holdings in excess of £100,000 invested in that line; and all but two of that eighteen were Peers and Gents. Joseph Christy and James Alexander each held blocks valued at more than £600,000. Thomas Sutherland, chairman of the board of the Pacific and Orient, held £400,000, and two prominent British Jews had large holdings as well. Nathan de Rothschild, the first of his religion to be created a peer and the son of Lionel de Rothschild, the first Jew to take a seat in the House of Commons and the man responsible for the loans used by the British to purchase the controlling interest in the Suez Canal, owned £200,000. Leonard Lionel Cohen, the son of another early Jewish Member of Parliament (MP), held half again as much (£300,000).

The second most popular investment for those in the £100,000-plus cohort was the Merchant's Trust. Included on its share list were seven men – four merchants, two bankers, and a "gentleman," each of whom controlled shares valued at between £100,000 and £150,000.

Among those seven were two members of the Gibbs family – Alban and Vicary – both partners in Antony Gibbs and Sons; and Sir John Willoughby, fifth baronet, a soldier who served in Egypt and Matabeleland and who accompanied Dr. Jameson on his famous and ill-fated raid into the Transvaal.

Of the twenty-two investors who reported holdings in the £50 to £100,000 range, eight were Peers and Gents; four, bankers; four, businessmen; and one, a soldier. The latter, Major General John Clark, had served primarily in India, and he too put a part of his fortune (£94,800) into the Bengal and Nagpur Railroad. The favorite investment of this group, however, was the Merchant's Trust. Among the seven who held shares in that firm was Sir Everard Hambro, a director of the Bank of England and the son of the famous banker, Baron Hambro. Everard owned shares in the company worth £94,500. John Hays Hammond, the mining engineer, had served as the special expert for the U.S. Geological Survey team that surveyed the California gold fields and later had worked as a consultant to Cecil Rhodes. He invested £90,000 in the Bulwayo Waterworks. Of the nineteen shareholders in the £25,000 to £50,000 class, nine were Peers and Gents; and among that group railroads were the favorite choice.

It is evident that experience in the Empire helped motivate investment in the colonies, usually in an area where the investor had served. Thus, General Clark, who had been stationed in India, held shares in the Bengal Nagpur Railroad. Sir John Willoughby, long involved in Rhodesia, invested in the Bulwayo Waterworks, as did Rhodes's advisor, John Hammond. James Alexander, who held the largest block of Bengal Nagpur stock, had been the last agent for India in London. Thomas Russell, although residing in Eaton Square, had been defense minister for New Zealand; and he held £82,258 worth of shares in the New Zealand Mines Trust. Lieutenant General George Jackson, who had served in the Punjab, however, preferred to place his trust in London's Maypole Dairy!

Of the total of almost 80,000 shareholders, at least 323 had sat in the House of Commons (out of the total of 3,768 men who sat between 1860 and 1914). At first blush this seems a small number, but they represented not only 8 percent of the total house membership but also 1.5 percent of the value of all stock in the sampled companies. It is difficult to judge exactly the degree to which MP participation compares with the involvement of other groups in similar circumstances, but it appears to have been substantially higher. Virtually none of the great names of British politics appear on the roster of stockholders, and when they do their holdings were small. Joseph Chamberlain, a man of great wealth, showed his faith in the Empire of which he was the leading prophet, by investing £15,000 in the Royal Niger Company, £9,500 in the National Africa Company, and £500 in the Kleksdorp Estate. Arthur Balfour, another man of great means, limited himself to £3,000 in the Floating Dock of St. Thomas and £636 in the Colonies Securities Trust. Henry Labouchere, the fierce opponent of Empire, on the hand, held £12,500 worth of stock in the Boston Consolidated Mine (an American enterprise).

Of the 15,000 odd stockholders in the sampled domestic companies, 29 were MPs and they held shares to the value of £208,000 (1.3 percent of the number of outstanding shares and more than 2 percent of their value). This figure is in some sense reduced, however, when it is realized that one MP, William Cuthbert Quilter, the innovative accountant, owned £100,000 worth of securities in a single company, the Railway Rolling Stock Trust. Just over 2 percent of the value of shares (£715,000) in sample foreign companies were held by MPs. Eighteen together owned almost 4 percent (£26,000) of the outstanding stock in the Pekin Syndicate; and three held almost 20 percent (£44,000) of the Chile Telephone Company; but again, £348,000 of the £715,000 was held by Quilter.

It must be reiterated that of the 104 firms in which MPs held shares, only 14 were domestic (about one-fourth the total). Foreign investment was more popular; there were 113 MP shareholders in 39 different companies (over half the total number was represented). However, 181 owned shares (valued at £1,520,000) in 51 Empire firms out of a total of almost 40,000 stockholders who had invested almost 118 million pounds in 126 firms. Of the MPs' investment, £1,115,000 was invested in the Bengal Nagpur Railroad alone. Of that total, Bernhard Samuelson held £400,000; William Henry Smith, £300,000; and Frederick Thorpe Mappin, £200,000.

In interpreting these data, it soon becomes clear that because of the large holdings of a few individuals, the value of shares held by MPs is not a very useful measure. In terms of the location, the foreign and Empire sectors certainly held pride of place over the domestic. As to the percentage of companies with MP shareholders, the foreign sector has the highest figure with 52 percent, followed by Empire with 40, and domestic with 23. When it comes to the percentage of MPs among all shareholders in the total, the results are similar – foreign, 0.5; Empire, 0.4; and the United Kingdom, 0.2 percent.

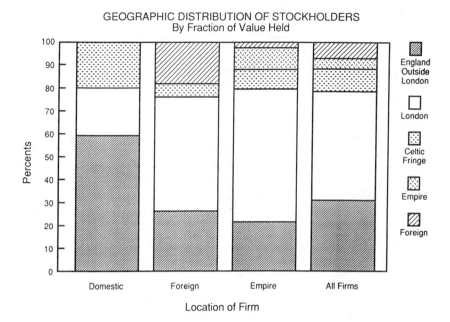

GEOGRAPHIC DISTRIBUTION OF STOCKHOLDERS
By Fraction of Value Held

Chart 7.1

III. The geographical distribution of stockholders

Any thought that British domestic firms depended on overseas investors is immediately dispelled by a glance at Chart 7.1; and the contribution of those investors to British enterprise in the foreign and Empire sectors, while somewhat larger, was far from dominant, by any stretch of the imagination. The proportion of overseas investment of firms located in the foreign sector is about one-sixth, and of Empire firms, no more than one-tenth.

In the Celtic fringe, Irish investment in no sector exceeded 1.5 percent. The Welsh and the Scots, however, made a substantial contribution to domestic industry, and the Scots owned almost 5 percent of foreign and more than 7 percent of Empire securities as well. The pattern suggested by the Scottish and Welsh experience is underscored when attention is focused on England. Depending on how one treats the City of London, as much as one-fifth or as little as one-tenth of domestic shares were held in London and the rest were owned by stockholders living outside the metropolis. Domestic shares were very broadly held, with stockholders spread fairly evenly from Land's End to John O'Groats. There were greater than average concentrations in the South and Southwest, in Yorkshire, and in the North, and less than typical concentrations in the Home Counties and the East; but British industry was truly domestic industry.

In the case of the foreign sector, only Lancashire, of the nonmetropolitan regions, stands out. Residents of the capital, however, held about a sixth of the foreign shares, if the City is excluded, and more than one-half, if it is not. In the case of the Empire firms, there was no secondary concentration in Lancashire, and, depending on the measure, the London proportion ranges from one-fifth to three-fifths of the total. If holdings are adjusted for population differences, it appears that a Londoner was more likely to invest in equities than his "country" cousin, but there was also a sharp contrast between London and the rest of the country when it came to selecting where to invest. A Londoner was about twice as likely as a nonmetropolitan resident to make an investment in domestic equities; but the population-adjusted index for London was only slightly higher than the Yorkshire (the next highest) figure. Those same Londoners, however, were twelve times as likely to buy foreign securities as their nonmetropolitan countrymen and eighteen times as likely to buy Empire securities. Nor were there other regions with indices close to London's. In the foreign sector, Lancashire residents displayed the second highest investment propensity (thanks to the citizens of Manchester and Liverpool), but that figure was only one-sixth the London number. In the case of the Empire, the scenario is similar. It was not residents of Lancashire but residents of the Home counties who bought Empire shares more frequently than any other nonmetropolitan group (and one can wonder whether many were not actually Londoners), but their average propensity to absorb imperial equities was only one-seventh that of their London neighbors.

One conclusion is obvious: While Britain was a very important market for equities, it was not one capital market, but two. Domestic firms enjoyed the savings of London residents, but they could not have survived without the accumulations of investors in Cornwall, Birmingham, and rural Rutland. In 1901, 26 million of England's 31 million people lived outside the capital, but, in terms of foreign equities, the contribution of that 26 million was only one and one-half times as large as that of the residents of greater London, even if the entire holdings of investors giving City addresses (East Central London) are removed from consideration. Moreover, in the case of the Empire, the total contributions of the two groups (one, five and a half times as large as the other) were almost equal. If the EC residents are counted, then the 4.6 million London residents contributed twice as much to foreign, and two and three-quarters times as much to Empire, finance as all of the rest of the citizens of England. To help place these conclusions in the context of British history, it appears useful to point out that of the 57 millionaires who lived and died in Great Britain in the last two decades of the nineteenth century, 11 claimed the City as their home and another resided elsewhere in greater London. After those 12, the next largest concentrations were in Merseyside (8) and in Clydeside and the Notthingham–Derby area (4 each). Greater Manchester, despite its contribution to British economic growth, claimed only 2.[9]

IV. Conclusions

The analysis presented in this chapter is designed to uncover any differences between those stockholders who invested in the Empire and ones who chose domestic or foreign equities. It appears that there were substantial contrasts between investors in domestic enterprises and those who bought shares in overseas companies, and almost equally important differences between investors who chose the Empire and those who preferred investments in lands not owing fealty to the British Crown. Given the way that the data were collected it is difficult to investigate the composition of the "investment portfolios" of the occupational groups; however Charts 7.2, 7.3, and 7.4 provide an index of relative portfolio holdings for the Elite and Business classes.[10]

While there were some important interoccupational differences, businessmen were twice as likely to invest in domestic as Empire securities, and about a sixth more likely to invest in domestic than in foreign securities. Of that group, merchants held the highest proportion of their "portfolios" in overseas investments, but as far as the Empire was concerned, the proportion was still below that held by any Elite subgroup except the military, and it was equal to that. Such reticent behavior was, however, not typical of their attitude toward foreign investments. Merchants displayed a very strong affinity for those securities; and Financiers and Miscellaneous Elites aside, they were more likely to invest in the foreign sector than any other occupational group. Removal of the merchants from the calculations, for example, reduces that foreign index for the Business group from 86 to 53. Manufacturers, on the other hand,

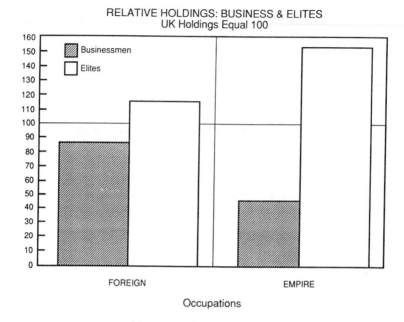

RELATIVE HOLDINGS: BUSINESS & ELITES
UK Holdings Equal 100

Chart 7.2

displayed the least interest in overseas, and particularly Empire, investment. Members of that group were eight times as likely to invest in domestic as in Empire securities.

The Elites appear to have been somewhat more inclined to invest in foreign, but very much more likely as a group to invest in Empire, than in domestic issues. In the Empire case the investment index is more than half again the domestic figure. Oddly enough, the military seems to resemble the Business group far more than the other Elites. They displayed a fairly strong preference for domestic as opposed to any overseas investments. In the overseas arena, the financiers appear to have much preferred foreign investment, and their index for Empire commitments was slightly below their domestic baseline. Miscellaneous Elites showed the strongest preference for overseas investment; they acquired foreign securities at rates more than twice as high as domestic, and Empire shares at rates two and a half times that level. Finally, the numerically largest group, the Peers and Gents, displays no particular predilection for foreign shares (their index was slightly less than 100) but a strong (more than 60 percent above domestic) preference for Empire investments.

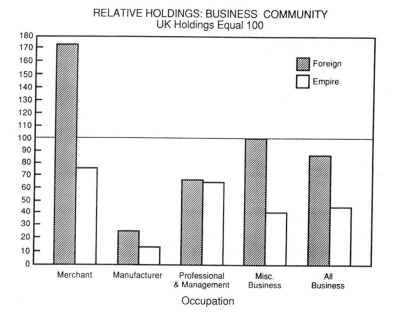

RELATIVE HOLDINGS: BUSINESS COMMUNITY
UK Holdings Equal 100

Chart 7.3

The conclusions are quite clear. Businessmen did invest abroad, but their major interest was the domestic economy. While the merchants should have been interested in foreign political developments, they, like the rest of the businessmen, were more oriented toward domestic than Empire problems. For the Elites the opposite was true, although military officers were an exception. If, however, the success of Empire ventures was linked to political policies at home, the Elites (and particularly the Miscellaneous and Peers and Gents) must have been more concerned with the shape of those imperial policies than were their counterparts in the world of Business.

The aggregate figures do not tell the whole story; there were substantial interindustry deviations from the All-Firms average. Businessmen were more heavily involved in some industries and the Elites in others. A measure of relative affinity is presented in Table 7.3. For the industries that have firms in all three sectors, the table provides a rank ordering of the investment preferences of the Elites relative to the business community. Thus, a rank of 1 (say for U.K. mines) indicates that among all domestic industries mines were

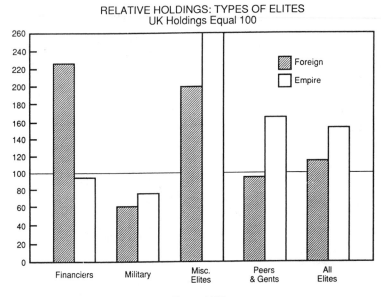

RELATIVE HOLDINGS: TYPES OF ELITES
UK Holdings Equal 100

Chart 7.4

Table 7.3. *Rank order of relative attractiveness, elites to businessmen, by industry*

Industry	U.K.	Foreign	Empire
Commercial banks	4	7	2
Breweries and distilleries	10	2	7
Commercial & industrial	11	10	10
Financial land & development	2	3	1
Financial trust	5	4	6
Gas and light	8	10	4
Iron, coal, and steel	7	5	5
Mines	1	6	8
Shipping	6	11	11
Trams and omnibuses	3	1	3
Canals and docks	9	8	9

most preferred by elite investors (and, therefore, least preferred by Business). A rank of 11, on the other hand, is associated with an industry (commercial and industrial) that was most preferred by Business and least favored by the Elites. One word of caution. The table includes only the eleven industries that were represented in all three sectors, and it excludes two Empire industries that were strongly preferred by Elites (railroads and telephones and telegraphs), one that was moderately preferred (waterworks), and one that the Elites viewed with positive distaste (tea and coffee). In the Empire, those industries would have ranked first, third, sixth, and thirteenth (out of fifteen).

Again, it appears that preferences at home were not identical to those in overseas investments: The rank order correlation between home and foreign was .37, and between home and Empire, .50.

The Elites' interest in Empire was strongest in railroads, commercial banks, and financial land and development companies, and the "public utilities" – gas and light, tramways and omnibuses, and waterworks. Businessmen, however, tended to focus their Empire investments in the "private" sector: in shipping lines, canals and dock companies, commercial and industrial firms, and tea and coffee plantations. While the Empire connection was important, these were competitive industries, and profits must have depended far less directly on the particular form of the political structure. As Schumpeter has observed:

> ... where free trade prevails no class has an interest in forceable expansion.... Where the cultural backwardness of a region makes normal intercourse dependent on colonization, it does not matter, assuming free trade, which of the civilized nations undertakes the task of colonization. Dominion of the seas, in such a case, means little more than a maritime traffic police. Similarly, it is a matter of indifference to a nation whether a railway concession in a foreign country is acquired by one of its own citizens or not – just as long as the railway is built.[11]

Overseas residents showed little inclination to invest in domestic securities; those in foreign countries placed most of their accumulations in foreign concerns; and stockholders who lived in the colonies turned almost entirely to Empire firms. Ninety percent of the shareholders, however, resided in the United Kingdom, and it is their spatial distribution that is of most interest from the point of view of a study of the political economy of Empire. The average figures for Scotland, Ireland, and Wales would suggest that investors there looked much like the typical Briton living outside the capital, but that average masks very different behavior by the citizens of the three Celtic "nations." The Welsh were more English than the English and seldom invested in any overseas securities. The Irish were, as might be expected, far more catholic in their tastes; on average, however, they preferred domestic to Empire, and foreign to domestic shares. The Scots displayed a little more interest in foreign equities than the typical "non–London" Englishman, but they still preferred domestic investment. On the other hand, their preference for Empire shares was almost as strong as a resident of the City – and that is a marked preference indeed.

Interest, however, centers on the English investors since they accounted for more than 90 percent of U.K. and 80 percent of all holdings; and there were clearly two Englands: London and the provinces. To the extent that equity holdings provide an adequate measure of total investments, a Londoner's portfolio held less than one-quarter domestic, more than one-third foreign, and almost two-fifths Empire securities. Within Greater London, EC residents were powerfully attracted to foreign investments and relatively strongly attracted to the Empire. In London outside the City, the Empire was very popular but residents of Westminister, Chelsea, and the rest of the environs appear to have been largely indifferent when it came to choosing between home and foreign investment.

In the "country," both the Empire and foreign indexes are about half the domestic. The foreign sector figure was much inflated by the residents of Lancashire and the rural East, while that latter area and the Home counties kept the Empire index as high as it was. The areas outside London were not, however, all identical. In the North, in Yorkshire, and in the Midlands the domestic proportions ranged from more than two-thirds to four-fifths, and averaged about three-quarters of a typical investor's portfolio. Elsewhere, the domestic figure, though much lower, was still far above ratios recorded in London. Empire shares averaged less than 15 percent of all investment in the four northern regions (the North, Lancashire, Yorkshire, and the Midlands), but they were over two times that level in the four southern (Home, East, West, and South and Southwest). Even in the country, the "London disease" appears to have infected the contiguous regions.

The rank orderings displayed in Table 7.4 provide an indication of the relative attractiveness of particular industries to London and provincial investors for the eleven industries that include observations from the three geographic sectors. A low number (the 2 for Empire financial, land, and development companies, for example)

Table 7.4. *Relative attractiveness of industries (eleven comparable industries only)*
Ratio of index of London stockholders to non–London stockholders[a]

| | Rank order | | |
Industry	U.K.	Foreign	Empire
Commercial banks	8	6	10
Breweries and distilleries	10	4	9
Canals and docks	11	1	1
Commercial and industrial	6	5	6
Financial, land, and development	1	7	2
Financial trusts	2	10	8
Gas and light	7	3	11
Iron, coal, and steel	9	8	7
Mines	3	9	3
Shipping	5	11	5
Trams and omnibuses	4	2	4

[a]Non–London includes Scotland, Ireland, and Wales

indicates that the industry was relatively much more preferred by London than by provincial residents; and a high figure (the 11 for Empire gas and light firms), the reverse. Again it should be noted that four industries have been excluded. In the case of Empire investments the four include two (railroads and waterworks) for which London residents displayed a strong preference, and two (tea and coffee and telephones and telegraphs) that they disliked intensely. In an ordering of all fifteen, the four would have stood second, third, fourteenth, and fifteenth, respectively.

To the extent that the ranking captures the relative preferences, there appears to have been a marked difference of opinion about the "best" investments in the three sectors. The rank order correlation between the domestic and foreign ordering is a *negative* .50; and there appears almost no relation between the domestic and Empire or the foreign and Empire orderings (the correlation coefficients are .04 and .08). The results are also less sharp than for the occupational distributions. In the Empire, Londoners had a propensity to invest in canals and docks; financial, land, and development companies; and mines in the unregulated sectors; and railroads and waterworks, among the public utilities. The non–London investors, while gazing abroad far less frequently than their

Table 7.5. *Relative attractiveness home, foreign, and empire, by occupation and location, business and elites only*
Ratio is London to non–London

	Location of firm		
Occupation	U.K.	Foreign	Empire
Merchants	19	135	110
Manufacturers	44	140	162
Professional	22	114	126
Miscellaneous business	2	40	635
Total business	17	122	142
Financiers	61	105	103
Military	132	108	94
Miscellaneous elites	152	129	90
Gents and peers	49	102	105
Total elites	62	106	102

London peers, looked in different directions when their eyes did turn outward. In the Empire their investments, with the exceptions of gas and light and telephones and telegraphs, clustered about the nonregulated parts of the economy. They displayed above-average indexes for three of the five goods-producing sectors (brewing, iron, coal and steel, and tea and coffee), and in addition they invested above-typical amounts in commercial banks and shipping. In the "public" sector they showed greater than "average" interest in gas and light and telephone and telegraph companies.

Finally, given the two-nation character of imperial investment, it appears useful to examine the composition of the occupational "portfolios" in the two regions. Did London-based Empire investors come from the same occupational distribution as those Empire investors who resided in the country, or did members of an occupational group display a different investment strategy if they lived in London? Table 7.5 and Chart 7.5 provide some insights into that question. An entry greater than 100 indicates that Londoners had a stronger preference for the sector's securities than their provincial cousins, and a number less than 100 manifests a country investor preference.[12] If the behavior of the investors was similar in both regions, the ratios should be close to 100.

In the case of Business, it is apparent that Londoners behaved very differently. In every subcategory, London businessmen invested far less often in domestic industry and far more frequently

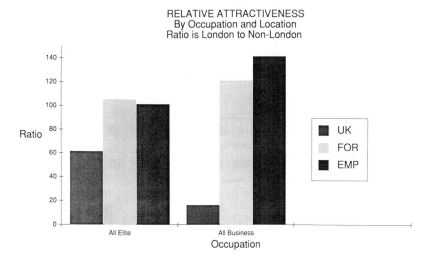

RELATIVE ATTRACTIVENESS
By Occupation and Location
Ratio is London to Non-London

Chart 7.5

in the Empire. The Miscellaneous-Business category aside, the same preference appears to hold for foreign investments as well. In the Business sector as a whole, the ratio of London to non–London indexes stood at less than 20 for domestic and almost 150 for Empire investment.

For the Elite category, the urban–rural differences are much less clearly marked. Every metropolitan subgroup appears somewhat more willing to invest in the foreign sector than were their counterparts outside London, but there is no such uniformity of feelings in the domestic and Empire sectors. In the former, although the overall Elite ratio for London is well below that for the provinces, both the military and miscellaneous groups tended to invest in domestic activities relatively more often than their country counterparts. In the case of Empire investment, the rates were similar for Londoner and non–Londoner alike. In London, Financiers and Peers and Gents appear to have viewed such investment as very slightly more attractive than did their rural confreres, but the opposite was true for the military and the Miscellaneous Elites.

Altogether, it appears that the London bias toward overseas investment, while in part accounted for by the somewhat greater concentration of Elite investment in the metropolis (Peers and Gents accounted for about 5 percent more of London than of "rural" investment), can in large measure be traced to the attraction of that overseas investment for London businessmen. Clearly that lure was less strong outside the capital, and the farther one traveled north from London the weaker it became. Overall, it appears that the Empire was the investment preserve of the nonmilitary Elites everywhere, and of London businessmen (particularly the merchants).

8   *The sources of government revenues*

I. Introduction

Empire investors appear to have come from the ranks of the elites and the London merchants. Outside London, what has traditionally been regarded as the British middle class, where the term is used to include both factory and shop owners, does not seem to have been heavily involved.[1] If the two former groups were the recipients of the imperial subsidy, who paid the bill? There is no more powerful policy tool available to a government than its budget, but the ability to spend is based to a large extent on the revenues raised through taxation. Those imposts are the subject of this chapter.

Empire investors found the imperial connection valuable, but some of that institution's value depended on the imperial subsidy. Its size was substantial, and its benefits not evenly spread. The middle class, particularly those members living in the Midlands and the North, received substantially less than their proportionate shares, while the financiers, government officials, the leisure classes, and the London merchants received more. In the Empire indigenous entrepreneurs fared even better since they paid none of the subsidy but received full measure of its rewards. It seems natural, therefore, to analyze the tax structure and discover which citizens paid and which citizens were relieved from those imposts. Neither task can be effected with complete precision, but the data yield some very suggestive hypotheses that have a substantial measure of support.[2]

II. The Empire

While most revenues came from taxes, a significant proportion originated in nontax sources (see Chart 8.1). The trends in total revenues are somewhat unexpected. Over time, revenues rose in the United Kingdom, in the colonies with responsible government, and in the two foreign sectors; but there is no evidence of any such increase in the dependent Empire. On average the largest revenues were raised in the United Kingdom (£2–16–5 per capita), but the figure for the colonies with responsible government was £2–13–7. For the

183

SOURCES OF GOVERNMENT REVENUE
Pounds Per Capita: All Years 1860-1912

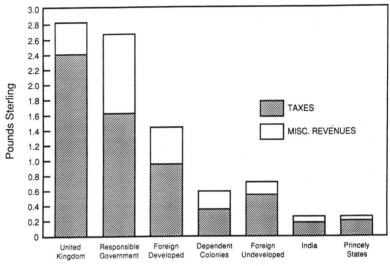

Chart 8.1

dependent colonies it was substantially less than £1, and that figure
was below the average burden in both the foreign developed and
underdeveloped countries. In India, however, while average revenues were well below those of the foreign underdeveloped countries
and in the dependent colonies, they were about equal to the average
figures for the Indian Princely States.

While the focus of this chapter is on tax revenues, given the important role played by nontax earnings in the Empire (where they
account for almost one-third of all revenue), those secondary revenue sources deserve a brief comment. Both dependent and self-
governing colonies drew heavily from licenses and fees – charges
that averaged about 3 shillings, 2 pence per person per year. That
figure compares with an average of 1 shilling and 7 pence among
developed, and 5 pence among underdeveloped countries. However, the bias toward licenses and fees, while accounting for a substantial portion of the extra nontax revenues in the case of the
dependent colonies, was a much less significant contributor to the
colonies with responsible government. For them (and to a lesser
extent in the dependent colonies) it was revenues from "natural

resources," and particularly from public land sales, that in large measure accounted for the high level of nontax receipts.

While the colonies with responsible government were clearly the greatest beneficiaries from the vastness of the imperial lands, the entire non–Indian Empire drew on these "public" resources far more than governments in the rest of the world. Revenues were highest in Australasia, but every self-governing colony received some. Overall they ranged from a high of £1–15–7 in New South Wales to a low of 5 pence in Canada. Of the dependent colonies five averaged more than 4 shillings per capita, and only twenty received nothing at all. Among the developed countries only five averaged as much as half the Canadian figure; and of the underdeveloped countries, just four – Argentina, Siam, Guatemala, and Venezuela.

When it comes to mining royalties, earnings were far less, but not surprisingly the figure for the Transvaal was almost twelve shillings and New Zealand and parts of Australia also received significant contributions. In the ranks of the dependent colonies, Southern Rhodesia and the Pacific possessions (Labuan, Sarawak, and the Gilbert and Ellice Islands) also drew fiscal resources from the "ground." Beyond the Empire, Norway, Russia, Greece, and Spain earned more than 2 pence, but of the underdeveloped countries only Bulgaria recovered anything near that amount. It is readily apparent that the colonies with responsible government benefited from the unoccupied lands within their borders – and to a lesser extent the minerals on those lands – and were able to turn those "free resources" into funds to support public expenditures without having to increase the burden of taxes.

The important questions, however, concern income derived from tax levies. Empire residents paid relatively high taxes, but they were less than might have been expected given their development and their levels of public expenditure. The trend in per capita taxes in the Empire was generally upward, and that movement marked the United Kingdom imposts as well. Not only was the tax burden increasing, but taxes in the home country remained among the highest in the world. Overall national taxes (excluding imposts levied by counties and cities) averaged almost 2 pounds and 10 shillings per person per year, but in the twentieth century the assessment was almost a pound higher than that figure. In those parts of the Empire with responsible government, the average tax burdens were very high when compared to almost any place in the world except Great Britain and a very few of the developed countries. The average assessment was below that in the United Kingdom, but it rose very rapidly and more than doubled between 1860 and 1912.[3] Only Western Australia, New Zealand, and Queensland levied as much as the United Kingdom; those governments received almost £1 per head more than the government in London. Of the others, Tasmania, Australia, Victoria, and the Transvaal all received more than £2 per capita per year, and except for Natal (14 shillings) per capita taxes in the other self-governing colonies ranged between £1–5–10 in Canada and £1–14–10 in New South Wales.

These figures are in sharp contrast to the levels that prevailed in the foreign developed countries, where the rate of increase was also rapid, but the average was less than £1. Of the sixteen countries in that group, none levied taxes that, on average were as high as £2 per head and in only seven (six in western Europe and the United States) did taxes reach half that level. Levies in the others ranged from 5 shillings (Portugal) to 18 shillings, 2 pence (Norway). In the colonies with responsible government where citizens were free to choose the weight of their tax burden, they appear to have been willing to shoulder very heavy loads. Natal aside, the voters in every one of the other such colonies opted to pay taxes that were, at minimum, a third higher than the average of all developed countries.

In the dependent colonies, the local residents had less voice, and the battles most often were fought between the London-based bureaucrats (in the Treasury and Colonial Office) and the colonial governor, whose views frequently reflected his own or local opinion. Over the period, taxes in those colonies were relatively low, averaging only 6 shillings and 10 pence; but there is every evidence that there was no single tax policy for all the dependent colonies. The residents of eleven colonies paid more than £1; the citizens of another twenty paid in excess of 10 shillings, but, in sixteen colonies, the average tax burden was less than 2 shillings per person. Moreover, there is little evidence of any increase in tax rates over time. Although partly a statistical artifact resulting from the nature of the new colonies added to the Empire, the average tax burden was actually lower in 1912 than it had been in 1860. In contrast, the average tax burden in the foreign underdeveloped sector was more than one and a half times as high as the rate in the dependent colonies, and that average levy had almost tripled between 1860 and 1912.

India differed markedly both from the rest of the dependent Empire and from the underdeveloped sector, but less sharply from the Princely States. Tax levies were much lower and, if there was any trend, it was downward. The average assessment was 3 shillings and 5 pence, but it fell from almost 4 shillings in the 1860s to about three-fourths that level in the twentieth century. The Princely States raised somewhat more, and the trend was upward. These results should be viewed with caution, however, since the data are marked by very wide state-to-state variation. Some (like Jobat, Manipur, and Dhar) averaged 7 pence or less – below all but two dependent colonies – while three (Rampur, Baroda, and Jam Khandi) averaged more than 6 shillings.

The analysis of public expenditures leads to the conclusion that to the extent service was correlated with cost, the level of public services provided by the government of India was quite meager. It is, however, equally clear that the taxes levied to support those services was also low. The average burden was, for example, only about one-third the 8 shillings and 7 pence levied in neighboring Siam. The dependent colonies too appear to have been relatively lightly taxed, although in their case the margin was smaller (about two-thirds of the 11 shillings prevailing in the foreign underdeveloped sector). On average, throughout the dependent Empire the level of tax imposts was not high, although some colonies were marked by substantial burdens. In the colonies where the tax level was a matter of local choice, however, the assessment was almost three-quarters of that in the home country and one and three-quarters times levels imposed in other developed countries.

Since all taxes do not fall equally on all social and economic groups, it is important to examine the Empire tax structure. See Chart 8.2. In the decade following the death of Victoria, the free-trade debate raged and was ultimately lost in Britain. In the colonies with responsible government, however, the issue had long been settled. Throughout the last four decades of the nineteenth century and despite continual pleas from the home country – at first for free trade and later for, at minimum, imperial preference – these colonies were at least as protectionist as Germany and the United States. In every self-governing colony, customs revenues were by far the most important source of tax revenue. On average, about a £1–5–0 per person per year were derived from taxes on foreign trade, and that figure represented over 3 in every £4 of tax income [Chart 8.3(a)]. While the trend in the proportion of customs in total taxes was downward (it fell from 90 to about 70 percent), the absolute burden had climbed, from about 15 shillings to more than twice that level by the end of the nineteenth century. Those tariffs were a matter of continual concern to the colonies' chief trading partner, the United Kingdom. As early as 1871 Kimberley lamented the impact of proposed legislation in New Zealand. In a letter to Gladstone he wrote: " . . . the

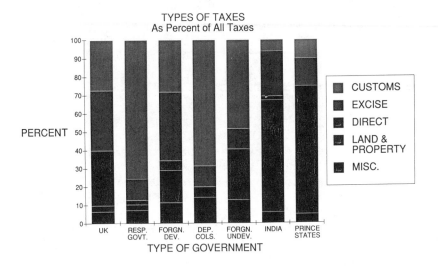

TYPES OF TAXES
As Percent of All Taxes

Chart 8.2

effect of the New Zealand Bill would undoubtedly be that New Zealand might admit Sydney made shoes free and charge any duty she pleased on shoes from Northhampton. . . . "[4]

The dependence on customs differed somewhat from colony to colony, but in none did it represent much less than 60 percent of all taxes. Newfoundland aside (tariffs were almost the only source of tax revenue in that colony), the dependence was greatest in Australasia, although after the birth of the Commonwealth that reliance was reduced somewhat. For the six Australian colonies the proportion ranged from 95 percent in Western Australia to 78 percent in New South Wales.[5] In New Zealand, the source of Kimberley's concern, the proportion was only 80 percent. Elsewhere dependence was somewhat less. After the formation of the Union of South Africa, the fraction raised in the four colonies stabilized at about three-fifths of the total tax bill. Earlier, however, the Cape had drawn 70 percent but the Orange River Colony a mere 57 percent. Canada lay somewhere between the extremes; its average was just over three in four. Differential tariff rates actually acted to deter political consolidation in South Africa. In 1880 Bartle Frere wrote:

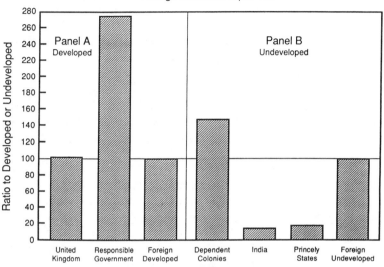

RELATIVE IMPORTANCE OF CUSTOMS
Foreign Countries Equal 100

Chart 8.3 (a)

> ... Natal has a low tariff. The Cape has raised its rates. . . . the difference and separation of interests has a bad effect on commerce in general and benefits only a few traders in Natal by enabling them to under-sell the Cape in quarters whose natural channel of supply would be via the Cape ports. . . . This is an obstacle to any union or confederation. . . . Natal does not want to give up its extensive power of lowering its rates, and thereby attracting a trade that would not otherwise come to its ports. . . . [6]

The responsibly governed colonies stand in stark contrast to the "developed" world, even though the latter is usually assumed to have been not only very protectionist but increasingly so. In those advanced nations the fraction of customs among all tax revenues averaged somewhere between a fifth and a third; and although the trend was upward, the movement, at least after 1880, was small. In absolute terms, the customs exaction was gradually increasing; however, that figure, which on average was perhaps £1–10 in the responsibly governed Empire, stood at only one-fifth that level in the developed countries. While no colony with responsible government raised less than 55 percent of its taxes from customs duties, only two developed countries (Switzerland and Norway) relied on customs duties so heavily. Among the others, only three (Denmark, Germany, and the United States) received as much as one-half of their tax revenues from this source and six received less than one-fifth (France, Netherlands, Italy, Belgium, Austria-Hungary, and Japan).

Without question, the dependence of the colonies with responsible government on customs revenues had implications for the imperial system. Much to Britain's chagrin, faith in the wonders of free trade was limited to the metropole. Import taxes were ultimately paid by the colonial consumers, but a substantial income must have found its way into the hands of local businessmen, rentiers, and workers able to operate under the protective umbrella. At the same time, British exporters and their employees faced sluggish sales as their products, burdened by oppressive customs duties, became steadily less competitive in the Empire markets.

While tariffs found much favor in the self-governing colonies, other excises did not [Chart 8.3(b)]. Where the government of the United Kingdom and other developed countries depended on these levies for about a third of their tax income, the colonies with responsible government drew little more than 10 percent. There, on average, excises produced no more than 4 shillings per capita a year; and although income from that source was increasing, even at the end of the period it was still far below the rest of the developed world. In Canada excises accounted for 23 percent of all national taxes, and in the Australian Commonwealth the figure was about half that amount. Those two aside, no other self-governing colony drew more than £1 in 12; and in six of the fourteen the level was £1 in 50 or less.

In contrast, in the foreign developed sector and despite the fact that total tax revenues were less than three-fifths those in the Empire of white settlement, excises brought in more than three times the proportion of the total. Only three countries turned to domestic excises for less than one-eighth (the responsible-government average) of their total tax returns, and five received more than £2 in 5. In the Empire, foreign producers (most often Englishmen) were heavily taxed, but the burden on domestic products was very light. Outside the Empire there were tariffs, but there were also domestic excises. In the case of alcohol taxes, for example, the colonies with responsible government received 7 pence per person per year but the foreign developed countries earned more than twice that amount.

As the nineteenth century wore on, the United Kingdom and, to

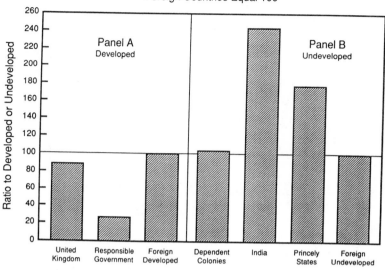

Chart 8.3 (b)

a lesser extent, other developed countries, turned increasingly to income and inheritance taxes [Chart 8.3(c)]. In the United Kingdom over the last four decades of that century, the national government derived about one-quarter of its total revenues from those taxes, and in the first decades of the twentieth century the figure was nearly two-fifths. In the foreign developed sector the change was more gradual, but the figures were still significant (something less than 5 percent in the nineteenth century and about a third more in the twentieth). In the colonies with responsible government income taxes were almost nonexistent before the late 1890s, but thereafter they were about equal to those in the foreign developed sector, and after 1895 inheritance taxes were higher. In those colonies, income and inheritance taxes together produced about 2 pence per capita in the years before 1895, but ten times that amount afterward.

The latter increase was particularly marked in the budgets of the Commonwealth of Australia and the Union of South Africa. In the twentieth century, the Island Continent received 13 percent of its revenues from these two sources and the Union, 8. The shift in colonial policy toward higher income taxes raised concern in the

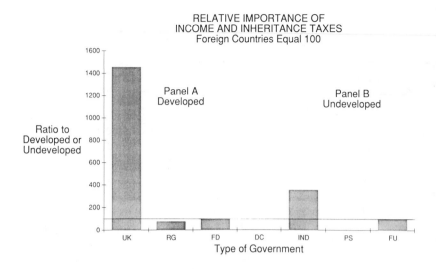

Chart 8.3 (c)

British Treasury. It noted that a British investor whose holdings were in South Africa was subject to double taxation, while a South African who invested in the United Kingdom was subject to only the United Kingdom income tax. Nor did there appear to have been any easy way out of the problem as long as Britain had no voice in South African tax policy.

> ... The profits made by Englishmen in our colonies are subject to local income tax, that our income tax does not apply, is knocking a big hole in our revenue, while the reciprocity extended by the colony is negligible. . . . There is no uniformity in the colonies. For instance, there is an income tax at the Cape and none in Canada. If we exempted a colony like the Cape from income tax in England, we should be giving a pull to the Cape; but Canada who chooses to raise her revenue in other ways than income tax, would get nothing.[7]

Australia and South Africa aside, the only other self-governing colonies to make significant use of these direct sources were the Orange Free State (when it was a separate colony), Victoria, New Zealand, and Tasmania. At the same time, three self-governing colonies had no income or inheritance taxes. In the foreign developed sector, Belgium and Italy displayed proportions (although not levels) only slightly less than those prevailing in the United Kingdom, nine na-

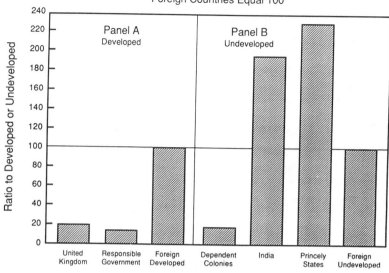

RELATIVE IMPORTANCE OF LAND & PROPERTY TAXES
Foreign Countries Equal 100

Chart 8.3 (d)

tions drew at least 3 percent of their tax revenues from these direct taxes, and only one country drew none at all.

The other major tax was the levy on property, and in this case the history in the colonies with responsible government was markedly different from the countries in the foreign developed sector [see Chart 8.3(d)]. The trend in per capita revenues was upward in both sectors, but the levels were much higher in the foreign countries. In those parts of the Empire allowed to choose their own tax patterns, the property tax on average brought in only about 3 percent of the total tax revenue, as compared with almost one-fifth in the foreign developed nations. The British government expressed concern with the disinclination of its white colonies to tax property. In the case of the Orange River Colony, for example, Milner pointed out to the colony's treasurer that:

> ... having regard for the fact that the Orange River Colony though a bad subject for taxation, has hitherto had very little that could be called taxation at all. I do not think for example, that a charge of one shilling on every 100 acres should be called a tax, and indeed I believe it is not. . . . It may be worth considering as

> we have to restart the agriculture of the whole colony, [that] the opportunity might be taken for insuring some larger permanent revenue to the State from the land. . . .[8]

In the developed countries, revenues from the property tax doubled over the last four decades in the nineteenth century; and, although declining as a share of all taxes, they remained an important component of the total revenue package. In the self-governing Empire, on the other hand, only South Australia, New Zealand, and Tasmania derived more than 6 percent of their tax revenues from property, and eight of those colonies received less than 1 percent. Only four of the developed countries derived no income from property levies, and nine garnered more than a fifth of their tax revenues from that source.

Miscellaneous taxes increased sixfold over the fifty-three years and accounted for about a tenth of all tax revenues in the colonies with responsible government [Chart 8.3(e)]. The category miscellaneous taxes is a catchall containing a multitude of imposts not captured elsewhere. The most important was the stamp tax; but, as the period wore on, the total was swollen by revenues from the native-hut tax imposed in many of the African colonies. Given the calamitous effects of the American revolution, it is not surprising that stamp imposts were not important on the North American continent. Elsewhere, however, they were ubiquitous and accounted for more than 4 shillings per capita in Queensland, New Zealand, and the Transvaal.

Less politically explosive in the nineteenth century, but the subject of far more political rhetoric in the twentieth, was the hut tax. That tax (almost exclusively an African impost) was unimportant in the Cape with its relatively small indigenous tribal population; however, it produced 1 shilling and 7 pence in Natal, 2 shillings and 2 pence in the Orange Free State, and 7 shillings (almost a fifth of *all* tax revenues) in the Transvaal. Critics have recently argued that the tax was a device designed to force native workers into the ranks of labor. The tax had that effect; but while a desire to coerce a redistribution of the labor force may have provided some part of the policy makers' motivation, it was not the only reason. The hut tax raised a significant amount of money; and, perhaps more important, it helped to convince the white settlers that they were not, from the government's point of view, the only game in town. In 1875, for example, Wolseley wrote Carnarvon:

> . . . There will be little difficulty passing the land tax on the property of the white settlers when it is understood that the natives

RELATIVE IMPORTANCE OF MISCELLANEOUS TAXES
Foreign Countries Equal 100

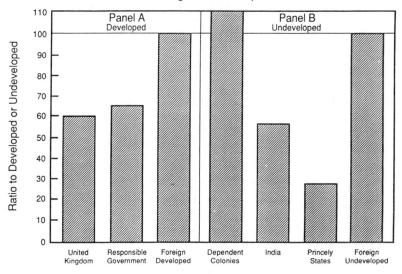

Chart 8.3 (e)

will have to bear a small proportion of the burden imposed upon the Colony by railway construction. The hut tax imposed by the Cape upon our neighboring province of Basutoland is £1 per hut and elsewhere in the Cape Colony it is 10 shillings a hut. . . . [9]

Among the developed countries, miscellaneous taxes increased at about the same rate as taxes in general, and also accounted for about £1 in 10 of tax income. As in the Empire, the category is a broad one, but there too the most important single component was the stamp tax. While not every country depended to any important extent on stamp taxes, to some it represented a sizeable source of income. That tax brought in about 6 shillings per capita in France and the Netherlands and more than 1 shilling in nine more countries.

The conclusions are obvious. The colonies with responsible government depended very heavily on customs duties and made limited use of domestic excises. These findings stand out whether the yardstick for comparison is the United Kingdom or the independent nations in the foreign developed sector. Given the limited but still significant role of the self-governing colonies in Britain's trade, it is hardly surprising that two generations of British politicians railed against colonial tariffs.

The countries in the underdeveloped foreign sector depended on customs duties for about one-half of their tax revenues. That figure contrasts with about one-quarter in the United Kingdom and the foreign developed sectors. Dependence on customs revenues were highest in South America. None of the sampled countries on that continent except Peru derived much below 10 shillings per capita per year from the tax on trade, and Uruguay and Argentina averaged more than £1–10. At the other end of the scale, a few countries (including Tunisia, Siam, and Haiti) drew no revenues from foreign commerce. The nations of Central America fell about halfway between these extremes, while Turkey, Liberia, and Japan were concentrated toward the lower end.

Since the British had granted the responsibly governed colonies control of their own finances, they were unable to force them to adopt a more acceptable fiscal package. In the dependent Empire, however, given British economic interests, it would have been expected that the colonies would have displayed far less dependence on tariffs than the underdeveloped nations, but such was not the case. In fact, the dependent colonies relied much more heavily on customs revenues than their independent brethren, although that reliance was slightly less than their self-governing cousins. Over the period, the typical colony drew just less than 70 percent of its tax revenue from tariffs, and while the figure declined somewhat as the Central African colonies were added to the Empire, it still represented about two-thirds of total tax receipts at the outbreak of World War I. Moreover, while six of the dependent colonies (including Hong Kong, the Federated Malay States and Egypt – not technically a colony) raised no money at all from customs, ten raised £1 or more.

There was almost certainly less opportunity for direct import substitution in the dependent colonies than in the Dominions, and therefore tariffs probably provided less protection for indigenous entrepreneurs. Still, such imposts must have cost British businessmen some sales. Despite an official commitment to free trade, simplification of collection and minimization of political turmoil appear to have carried more weight with the Treasury and Colonial Office than the words "comparative advantage" as enunciated by John Stuart Mill.

The private papers of officials are replete with complaints from the colonial governors about the difficulty of imposing their fiscal views on the colonies they governed. For example, in 1871 Hamilton Gordon, the Governor of Mauritius, lamented:

... You know that I am no financier, but I am appalled by the incidence of taxation on the island. It falls almost wholly on the poor, who are made to pay in almost every conceivable way, while the rich are pretty well exempt from taxation.

If, for my sins, I am compelled to remain any time in this detestable place (which I devoutly trust I may not be) I shall feel compelled to make an attempt to remedy this evil. It will be difficult work as the whole of the membership of the Legislative Council are directly interested in keeping up the present system, and I shall ... encounter the most violent opposition.... [10]

Costs had to be kept down and local grievances were often more immediate than scattered discontent in the British hinterlands.

In the foreign underdeveloped sector, domestic excises produced something just less than 10 percent of all tax revenues, and these levies became more important after the mid-1870s. In the dependent colonies, while the typical proportions were slightly higher than in the foreign sector, those taxes appear to have become less important after the turn of the century. Among the foreign underdeveloped countries five (23 percent) derived less than 2 pence from domestic excises and five received more than 4 shillings from that source. Of the dependent colonies, no less than forty-one (65 percent) earned less than 2 pence, and only five (8 percent) derived more than 4 shillings. The latter group included the Territory of the North Borneo Company, Egypt, Trinidad, Honduras, and St. Lucia.

Income and inheritance taxes were not a significant part of the fiscal package of any dependent colony; and the same can be said for the underdeveloped nations. That latter group of countries, however, did turn to property levies as the major supplement to customs receipts; and such taxes produced more than 3 shillings per capita and accounted for more than £1 in 4 of tax revenues. In the dependent colonies the reliance on land and property was much smaller. The level was less than a fifth of that in the foreign underdeveloped sector, and those imposts accounted for less than 5 percent of tax revenues. While, at the lower end of the scale, about the same proportion of colonies and countries had no property taxes, at the upper, five times as large a proportion of underdeveloped countries as dependent colonies received more than 4 shillings from property taxes.

Finally, although smaller budgets meant lower levels, special and miscellaneous taxes were slightly more significant in the budgets of the dependent colonies than they were in those of the underdeveloped countries. The stamp tax was somewhat more important among the underdeveloped countries but the differences are not marked. The Colonial Office liked the tax; it was easy to collect and administer; and, erstwhile North American subjects aside, it appeared to generate less political opposition than most alternatives. From the Bahamas the governor wrote:

> ... I propose ... to ask the assembly to sanction the imposition of a stamp duty as far as cheques are concerned. ... It is the end of the wedge and once people have gotten used to it, the duties can be extended to receipts, bills of lading, etc., and be made a very fruitful source of income.[11]

The native-hut tax, however, absent from the budgets of the underdeveloped countries, produced 2 pence or more per person per year in twelve dependent colonies and protectorates. Moreover, for two (Swaziland and Southern Rhodesia) the yield was more than 6 shillings, and for another three (Basutoland, Bechuanaland, and Fiji), more than 2 shillings and 10 pence.

It is worth reiterating that the most striking feature of the tax history of the dependent colonies is the reliance on tariffs. Those levies were somewhat less important in the independent underdeveloped nations, and those countries were interested in protecting local business. In the dependent Empire the protective walls were raised in large part against British business; and the British business community, to the extent it objected to these discriminatory levies, appears to have gone largely unheard or unanswered in Whitehall.

For Britain, however, India was another matter. As the British spread their influence across the subcontinent, they assumed an existing institutional baggage that included a significant fiscal component, and they were forced to deal with an Indian elite with strongly held views on appropriate tax policies. India was not Africa or the sugar islands of the Caribbean. By the standards of the dependent Empire, it was relatively well developed; and, most importantly, it had a business community that was prepared to compete with the British in providing a wide range of products and services and that was nearly competitive, even, in some manufacturing industries. India not only exported entrepreneurial talent to many corners of the dependent Empire, but had begun to compete with the British in such traditionally British industries as cotton textiles and, by the end of the period, steel. Finally, the "country" was the domicile of a significant (and certainly vocal and political) number of "temporary expatriates," and they had very definite ideas about an appropriate fiscal structure. These institutional constraints, coupled with a population near and often pushed over the margin of subsistence by floods and famines, produced schizophrenia in a succession of otherwise able Governors General, and a fiscal apparatus that was unlike anything else in Britain or the rest of the Empire.

The Indian fiscal system can, perhaps, best be viewed as a revolving prism reflecting the interests of the subcontinent, Parliament, and the India Office. The British were concerned with the regressivity of the tax structure, but attempts to alter that structure ran into both legal and political problems. John Lawrence captured the view of the Indian elite: " . . . At present the ideas of many influential men are in practice to increase the taxation on the poor and to spare those that are well off. . . . "[12] In a similar vein the technical difficulties were summarized by another frustrated British official:

> . . . what weighs heavily on my mind is the fact that taxation in India presses with undue severity on the poorer classes. The reason no doubt in part that it is so difficult to apply taxation in the East; you have to hit your man where you can hit him, through salt in India. . . . Salt and cotton duties press on the poor man, customs and income tax are largely paid by Europeans, your wealthy native does not contribute his fair share, I have been considering whether you could get at him through death duties, but the structure of native societies precludes this. . . . [13]

The goals of British policy appeared straightforward and simple: " . . . The aim of our measures has been, and must be, to make each section of the community (with the exception of the European officials who are exempted for special reasons) contribute fairly and in just proportion towards the necessities of the state, each according to his means. . . . "[14] The European exemption was not based on any moral principle; instead it was only a reflection of political reality. Mayo outlined the problem in a discussion of the vote on a tax bill in the legislative council: " . . . The official members of the council [are] . . . much more bitter than the non official. This serves to show how much the European opposition comes from the employees of government who dislike the tax merely because they have to pay it. . . . "[15] Or, as Lawrence had earlier observed: " . . . The English community in India is really much more intolerant of taxation than are the natives. There is none to which they will submit, if they can help it. But they do not mind the natives being taxed, if they are themselves exempted. . . . "[16]

Policies were one thing, effecting them another. Existing agreements sorely limited the British in their attempt to tax the Zamindars of Bengal, and the threat of political upheaval made them tread very warily in their attempts to increase the taxes on other wealthy Indians. Both constraints were much on the mind of Lytton when he asked:

> ... permission to extract from the Zemindars of Bengal a somewhat fairer proportional contribution than they have made, towards the necessities of the State. This would be quite in accordance with the principle which I think you are disposed to approve of, in endeavoring to put at least some portions of the burden of taxation more directly on the wealthy classes. Professor Rojlis's postulate that the native princes ought to be taxed is very plausible ... but I have been led to the conclusion that such a policy is not practical; and the attempt to carry it out might, I think (as you suggest), be dangerous. ... [17]

The frustrated pleas of Randolph Churchill almost a decade later showed the continuing resistance to change:

> ... They [the Zamindars] surely may be required to pay a reasonable amount of taxation for the military protection of the free trade and prosperity which they enjoy while contributing a mere fraction to the public revenue. The difficulty of taxing them will not decrease with the delay which creates the idea of a prescriptive right to immunity. [18]

Nor were all the problems Indian. At home, the business community was always ready to bring pressure directly on Whitehall (or Downing Street) should Indian tax policy threaten to adversely affect their profits. Curzon warned of the effects of these political decisions:

> ... One thing the home government must be particularly careful to avoid, and that is to make the fiscal system of India the sport or victim of political or fiscal exigencies at home. Public opinion has never gotten over the excise duty placed on our cotton manufacture in order to placate the Lancashire members, and any revision of Imperial policy which tends to place India more instead of less under the hands of the Great Britain would excite bitter and hostile feelings here. ... [19]

The result of all these pressures and counterpressures was a hybrid fiscal system very different from any other. Policy was almost always sacrificed to expediency. In the words of John Lawrence: " ... There is no doubt that direct taxation in India is especially odious, while indirect taxation beyond what we have now, is almost impractical. . . ."[20] The pressure for immediacy produced decisions like the one to raise the export duty on corn simply because: " . . . such a measure would be popular with the natives, and not unpopular with the English merchants who don't engage much in this trade. . . ."[21]

The Indian government, like its counterparts in the dependent Empire, was usually more than willing to solve the continuing financial crises through the imposition of tariffs on imported products; however, attempts to place even small imposts were met with loud and frequently effective complaints from British manufacturers and merchants. In "free-trade" England, customs duties accounted for somewhat more than one-quarter of all tax revenues; in the increasingly protectionist foreign developed sector, the figure had by 1900 surpassed 30 percent; in the foreign underdeveloped countries, it averaged just less than 50 percent; and in the colonies dependent or self-governing it was more than two-thirds. In India, on the other hand, tariffs represented only 6 percent of all tax revenues, and never exceeded 5 pence per capita per year.

The conflict between the need for revenues and the interests of the Midlands workers, manufacturers, and merchants is neatly captured in the history of the cotton duty (i.e., the tariff on cotton imported to India). From 1859 to 1869 the rate was set at 10 percent, but at that later date, because of political grumbling in England, it was cut in half. Even that low level did not satisfy the Lancashire businessmen, and in 1877 a House of Commons resolution demanded the total abolition of the duty. Two years later it was gone, and in 1882 all import duties were abolished. Within a decade, however, India's financial position was critical and as Kimberley wrote Gladstone:

> . . . The financial position of India is such that we shall be compelled, if the exchange does not rise, to increase taxation or borrow. . . . Everyone is agreed that to increase taxation would be most dangerous politically, nor could we get any significant addition to revenue, except by raising the salt tax, a hateful expedient and one that would deprive us of our only resource in the event of war or other great emergency. I put out of the question recurrence of import duties, in India their reimposition would, it is true, be generously approved, but the Lancashire opposition would be too strong, not to mention the economic objections to such duties. . . .[22]

But the pressures did not abate, the exchanges did not improve, and the British government was forced to reassess its position. Opposition was, as predicted, strong, and the outcome was a compromise. In Northbrook's words: "... As I gather from his [Fowler's] budget speech, the government are disposed to withdraw their objections to imposing import duties on cotton manufacture if an equivalent excise is put on Indian manufacture. ... "[23] As Curzon later remarked, the decision was not a popular one in India, but the tariff and the countervailing excise were introduced.

It is interesting to note that while on average customs duties produced only a slightly smaller fraction of revenue in India than they did in the Princely States, the time pattern is very different. In the states, tariffs were a regular part of the budgetary package, and tariff revenues appear in the budgets year in and year out. In India they were temporary measures and subject (as the history of the cotton duties indicates) to substantial year-to-year variation. There were no tariff revenues in the Indian budget in the second half of the 1880s nor in the first half of the 1890s, but they constituted 12 percent of all tax revenues over the eight years ending in 1912.

The absence of a customs base meant that the Indian government had to look to other revenues, and to a large extent they turned to the same source that had supported the Mogul princes in the days before the Raj: the land tax. At home, land taxes counted for less than 3 percent of "national" revenues; in those parts of the Empire with responsible government the figure was about the same; and even in the dependent colonies it was still less than 6 percent. In the foreign sector, it was more important, accounting for perhaps a quarter of the tax revenues in the underdeveloped sector and about one-fifth in the developed. In India, however, the average was 2 shillings per person per year – more than £3 in every 5. The figure would probably have been even larger had the government not been constrained by earlier agreement with the Bengal taxfarmers. As Lytton searched for revenue sources to replace the cotton duties he complained:

> ... But the Bengal Zemindars, who virtually constitute the British Indian Association, are the most pampered, pretentious, disloyal set of rascals in India. That unfortunate permanent settlement of Lord Cornwallis has deprived the government of India of probably not less than 3 million of revenue, which it can ill afford to forgo, in a time of financial difficulty at the present, and from the remission of which the country in general derives absolutely no benefit. ... [24]

Only in the Princely States, where such taxes yielded upward of 70 percent of all revenues, was there greater dependence on the "fruits of the land." In India, however, some changes were underway, and the taxes that had supported emperors and princes centuries before the arrival of the British declined from about 2 shillings and 5 pence in the 1860s to 1 shilling and 7 pence in the twentieth century. In terms of importance, the fall was from almost two-thirds to less than half of all tax revenues.

Domestic excises were the second most important source of Indian tax revenues. The salt tax alone produced about three-fourths of the 10 pence per person per year that the government garnered from such indirect imposts. While officials in the government of India spoke against the incidence of the salt tax, they also recognized that it was a tax that could "hit" the Indians where they could be "hit" and which could be depended upon to produce revenue when needed. As Lytton wrote:

> To no one do I dare openly reveal the full importance which, personally, I attach to a *low uniform* salt duty; as being in the absence of an income tax (and more prolific than any *possible* income tax) permanently the source of revenue which at any moment, we can augment almost indefinitely without any appreciable pressure on the community, by simply turning on the screw, *anna per anna*. Even the recognition of such a possibility, however, must not be whispered in any of the cities of Philistia. . . .[25]

Taken together, excise taxes accounted for about one-fourth of tax revenues – a proportion that, while below typical levels in the United Kingdom, was well above those prevailing elsewhere in the Empire or, for that matter, in the foreign underdeveloped sector. The Indian excise levels were also somewhat above those levied in the Princely States, whether the measure chosen is the per capita charge or the proportion of the total tax bill.

There were no inheritance taxes on the subcontinent, but the income tax had a stormy history. Because of the difficulties of assessment and a series of agreements and protocols, the tax fell most heavily on members of the British community (traders and government officials); and that was not a group that acceded easily to any taxation. The tax was levied in the early 1860s (it produced £800,000 in 1860 and £692,000 in 1865), but because of the objections of British expatriates, it was dropped.[26] A succession of Governors General, each concerned with the perennial problem of balancing the budget, agitated for reimposition, despite the objections of the British businessmen and officials in India. Within three years of the abolition, Mayo lobbied for Parliamentary action on a bill that would tax not only incomes in India but would "subject the whole of the Indian debt and all salaries paid out of Indian funds at home to income tax." He made this proposal despite his recognition of the "very strong feeling that exists in Council against the income tax in any shape and which I believe is shared by the majority of the people able to form an opinion on such subjects."[27] As it turned out, these opinions were too strong to ignore. A few years later Lytton again toyed with the idea of reimposing the tax, but once more he was forced to conclude that the political problems were too difficult to overcome. In 1876 he declared:

> I believe that the country can very well bear two millions worth of additional taxes; and, if we can succeed in devising some form of imperial taxation which will directly meet the purpose of the income tax without directly exciting from the European and official community the opposition to which the income tax was sacrificed . . . the object could be met.[28]

But finding no acceptable way to mask such a tax he wrote in the next year:

> . . . As regards to the rest of Salisbury's program, you know I have always regretted the abolition of the income tax, but I am quite confident that to reimpose it now, with the European community here so hard hit by the depreciation of the exchanges, would be a practical impossibility.[29]

As the financial crises deepened, the government turned its thoughts time and again to the income tax, but each approach from London brought complaints from high officials in India. For example, in 1885 the Governor of Bombay wrote Churchill:

> The increase of taxation would certainly be unpopular but I am not convinced that the outcry against it would not have reason on its side. . . . The fall of the rupee hits all Englishmen who have to remit for the education of their children or the support of relatives very hard, and an income tax on salaries would contribute more or less to a grievance to them. . . . [30]

Nevertheless, the income tax was reimposed in 1886, but agricultural incomes were to a large extent exempted. In the first decade of the present century, an average of more than 6 percent of all taxes were drawn from that source; and while income taxes were never as important a source of revenue as it was in the United Kingdom, they did produce more than £1 million a year by 1912 and at that time they represented as large a fraction of all taxes as such levies did in the foreign developed sector.

Despite the increasing progressivity in the tax structure at home, the Indian income tax remained proportional. It was not that the government was uninterested in generating more tax revenues and in shifting the tax burden to the upper income groups; rather, it was just a question of who paid the tax. In 1911 Hardinge wrote to Crewe:

> Montague has written to Fleetwood Wilson suggesting the imposition of a graduated income tax. I wish to keep an open mind to the subject until I have received full information as to what its effects and results would be. Since I have been here I have heard on all sides that the income tax which produces at present about one million sterling, is levied almost entirely upon Government officials and European traders. None of the landed aristocracy pay anything although they are the richest people in the land, while it is impossible to ascertain what is the income of the native traders.[31]

One thing is clear, while the government of India was more sensitive to the interests of the British business community than the India Office seems to have been, the fiscal package that was adopted reflected the interests of the Indian elites and the British in India at least as much as it reflected the opinions of the Midlands manufacturers. It appears that it was only the welfare of the Indian peasants that was not directly represented in the formation of tax policy, but the natives received at least some indirect benefits from Lancashire businessmen's insistence on something approximating free trade.

In the Empire the principal sources of revenue were consumption taxes. In the absence of the "imperial subsidy" would the colonies have increased domestic imposts or would they have reduced spending? If they chose the former course, to what sources would they have turned? In the colonies of white settlement, the colonies that, after all, profited the most from the generosity of the British taxpayer, it is likely that there would have been some substantial reduction in spending as well as some tax increases. If the experience of the developed nations offers any clues, domestic excises would have been increased. In addition, the imposition of direct taxes (income and inheritance) would likely have been accomplished with greater alacrity and levied at higher levels than actually maintained. Whatever the case, the colonial business community and its British partners would have had to shoulder a greater fraction of the tax burden.

Again, if the underdeveloped countries provide a touchstone, it would appear that the dependent colonies would have been driven to adopt the strategy forced on their autonomous fellows – cuts in spending and increases in domestic excises and property taxes. Although the colonial governments would probably have chosen to develop new instruments like the hut tax, designed to increase the tax burden on persons not normally a part of the market economy, it is difficult to see how these innovations would have prevented indigenous and British businessmen from paying at least a few pounds more for the services of government.

In India the situation would likely have developed quite differently. It seems evident that had the Indian "elites" had a greater voice in the nature of the subcontinent's tax structure, they would have raised tariffs. Such a change would, at least in the short run, have produced an increase in business profits and, in the long run, a greater proportion of resources devoted to the production of commodities, particularly those, like textiles, that were directed toward the mass market. Since these new firms and industries would have been "high-cost" producers in comparison to their foreign (that is, British) competitors, both the increase in short-run profits and the rise in long-term prices would have raised the "tax" burden disproportionately on the lower classes. Americans have recently had a chance to observe this phenomenon at first hand as they have watched import restrictions on Japanese Nissans and Toyotas let auto makers push up the price of domestic automobiles.

Indian nationalists of yesteryear argued that manufacturing (and particularly textiles) were "infant" industries, and that those infants needed tariff protection to let them grow to maturity and become competitive. If tariffs would have permitted Indian firms to grow until they were large enough to exploit some inherent economies of scale and, thus, become truly competitive, British policy might have imposed a severe long-run cost on the Indian masses. There is, however, little evidence that, for the industries in question, protection would have produced a comparative advantage where none had existed before. An analysis of the effects of tariffs on the American economy indicates that only the silk industry ever developed such an advantage behind tax barriers; and the experience of Canada and New Zealand provide even less support for the argument. In those members of the Commonwealth the bulk of the industrial sector has survived only because of tariff protection and has required a continuing subsidy – one paid by consumers in the form of higher prices. The infants never seem to grow up.

III. The United Kingdom

As the "subsidy" was funded in Britain, the question of the incidence of taxes in the United Kingdom becomes particularly important. Taxes in England were high, two and a half times higher than the average on the developed world. Nor was the rest of the developed world catching up – if anything, British taxes were relatively higher in 1912 than they had been in the 1860s.

In terms of structure, the United Kingdom and the foreign developed sector look similar, but there were some important differences. Both depended on customs receipts for about one quarter of their tax revenue; but while that dependence was increasing abroad, it was decreasing at home. Tariff receipts accounted for more than one-third of all U.K. tax receipts in the 1860s but less than one-quarter in the years from 1905 to 1912. Moreover, tobacco aside, the decline was spread across most taxed imports. Between 1860 and 1908 the duty on tea declined from 17 to 5 pence per pound, that on coffee from 3 pence to 2, and the one on sugar from 16 shillings to less than 2 shillings a hundred-weight (and there was *no* sugar tariff between 1874 and 1902).[32] A contemporary economist observed that by the end of the century duties on necessities had been largely abolished. Consumers might not have entirely agreed with his conclusions, but customs duties had certainly been reduced.

Dependence on domestic excises was probably somewhat less in the United Kingdom than in the foreign developed sector; however, the picture is clouded because in the foreign sector excises were frequently on products subject to the tariff in Britain. There is little evidence of trend in the burden of those imposts in either sector, but in the United Kingdom those revenues were subject to substantial year-to-year fluctuations. The most important of the domestic excises were the taxes on beer and spirits, and both rose over the period. The duty on hard liquor increased by only a moderate 10 percent, but the beer duties rose by a substantial 40.[33] While some might argue that beer is not a necessity, it is obvious that the increase in the beer levies fell to a large extent on the lower income groups.[34]

The most striking difference between the United Kingdom and the countries that made up the foreign developed sector, however, was the dependence in Britain on direct income and inheritance taxes. Abroad, these levies gradually increased from less than 5 percent of the total tax bill in the 1860s to just less than twice that level at the outbreak of the First World War. In Britain, in contrast, the comparable figures were more than 25 and almost 45 percent. As late as the fourth decade of the nineteenth century British taxes were indirect and very regressive. In 1840 in a speech on the corn laws Sir Robert Peel had argued:

> ... It is inevitable with a system of indirect taxation that families earning less than 30s a week must pay heavily; but I know if the burden presses unjustly upon them, it is not from want of sympathy on the part of the gentlemen of England; it is, however, inevitable. We must raise a great part of our taxation by indirect taxes and the burden will be unequally distributed. . . . [35]

The country had experimented with both income and inheritance taxes; the former was viewed as at best a temporary measure and the latter as no more than a minor income source. The first inheritance tax antedated the American Revolution, but it was so unimportant that the revenues it earned were not officially segregated from those received from the stamp duties until 1870. The income tax was almost as old. It was first imposed in 1799 as an emergency measure to help finance the Napoleonic wars, and it was repealed soon after Waterloo. In the 1840s, however, the political profile of Britain began to change, and with it the tax structure changed as well. Once the process had begun, politicians found it impossible to stop it, let alone reverse it. The first permanent income tax was imposed in 1842, and within a decade the tax had become not only permanent but also heavy. Moreover, in 1852 Gladstone, then Chancellor of the Exchequer, introduced legislation designed to expand the domain of the death duties to encompass real as well as personal property. The changes had proceeded so far by 1874 that Northcote complained to Disraeli: " . . . The truth is that the income tax has lost its terrifying character and become a fixed element in our financial system. . . . "[36]

In the case of the income tax, although rates were proportional to income, exemptions and abatements meant that almost none of the tax fell on working-class incomes.[37] It is, for example, estimated that less than 2 percent of the population (850,000 out of 43 million) paid the tax in 1903.[38] More importantly, from the viewpoint of those at the lower end of the income distribution, the exemptions and abatements increased as time passed. The Act of 1853 had exempted all incomes below £100, but that figure was increased to £150 in 1877 and to £160 in 1893. In addition, abatements on higher incomes were permitted, and by 1897 they provided at least some relief for persons earning incomes as high as £700.[39]

Death duties did not increase from 1853 to 1888, and even the

1888 reform imposed relatively small changes. In 1894, however, a progressive rate was imposed, and the entire tax structure was shifted dramatically upward. The new graduated scale began at 1 percent on estates valued at £100 and went up to 8 percent on those with a value over £1,000,000. Progressivity was further extended in 1907, and any estate valued at over £3,000,000 was charged £300,000 plus 15 percent of the excess above £1,000,000.

The new direct taxes had become, as Northcote feared, a permanent part of the fiscal system, and politics dictated that they should remain so. In a 1907 review of changes in tax policy over the previous two decades Bernard Mallet, noted:

> ...It is interesting to see how the tendency all through until the Boer War, was to substitute direct for indirect taxation increasingly; avowedly because of the disproportionate pressure of the latter on the poorer classes. To turn our back on this seems really impossible. The working classes know too much about it in this country....[40]

So far had the country traveled that politicians came to view the tax policy as a benefit for the wealthy. In 1908 Haldane wrote:

> The more boldly such a proposition is put the more attractive, I think, it will prove. It will recommend itself to many people as a bulwark against Nationalization of wealth....[41]

Over the entire period revenues from the income tax averaged 8 shillings and 10 pence, and those from the estate duties 5 shillings and 10 pence, per person per year, and in the years 1910 to 1912 the figures were twice those. The total (£1–8–10) was 10 percent more than the *entire* tax bill in the foreign developed sector.

The movement away from dependence on customs and excises and toward income and inheritance taxes meant that taxes were becoming less regressive and that the burden was shifting away from the working classes. It is possible to get some feeling for the effects of that redistribution by examining the three tax profiles – estimates of the tax burden by income group – presented in Charts 8.4(a) and 8.4(b). Each panel provides an estimate of the percentage of a taxpayer's income devoted to taxes in three years (1863–4, 1883–4, and 1903–4); panel B reflects the rate paid by a taxpayer whose earnings came entirely from wages and salaries, and panel A the rate for a taxpayer receiving half his income from wages and salaries and half from property. The difference between the two, of course, captures the effects of the increasingly stringent inheritance tax.[42]

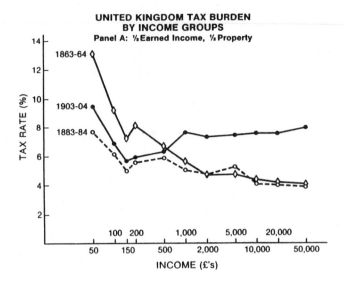

Chart 8.4 (a)

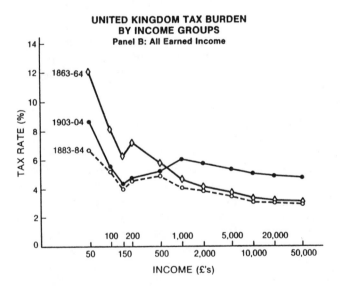

Chart 8.4 (b)

In each of the three years the tax burden bore most heavily on the lowest income classes–a result of the heavy reliance on very regressive customs duties and excise taxes. Times were, however, changing; and the workers found their tax burdens significantly reduced between 1863 and 1884. Even the new taxes imposed to finance the Boer War (although again falling heavily on the working class) left that class's relative exaction well below the level of the 1860s.

The working classes were not, however, official players in the imperial game under the rules propagated by Lenin and Hobson; and to understand the tax structure in that context it is necessary to refocus attention toward the upper end of the income scale. In each year, although the highest rates were associated with the lowest incomes, there was a secondary peak in the middle income range.[43] For incomes above that middle income peak, rates fell as income rose, although the decline was tempered at the very end of the income scale.[44]

Overall, there is clear evidence of declining regressivity, if not of increasing progressivity. In 1863 every income class except £200 paid at a lower rate than the class beneath them; by 1904 that pattern held only for classes below £150. The reduction in regressivity attained in the 1860s and 1870s was achieved largely through decreases in the rates levied on low and middle income groups – there was essentially no change in the rates imposed on upper income recipients. In the second period (1884 and 1904), however, the rates imposed on the upper middle income groups were increased substantially, and those charged the upper classes were pushed up even more precipitously. This change can, in large part, be attributed to the new estate duties. Between 1884 and 1904 a taxpayer who received £50,000 or more of earned income was faced by an increase of rates of about 65 percent; but his fellow subject who drew half his income from property was faced by a doubling of the rate he was expected to pay.

Although the results are somewhat speculative, it is important to attempt to apportion the nineteenth-century tax burden between the working and the middle and upper classes. R. Dudley Baxter has concluded that in 1867 the 23 million members of the working class paid 35 percent of all taxes and the 6.7 million members of the middle and upper classes paid the remaining 65 percent.[45] Leon Levi argued that the figures were somewhat different (41 and 59 percent) in 1882.[46] Although both estimates are likely subject to some error, the mistakes would have to have been of massive proportions to reverse the central finding: that it was to the middle and upper classes that the government turned for at least one-half and perhaps as much as two-thirds of its tax revenues. Since the proportion of income accruing to the working class did not change significantly between the 1860s and the First World War, and, given the shifts in the incidence of the taxes that were levied, it appears that the proportion borne by the middle and upper groups was no lower, and was almost certainly higher, at the end of the period.[47]

For the central thesis of this study, however, the question still remains: How was the tax burden distributed between the middle and upper income classes? Before it is possible to answer that question, however, it is necessary to agree on what is meant by "middle" and "upper" classes. As the terms are generally perceived and as they have been used in the analysis of stock ownership in this study, those classifications carry certain sociological connotations. The evidence, however, is cast in terms of income groups; and there is at best an imperfect correlation between the economic and sociological definitions.[48] There were impoverished aristocrats, and there were more than a few merchants and manufacturers with incomes well in excess of £5,000 a year.[49] Despite these obvious caveats, it appears that the occupational upper class (that is, the Elites of Chapter 7) tended to be concentrated at the higher, and the middle class toward the lower, end of the income scale. Assuming then that income provides an adequate, if not perfect, guide to class, it is possible to estimate the proportion of the total tax bill borne by the two groups.

There are estimates of the total income accruing to the members of various income cohorts for 1867, 1880, and 1906; and, from those distributions and a knowledge of the tax system, it is possible to construct an estimate of the relative tax burden on the middle and upper classes.[50] If, in addition, we assume that together the middle and upper classes paid 62 percent of all taxes (the average of Baxter's and Levi's estimates), a simple multiplication provides an estimate of the total amount of taxes paid by each group. Writing at the end of the 1860s, Baxter drew the demarcation between the middle and upper classes at an annual income of £1,000; and, as incomes grew over the next half century, the dividing line almost certainly rose (Levi a decade and a half later put it at twice that level). Thus, employment of the the £1,000 figure to divide the two classes provides the basis for a minimum estimate of the middle-class burden. The results of these calculations are displayed in Table 8.1.

For 1867 and 1880 the results are remarkably similar. The middle class contributed almost two and a half times as much to the gov-

Table 8.1. *Distribution of the tax burden, middle and upper classes only (percentage)*

Class	1867	1880	1906
Middle	70.6	70.6	83.1
Upper	29.4	29.4	16.9

ernment coffers as the upper class. The estimates for 1906 are even more extreme and place the ratio at close to five to one. The estimates are certainly subject to a substantial margin of error; but, again, it would take a series of massive mistakes to reverse the central finding: The middle-class tax bill was several times as large as that presented to the aristocracy, the landed gentry, the government servants, and the bankers who made up the bulk of the upper class.

To paraphrase Gertrude Stein, "a pound is a pound is a pound"; and there is no correct way to link particular governmental receipts to particular governmental expenditures. Still, given the magnitude of the relative tax burden, there is a strong presumption that the middle class paid far more than its share of the imperial subsidy; and, given the class composition of imperial stockholders, it should be apparent that they did not receive an equal share of its benefits.

Probably no one will ever know for certain just how much the middle class lost and the upper class gained from the imperial "lottery"; but it is possible to obtain a feel for the magnitude of those interclass transfers through an exercise in synthetic history. If the stock-ownership figures are adjusted for Other and non–United Kingdom holders, it appears that businessmen held about 38 and the elites about 50 percent of Empire shares. The British subsidy to the Empire has been estimated to have amounted to between 14 shillings and 2 pence and 19 shillings per capita per year – an annual total of between 31 and 41 million pounds.[51] If the amount of the subsidy is subtracted from total tax receipts, the residual is an estimate of the domestic portion of taxes. Since total taxes in 1906 were 130 million, the domestic figure would fall between 90 and 91 million pounds.

The estimates in Table 8.2 suggest that the elites paid £13.1 million in taxes on their income of £172.1 million. If they received about one-half of the Empire subsidy, their share should have been between fifteen and twenty million pounds – an amount that exceeds their total tax bill by between £2 million and £7 million. Thus, the elites appear to have been "net winners," even if they received no

Table 8.2. *Tax burdens and income estimates, 1906, middle and upper classes only*

Class	Burden (%)	Taxes paid (£s millions)	Estimated income (£s millions)
Middle	83.8	67.6	1086.1
Upper	16.2	13.1	172.0

benefits from the "domestic taxes." And, to the extent that they benefited from the domestic services provided by government, they paid nothing for them.

For the middle classes, however, the picture appears less alluring. Their share of the imperial subsidy lay somewhere between £12 million and £19 million, but they paid taxes of £68 million. A simple subtraction indicates that they paid taxes for "domestic" purposes of between £52 million and £56 million. If they received domestic benefits in proportion to their numbers, the value of those benefits should have fallen between £20 million and £22 million; and, if the benefits were distributed in proportion to income, their share would have come to somewhere between £48 million and £53 million. Thus, even under the most extreme assumptions, the middle class were net losers by more than £2 million; and the figure could have been several times that amount.

9   Empire, the special interests, and the House of Commons

Despite those wags who conjectured that the British Empire had been conceived in a fit of absence of mind and its progress solely dictated by the whims of the man on the spot without benefit of a coherent governing philosophy, Parliament, and especially the House of Commons, scrutinized the affairs of Britain's far-flung possessions with some care. No major change in fiscal or administrative policy could in practice be effected without the House's scrutiny. But power is never absolute, especially in a democracy, and it is the purpose of this chapter to determine, to the degree possible, the extent to which special interests modulated and influenced the decisions of the representatives of the people.

I. The special interests

Firms acting independently or in concert through trade associations and chambers of commerce continuously bombarded Parliament with pleas for action on their pet projects. If the concerns included in this study are representative, the most active were the utilities and transportation companies. They maintained a drumfire of pressure for the extension of their powers, the limitation of governmental control and the curtailment of competition. In 1871, the Sunderland and South Shields Water Company, "bent every effort" to protect itself from proposed legislation that would have limited its ability to lay pipe over certain bridges; later, it demanded Parliament defeat the Sunderland Corporation Act; and later still, it acted against the Durham County Electricity Supply Bill. Success was sporadic, but in the latter case the company's solicitor did report that the bill's agents had assured him the measure would be amended before it reached the second house.[1] Generally, gas companies resented the introduction of electricity, the street railroad companies fought the advent of the Underground, and the established railroads attacked the chartering of new ones. Although Parliament usually smiled on requests for recapitalization and the expansion of service, it was less cooperative in other directions.

Collieries and steel companies also often lobbied Parliament. Sam-

215

uel Fox, the steel maker, felt endangered by removal of water from the River Don; and in August 1874, the directors reported that the company had successfully opposed two bills that would have reduced the available water. More than two decades later the issue was still not resolved, but the company's officers were again able to report that new legislation had been amended to their satisfaction.[2] It was, however, labor legislation that most concerned these companies. When the iron industry lost the battle against the workmen's compensation act, the management of the Shotts Iron Company lamented, "This obnoxious act of Parliament comes into operation on January 1."[3] The directors of the Stavely Coal and Iron Company urged strong opposition to the establishment of a minimum-pay scale for miners and suggested the organization of a unified crusade on the national level.[4]

Breweries fought continuously against government regulation, and that battle was particularly vicious when the Liberals were in power. The Barclay Perkins Brewery, threatened by licensing legislation, urged its customers to write their MPs: "We would press on you the desirability of your urging your members to support any action in Parliament which has as its object the *equitable protection of licensed property* and the recognition of the *principal that all interest in a license, taken away for no fault of the licensee shall be fully compensated.*"[5] The breweries may have slowed the process, but like the iron and steel companies they largely failed to halt government's determination to control them and their clientele. Still, the Conservative party drew substantial financial support in the process.

Not surprisingly, the more a firm's business depended on a particular property right, vested by a government license or a charter, the more determined the firm was to bend the direction of government policy in its favor; and the more formidable its base of support, the greater were the chances of success. At the 1906 meeting of the proprietors of City and West End Properties, it was reported:

> Last year the County Council introduced a bill in Parliament entitled "London Builders Act of 1894, Amendment Act." This bill was of a very far reaching and drastic nature and your directors carefully studied it once they saw that if the bill was carried it might interfere largely with some of your properties and more likely cause considerable expense. We therefore drew up a petition which was presented to the City of London and enlisted their sympathies. They, with their powerful backing, opposed the bill in Parliament and as you know, I dare say, the result of the discussion was that the bill was withdrawn. . . .[6]

For those well placed in the establishment, the technique was familiar and direct. Alban Gibbs of the international banking and commercial house of Antony Gibbs and Sons was able to write the prime minister, Arthur Balfour, on familiar terms. "My Dear Arthur," he wrote, "I am sorry to have to trouble you with a long letter, but the state of irritation and strain in the City is such as I feel compelled to do so." Gibbs then proceeded to complain about the Port of London, employment of children, education, and preferential tariff measures before Parliament, and to declare that he did not want a free-trade candidate winning in the City in the next election.[7]

Perhaps more telling, a member of the same firm wrote the prime minister, Herbert Asquith: "You may remember that when you were good enough to lunch with me back at the Savoy to meet some City friends, you gave me permission to inform them that I would send you the list of subscribers to the General Election Appeal. In fulfillment of that promise I therefore enclose my list, the total of which is £134,887,110. . . ."[8]

Some two years later, Herbert Gibbs attempted to call in the debt:

> There is one thing which I think necessary to make an appeal for funds a success, and that is that we should know that when Ministers come to power they will devise some permanent constitutional check on the unlimited power of the House of Commons over the money of the rich.

> The death duties have done much damage to the country and the uncertainty as to their increase has done and is doing more and from a business point of view it is not good business to spend money in supporting a Party which does not take the matter up, but I think people will agree that it *was* good business to support a party that did. . . .[9]

The income tax law of 1912, however, suggests he was not entirely successful.

Shortly thereafter Herbert Gibbs gained an interview with Lloyd George, then the Chancellor of the Exchequer. His concern was a tax imposed on nitrate companies' depreciation funds. Gibbs reported that the Chancellor was at first not very sympathetic but that, after a prolonged discussion, he had finally admitted that the effects were a "bit stiff." Gibbs concluded that his arguments had convinced Lloyd George that the heavy amortization of nitrate gounds was linked to their short life (as compared with, for example, coal mines), not to an attempt by the companies to earn unfair profit. The chancellor agreed to review the situation.[10]

The explosion of economic activity in Britain during the last half of the nineteenth century produced not only the limited liability company and the worldwide flows of symbolic capital, but numerous attempts to lessen the competitive edge of the laissez faire environment. Workers pursued their goals through trade unions, and management and investors expressed their interests through chambers of commerce and trade associations.

In the years after 1860, the chambers had grown greatly in number; and, as Clapham noted, they "were always more concerned with dealing than with making."[11] The chambers attempted to influence both government policy and specific legislation; and the Empire and foreign sectors were very important to some business at least. In 1877, the Association of Chambers of Commerce of the United Kingdom resolved: "... that a memorial be sent to the First Lord of Her Majesty's Treasury, calling the attention of the government to the very unsatisfactory position of the long pending project of a direct land route for commerce between Rangoon ... [and] the southwest frontier of China.[12] Similarly, on June 12, 1896, and following earlier resolutions of the Manchester and the London chambers, the association urged the government to support railway construction in Uganda and West Africa.

Any expansion of the Empire that might benefit business and commerce was usually favored by the chambers, although the degree of ardor varied with the importance of colonial trade in the region's economy. London and the port cities tended to be the most vocal. In 1885, for example, the Glasgow Chamber of Commerce advocated the British annexation of Upper Burma and inveighed against the dangers of Chinese commercial competition.[13] The closer the bonds of Empire, and the more fully developed the precepts of imperial reciprocity, the better it was for business. Hence, the Liverpool Chamber urged that "with the feeling of imperial citizenship throughout the Empire, and the sense of union already obtained between the Mother Country and her colonies," an imperial consultative assembly representing Britain and her colonies be formed at the earliest possible date.[14] In addition, the Liverpudlians recommended the appointment of a Royal Commission with members drawn from Britain, India, and the colonies to consider the enhancement of trade relations between the various parts of the Empire.[15] In 1903, the fifth Congress of Chambers of Congress of the

British Empire was convened in Montreal. Its policy resolutions, dealing with imperial defense, enhanced trade relations within the Empire, imperial reciprocity, and the need for improved communications reflected closely those placed previously on the record both by the Association of Chambers of Commerce and the various municipal chambers.

The chambers supported measures designed to increase Empire trade and demanded a greater mercantile presence on appointed organs of government (the India Council, for example). Profits were, however, profits, and domestic policy also occupied some fraction of their time. They scanned proposed legislation with a watchful eye and became increasingly restive as political and social reform captured an ever larger fraction of the legislative agenda. Any improvement in the lot of the working man (or woman or child), if it might cost a farthing (and sometimes even if it did not), was frowned upon by the chambers. In 1872, for example, the Glasgow Chamber fought against a bill aimed at restricting the hours children could work.[16] Political rights for the proletariat, working conditions and hours of labor, the right to organize, were issues the chambers were prepared to combat with all the political power at their command.

A detailed perusal of the records of the Glasgow, Birmingham, Liverpool, Manchester, and London Chambers of Commerce manifests the underlying homogeneity of the British mercantile community. Free trade was perceived as the basis of British prosperity, and it was the cornerstone of the chambers' philosophic position. Thus, laws judged to be in restraint of trade in whatever guise, whether domestic, colonial, or foreign, were continually attacked. No measure was too insignificant to arouse the chambers' ire. The London Chamber railed against the death duties act in New South Wales. Birmingham noted with concern French tariffs on "velocipedes" and brass fittings for umbrellas, and protested against a Natal law requiring the payment of a tax by commercial travelers.[17] London was more interested in questions of imperial cohesion and defense than the others, but those were fairly common themes in most of the port cities. As the issues expanded from Empire to overseas trade, the other chambers raised their voices with increasing frequency. Questions regarding the opening of the Congo, West Africa, and China to British commerce, the construction of railways in Africa, India, and China, and opposition to foreign subsidies for shipping and sugar, all appeared on the list of resolutions supported by a variety of local chambers. Trade yes, politics maybe – as Schumpeter had noted, in a world of free trade it makes no difference to business who opens new markets or constructs new railroads as long as the markets are open and the railroads built.

It is difficult to provide a precise measure of the effectiveness of the chambers in their attempts to influence imperial policy; but it is clear that sometimes, at least, they proved quite persuasive agencies of political manipulation. The best example of a successful exercise of political power on a matter of imperial concern can be found in the chambers' campaign to eliminate the Indian duties on British cotton. In that case the organizations were pitted against the entire Indian establishment. The government of India wanted the tariffs for fiscal purposes and the Indian business community hoped to expand domestic enterprise behind those barriers.

In the early 1860s, the government of India had imposed a tariff of 10 percent on all imports. Although this figure was reduced in 1864 and again in 1875, the Midlands textile interests remained outraged. John Morley, the future Secretary of State for India, wrote the Second Lord Lytton, the then viceroy, in 1876: "At this moment... not a seat in Lancashire can beget a man who did not go for total and immediate repeal of the import duty on cotton...."[18] At a time when the government majority was fifty-two and the Lancashire and Yorkshire seats totaled seventy-one, Lord Cranbrook, the Secretary of State for India, wrote Lytton in a similar vein:

> A great deputation from Lancashire on the cotton duties has just left me and they are backed by a formidable force. The question occupies the minds of manufacturers and operatives and the import duties is looked upon as the main cause of their distress. The subject may materially influence the Lancashire elections at present so much in our favour....[19]

Increasingly alarmed, Cranbrook again wrote the Viceroy: "I continue to be picked upon about the cotton duties. Mr. Chancellor of the Exchequer has just sent over four Lancashire letters which speak of the loss of fourteen seats as inevitable unless remission is commenced...."[20]

Responding to the determination of the chambers, the manufacturers, and the Lancashire members, the House of Commons denounced the Indian duties on cotton as protective and demanded their abolition. Succumbing to the pressure, the government of India removed the duty of the coarser grades of cotton (the most common import) and later abolished virtually all tariffs. Revenue shortfalls prompted by these "reforms" forced the Indian authorities to reinstitute a general 5-percent duty in 1894; but to mollify the critics, an equivalent excise tax was levied on all cotton goods manufactured in India. Even that compromise proved politically unacceptable, and in 1896 both the import and the excise taxes were reduced.

In this instance, both the legislative and bureaucratic response would have pleased even the most resolute chamber member; however, it is far from clear that the same result would have been achieved on a different issue. The Indian cotton tariff flew in the face of a generally accepted view on the efficacy of free trade; and in addition the chambers were allied with a highly vocal group of manufacturers and workers who were capable of bringing very focused electoral pressure to bear on a government whose working majority was not large. Besides, the issue did not adversely affect any significant British interest group. The lesson is quite clear: Parliament could under certain circumstances be influenced. In the main, however, successful manipulation demanded considerable political muscle and sympathetic opinion in both houses.

The chambers' attack on tariffs both in the Empire and abroad was hardly less vociferous; but, because of a lack of support in the Empire and the obvious constitutional limitations on the power of Parliament, it was largely doomed to failure. Of the various chambers, Birmingham's was clearly the most concerned about the tariff issue; but Liverpool was only somewhat less so. Both took great exception to the behavior of the Canadian, Australian, New Zealand, and South African governments. No perceived affront was beneath notice. In 1907, the Birmingham Chamber, for example, resolved to contact the Colonial Office in regard to the customs duty charged by the South African Colonies on the importation of British catalogs and price lists. While other cities worried less about the Empire, foreign tariffs were of greater general concern. In London, a third of all deliberations concerned that latter issue, and for the chambers as a whole, the figure was almost one-fifth. The attacks were numerous, but in both the Empire and foreign sectors they appear to have met with little success.

If the London Chamber's greatest concern was with imperial unity (a concern based to a large extent on questions of imperial cost and the need for defense), its Glasgow counterpart was the most bellicosely expansionist. It strongly supported British advance into New Guinea, Swaziland, and the Northern Gold Coast and inveighed against the Germans in the Cameroons. There is no doubt, however, that the London Chamber manifested a more continuing and stronger interest in imperial affairs than did any of its provincial

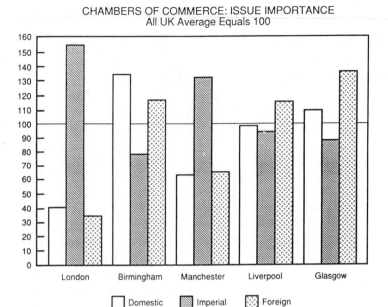

Chart 9.1

counterparts. Over the years 1891 to 1912, for example, the City's index of imperial activity stood at one and one-half times the "All-U.K." average. The figure for Manchester was 132 (but a large fraction of the resolutions dealt with Indian duties with a secondary and somewhat surprising focus on the cost of Empire), and in sharp contrast the figure for Liverpool was 94, for Glasgow 80, and for Birmingham but 78. (See Chart 9.1.) In a broader context, the chambers directed about one-fifth of their efforts (if discussions and resolutions can be used as a proxy for effort) in support of the extension of foreign and colonial trade and another one-fifth urging subsidies for mail and telegraph communications and general government support of business. Empire tariffs and imperial preference, although of relatively little interest to the London and Glasgow chambers, were very important to Liverpool's and to the other Midlands' chambers. Indian tariffs on British textiles were almost the sole imperial concern of the Manchester Chamber in the 1870s, and the subject occupied a surprisingly large proportion of all its deliberations for the entire period (see Chart 9.2).

As with the chambers of commerce, so with the trade associations,

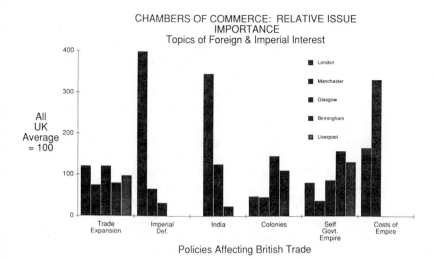

CHAMBERS OF COMMERCE: RELATIVE ISSUE
IMPORTANCE
Topics of Foreign & Imperial Interest

Chart 9.2

although each association had its own specific policy agenda. The associations covered many fields of enterprise, and their number increased greatly in the last half of the century. Only occasionally interested in questions of broad imperial policy, they usually became intimately involved when specific legislation appeared to directly affect their prospects. Not surprisingly, the Oldham cotton spinners, for example, were immersed in the protest against Indian tariffs. More often, however, the association's concerns were domestic but no less narrow. Most of their efforts were devoted to specific pieces of legislation, to opposition to foreign competition, and to the design of institutional arrangements that could allow them to effectively control wages and maintain monopoly prices.

Trade associations varied in their level of effectiveness and or-ganization. Some were so loosely knit that they met only once a year and then to little purpose. Others were active not only in rhetorical efforts to effect wage and price controls but in attempts to limit production as well. Examples of these associations spanned the in-dustrial spectrum. They included, for example: the Master Cotton Spinners' Association of Oldham, the Midland Flint Glass Manufacturers, the London Master Printers, the London Master Builders, the Cleveland Ironmasters' Association, the South Staffordshire Association (Iron), the Steam Coal Association of Tyneside, the Lancashire Cornish Boilerplates Association, and the Dundee Spinners and Manufacturers Association.

Purely regional trade associations were followed by more broadly based ones – a development that paralleled the evolution of the chambers of commerce. On March 2, 1899, for example, the North Staffordshire, the Lancashire, and the North Wales Colliery Owners' Associations met to merge their organizations and one representing Cheshire into a single unit. The aim was to broaden the effectiveness of their political activity. The General Builders' Association, the North of England Iron Manufacturers' Association, the association of tin plate manufacturers, the wire trade association, the English and Scottish Steelmakers (Founders), the Scottish Steelmakers, the Association of Steel Rail Makers, the tire and axlemakers' association, the steel smelters association, the steel plate manufacturers' association, the steel wheel centers association, and organizations representing sugar refiners, alkali manufacturers, leather manufacturers, and papermakers were all examples of voluntary cooperation along increasingly comprehensive lines.

II. Interaction between Whitehall and British business overseas

It seems appropriate to examine the interrelationship of government (in this case Whitehall more than Westminster) and business in the Empire and in those parts of the foreign overseas sector where British influence was sufficiently strong to possibly deem them parts of Robinson and Gallagher's conception of an "informal Empire."

Although the government of India tended to prefer public to private enterprise, there was an inclination, even under "free-trade" policies, to favor British over foreign business. In 1903, Lord Kilbracken, the former Permanent Undersecretary at the India Office, wrote St. John Brodrick, the Secretary of State for India:

> ...We constantly get from foreign firms tenders which are far below those from English firms in respect to price, which as to quality we are often told there is little or nothing to choose.... Lord George Hamilton was always most unwilling to place an order abroad; and as a rule we have managed to avoid it, though occasionally it is by no means easy to do so.... At the same time the charge thrown upon interior revenue is sometimes very heavy....[21]

Earlier, when Standard Oil competed for a contract in India, it was turned down and Hamilton, then the Secretary of State for India, wrote Curzon, the Viceroy, that despite the undoubted benefits which would have accrued to the consumer due to lowered prices,

> ...I think you are perfectly correct in refusing the concession to the American Standard Oil Company. Great commercial organizations such as Standard Oil, become the depository of gigantic potential forces, which might at any moment be used to the detriment of some vast community or nation which those managing the monopoly wish either to spite or squeeze....[22]

And this xenophobic view was also reflected in a Parliament that was ready to rise in wrath against the implementation of a mild import duty on British cotton going into India. "...This outcry against protection," Kilbracken wrote Lord Elgin, the Viceroy, "comes very ill from a House of Commons which is ready to pass a vote of censure on the Secretary of State, if the guaranteed Indian Railway Companies are allowed to save £1,500 on an order of steel sleepers by placing it in Belgium."[23] Clearly, as far as India was concerned free trade was not always the eleventh commandment, and it was at times worshipped only when it did not interfere with profits and self-interest. Either the right hand did not know what the left was doing, or India was sui generis and treated like no other colony. In the case of the dependent colonies, the Crown Agents made purchases on behalf of India's imperial bretheren at the lowest price they could find even if the vendor was foreign!

The history of the debate over the Indian tariffs has already been related. Despite their victory, the textile manufacturers did not relax their vigilance. Somewhat incredulously, Lord Cross, the Secretary of State for India, wrote Lord Landsdowne, the Viceroy, that a large deputation from Lancashire had called upon him to protest the passage of the Indian factory acts. The secretary of state was not sure he had convinced his callers "that the purpose of the acts was to protect women and children and not trade."[24] Similarly, two decade later, Lord Hardinge, then the viceroy, understood that the Indian cotton duties, despite being smaller than the British free-trade government's equivalent, could not survive because the Indian tariff had hurt firms whose Parliamentary support the government needed.[25]

But India appears to have been an anomaly. In general, when it came to British business operating abroad, the official attitude was different. Overseas, Whitehall manifested great reluctance to support British commercial enterprises. With few exceptions, British diplomats were willing to offer their good offices but little else. An official philosophy that asked only the protection of international law and equal but not favored treatment for British subjects and the social prejudices of the day both played a role. Laissez faire was the state religion, at least outside India; and government's interference on behalf of business was anathema. In addition, most government bureaucrats were drawn from a social class that looked down on commerce as not altogether respectable. Philosophy and prejudice together produced a set of policies neatly summarized in a letter from Sir Robert Morier, the British Ambassador to Russia, to Rosebery, the Foreign Secretary: "No rule as been more absolutely insisted upon in the dealings of Her Majesty's Missions abroad than this one, that, unless there is a denial of justice, or treatment of British subjects engaged in mercantile transactions contrary to Treaties, or to the spirit of Treaties, no assistance shall be rendered to further private interests."[26] Three years later, the Treasury expressed essentially the same view when it said in a letter to the Foreign Office: "It has been and is My Lords' conviction that it is unsound commercial policy to seek to assist the British enterprise in its struggle with foreign rivals out of the pocket of the general taxpayer."[27]

So-called foreign bondholders were held in particular contempt as they were deemed to have diverted useful resources for the unilateral benefit of a foreign state.[28] Thus, their cries for support and protection from foreign default tended to go unheeded and to evoke little sympathy. The voluminous records of the Council of Foreign Bondholders, the association formed to protect their interests, show little evidence of government sympathy. In a letter to the Earl of Ripon, then Colonial Secretary, Robert Meade, an undersecretary in that Office, reflected prevailing official opinion when he wrote: "H.M.'s Government must expect pressure from the bondholders who will like to be relieved of their bad investment and this pressure they must be prepared to resist."[29]

On rare occasion, however, the government did provide some assistance to British business operations in the foreign sector. When trouble erupted at Antony Gibbs and Sons' nitrate works in Quique, Peru, the company requested a British naval presence. Whether as a consequence of the company's efforts or mere happenstance, Herbert Gibbs was able to write in December 1907: " . . . I have just received your letter telling me that the Admiralty are sending a ship at once, and I can only confess the gratitude of my firm and the Nitrate Industry for the kind assistance of the Foreign Office in the protection of our interest."[30] The Gibbs family, of course, had very good political connections; but the records provide few other examples of such favorable responses.

A more typical example of the usual support was an incident in Peru described in the minutes of the board of directors of the Corporation that bore that country's name:

> Acting upon instructions received from this government, the British legation in Lima addressed the Peruvian minister of foreign affairs upon the date of 7 January, 1898, in a letter intimating that Her Majesty's Government could not consent to the infraction of British rights of property involved in the decision and degrees of the Peruvian government. . . .[31]

No doubt fully aware that the British lion had no intention of unsheathing his claws, the Peruvian minister of foreign affairs duly acknowledged the communication but "at the same time reiterated the views held by the Peruvian government on the subject." And the minutes concluded: "There the matter at present rests," and there it would continue to rest.[32] As Salisbury, then the Secretary of State for Foreign Affairs, had declared when pressed to intervene in South America, Her Majesty's government was not willing to relinquish the principle of nonintervention that had been in operation since the time of Canning. "We have been pressed . . . to undertake the part of arbitrator, of compulsory arbitrator, in quarrels in the west of South America. . . . We have been earnestly pressed, also . . . to undertake the regeneration of Argentine finance. On neither of these subjects are Her Majesty's Government in the least degree disposed to encroach on the function of providence."[33]

When British interests in Chile's Atacama Desert seemed threatened, the government would offer only "tacit diplomatic support" and no gunboats.[34] In the case of British economic relations with Uruguay, "even the Baring Crisis of 1890, where greater British economic interests were at stake than in Egypt a decade before, did not lead to British intervention."[35] The records of the Lautaro Nitrate Company are filled with reports of litigation in Chilean courts with no evidence of British intervention or even diplomatic pressure on the firm's behalf. As D.C.M. Platt concludes: "In practice, Government assistance was insignificant."[36] If the British de facto acquisition of Egypt in 1881 should spring to mind, it must be remembered that the motivation there was strategic and not commercial.

Nor do China and Thailand offer frequent examples of political support of British commercial activities. In the case of the former, Whitehall resisted the blandishments of business and refused to support British investment in China when it became convinced, "that the China trade would never be worth the expense of war or sovereignty. . . . "[37] As one expert wrote, "Economic criteria . . . may be applied as important determinants of the existence of informal empire . . . [but] for China the evidence suggests that such factors did not exist."[38] The official position on intervention is underscored by the reaction to an apparently innocent request from the British legation in China for assistance in obtaining copies of imperial decrees that had authorized certain loans made by British financiers. On May 22, 1885, the British chargé d'affaires in Peking was peremptorily ordered not to cooperate and instructed in no way "however remotely" to assist the representatives of British finance in China.[39]

Writing about Thailand, James Ingram concludes that: "The British desire to keep Thailand as a buffer state between British and French possessions in British hands, was largely responsible for the use of British diplomacy to preserve the independence of Thailand. . . . "[40] And indeed Rosebery then holding the Foreign Office had written Gladstone: "Our interest in Siam is twofold: for we do not desire to see her absorbed by France, a circumstance which would place . . . their great military power on our eastern frontier, and as we have practically a monopoly of Siamese commerce we do not wish to see our trade destroyed by the tariff the French erect around their possessions."[41] The imperialism of free trade is an elusive concept, and perhaps never more so than in the case of Thailand.

Turning to Africa, it appears that, even in the dependent Empire outside of India, British business did not fare well. The Bathurst Company, with its primary operations in West Africa, frequently importuned Whitehall for intervention on its behalf. Rather than offering support, Her Majesty's government ceded the port of Yarbutenda on the Gambia River to the French. The directors of the company could but dejectedly note: "The monetary interests which the company has created on the River Gambia in the firm belief . . . that the colony in its entirety would always remain under the sovereignty of the British Crown has been adversely affected by the unexpected concession."[42] Other examples abound. Sir William MacKinnon, the President of the Imperial British East Africa Company pointed to the vast support afforded their respective imperial enterprises by the Germans and Belgians and how niggardly in contrast was that of the British government.[43] But the company was not above using every means of improving its position. George Mackenzie, one of the company's officers, wrote Sir Murdoch Smith:

...it has occurred to me that perhaps you might be able to find some influential party... to get some leading men, personally known either to Lord Rosebery or Mr. Gladstone, to approach them, as entirely outside the Company, without in any way indicating that they were inspired from here as to the desirability of Government now coming forward to give some support....[44]

The Pacific Steam Navigation Company seldom ceased to bemoan the lack of government help against foreign competition. At the general meeting of May 29, 1899, the chairman reported: "I am sorry to say, with the exception of the Foreign Office, it is Inland Revenue, with its refusal to allow a just deduction for depreciation, and imposition of taxes on transfer, or the Agriculture Department, who do all they can to prevent us carrying sheep and cattle; or the Post Office... or the Board of Trade.... They are all alike it seems to me...."

Apparently driven to the limits of tolerance, the National Africa Company at a meeting of its board of September 23, 1885, resolved:

And whereas the Directors have in ways that are well known to H.M.G. already made as great a sacrifice as they could justify to their shareholders in order to make the Niger a British river, and to keep open to British influence and to British freight, the only practical commercial river route to the vast populations of the Central Sudan, and whereas after unexampled patience and mature consideration, the directors cannot but conclude to their deep regret that H.M.G. will continue to procrastinate (although admittedly long convinced of the necessity of immediate action) until after the occurrence of a complete catastrophe, the forerunning disturbances of which had long since been reported to them. Resolved: that negotiations be opened with a foreign power with the following objects, a) the transfer to the foreign power of the independent treaties of the company; b) the effective occupation of the countries thus transferred; c) the placing of the country under the flag of a foreign power; and d) the obtaining of such conditions as shall be most advantageous to the shareholders....

There was no doubt a good deal of bluff in this series of threats coming as they did at a time when the negotiations for a Royal Charter for what was to become the Royal Niger Company were underway, but there was an element of real frustration as well.

The entire position on foreign investment was neatly summarized by Salisbury: "On general principles," he wrote, "Her Majesty's Government always decline to place the power of the country at the disposal of individual investors to secure investments which they may think fit to make in the territory of another power."[45] In the Empire formal and informal, India aside, the same attitude seems to have prevailed.

III. The House of Commons and the imperial enterprise

Although the Lords could exercise more influence than they can today, and the Crown retained a strong voice in military appointments, by the third quarter of the nineteenth century, political power in Britain had centered in the House of Commons. Since the imperial enterprise, while profitable for some, was almost certainly a losing proposition for the average British citizen, was Parliament the institutional mechanism used by the economic imperialists to turn private gain into public policy? There are, of course, other possible explanations: Imperial policy might have been effected through the political parties, it might have been accomplished by the bureaucracy operating largely independently of the political process, or it might not have been achieved at all. The Empire might have been a consumption good purchased and consumed by the typical voter because he liked it better than beer or fish and chips.

Between January 1, 1860, and December 31, 1912, 3,768 men were elected and served in the Commons. Those elected representatives had an opportunity to express their views on imperial matters through the votes they cast on some 125 imperial bills that came before the House. A member's voting behavior, of course, reflected not only his own personal views and financial status but the position of his party and the stance and pocketbooks of his constituents. Thus a complete analysis of parliamentary behavior would include an examination of each member's occupation, wealth, imperial investments, education, and social relations. In addition it would examine the socioeconomic and demographic characteristics of his constituency and the electoral process that tied him to that constituency. It would also examine questions of party policy formation. Between a theoretic ideal and practical reality there is almost always a considerable gap and few are wider than this one. These explorations are at best preliminary; and, while the results are suggestive, they are at most tentative and certainly far less conclusive than either science or scholarship demands.

It has been averred that during the nineteenth century nothing was so likely to send members of Parliament to the local pub or even farther than an imperial measure on the floor. The evidence indicates

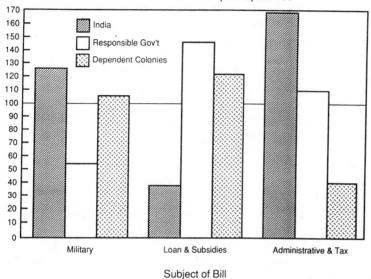

Chart 9.3

that they were partly right, but only partly. Overall about 37 percent of the eligible MPs voted on a typical imperial bill, and the figure for Conservatives was over 40. Moreover, there is a decided upward trend in the participation of both parties. The average over the Parliaments that met after the great redistricting of 1885 was more than 45 percent, and even the liberals were present more than two times in five.

Between 1860 and 1910 (no significant imperial issues came before Parliament between 1910 and 1912) there were eleven parliaments: (1) 1859 to 1865, (2) 1865 to 1868, (3) 1858 to 1874, (4) 1874 to 1880, (5) 1880 to 1885, (6) 1885 to 1886, (7) 1886 to 1892, (8) 1892 to 1895, (9) 1895 to 1900, (10) 1900 to 1906, and (11) 1906 to 1910.[46] Over the entire period, of the 125 imperial divisions,[47] 55 dealt with military matters, 48 with loans and nonmilitary subsidies, and 23 with administration and taxes; 42 dealt with India, 30 with the dependent colonies, and 53 with those colonies that had been granted responsible government (see Chart 9.3 and Appendixes 9.1 and 9.2).

Parliament was, however, faced by a different mix of problems in each of the three parts of the Empire. Administrative and tax problems in India came to the attention of the House relatively much more frequently than those questions in the rest of the Empire; and, to a less extent, the same was true of military issues. On the other hand, Parliament acted only rarely on questions of loans or subsidies to the subcontinent. The problems of loans and subsidies to the dependent Empire were brought to the members' attention quite frequently; and those of a military nature (thanks to Egypt and the Sudan) somewhat more often than chance would dictate; but the House was very seldom forced to confront issues of colonial administration and taxes that so dominated the Indian agenda. Finally, in their dealings with the responsibly governed colonies, it was questions of loans and subsidies that attracted the MPs' attention, while issues of administration and taxes were heard almost as infrequently as were questions of Indian loans and subsidies.

Over time the nature of "imperial issues" changed as well. In the first Parliament the major concern was financial – military expenditures and loans. In the second, the majority of bills dealt with steamship subsidies and railroad construction; but it was loans again that dominated the imperial agenda in the third (1868 to 1872). The members divided twenty-one times in the fourth (Disraeli's) Parliament; and the issues, as befitted the great imperalist, touched the Afghan and Zulu wars, the annexation of Fiji, and that perennial hot potato, the Indian cotton duties. Gladstone was the prime minister in the fifth–sixth session, and he was confronted by issues arising from the troubles in Egypt and the Sudan.

In the "almost" newly reapportioned seventh Parliament, the most important imperial issue appears to have been naval defense; in the next it was loans and subsidies to India and the dependent colonies in East Africa. The Empire was a major concern of the members of the ninth session; and an initial concern with the financial affairs of Cyprus and the construction of the Ugandan Railway was soon overshadowed by the growing crisis in South Africa. In the new century South Africa remained the single most important issue of imperial concern; but, as the conflict cooled and European politics heated, questions relating to the defense of the Dominions came under scrutiny. Finally, of the five imperial divisions in the eleventh Parliament, two dealt with free trade and imperial preference and two with loans – to India and the Transvaal.

Although the Conservatives were somewhat the more imperial party, the Liberals were not profoundly different. Given the marked homogeneity and the distinctly patrician flavor of nineteenth-century Parliaments, similarity is hardly remarkable. Of the total of

3,768, almost half were drawn from the elites (the City, peers and gents, military officers, the civil service, and the clergy); nearly 30 percent were businessmen or professionals; and more than a fifth, barristers or solicitors. At the other end of the economic spectrum, only 2 percent considered themselves "workers." Over time, the elite's dominance declined, and the number of business and professional men increased. The elites were, hardly surprisingly, distinctly Conservative; but the businessmen were even more devoutly Liberal. Lawyers, as one might guess, were fairly evenly divided between the two major parties.

If any other proof of the class structure of the members of the House is required, it can be found in their educational record. More than two in five attended either Oxford, Cambridge, Edinburgh, or Trinity College Dublin; and 35 percent had gone to Eton, Harrow, or one of the other major public schools. After 1885, however, there was a shift away from Oxbridge to a somewhat more egalitarian pattern. University College London, for example, trained sixty-five MPs, far less than the numbers from either Oxford or Cambridge, but well in excess of nearly all of the colleges that made up those august institutions.

Finally, memberships in that famous British institution, the club, provides yet another piece of evidence on the social structure of the House. The men who served in the House of "Commons" held at least 8,537 club memberships – an average of well over two per member, and that average did not change after 1885.

IV. The House of Commons: influences on members' voting behavior

With voting records, the members' biographies, election returns, and some socioeconomic data in hand, it should be possible to begin to explore the factors that influenced an MP's vote on imperial issues. The statistical technique to be employed is called multiple regression analysis. This is neither the time nor the place to discuss the model and its assumptions; but for the uninitiated let it merely be said that the technique measures, under certain assumptions, the degree of association between certain independent and one dependent variable. In this case the dependent variable is a measure of the member's voting record on imperial issues and the independent variables proxies for the "factors" that influenced his votes.

Since interest centers on the nonparty factors that influenced a member's vote, and his record on imperial issues was conditioned on the support for the issue given by his party, Liberals and Conservatives are treated separately. The measure of a member's imperial voting record chosen is the percentage of time in a session of Parliament that he supported the pro-imperial position divided by the percentage of time that his party supported that position. The "independent" factors that are assumed to have influenced his deviation from his party's position include: (1) the proportion of times that he supported the party position on domestic issues (a proxy for the general effect of party discipline on the member); (2) the margin by which he won his seat (a measure of his vulnerability to constituent discontent); (3) the location of his seat (a measure of the economic interests of his constituents); (4) his occupation (a measure of his economic interests); (5) the number of clubs to which he belonged (a proxy for his wealth); (6) his education, and (7) the types of clubs to which he belonged (measures of his noneconomic connections and interests) (see Appendixes 9.3 through 9.9).[48]

It should be emphasized that the explanatory power of this model is not great. There were obviously a great many more things influencing a member's voting behavior than the factors encompassed in this specification. It is certainly legitimate to wonder if the proxies capture the factors that they were designed to treat. Moreover, even within the category of "not very powerful," there is a considerable degree of inter-Parliament variation. Over the ten Parliaments the model can be said to "explain" on average something more than 10 percent of a Conservative member's votes and about half again that much for a typical Liberal's. That average, however, encompasses individual Parliaments, with explanation ratios ranging from less than 5 to more than 25 percent.

While its explanatory power is weak, the model is suggestive. For Conservatives the level of support for their party on imperial issues is positively associated with the intensity of their support for that position on domestic questions. For Liberals the relationship is even stronger, but it runs in the opposite direction. Often the Liberals who were most loyal to their party on domestic issues were the ones who were most likely to defect when the question involved the Empire.

The margin by which a member won his seat in the last election is weakly (but positively) linked to the strength of his pro-imperial position. The connection is, however, stronger for Conservatives than for Liberals. To the extent that the number of clubs to which a member belonged is an adequate proxy for wealth, at least to some small degree, the richer he was the more strongly he supported the Empire.

With qualitative variables – occupations (a member was either a merchant or he was not), the location of a seat, the fact that a member belonged to a literary club, or was a graduate of Eton – there is a need for a basis of comparison. In this analysis occupational behavior was measured against the votes of solicitors and barristers; the effects of education against the behavior of those who attended neither a university nor a major public school; the effect of the kind of club against the voting pattern of those MPs who belonged only to political clubs; and the behavior of members from most constituencies against those who represented seats in the industrial Midlands.

Conservative businessmen of any calling tended to support the Empire no more strongly than the solicitors and barristers; but when it comes to Liberals, both merchants and professional people proved substantially less interested in imperial aggrandizement than their legal colleagues. Among the Conservative elites, speculations to the contrary, both financiers and the leisure classes were less imperially minded than those who practiced the law. Liberal behavior was very similar, except that even the military officers in that party joined the financiers and the gentlemen in their relatively anti-imperial position.

The relationship between imperialism and education was basically similar on both sides of the political aisle, but the relationship for the Liberals appears stronger. It is worthy of note, however, that for the Conservatives both university-educated members and those who had ended their education in Public School were more strongly anti-imperial in the seventh Parliament (1892–5) than their colleagues with different educational backgrounds. University-educated Liberal MPs were the most anti-imperial of any group when education is the measure, but Liberal old boys from Public Schools who did not go on to university were more favorable to imperialism than the Liberals with other educational backgrounds.

Regional differences in imperial attitudes were more marked among Liberals than Conservatives. For the former, the most anti-imperial legislators represented the Celtic fringe and the rural regions of the Midlands and Southwest, while the strongest supporters of the Empire came from London and the Home Counties. Among the Conservatives, the Irish representatives proved to be the least imperialistic and those from London and the Home Counties the most frequent supporters of imperial legislation.

On average the Conservatives tended to provide more legislative support for the Empire than the Liberals; but from 1886 to 1895 and again from 1906 to 1910, it was the Liberals who contributed a disproportionate share of the pro-imperial votes. Since the issues addressed changed from Parliament to Parliament, some clues about the factors underlying voting behavior may be found by looking at the ten sessions in turn.

The party-support variable is designed to capture the idiosyncratic component of a member's voting behavior; and the results are surprising. It was sometimes the case that the strongest supporters of their party's position on domestic matters were the same MPs who voted most often with the party on matters imperial. But in more than half of the Parliaments the typical relationship ran in the other direction; and the reason lay in the behavior of the Liberal members. For them the inverse relationship was particularly strong in periods of war or impending hostilities (the fourth, sixth, eighth, and ninth sessions). Only in one instance (the second Parliament) did the Conservatives display this inverse behavior, and at that time the votes involved questions of colonial loans and subsidies. In three sessions (the first, fifth–sixth, and eleventh) Liberal MPs behaved as might be expected, but their attitude in the last session was clearly related to the issues involved – financial measures to rebuild the war-ravaged lands in South Africa and the defense of free trade.

Given the Liberal tradition, it may not be surprising that very often the members who most strongly supported the party's position on domestic affairs, the really true believers, also opposed bellicose and imperialistic tendencies when they recognized them in the official position taken by their party – a party whose manifestos had traditionally opposed war and overseas expansion. More surprising, perhaps, was the presence of a group of MPs who opposed their party's domestic policies but were distinctly pro-imperial. The behavior of this group is very marked in the early years, but disappears after the Liberal Unionists and the Irish Nationalists split off from the party in the later 1880s.

Neither a generous position on reparations nor the activities of a small group of imperially minded conservative Liberals explains the strong positive association between party domestic policy and imperial support that emerged during the fifth–sixth Parliament – a Parliament dominated by measures supporting war in Egypt and the Sudan and hostilities in Burma. No really credible explanation is close at hand. Possibly even the staunchest Liberals, who were in spite of everything still patriots, found these events sufficiently threatening to cause them to rally round the flag. Possibly they found the voters, who were certainly loyal to the Crown, sufficiently threatening to cause them to jump on the bandwagon regardless of what they really thought. It is interesting to note that the Liberals joined the Conservatives in strongly supporting resolutions of thanks to those officers responsible for British victories and in defeating a resolution regretting the overthrow of the Mahdi. On the other hand, they voted 270 to 3 in favor of withdrawing British forces from Southern Afghanistan – a measure the Conservatives opposed 191 to 29. Both parties voted unanimously in favor of providing an addition £1,000,000 for the army, but the Conservatives opposed the guarantee of a £135,000 loan to Egypt for essentially peaceful purposes – a loan the Liberals supported 243 to 3.

The apparent effects of electoral competition also raise interesting questions. For the Liberals there is an obvious relationship, but for the Conservatives, in the years before the redistricting, the most strongly imperial members came from the safest seats. After 1886, however, there is little evidence of any relationship except during the eighth session, marked by the eruption of the Anglo–Boer War. At that time it was the Conservative MPs who had survived the closest elections who tended to support imperial issues the most fervently.

Counter to the usual arguments about the economic basis of imperialism, a member's occupation was not strongly associated with his level of imperial support; and what connection there was appears to indicate that the groups that might have been assumed to be the strongest supporters of the Empire (merchants and peers and gentlemen) were relatively anti-imperial. Nor does the examination of the individual Parliaments appear to provide any additional support for the economic hypothesis.

In the case of merchants, the first Parliament aside, the only noticeable association occurred among the Liberal members in the second and eighth sessions; and in both instances those merchant MPs tended to be less imperially minded than their legally trained colleagues. In fact in the first of those two parliaments the votes were on questions of railroad and steamship subsidies – issues that might have been thought of particular concern to the mercantile community. In the second case, the Anglo–Boer War appears to have affected all Liberal businessmen in a similar fashion – they became substantially less imperially minded than the barristers and solicitors in their party.

For manufacturers again there is little difference between their legislative behavior and that of the legally trained members of their party except during the first, fourth, and eleventh Parliaments in the case of the Conservatives and the first and eighth sessions for the Liberals. In the first and fourth Parliaments both Liberals and Conservatives became more strongly pro-imperial, but the eighth and eleventh saw the behavior of both groups shift in the other direction. The first Parliament was concerned with imperial defense and with loan guarantees, the fourth with defense and the Indian cotton duties. The eighth was the Boer War Parliament, of course; and the eleventh underscored some of the costs of the imperial enterprise.

In the case of the elites, there is no evidence from any parliament that they were particularly imperialistic; and, if the fourth session is excluded, financiers, military officers, and the "leisure classes" were almost certainly less dedicated to the empire than their colleagues from the legal profession. The anti-imperial sentiment of the elites is particularly marked in the second and seventh Parliaments. Again, it appears what differences there were rest with the Liberals. To have been a Liberal and a member of the elites meant, after 1880, to have voted in favor of imperial policies less often than the rest of your party.

The data are weak and the analytical results offered with a great many caveats. More work could be done, and it probably should be; but, barring a very major reversal of these results, it appears doubtful that Parliament provided the constitutional mechanism that was used to protect the profits of imperial investors and businessmen.

V. Conclusion

Individual companies, the chambers of commerce, and the trade associations were interested in politics largely in relation to questions involving trade and commerce. In that arena, the evidence leaves little room for doubt that firms operating either individually or in concert (often through formal organizations like the Chambers of Commerce and trade associations and occasionally through informal and, frequently, short-lived coalitions) were at times able to influence government policy. The essential elimination of Indian tariffs on textiles is a case in point. On the other hand, the number of resolutions on colonial and foreign tariffs, and regulations adverse to business that were not followed by government action, and the number of times a minister noted that he had been called on by a "delegation" of businessmen to whom he offered nothing but sympathy, indicate that their success was very far from complete. Questions of tariffs in the responsibly governed colonies and imperial preference together were the subject of almost a third of the chambers' imperial business and there is no evidence that their actions had any positive effect.

Although the evidence is not totally compelling, it seems possible to speculate about the explanation of the relative success of some business-supported lobbying. It is clear that the British government displayed a greater willingness to deploy its services in support of Indian rather than foreign-sector activities. In the case of the remainder of the dependent Empire the evidence is much less clear. To a considerable degree, whatever tendency to intervene the government displayed was, in part, the result of domestic political realities; but it also appears to have reflected, first, the much lower cost of Empire involvement and, second, some official questioning of the usefulness of foreign, as opposed to imperial or domestic, investment. It was probably also, however, indicative of something more fundamental. During the time when Britain was powerful enough to interfere in the foreign sector without engendering serious responses from other developed countries, there was a general, and almost certainly correct, belief that its commerce and industry were sufficiently competitive to allow British businessmen to triumph, if they were guaranteed equal access to markets. On the question of the right to compete unimpeded, the London government was firm. By the turn of the century, however, competitive success was no longer assured, but, by then, the costs of intervention had risen. It is interesting to note that the Indian examples of government interference all come from that later period.

In the public sector, by and large, complaints by disgruntled British investors were directed toward foreign, not Empire, governments. In the Empire, government had already adopted a set of policies that protected the investors interests almost as well as any set of regulations those investors themselves might have designed. Indian debt was British debt, and elsewhere there were certainly de facto government guarantees in the years before 1900, and de jure ones thereafter. In its relation with the private sector, in India, at least, the government did informally act to reduce foreign (that is, non–British) competition.

Neither in India nor elsewhere, however, is there evidence that markets were not open to all British and indigenous entrepreneurs. Moreover, over most of the period the British competitive advantage in manufactures was so great that foreign exclusion, if it existed at all, must have entailed, at most, trivial costs. After the turn of the century, such was no longer the case.

The Indian government may have acted to stifle foreign competition, but the same was not true in the dependent colonies. The Crown Agents, when acting as colonial purchasing agents, actively sought foreign bids when they thought domestic prices excessive. Finally, when it came to those parts of the Empire with responsible government, the business lobbyists were almost uniformly unsuccessful. Despite the continued pleas of manufacturers, alone or joined together, and of almost every local Chamber of Commerce, the Dominions continued to increase the level of those tariffs aimed at excluding British business from colonial markets. In the words of one member of the free-trade Manchester school: "The worst offenders against us are our own kinsfolk, whom we have defended in their infancy at our cost, and who retort on us by repudiating all the projects of our industry but our money. . . ."[49] Or as it was put, more stridently, by an economist arguing for dissolution of the Empire: " . . . Retain our colonies? What is there left to retain? Retain the privilege of spending nearly 4,500,000 pounds sterling on their prohibitive tariffs and 'ironical allegiance.' "[50] British businessmen could call on their representatives and the Chambers could rally and rail; but the colonial response was higher, not lower, tariffs. All that was left for a laissez faire economist was to bemoan the granting of self-government to colonies – grants made without restrictions on the ability of colonial Parliament to protect infant (or any other) industries through the erection of "mischievous tariff barriers."[51] Britain had attempted to tie the hands of the Canadian Parliament, but to no avail. No Dominion had higher tariffs than Canada.

It appears that three conditions characterize the most successful lobbying operations of the business community. First, the agitation had to be focused: That is, a substantial concentration of affected businesses capable of commanding a pivotal coalition needed to be concentrated in some geographic area. Second, the probability of achieving the desired end was greatest when there was no countervailing pressure within the United Kingdom. Third, the chances of gaining governmental support tended to be highest when the costs of the effort were low, as, for example, in cases where demands were consistent with established British policy.

As for Parliament itself, it is hard to find much connection between MP self-interest and voting behavior on imperial issues. For the moment one must conclude that the Empire's development, at least in the political sphere, was largely unrelated to the search for economic profit.

IMPERIAL DIVISIONS IN STUDY
1860-1910

Parliament	Party Strength	Bill Number and Title	Conservatives Aye	Conservatives Nay	Liberals Aye	Liberals Nay
I (1859-65)	Conservative 307	1 European Forces India Bill	95	26	157	21
	Liberal 347	2 Fortifications--Provision for Expenses	51	3	68	24
		3 Fortifications--Provision for Expenses	66	10	75	42
		5 Fortifications--Provision for Expenses	54	12	70	42
		7 Ashanti War, Health of Troops Critical	17	188	192	16
		8 New Zealand Guarantee of Loan	29	11	45	16
		9 Indian Medical Service	5	26	36	14
		10 Indian Army Officers Grievances	32	6	12	27
		1008 New Zealand Guarantee of Loan	33	8	47	20
		2008 New Zealand Guarantee of Loan	22	21	59	29
II (1865-68)	Conservative 299	13 Counsel to the Secretary of State for India	0	47	32	6
	Liberal 359	14 Canada Railway Loan	157	3	55	35
		17 East Indian Troops & Vessels, Abyssinian Campaign	109	2	62	17
		18 India, China & Japan Mails	42	0	8	12
		1018 India, China & Japan Mails	11	75	176	2
III (1868-74)	Conservative 279	21 Canada Loan--Rupert's Land	12	1	46	8
	Liberal 379	24 Emigration--Paupers to Colonies	23	27	20	113
		26 Common Nationality--Colonies	53	10	8	94
		27 East India Opium Revenue	11	53	29	85
		30 East India Company Claims of Former Officers	94	11	10	76
		33 Canada Guarantee of Loan	24	3	36	12
		40 Fiji Protectorate	69	56	8	73
		43 Canada Loan Guarantee	36	6	74	12
		501 East India Loan Bill	22	22	55	16
IV (1874-80)	Conservative 352	47 Gold Coast Withdrawal	207	14	77	49
	Liberal 300	52 India Councils	127	6	26	39
		53 Fiji Annexation Approval	62	5	13	20
		54 P&O Contract Approval	108	1	27	15
		55 East India Home Government	116	8	3	57
		63 Council of India Professional Appointments	110	4	25	30
		69 Appointment Select Committee Indian Finances	10	154	94	2
		70 Supplementary £40,500 for Colonial Expenses	7	128	74	4
		71 Supplementary £44,500 for Colonial Expenses	4	103	48	5
		77 Motion £23,176 to Defray Colonial Expenses	2	90	10	34
		83 Indian Vernacular Press Act	10	176	127	6
		84 Afghan Expenses of Military Operations Charged to India	206	7	7	104
		85 Zulu War, Regret British Actions	20	271	202	4
		87 Afghan War Expenses not to Delay Remission of Indian Cotton Duty	11	145	64	4
		88 Reduction in Cotton Duties, Good First Step	7	139	49	6
		89 Lytton Condemned for Actions Against Indian Population	137	1	57	30
		91 Thanks Lytton/Haines for Afghan War--Lytton Exclud Amend	103	2	26	24
		92 Vote of Thanks to Lytton & Haines for Afghan War	101	2	20	19
		502 Against India Trade Licences Tax	11	127	73	13
		503 Regrets Increased Salt Duty in Bombay & Madras	8	130	70	13
		504 India Overcharged for Afghan War	117	13	4	98

Parliament	Party Strength	Bill Number and Title	Conservatives Aye	Conservatives Nay	Liberals Aye	Liberals Nay
V (1880-86)	Conservative 238					
	Liberal 414					
		100 India Office Sale of Superfluous Land	0	23	3	44
		103 Afghanistan Against Withdrawal from South	191	29	3	270
		107 Vote of Thanks for Haines Afghan Military Operations	136	0	139	5
	Election of 1885:					
	Conservative 250	112 India to Bear Costs of Her Troops in Egypt	35	3	94	13
	Liberal 334	113 Thanks to Seymour for Attack on Alexandria	148	0	174	4
	Irish Nationalist 86	114 Thanks to Wolseley for Tel El Kebir	85	2	124	8
		115 Condemning Additional Financial Burdens Due to Egypt	21	4	66	11
		116 £274,000 More for Navy Due to Egypt	6	30	6	114
		120 Reduce Indian Expenditure--Adjournment of Debate	33	8	35	0
		132 £324,000 for Navy in Egypt	12	0	48	4
		135 East India Expenses--Military Expedition to Sudan	12	3	65	7
		136 Guarantee of £315,000 Loan for Egypt	28	193	243	3
		505 Army Supply £1,000,000 for Nile Expedition for Year Ending 1885	12	0	56	0
		506 Replace £330,000 for Building New Ships Because of Nile by $80,000	0	12	2	48
		507 3,000 Extra Men for the Army	0	1	0	8
		508 Replace Proposed 35,000 New Men for the Army with 12,000	1	72	7	14
		510 Regrets Use of Power to Overthrow Mahdi	4	210	63	186
		511 Government's Sudan Policy Does Not Justify Confidence of House	198	25	10	238
VI (1886-92)	Conservative 316	144 Criticism of Indian Frontier Policy	4	115	51	4
	Liberal 191	148 U.K. Australasia Naval Defence Pact Ratification	86	0	4	33
	Irish Nationalist 85	149 £185,000 for Vessels Under Australasian Agreement	127	0	84	35
	Liberal Unionist 78	150 £2,600,000--Imperial Defense, Ports, Coaling Stations	180	0	21	41
		155 £2,130,000 for Navy	217	1	26	56
		156 £21,500,000 for Navy	198	0	7	91
		157 Naval Defence	250	1	14	113
		158 Telegraph Contract, Halifax & Bermuda	1	0	23	5
		509 Indian Revenues for Burma Expedition	169	140	112	57
		513 £28,375 for Telegraph Subsidy	69	5	1	23
		1151 Indian Revenue Accounts	0	101	21	3
VII (1892-95)	Conservative 268	192 East India Loan £100,000,000	2	63	102	2
	Liberal 271	515 $50,000 for Uganda	99	1	96	30
	Irish Nationalist 81	516 India Pays Excessive Military Costs	8	18	61	5
	Liberal Unionist 47	517 £29,000 for Cyprus	109	1	111	15
	Labor 3	518 $80,000 for IBEAC	128	1	93	34

Parliament	Party Strength	Bill	Number and Title	Conservatives Aye	Conservatives Nay	Liberals Aye	Liberals Nay
VIII (1895-1900)	Conservative 341	207	Naval Works	204	1	42	17
	Liberal 177	208	Naval Works	157	0	22	14
	Irish Nationalist 82	214	Uganda Railway	200	1	22	56
	Liberal Unionist 70	226	Recent Hostilities Beyond India not to be Charged	3	170	62	4
		229	Expedient that Loan of £798,802 to Egypt Not to Repaid	134	5	3	58
		235	Thanks for Sudan Expedition	231	0	92	2
		236	To Disallow Indian Tariff Act	7	254	113	3
		241	Royal Niger Company	150	0	13	58
		242	Colonial Loans	102	0	5	49
		248	War Loan	183	0	65	2
		250	Uganda Railway	157	0	45	36
		519	£182,432 for Uganda, West & Central Africa and Uganda Railroad	119	0	9	34
		520	£1,000 for Cyprus	120	1	7	21
		521	£104,000 Grant for Uganda East & Central Africa	144	0	8	29
		522	Approves Uganda Railway and Votes $3,000,000	210	0	23	58
		523	India to Pay for Its Troops in Africa	242	21	1	134
		524	India to Pay for Its Troops in Africa (Main Q)	226	5	1	62
		525	£1,000 Grant for Cyprus	119	0	8	20
		526	£154,463 for Uganda, East & Central Africa and Uganda Railroad	94	1	1	27
		527	£1,000 for Cyprus	176	1	12	49
		528	£1,000 for Cyprus	174	2	2	56
		530	£805,000 for Payments to Niger Co. (Orig)	193	1	4	76
		531	£805,000 for Payments to Niger Co. (Orig)	194	1	3	91
		550	£10,000,000 for India	175	0	32	63
		551	£120,000 for Army and $13,000,000 for War in South Africa	191	0	58	2
		552	Supplemental $11,500,000 for Army in China and South Africa (Against)	0	74	1	7
		1551	Colonial Supply	158	0	36	2
		2551	Colonial Supply	128	0	28	1
IX (1900-06)	Conservative 334	261	Colonial Loan	193	0	7	46
	Liberal 184	262	Thanks to Imperial Forces in South Africa	238	1	108	0
	Irish Nationalist 82	272	Sugar Convention	201	10	5	109
	Liberal Unionist 68	275	Brussels Sugar Convention, Negative View	6	182	97	3
	Labor 2	279	East Indian Revenues for Any Tibet Expense	210	1	35	15
		289	Cunard Agreement Money	124	2	4	23
		305	Naval Works	190	1	1	59
		553	$5,000,000 for Army for South African War	166	0	38	16
		554	Vote for Land Forces of 420,000	176	0	7	33
		555	£1,016,000 for Colonial Services Inc. Grants	146	0	2	71
		556	£26,500 for Colonial Expenses Inc. Grants	162	1	4	55
X (1906-10)	Conservative 156	309	Anti-Free Trade	101	2	1	306
	Liberal 374	336	Favors Imperial Preference	81	4	6	328
	Irish Nationalist 83	339	Transvaal Loan Guarantee		49	172	5
	Labor 52	368	East India Loans	6	21	96	15
		557	£29,050 for Colonial Expenses Inc. Grants	3	69	265	3

APPENDIX 9.2

IMPERIAL DIVISIONS ANALYZED
1859-1910

NUMBER OF DIVISIONS

Parliament	India Military	India Loans and Non-Military Subsidies	India Admin. and Taxes	Responsible Government Military	Responsible Loans and Non-Military Subsidies	Responsible Admin. and Taxes	Dependent Government Military	Dependent Loans and Non-Military Subsidies	Dependent Admin. and Taxes	All Empire Military	All Empire Loans and Non-Military Subsidies	All Empire Admin. and Taxes	Empire Total	Domestic Total	All Bills Total
1859-65	6	0	0	0	3	0	1	0	0	7	3	0	10	2	12
1865-68	0	2	1	0	1	0	1	0	0	1	3	1	5	6	11
1868-74	1	0	0	0	4	2	0	0	2	1	4	4	9	21	30
1874-80	5	0	8	0	1	0	2	4	1	7	5	9	21	27	48
1880-86*	4	1	1	0	0	0	11	1	0	15	2	1	18	30	48
1886-92	2	0	2	3	1	0	3	1	0	8	2	2	12	36	48
1892-95	1	1	0	0	0	0	0	3	0	1	4	0	5	20	25
1895-1900	3	1	1	4	0	0	2	15	1	9	16	2	27	29	56
1900-06	1	0	0	0	6	2	4	0	0	5	6	2	13	36	49
1906-10	0	1	0	0	1	2	0	1	0	0	3	2	5	45	50
All Parliaments	23	6	13	7	17	6	24	25	4	54	48	23	125	252	377

PERCENT OF IMPERIAL DIVISIONS BY PARLIAMENT

Parliament	India Military	India Loans and Non-Military Subsidies	India Admin. and Taxes	Responsible Government Military	Responsible Loans and Non-Military Subsidies	Responsible Admin. and Taxes	Dependent Government Military	Dependent Loans and Non-Military Subsidies	Dependent Admin. and Taxes	All Empire Military	All Empire Loans and Non-Military Subsidies	All Empire Admin. and Taxes	Empire Total
1859-65	100	0	0	0	100	0	100	0	0	70	30	0	100
1865-68	0	67	33	0	100	0	100	0	0	20	60	20	100
1868-74	100	0	0	0	67	33	0	0	100	11	44	44	100
1874-80	38	0	62	0	100	0	33	67	0	33	24	43	100
1880-86*	67	17	16	0	0	0	92	8	0	83	11	6	100
1886-92	50	0	50	75	25	0	75	25	0	66	17	17	100
1892-95	50	50	0	0	0	0	0	100	0	20	80	0	100
1895-1900	60	20	20	100	0	0	11	83	6	32	60	8	100
1900-06	100	0	0	0	75	25	100	0	0	39	46	15	100
1906-10	0	100	0	0	33	67	0	100	0	0	60	40	100
All Parliaments	55%	31%	14%	23%	57%	20%	45%	47%	8%	44%	30%	18%	100%

*Includes both 1880-85 and 1885-86 sessions.

APPENDIX 9.3

AVERAGE PARTY SUPPORT ON NONIMPERIAL ISSUES

(Percentages)

PARLIAMENT	CONSERVATIVE	LIBERAL
1859-65	.704	.740
1865-68	.913	.871
1868-74	.880	.936
1874-80	.930	.789
1880-85	.878	.892
1886-92	.943	.892
1892-95	.950	.929
1895-1900	.947	.895
1900-06	.949	.965
1906-10	.917	.913

MP SUPPORT SCORES

CONSERVATIVES

Parliament Number	R²	SNI	WM	# Clubs	BUSINESS			ELITES				EDUCATION		CLUBS			No Clubs		REGIONS				
					Comm	Bus/Mfg	OB	Fin	Mil	Aris	OE	Univ	MPS	Emp	Soc	Lit	Clubs	Other	S&W	Ire	N&L	RS	L&H
1	.17		+.22		+	+								+	-.29	+.29	+.73		+		+	+.17	+.31
2	.13	-.32	+.27		+	+		-.46		-.16	-.65		-.29	+.14	+	+	+	+.23	+.37	-.20		+.17	-
3	.15	+.60		+.04		+.18			-	-	+.26		-.11	+	-	+.44	+.44						
4	.09	+.45	+.13	-.04					+	-	+.26	+		+	+	+	-.11		-			-	-
5	.04	-		-	-	+	-		+	-	+	-		+	+								
6	.06	+.14	+		-	+	+		+	-	+	-.34	-.68	+	+	+		+		-.03	+		-
7	.17	-			+.04		+.03	+.09	+	+	+								-	-	+		-.02
8	.07	+.15	-.05				+		-	+	+		+.06	+		+	+	+		+	+.41	+.31	+
9	.09	+.15	+							-	+									-			
10	.11				-	-.61				-	+						-						

LIBERALS

Parliament Number	R²	SNI	WM	# Clubs	BUSINESS			ELITES				EDUCATION		CLUBS			No Clubs		REGIONS				
					Comm	Bus/Mfg	OB	Fin	Mil	Aris	OE	Univ	MPS	Emp	Soc	Lit	Clubs	Other	S&W	Ire	N&L	RS	L&H
1	.25	+.20	+.62	+.06	-.20	+.25	+.30	-.39	+	+.17	+	-	+	-.32			-.19	-.19		-.14			
2	.10	-.02	-.25	+.04		+	-	-1.07	-.24	-.18	-						-.19	+.13	-.21	-.25	-.30	-.30	-
3	.06				+	+	-	+.25	+.25	+	+							+	+.09	+.10	+.10	-.36	+
4	.18	-.34			-	-	-	-.20	-.20	-	-	-.13	+.14	-.09	-.15	-.32	-.32	-.13	-.11					
5	.12	+.39		+.07		-		-.47	-.47	-.39	+	-.22	+.53	-.37		-.13				-.23		-.19	-.19	
6	.17	-.78	-.59						+		+				-.23						-.21		
7	.12				-.28	-.25	-.29	-	-	-	+	-.25	+.34	+	+	+	+	-	-.26		+	+	
8	.20	-.68	+.67		-	-	-	-	-	-.33	+	+.08	+.14					-	-.12	-	+.11		
9	.16	-.67			+	+	-.29			-.41	-													
10	.09	+.49	+.25	+	+	+	+.12							+		+	+	-					

Aris: Aristocrats
Bus/Mfg: Business and Manufacturing
Clubs: Number of Club Memberships
Comm: Commerce
Emp: Empire
Fin: Finance
Ire: Ireland

L&H: London and Home Counties
Lit: Literary
Mil: Military
MPS: Major Public Schools
N&L: North and Lancashire
OB: Other Business
OE: Other Elites

RS: Rural South
S&W: Scotland and Wales
SNI: Support on Non-Imperial Issues
Soc: Social
Univ: Universities
WM: Winning Margin

APPENDIX 9.5

MP OCCUPATIONS

PANEL A: FREQUENCIES

OCCUPATIONS	ALL YEARS			1860-1885 ALL MPs ELECTED BEFORE 12/85 AND SITTING			1886-1910 ALL MPs SITTING			1886-1910 MPs ELECTED FIRST TIME AND SITTING		
	A	B	C	A	B	C	A	B	C	A	B	C
Medical	48			25			38			23		
Education	71			30			63			41		
Newspapers	158			64			134			94		
Miscellaneous Professions	32			11			27			21		
Professions Group Subtotal	(309)	297		(130)	128		(262)	250		(179)	169	
Merchants	316			196			186			120		
Retail & Business Services	40			19			35			21		
Sales & Agency	36			22			25			14		
Trade & Commerce Group Subtotal	(392)	382		(237)	231		(246)	238		(155)	151	
Miscellaneous Manufacturing	309			177			202			132		
Engineering & Construction	70			35			49			35		
Brewers & Distillers	51			33			32			18		
Manufacturing Group Subtotal	(430)	425		(245)	241		(283)	280		(185)	184	
Marine, Transport, etc.	62			34			41			28		
Management	3			2			2			1		
Agriculture	48			16			42			32		
Mining	56			31			44			25		
Business Unspecified	90			24			83			66		
Misc. Business Group Subtotal	(259)	256		(107)	107		(212)	209		(152)	149	
BUSINESS CLASS TOTAL	((1390))	(1360)	1199	((719))	(707)	605	((1003))	(977)	870	((671))	(653)	594
Finance	112	112		69	69		72	72		43	43	
Peers & Gents	1030	1030		751	751		458	458		279	279	
Military	559	559		375	375		265	265		184	184	
Civil Service	118	138		63	73		82	98		55	65	
Clergy	20			10			16			10		
ELITES CLASS TOTAL	((1839))	(1839)	1815	((1268))	(1268)	1257	((893))	(893)	875	((571))	(571)	558
Barristers	771	771		449	449		495	498		320	322	
Solicitors	124	124		51	51		100	97		75	73	
LEGAL CLASS TOTAL	((895))	(895)	883	((500))	(500)	495	((595))	(595)	584	((395))	(395)	388
Labor Leaders	41	41		2	2		40	40		39	39	
Laborers	62	62		23	23		59	59		39	39	
LABOR CLASS TOTAL	((103))	(103)	87	((25))	(25)	24	((99))	(99)	83	((78))	(78)	63
ALL CLASSES TOTAL	4227	4197	3984	2512	2500	2381	2591	2564	2412	1715	1697	1603

PANEL B: PERCENTS

OCCUPATIONS	ALL YEARS			1860-1885 ALL MPs ELECTED BEFORE 12/85 AND SITTING			1886-1910 ALL MPs SITTING			1886-1910 MPs ELECTED FIRST TIME AND SITTING			RELATIVE ELECTED PRE-1885 / ELECTED POST-1885		
	A	B	C	A	B	C	A	B	C	A	B	C	A	B	C
Medical	1.1			1.0			1.5			1.3			77		
Education	1.7			1.2			2.4			2.4			50		
Newspapers	3.7			2.5			5.2			5.5			45		
Miscellaneous Professions	0.8			.4			1.0			1.2			33		
Professions Group Subtotal	(7.3)	7.1		(5.2)	5.1		(10.1)	9.8		(10.4)	10.0		(50)	51	
Merchants	7.5			7.0			7.2			7.0			111		
Retail & Business Services	.9			1.4			1.4			1.2			67		
Sales & Agency	.8			1.0			1.0			.8			112		
Trade & Commerce Group Subtotal	(9.3)	9.1		(9.4)	9.2		(9.5)	9.3		(9.0)	8.9		(104)	103	
Miscellaneous Manufacturing	7.3			7.0			7.8			7.7			91		
Engineering & Construction	1.7			1.4			1.9			2.0			70		
Brewers & Distillers	1.2			1.3			1.0			1.0			130		
Manufacturing Group Subtotal	(10.2)	10.1		(9.8)	9.6		(10.9)	10.9		(10.8)	10.8		(91)	89	
Marine, Transport, etc.	1.5			.1			1.6			1.6			88		
Management	.1			.1			.1			.1			100		
Agriculture	1.1			.6			1.6			1.9			32		
Mining	1.3			1.0			1.7			1.5			80		
Business Unspecified	2.1			2.5			3.2			3.8			26		
Misc. Business Group Subtotal	(6.1)	6.1		(4.3)	4.3		(8.2)	8.2		(8.9)	8.8		(48)	49	
BUSINESS CLASS TOTAL	(32.9)	(32.4)	30.1	(28.6)	(28.3)	25.4	(38.7)	(38.1)	36.1	(39.1)	(38.5)	37.1	(73)	(74)	68
Finance	2.6			2.7			2.8			2.5			108		
Peers & Gents	24.3			29.8			17.7			16.3			183		
Military	13.2			14.9			10.2			10.7			139		
Civil Service	2.8			2.5			3.2			3.2			78		
Clergy	.5			.5			.6			.6			67		
ELITES CLASS TOTAL	(43.5)	(43.8)	45.5	(50.4)	(50.7)	52.8	(34.5)	(34.8)	36.3	(33.3)	(33.6)	34.8	(151)	(151)	152
Barristers	18.3			17.8			19.1			18.6			95		
Solicitors	2.9			2.1			3.7			4.3			47		
LEGAL CLASS TOTAL	(21.2)	(21.3)	22.2	(19.9)	(20.0)	20.8	(23.0)	(23.2)	24.2	(23.0)	(23.3)	24.2	(87)	(86)	86
Labor Leaders	1.0			.1			1.6			2.3			4		
Laborers	1.5			.9			2.3			2.3			39		
LABOR CLASS TOTAL	(2.5)	(2.5)	2.2	(1.0)	(1.0)	1.0	(3.9)	(3.9)	3.4	(4.6)	(4.6)	3.9	(22)	(22)	26

COLUMN A reflects the distribution of MP occupations across 25 career categories, with each MP counted once for each career in a different category (but no more than once in any one category). Computed on this basis, the subtotals for each occupational group (excluding those which consist of only one category) are given, enclosed by a single set of parentheses. The class totals computed on this basis are also given, enclosed in a set of double parentheses.

COLUMN B contains the group subtotals, and the class totals (enclosed in a single set of parentheses) for MP occupations, counting each MP no more than once for multiple occupations held within the same group, regardless of any distinctions which are made at the category level.

COLUMN C contains class total figures only, counting each MP no more than once in any of the four classes, regardless of any distinctions made at either the group or category level.

APPENDIX 9.6

MP OCCUPATIONS BY PARTY

PANEL A-1: ALL YEARS FREQUENCIES

OCCUPATIONS	CONSERVATIVES			LIBERALS			LABOR			IRISH NATIONALISTS			OTHERS		
	A	B	C	A	B	C	A	B	C	A	B	C	A	B	C
Medical	8			28			2			10			0		
Education	14			46			1			10			0		
Newspapers	33			78			6			41			0		
Miscellaneous Professions	12			18			0			2			0		
Professions Group Subtotal	(67)	65		(170)	164		(9)	9		(63)	59		(0)	0	
Merchants	80			200			1			35			0		
Retail & Business Services	17			13			0			10			0		
Sales & Agency	11			18			0			7			0		
Trade & Commerce Group Subtotal	(108)	107		(231)	228		(1)	1		(52)	46		(0)		
Miscellaneous Manufacturing	92			204			5			8			0		
Engineering & Construction	27			34			4			5			0		
Brewers & Distillers	30			14			0			2			0		
Manufacturing Group Subtotal	(149)	149		(251)	253		(9)	9		(15)	15		(0)	0	
Marine, Transport, etc.	32			28			0			2			0		
Management	2			0			0			1			0		
Agriculture	6			14			0			28			0		
Mining	20			34			0			2			0		
Business Unspecified	40			45			0			5			0		
Misc. Business Group Subtotal	(100)	97		(121)	121		(0)	0		(38)	38		(0)	0	
BUSINESS CLASS TOTAL	((424))	(417)	372	((779))	(766)	668	((19))	(19)	17	((168))	(158)	142	((0))	(0)	0
Finance	67			65			0			2			0		
Peers & Gents	586			407			2			35			0		
Military	394			159			3			6			0		
Civil Service	55			55			0			5			0		
Clergy	0			19			0			1			0		
ELITES CLASS TOTAL	((1102))	(1102)	1083	((683))	(683)	678	((5))	(5)	5	((49))	(49)	49			
Barristers	356			375			1			33			1		
Solicitors	43			67			0			20			0		
LEGAL CLASS TOTAL	((399))	(398)	394	((442))	(442)	435	((1))	(1)	1	((53))	(53)	52	((1))	(1)	1
Labor Leaders	2			9			26			4			0		
Laborers	2			29			27			5			0		
LABOR CLASS TOTAL	((4))	(4)	4	((38))	(38)	34	((53))	(52)	40	((9))	(9)	9	((0))	(0)	0
ALL CLASSES TOTAL	1929	1921	1853	1942	1929	1815	78	77	63	279	269	252	1	1	1

APPENDIX 9.6 (Continued)

PANEL A-2: 1859-1885 FREQUENCIES; ALL MPs ELECTED BEFORE 12/85 AND SITTING

OCCUPATIONS	CONSERVATIVES A	B	C	LIBERALS A	B	C	LABOR A	B	C	IRISH NATIONALISTS A	B	C	OTHERS A	B	C
Medical	3			18			0			4			0		
Education	4			24			0			2			0		
Newspapers	10			32			0			22			0		
Miscellaneous Professions	4			6			0			1			0		
Professions Group Subtotal	(21)	21		(80)	78		(0)	0		(29)	29		(0)	0	
Merchants	51			130			0			13			0		
Retail & Business Services	6			7			0			6			0		
Sales & Agency	8			11			0			3			0		
Trade & Commerce Group Subtotal	(65)	64		(150)	148		(0)	0		(22)	19		(0)	0	
Miscellaneous Manufacturing	46			129			0			2			0		
Engineering & Construction	12			21			0			2			0		
Brewers & Distillers	20			12			0			1			0		
Manufacturing Group Subtotal	(78)	78		(162)	158		(0)	0		(5)	5		(0)	0	
Marine, Transport, etc.	19			15			0			2			0		
Management	1			0			0			6			0		
Agriculture	1			9			0			0			0		
Mining	9			22			0			0			0		
Business Unspecified	9			14			0			1			0		
Misc. Business Group Subtotal	(39)	39		(60)	60		(0)	0		(8)	8		(0)	0	
BUSINESS CLASS TOTAL	((203))	(202)	175	((452))	(444)	376	((0))	(0)	0	((64))	(61)	54	((0))	(0)	0
Finance	42			27			0			0			0		
Peers & Gents	421			315			0			15			0		
Military	249			123			0			3			0		
Civil Service	27			34			0			3			0		
Clergy	0			9			0			1			0		
ELITES CLASS TOTAL	((739))	(739)	730	((508))	(508)	506	((0))	(0)	0	((21))	(21)	21	((0))	(0)	0
Barristers	186			244			0			15			0		
Solicitors	21			25			0			9			0	(1)	
LEGAL CLASS TOTAL	((207))	(206)	205	((269))	(269)	266	((0))	(0)	0	((24))	(24)	23	((1))	(1)	1
Labor Leaders	0			2			0			0			0		
Laborers	0			20			0			3			0		
LABOR CLASS TOTAL	((0))	(0)	0	((22))	(22)	21	((0))	(0)	0	((3))	(3)	3	((0))	(0)	0
ALL CLASSES TOTAL	1149	1147	1110	1251	1243	1169	0	0	0	112	109	101	1	1	1

PANEL A-3: 1886-1910 FREQUENCIES; ALL MPs SITTING

OCCUPATIONS	CONSERVATIVES A	B	C	LIBERALS A	B	C	LABOR A	B	C	IRISH NATIONALISTS A	B	C	OTHERS A	B	C
Medical	8			18			2			10			0		
Education	14			38			1			10			0		
Newspapers	30			59			6			39			0		
Miscellaneous Professions	11			14			0			2			0		
Professions Group Subtotal	(63)	61		(129)	123		(9)	9		(61)	57		(0)	0	
Merchants	43			108			1			34			0		
Retail & Business Services	15			10			0			10			0		
Sales & Agency	8			10			0			7			0		
Trade & Commerce Group Subtotal	(66)	66		(128)	126		(1)	1		(51)	45		(0)	0	
Miscellaneous Manufacturing	65			125			5			7			0		
Engineering & Construction	19			21			4			5			0		
Brewers & Distillers	20			10			0			2			0		
Manufacturing Group Subtotal	(104)	103		(156)	154		(9)	9		(14)	14		(0)	0	
Marine, Transport, etc.	21			18			0			1			0		
Management	1			0			0			2			0		
Agriculture	5			9			0			28			0		
Mining	18			24			0			2			0		
Business Unspecified	39			39			0			5			0		
Misc. Business Group Subtotal	(84)	81		(90)	90		(0)	0		(38)	38		(0)	0	
BUSINESS CLASS TOTAL	((317))	((311))	282	((503))	((493))	433	((19))	((19))	17	((164))	((154))	138	((0))	(0)	0
Finance	45	45		25	25		0	0		2	2		0	0	
Peers & Gents	263	263		160	160		2	2		33	33		0	0	
Military	206	206		54	54		2	2		5	5		0	0	
Civil Service	43	43		31	31		3	3		5	5		0	0	
Clergy	0	0		16	16		0	0		0	0		0	0	
ELITES CLASS TOTAL	((557))	(557)	52	((286))	(286)	283	((5))	(5)	5	((45))	(45)	45	((0))	0	0
Barristers	256	256		208	211		1	1		30	30		0	0	
Solicitors	30	30		51	48		0	0		19	19		0	0	
LEGAL CLASS TOTAL	((286))	(286)	22	(259)	(259)	253	((1))	(1)	1	(49)	(49)	48	(0)	0	0
Labor Leaders	2	2		8	8		26	26		4	4		0	0	
Laborers	2	2		27	27		27	26		4	4		0	0	
LABOR CLASS TOTAL	((4))	(4)	4	(35)	(35)	31	((53))	((52))	40	(8)	(8)	8	(0)	0	0
ALL CLASSES TOTAL	1164	1158	110	1083	1073	1000	78	77	63	266	256	239	0	0	0

PANEL A-4: 1886-1910 FREQUENCIES; ALL MPs ELECTED FIRST TIME AND SITTING

OCCUPATIONS	CONSERVATIVES			LIBERALS			LABOR			IRISH NATIONALISTS			OTHERS		
	A	B	C	A	B	C	A	B	C	A	B	C	A	B	C
Medical	5			10			2			6			0		
Education	10			22			1			8			0		
Newspapers	23			46			8			19			0		
Miscellaneous Professions	8			12			1			1			0		
Professions Group Subtotal	(46)	44		(90)	86		(12)	12		(34)	30		(0)	0	
Merchants	29			68			5			22			0		
Retail & Bus.Services	11			6			2			4			0		
Sales & Agency	3			7			0			4			0		
Trade & Commerce Group Subtotal	(43)	43		(81)	80		(7)	7		(30)	27		(0)	0	
Miscellaneous Mfg.	46			75			9			6			0		
Engineering & Construction	15			13			4			3			0		
Brewers & Distillers	10			7			1			1			0		
Manufacturing Group Subtotal	(71)	70		(95)	95		(14)	14		(10)	10		(0)	0	
Marine, Transport, etc.	13			13			0			2			0		
Management	1			0			1			0			0		
Agriculture	5			5			0			22			0		
Mining	11			12			0			2			0		
Business Unspecified	31			31			1			4			0		
Misc. Business Group Subtotal	(61)	58		(61)	61		(2)	2		(30)	30		(0)	0	
BUSINESS CLASS TOTAL	((221))	(215)	197	((327))	(322)	292	((35))	(35)	31	((104))	(97)	88	((0))	(0)	0
Finance	25	25		16	16		2	2		2	2		0	0	
Peers & Gents	165	165		92	92		7	7		20	20		0	0	
Military	145	145		36	36		0	0		3	3		0	0	
Civil Service	28	28		21	21		5	5		3	3		0	0	
Clergy	0			10	10		0			0			0		
ELITES CLASS TOTAL	((363))	(363)	353	((175))	(175)	172	((14))	(14)	14	((28))	(28)	28	((0))	(0)	0
Barristers	170	170		131	133		5	5		18	18		0	0	
Solicitors	22	22		42	40		1	1		11	11		0	0	
LEGAL CLASS TOTAL	((192))	(192)	189	((173))	(173)	169	((6))	(6)	6	((29))	(29)	29	((0))	(0)	0
Labor Leaders	2	2		7	7		26	26		4	4		0	0	
Laborers	2	2		9	9		27	26		2	2		0	0	
LABOR CLASS TOTAL	((4))	(4)	4	((16))	(16)	13	((53))	(52)	40	((6))	(6)	6	((0))	(0)	0
ALL CLASSES TOTAL	780	774	743	658	653	616	78	77	63	167	160	151	0	0	0

PANEL 8.1: ALL-YEARS' PERCENTAGES

OCCUPATIONS	CONSERVATIVES			LIBERALS			LABOR			IRISH NATIONALISTS			OTHERS		
	A	B	C	A	B	C	A	B	C	A	B	C	A	B	C
Medical	0.4			1.4			2.6			3.6			0.0		
Education	0.7			2.4			1.3			3.6			0.0		
Newspapers	1.7			4.0			1.7			14.7			0.0		
Miscellaneous Professions	0.6			0.9			0.0			0.7			0.0		
Professions Group Subtotal	(3.5)	3.4		(8.7)	8.5		(11.6)	11.7		(22.6)	21.9		(0.0)	0.0	
Merchants	4.2			10.4			1.3			12.5			0.0		
Retail & Business Services	0.9			0.7			0.0			3.6			0.0		
Sales & Agency	0.6			0.9			0.0			2.5			0.0		
Trade & Commerce Group Subtotal	(5.6)	5.6		(12.0)	11.8		(1.3)	1.3		(18.6)	17.1		(0.0)	0.0	
Miscellaneous Manufacturing	4.8			10.5			6.4			2.9			0.0		
Engineering & Construction	1.4			1.8			5.1			1.8			0.0		
Brewers & Distillers	1.6			1.3			0.0			0.7			0.0		
Manufacturing Group Subtotal	(7.7)	7.7		(13.6)	13.1		(11.5)	11.7		(5.4)	5.6		(0.0)	0.0	
Marine, Transport, etc.	1.7			1.4			0.0			0.7			0.0		
Management	0.1			0.1			0.0			0.4			0.0		
Agriculture	0.3			0.7			0.0			10.0			0.0		
Mining	1.0			1.8			0.0			0.7			0.0		
Business Unspecified	2.1			2.3			0.0			1.8			0.0		
Misc. Business Group Subtotal	(5.2)	5.1		(6.2)	6.3		(0.0)	0.0		(13.6)	14.1		(0.0)	0.0	
BUSINESS CLASS TOTAL	((22.0))	(21.7)	20.1	((40.5))	(39.7)	36.8	((24.4))	(24.7)	27.0	((60.2))	(58.7)	56.4	((0.0))	(0.0)	0.0
Finance	3.5	3.5		2.2	2.3		0.0	0.0		0.7	0.7		0.0	0.0	
Peers & Gents	30.4	30.5		21.0	21.1		2.6	2.6		12.6	13.0		0.0	0.0	
Military	20.4	20.5		8.2	8.3		0.0	0.0		2.1	2.2		0.0	0.0	
Civil Service	2.8	2.9		2.8	3.7		3.8	3.8		1.8	1.8		0.0	0.0	
Clergy	0.0	0.0		1.0	0.0		0.0	0.0		0.4	0.4		0.0	0.0	
ELITES CLASS TOTAL	((57.1))	(57.4)	58.4	((35.2))	(35.4)	37.4	((6.4))	(6.4)	7.9	((17.6))	(18.2)	19.4	((0.0))	(0.0)	0.0
Barristers	18.5	18.6		19.3	19.6		1.3	1.3		11.8	12.3		100.0	100.0	100.0
Solicitors	2.2	2.1		3.4	3.3		0.0	0.0		7.2	7.4		0.0	0.0	
LEGAL CLASS TOTAL	((20.7))	(20.7)	21.3	((22.7))	(22.9)	24.0	((1.3))	(1.3)	1.6	((19.0))	(19.7)	20.6	((100.0))	(100.0)	100.0
Labor Leaders	0.1	0.1		0.5	0.5		33.3	33.8		1.4	1.5		0.0	0.0	
Laborers	0.1	0.1		1.0	1.5		34.6	33.8		1.8	1.9		0.0	0.0	
LABOR CLASS TOTAL	((0.2))	(0.2)	0.2	((1.5))	(2.0)	1.9	((67.9))	(67.6)	63.5	((3.2))	(3.4)	3.6	((0.0))	(0.0)	0.0
ALL CLASSES TOTAL	100.0	100.0	100.0	99.9	100.0	100.1	100.0	100.0	100.0	100.1	100.0	100.0	100.0	100.0	100.0

253

APPENDIX 9.6 (Continued)

PANEL B-2: 1859-1885 PERCENTS; ALL MPs ELECTED BEFORE 12/85 AND SITTING

OCCUPATIONS	CONSERVATIVES A	B	C	LIBERALS A	B	C	LABOR A	B	C	IRISH NATIONALISTS A	B	C	OTHERS A	B	C
Medical	0.3			1.4			0.0			3.6			0.0		
Education	0.3			1.9			0.0			1.8			0.0		
Newspapers	0.9			2.6			0.0			19.6			0.0		
Miscellaneous Professions	0.3			0.5			0.0			0.9			0.0		
Professions Group Subtotal	(1.8)	1.8		(6.4)	6.3		(0.0)	0.0		(25.9)			(0.0)	0.0	
Merchants	4.5			10.4			0.0			11.6			0.0		
Retail & Business Services	0.5			0.6			0.0			5.3			0.0		
Sales & Agency	0.7			0.9			0.0			2.7			0.0		
Trade & Commerce Group Subtotal	(5.7)	5.6		(11.9)	11.9		(0.0)	0.0		(19.6)			(0.0)	0.0	
Miscellaneous Manufacturing	4.0			10.2			0.0			1.8			0.0		
Engineering & Construction	1.1			1.6			0.0			1.8			0.0		
Brewers & Distillers	1.7			1.0			0.0			0.9			0.0		
Manufacturing Group Subtotal	(6.8)	6.8		(12.8)	12.7		(0.0)	0.0		(4.5)	4.6		(0.0)	0.0	
Marine, Transport, etc.	1.6			1.2			0.0			0.0			0.0		
Management	0.1			0.0			0.0			0.9			0.0		
Agriculture	0.1			0.7			0.0			5.3			0.0		
Mining	0.8			1.8			0.0			0.0			0.0		
Business Unspecified	0.8			1.1			0.0			0.9			0.0		
Misc. Business Group Subtotal	(3.4)	3.4		(4.8)	4.8		(0.0)	0.0		(7.1)	7.3		(0.0)	(0.0)	
BUSINESS CLASS TOTAL	((17.7))	(17.6)	15.8	((35.9))	(35.7)	32.1	((0.0))	(0.0)	44.4	((57.1))	(56.1)	53.5	((0.0))	(0.0)	
Finance	3.7	3.7		2.2	2.2		0.0	0.0		0.0	0.0		0.0	0.0	
Peers & Gents	36.6	36.7		25.2	25.3		0.0	0.0		13.4	13.8		0.0	0.0	
Military	21.7	21.7		9.8	9.9		0.0	0.0		2.7	2.8		0.0	0.0	
Civil Service	2.3	2.3		2.7	3.5		0.0	0.0		1.8	2.7		0.0	0.0	
Clergy	0.0			0.7			0.0			0.9			0.0		0.0
ELITES CLASS TOTAL	((64.3))	(64.4)	65.8	((40.6))	(40.9)	43.3	((0.0))	(0.0)	0.0	((18.8))	(19.3)	20.8	((0.0))	0.0	
Barristers	16.2	16.4		19.9	19.7		0.0	0.0		13.4	13.8		0.0	0.0	
Solicitors	1.8	1.6		1.9	1.8		0.0	0.0		8.0	8.2		100.0	100.0	
LEGAL CLASS TOTAL	((18.0))	(18.0)	18.5	((21.8))	(21.6)	22.8	((0.0))	(0.0)	0.0	((21.4))	(22.0)	22.8	((100.0))	(100.0)	100.0
Labor Leaders	0.0	0.0		0.2	0.2		0.0	0.0		0.0	0.0		0.0	0.0	
Laborers	0.0	0.0		1.5	1.6		0.0	0.0		2.7	2.7		0.0	0.0	
LABOR CLASS TOTAL	((0.0))	(0.0)	0.0	((1.7))	(1.8)	1.8	((0.0))	(0.0)	0.0	((2.7))	(2.7)	3.0	((0.0))	(0.0)	0.0
ALL CLASSES TOTAL	100.0	100.0	100.0	100.0	100.0	100.0	0.0	0.0	0.0	100.0	100.0	100.1	100.0	100.0	100.0

PANEL B-3: 1886-1910 PERCENTS; ALL MPs SITTING

OCCUPATIONS	CONSERVATIVES A	B	C	LIBERALS A	B	C	LABOR A	B	C	IRISH NATIONALISTS A	B	C	OTHERS A	B	C
Medical	0.7			1.7			2.6			3.8			0.0		
Education	1.2			3.5			1.3			3.8			0.0		
Newspapers	2.6			5.4			7.7			14.7			0.0		
Miscellaneous Professions	1.0			1.3			0.0			0.8			0.0		
Professions Group Subtotal	(5.4)	5.3		(11.9)	11.5		(11.6)	11.7		(22.9)	22.3		(0.0)	(0.0)	0.0
Merchants	3.7			10.0			1.3			12.8			0.0		
Retail & Business Services	1.3			0.9			0.0			3.8			0.0		
Sales & Agency	0.7			0.9			0.0			2.6			0.0		
Trade & Commerce Group Subtotal	(5.7)	5.7		(11.8)	11.7		(1.3)	1.3		(19.2)	17.6		(0.0)	(0.0)	0.0
Miscellaneous Manufacturing	5.6			11.5			6.4			2.6			0.0		
Engineering & Construction	1.6			1.9			5.1			1.9			0.0		
Brewers & Distillers	1.7			0.9			0.0			0.8			0.0		
Manufacturing Group Subtotal	(8.9)	8.9		(14.3)	14.4		(11.5)	11.6		(5.3)	5.5		(0.0)	(0.0)	0.0
Marine, Transport, etc.	1.8			1.7			0.0			0.8			0.0		
Management	0.1			0.0			0.0			0.4			0.0		
Agriculture	0.4			0.8			0.0			10.5			0.0		
Mining	1.6			2.2			0.0			0.8			0.0		
Business Unspecified	3.4			3.6			0.0			1.9			0.0		
Misc. Business Group Subtotal	(7.2)	6.7		(8.3)	8.4		(0.0)	(0.0)		(14.3)	14.8		(0.0)	(0.0)	0.0
BUSINESS CLASS TOTAL	((27.2))	(26.9)	25.4	((46.3))	(46.0)	43.3	((24.4))	(24.6)	27.0	((61.7))	(60.2)	57.7	((0.0))	(0.0)	0.0
Finance	3.9	3.9		2.3	2.3		0.8	0.8		0.8	0.8		0.0	0.0	
Peers & Gents	22.6	22.7		14.8	14.9		2.6	2.6		12.4	12.9		0.0	0.0	
Military	17.7	17.8		5.0	5.0		0.0	0.0		1.9	2.0		0.0	0.0	
Civil Service	3.7	3.7		2.9	4.4		3.8	3.9		1.9	2.0		0.0	0.0	
Clergy	0.0			1.5			0.0	0.0		0.0			0.0		
ELITES CLASS TOTAL	((47.9))	(48.1)	48.8	((26.5))	(26.6)	28.3	((6.4))	(6.5)	7.9	((16.9))	(17.6)	18.8	((0.0))	(0.0)	0.0
Barristers	22.0	22.1		19.2	19.7		1.3	1.3		11.3	11.7		0.0	0.0	
Solicitors	2.6	2.6		4.8	4.5		0.0			7.1	7.4		0.0	0.0	
LEGAL CLASS TOTAL	((24.6))	(24.7)	25.4	((24.0))	(24.2)	25.3	((1.3))	(1.3)	1.6	((18.4))	(19.1)	20.1	((0.0))	(0.0)	0.0
Labor Leaders	0.2	0.2		0.7			33.3	33.8		1.5	1.6		0.0		
Laborers	0.2	0.2		2.5			34.6	33.8		1.5	1.6		0.0		
LABOR CLASS TOTAL	((0.3))	(0.4)	0.4	((3.2))	(3.2)	3.1	((67.9))	(67.6)	63.5	((3.0))	(3.1)	3.4	((0.0))	(0.0)	0.0
ALL CLASSES TOTAL	100.0	100.0	100.0	100.0	100.0	100.0	100.0	100.0	100.0	100.0	100.0	100.0			0.0

APPENDIX 9.6 (Continued)

PANEL B-4: 1886-1910 PERCENTAGES: ALL MPs ELECTED FIRST TIME AND SITTING

OCCUPATIONS	CONSERVATIVES			LIBERALS			LABOR			IRISH NATIONALISTS			OTHERS		
	A	B	C	A	B	C	A	B	C	A	B	C	A	B	C
Medical	0.6			1.3			2.6			3.6			0.0		
Education	1.3			3.2			1.3			4.8			0.0		
Newspapers	3.0			6.7			7.7			11.4			0.0		
Miscellaneous Professions	1.0			1.9			0.0			0.6			0.0		
Professions Group Subtotal	(5.9)	5.7		(13.1)	12.5		(11.6)	11.7		(20.4)	18.8			0.0	
Merchants	3.7			9.8			1.3			13.2			0.0		
Retail & Business Services	1.4			0.9			0.0			2.4			0.0		
Sales & Agency	0.4			1.0			0.0			2.4			0.0		
Trade & Commerce Group Subtotal	(5.5)	5.6		(11.7)	11.7		(1.3)	1.3		(18.0)	16.9			0.0	
Miscellaneous Manufacturing	5.9			10.9			4.9			3.6			0.0		
Engineering & Construction	1.9			1.9			5.7			1.8			0.0		
Brewers & Distillers	1.3			1.0			0.9			0.6			0.0		
Manufacturing Group Subtotal	(9.1)	9.0		(13.8)	13.8		(11.5)	11.6		(6.0)	6.2			0.0	
Marine, Transport, etc.	1.7			1.9			0.0			1.2			0.0		
Management	0.1			0.7			0.0			0.0			0.0		
Agriculture	0.6			1.7			0.0			13.2			0.0		
Mining	1.4			4.5			0.0			1.2			0.0		
Business Unspecified	4.0			0.0			0.0			2.4			0.0		
Misc. Business Group Subtotal	(7.8)	7.5		(8.8)	8.9		(0.0)	0.0		(18.0)	18.7			0.0	
BUSINESS CLASS TOTAL	((28.3))	((27.8))	26.5	((46.9))	((46.9))	45.2	((24.4))	((24.6))	27.0	((62.3))	((60.6))	58.3			0.0
Finance	3.2	3.2		2.3	2.3		0.0	0.0		1.2	1.2		0.0	0.0	
Peers & Gents	21.2	21.3		13.3	13.4		2.6	2.6		12.0	12.5		0.0	0.0	
Military	18.6	18.7		5.2	5.2		0.0	0.0		1.8	1.9		0.0	0.0	
Civil Service	3.6	3.6		3.0	3.1		3.8	3.9		1.8	1.9		0.0	0.0	
Clergy	0.0			1.4	1.5		0.0	0.0		0.0	0.0		0.0	0.0	
ELITES CLASS TOTAL	((46.6))	((46.9))	47.5	((25.2))	((25.5))	26.6	((6.4))	((6.5))	7.9	((16.8))	((17.5))	18.5			
Barristers	21.8	22.0		19.0	19.4		1.3	1.3		10.8	11.2		0.0	0.0	
Solicitors	2.8	2.8		6.1	5.8		0.0	0.0		6.6	6.9		0.0	0.0	
LEGAL CLASS TOTAL	((24.6))	((24.8))	25.5	((25.1))	((25.2))	26.2	((1.3))	((1.3))	1.6	((17.4))	((18.1))	19.2			
Labor Leaders	0.3	0.3		1.0	1.1		33.3	33.8		2.4	2.5		0.0	0.0	
Laborers	0.2	0.2		1.3	1.3		34.6	33.8		1.2	1.3		0.0	0.0	
LABOR CLASS TOTAL	((0.5))	((0.5))	0.5	((2.3))	((2.4))	2.0	((67.9))	((67.6))	63.5	((3.6))	((3.8))	4.0			0.0
ALL CLASSES TOTAL	100.0	100.0	100.0	100.0	100.0	100.0	100.0	100.0	100.0	100.0	100.0	100.0	0.0	0.0	0.0

APPENDIX 9.6 (Continued)

PANEL C-1: RELATIVES; SITTING PRE-1885 / SITTING POST-1885

(Percents)

OCCUPATIONS	CONSERVATIVES			LIBERALS			LABOR			IRISH NATIONALISTS			OTHERS		
	A	B	C	A	B	C	A	B	C	A	B	C	A	B	C
Medical	43			82			0			95					
Education	25			54			0			47					
Newspapers	35			48			0			133					
Miscellaneous Professions	30			38			0			113					
Professions Group Subtotal	(33)	34		(54)	55		(0)	0		(113)	119				
Merchants	122			104			0			91					
Retail & Business Services	39			67			0			139					
Sales & Agency	100			100			0			104					
Trade & Commerce Group Subtotal	(100)	98		(102)	102		(0)	0		(102)	99				
Miscellaneous Manufacturing	71			88			0			69					
Engineering & Construction	69			84			0			95					
Brewers & Distillers	100			111			0			113					
Manufacturing Group Subtotal	(76)	76		(90)	88		(0)	0		(85)	84				
Marine, Transport, etc.	89			71			0			0					
Management	100			0			0			225					
Agriculture	25			88			0			51					
Mining	50			82			0			0					
Business Unspecified	24			32			0			47					
Misc. Business Group Subtotal	(47)	51		(58)	57		(0)	0		(50)	49				
BUSINESS CLASS TOTAL	((63))	(65)	62	((78))	(78)	82	((0))	(0)	0	((93))	(93)	93			
Finance	95			96			0			0	0				
Peers & Gents	162			170			0			108	107				
Military	123			196			0			142	140				
Civil Service	62			93			0			95	135				
Clergy	0			47			0			0	0				
ELITES CLASS TOTAL	((134))	(134)	135	((153))	(154)	153	((0))	(0)	0	((111))	(110)	111			
Barristers	74			104			0			119	118				
Solicitors	69			46			0			113	111				
LEGAL CLASS TOTAL	((73))	(73)	73	((91))	(89)	90	((0))	(0)	0	((116))	(115)	113			
Labor Leaders	0			29			0			0					
Laborers	0			60			0			180	169				
LABOR CLASS TOTAL	((0))	(0)	0	((53))	(56)	58	((0))	(0)	0	((90))	(87)	88			
ALL CLASSES TOTAL	100	100	100	100	100	100	0	0	0	100	100	100			

APPENDIX 9.6 (Continued)

PANEL C-2: RELATIVES; ELECTED PRE-1885, ELECTED POST-1885

(Percents)

OCCUPATIONS	CONSERVATIVES			LIBERALS			LABOR			IRISH NATIONALISTS			OTHERS		
	A	B	C	A	B	C	A	B	C	A	B	C	A	B	C
Medical	50			93			0			100					
Education	23			54			0			38					
Newspapers	30			39			0			172					
Miscellaneous Professions	30			29			0			150					
Professions Group Subtotal	(31)	32		(49)	50		(0)	0		(127)	142				
Merchants	122			106			0			88					
Retail & Bus. Services	36			67			0			221					
Sales & Agency	175			90			0			113					
Trade & Commerce Group Subtotal	(104)	100		(102)	102		(0)	0		(109)	103				
Miscellaneous Mfg.	68			94			0			50					
Engineering & Construction	58			79			0			100					
Brewers & Distillers	131			100			0			150					
Manufacturing Group Subtotal	(75)	76		(93)	92		(0)	0		(75)	74				
Marine, Transport, etc.	94			63			0			0					
Management	100			0			0			0					
Agriculture	17			100			0			40					
Mining	57			106			0			0					
Business Unspecified	20			24			0			38					
Misc. Business Group Subtotal	(44)	45		(55)	54		(0)	0		(39)	39				
BUSINESS CLASS TOTAL	((63))	(63)	60	((77))	(76)	78	((0))	(0)	0	((92))	(92)	92			
Finance	116	116		96	96		0	0		0	0				
Peers & Gents	173	173		189	189		0	0		112	110				
Military	117	116		188	190		0	0		150	147				
Civil Service	64	59		90	113		0	0		100	142				
Clergy	0	0		50			0	0		0	0				
ELITES CLASS TOTAL	((138))	(137)	139	((161))	(160)	163	((0))	(0)	0	((112))	(110)	112			
Barristers	74	75		105	102		0	0		124	123				
Solicitors	64	57		31	33		0	0		121	119				
LEGAL CLASS TOTAL	((71))	(73)	73	((87))	(86)	87	((0))	(0)	0	((123))	(122)	119			
Labor Leaders	0	0		20	18		0	0		0	0				
Laborers	0	0		115	123		0	0		225	208				
LABOR CLASS TOTAL	((0))	(0)	0	((74))	(75)	90	((0))	(0)	0	((75))	(71)	75			
ALL CLASSES TOTAL	100	100	100	100	100	100	0	0	0	100	100	100			

COLUMN A reflects the distribution of MP occupations across 25 career categories, with each MP counted once for each career in a different category (but no more than once in any one category). Computed on this basis, the subtotals for each occupational group (excluding those which consist of only one category) are given, enclosed by a single set of parentheses.

COLUMN B contains the group subtotals, and the class totals (enclosed in a single set of parentheses) for MP occupations, counting each MP no more than once for multiple occupations held within the same group, regardless of any distinctions which are made at the category level.

COLUMN C contains class total figures only, counting each MP no more than once in any of the four classes, regardless of any distinctions made at either the group or category level.

APPENDIX 9.7

MP EDUCATION
LAST SCHOOL ATTENDED

PANEL A: TOTAL NUMBERS

	ALL YEARS						ELECTED 1860-1885						ELECTED 1886-1912					
	Cons	Lib	Lab	Nat	Other	Total	Cons	Lib	Lab	Nat	Other	Total	Cons	Lib	Lab	Nat	Other	Total
Medical School	5	14	1	5	0	25	1	9	0	3	0	13	4	5	1	2	0	12
Law School	372	394	2	33	1	802	200	262	0	15	1	478	172	132	2	18	0	324
Oxbridge, etc.	520	353	3	18	0	894	317	229	0	6	0	552	203	124	3	12	0	342
British Universities	50	89	1	20	0	160	19	47	0	9	0	75	31	42	1	11	0	85
Foreign Universities	36	38	1	6	0	81	10	14	0	1	0	25	26	24	1	5	0	56
Military Education	30	8	0	1	0	39	14	5	0	0	0	19	16	3	0	1	0	20
Major Public Schools	262	106	0	0	0	368	148	70	0	0	0	218	114	36	0	0	0	150
Other Schools	119	261	36	78	0	494	67	127	0	22	0	216	52	134	36	56	0	278
Private Education	42	82	2	14	0	140	11	19	0	5	0	35	31	63	2	9	0	105
Unknown	335	361	10	59	0	765	287	327	0	31	0	645	48	34	10	28	0	120
Total	1771	1706	56	234	1	3768	1074	1109	0	92	1	2276	697	597	56	142	0	1492

PANEL B: PERCENTAGES

	ALL YEARS						ELECTED 1860-1885						ELECTED 1886-1912					
	Cons	Lib	Lab	Nat	Other	Total	Cons	Lib	Lab	Nat	Other	Total	Cons	Lib	Lab	Nat	Other	Total
Medical School	0.3	0.8	1.8	2.1	0.0	0.7	0.1	0.8	--	3.3	0.0	0.6	0.6	0.8	1.8	1.4	--	0.8
Law School	21.0	23.1	3.6	14.1	100.0	21.3	18.6	23.6	--	16.3	100.0	21.0	24.7	22.1	3.6	12.7	--	21.7
Oxbridge, etc.	29.4	20.7	5.4	7.7	0.0	23.7	29.5	20.7	--	6.5	0.0	24.3	29.1	20.8	5.4	8.5	--	22.9
British Universities	2.8	5.2	1.8	8.6	0.0	4.2	1.8	4.2	--	9.8	0.0	3.3	4.5	7.0	1.8	7.8	--	5.7
Foreign Universities	2.0	2.2	1.8	2.6	0.0	2.1	0.9	1.3	--	1.1	0.0	1.1	3.7	4.0	1.8	3.5	--	3.8
Military Education	1.7	0.5	0.0	0.4	0.0	1.0	1.3	0.5	--	0.0	0.0	0.8	2.3	0.5	0.0	0.7	--	1.3
Major Public Schools	14.8	6.2	0.0	0.0	0.0	9.8	13.8	6.3	--	0.0	0.0	9.6	16.4	6.0	0.0	0.0	--	10.1
Other Schools	6.7	15.3	64.3	33.3	0.0	13.1	6.2	11.5	--	23.9	0.0	9.5	7.5	22.5	64.3	39.4	--	18.6
Private Education	2.4	4.8	3.6	6.0	0.0	3.7	1.0	1.7	--	5.4	0.0	1.5	4.5	10.6	3.6	6.3	--	7.1
Unknown	18.9	21.2	17.9	25.2	0.0	20.3	26.7	29.5	--	33.7	0.0	28.3	6.9	5.7	17.9	19.7	--	8.0
Total	100.0	100.0	100.0	100.0	100.0	100.0	100.0	100.0	--	100.0	100.0	100.0	100.0	100.0	100.0	100.0	--	100.0

Dash (--) = No Data

Cons: Conservative   Lab: Labor
Lib: Liberal   Nat: Irish Nationalist

MP EDUCATION

PANEL A: ALL SCHOOLS ATTENDED

	ALL YEARS						ELECTED 1860-1885						ELECTED 1886-1912					
	Cons	Lib	Lab	Nat	Other	Total	Cons	Lib	Lab	Nat	Other	Total	Cons	Lib	Lab	Nat	Other	Total
Medical School	6	22	2	9	0	39	2	16	0	5	0	23	4	6	2	4	0	16
Law School	395	416	3	38	2	854	208	275	0	18	2	503	187	141	3	20	0	351
Oxbridge, etc.	839	647	4	29	1	1520	488	429	0	11	1	929	351	218	4	18	0	591
British Universities	99	191	2	45	0	337	38	103	0	22	0	163	61	88	2	23	0	174
Foreign Universities	77	110	5	18	0	210	17	44	0	7	0	68	60	66	5	11	0	142
Military Education	76	27	0	2	0	105	29	12	0	1	0	42	47	15	0	1	0	63
Major Public Schools	860	442	1	6	0	1309	469	285	0	1	0	755	391	157	1	5	0	554
Other Schools	329	672	50	172	0	1223	145	309	0	57	0	511	184	363	50	115	0	712
Private Education	68	116	2	18	0	204	16	27	0	7	0	50	52	89	2	11	0	154
Unknown	335	361	10	59	0	765	287	327	0	31	0	645	48	34	10	28	0	120
Total	3084	3004	79	396	3	6566	1699	1827	0	160	3	3689	1385	1177	79	236	0	2877

PANEL B: PERCENT OF PARTY

	ALL YEARS						ELECTED 1860-1885						ELECTED 1886-1912					
	Cons	Lib	Lab	Nat	Other	Total	Cons	Lib	Lab	Nat	Other	Total	Cons	Lib	Lab	Nat	Other	Total
Medical School	0.2	0.7	2.5	2.3	0.0	0.6	0.1	0.9	--	--	0.0	0.6	0.3	0.5	2.5	1.7	--	0.6
Law School	12.8	13.9	3.8	9.6	66.7	13.0	12.2	15.1	--	11.3	66.7	13.6	13.5	12.0	3.8	8.5	--	12.2
Oxbridge, etc.	27.2	21.5	5.1	7.3	33.3	23.2	28.7	23.5	--	6.9	33.3	25.2	25.3	18.5	5.1	7.6	--	20.5
British Universities	3.2	6.4	2.5	11.4	0.0	5.1	2.2	5.6	--	13.8	0.0	4.4	4.4	7.5	2.5	9.8	--	6.1
Foreign Universities	2.5	3.7	6.3	4.6	0.0	3.2	1.0	2.4	--	4.4	0.0	1.8	4.3	5.6	6.3	4.7	--	4.9
Military Education	2.5	.9	0.0	0.5	0.0	1.6	1.7	0.7	--	0.6	0.0	1.1	3.4	1.3	0.0	0.4	--	2.2
Major Public Schools	27.9	14.7	1.3	1.5	0.0	19.9	27.6	15.6	--	0.6	0.0	20.5	28.2	13.3	1.3	2.1	--	19.3
Other Schools	10.7	22.4	63.3	43.4	0.0	18.6	8.5	16.9	--	35.6	0.0	13.9	13.3	30.8	63.3	48.7	--	24.8
Private Education	2.2	3.9	2.5	4.6	0.0	3.1	0.9	1.5	--	4.4	0.0	1.4	3.8	7.6	2.5	4.7	--	5.4
Unknown	10.9	12.0	12.7	14.9	0.0	11.7	16.9	17.9	--	19.4	0.0	17.5	3.5	2.9	12.7	11.9	--	4.2
Total	100.0	100.0	100.0	100.0	100.0	100.0	100.0	100.0	--	100.0	100.0	100.0	100.0	100.0	100.0	100.0	--	100.0

PANEL C: RELATIVES

	ALL YEARS		ELECTED 1860-1885	
	Cons	Lib	Cons	Lib
Medical School	33	180	100	182
Law School	90	126	111	133
Oxbridge, etc.	113	127	123	91
British Universities	50	75	72	141
Foreign Universities	23	43	37	94
Military Education	50	54	50	150
Major Public Schools	98	117	106	29
Other Schools	64	55	56	73
Private Education	24	20	26	94
Unknown	483	617	417	163

Cons: Conservative Lab: Labor
Lib: Liberal Nat: Irish Nationalist

Dash (--) = No Data

MP CLUB MEMBERSHIPS

PANEL A: NUMBER OF MPs

MEMBERSHIP	ALL YEARS						ELECTED 1860-1885						ELECTED 1886-1912					
	Cons	Lib	Lab	Nat	Other	Total	Cons	Lib	Lab	Nat	Other	Total	Cons	Lib	Lab	Nat	Other	Total
Political	2428	2356	7	89	0	4880	1388	1392	0	33	0	2813	1041	964	7	56	---	2068
Empire	274	187	0	4	0	465	180	149	0	4	0	333	94	38	0	0	---	132
Military	316	117	0	1	0	434	195	97	0	1	0	293	121	20	0	0	---	141
Business	54	38	0	2	0	94	31	28	0	1	0	60	23	10	0	1	---	34
Educational	203	165	1	1	0	370	131	136	0	0	0	267	72	29	1	1	---	103
Social	423	169	1	8	0	601	181	99	0	6	0	286	242	70	1	2	---	315
Literary	360	304	14	12	0	680	216	229	0	8	0	453	144	75	4	4	---	227
Regional	398	92	3	28	0	521	255	72	0	7	0	334	--	20	3	21	---	187
Sports & Recreation	250	132	0	13	0	395	56	24	0	3	0	83	194	108	0	10	---	312
Unclassified	41	50	6	4	0	95	14	34	0	3	0	51	27	16	0	1	---	44
No Clubs	89	185	47	138	1	460	65	140	0	53	0	259	24	45	49	85	---	201
Total	4836	3795	63	300	1	8995	2712	2400	0	119	0	5232	2124	1395	62	181	---	3763

PANEL B: PERCENT DISTRIBUTION BY PARTY

MEMBERSHIP	ALL YEARS						ELECTED 1860-1885						ELECTED 1886-1912					
	Cons	Lib	Lab	Nat	Other	Total	Cons	Lib	Lab	Nat	Other	Total	Cons	Lib	Lab	Nat	Other	Total
Political	50.21	62.08	11.11	29.67	0.00	54.25	51.18	58.00	0.00	27.73	0.00	53.77	49.01	68.53	11.29	30.94	---	54.63
Empire	5.67	4.92	0.00	1.33	0.00	5.17	6.64	6.20	0.00	3.36	0.00	6.36	4.43	2.70	0.00	0.00	---	3.51
Military	6.53	3.08	0.00	.33	0.00	4.82	7.19	4.04	0.00	.84	0.00	5.60	5.70	1.43	0.00	0.00	---	3.75
Business	1.12	1.09	0.00	.67	0.00	1.05	1.14	1.16	0.00	.84	0.00	1.15	1.08	.71	0.00	.55	---	.90
Educational	4.20	4.34	1.58	.33	0.00	4.11	4.83	5.65	0.00	0.00	0.00	5.47	3.39	2.07	1.61	.55	---	2.74
Social	8.75	4.45	1.58	2.67	0.00	6.68	6.67	4.13	0.00	5.04	0.00	8.66	11.39	5.01	6.45	1.10	---	8.37
Literary	7.44	8.01	6.34	4.00	0.00	7.56	7.96	9.54	0.00	6.72	0.00	6.38	6.78	5.37	4.83	2.21	---	6.03
Regional	8.23	2.42	4.76	9.33	0.00	5.79	9.40	3.00	0.00	5.88	0.00	1.59	6.73	1.43	3.79	11.60	---	4.97
Sports & Recreation	5.17	3.47	0.00	4.33	0.00	4.39	2.06	1.00	0.00	2.52	0.00	.97	9.13	7.74	0.00	5.52	---	8.29
Unclassified	.85	1.31	0.00	1.33	0.00	1.06	.52	1.41	0.00	2.52	0.00		1.27	1.14	0.00	.55	---	1.17
No Clubs	1.84	4.87	74.60	46.00	100.00	5.11	2.40	5.83	0.00	44.54	100.00	4.95	1.13	3.22	37.12	46.96	---	5.34
Total	53.76	42.19	.70	3.34	.01	100.00	51.83	44.87	0.00	2.27	.02	100.00	56.44	37.07	75.80	4.81	---	100.00

PANEL C: PER CAPITA BY PARTY

MEMBERSHIP	ALL YEARS						ELECTED 1860-1885						ELECTED 1886-1912					
	Cons	Lib	Lab	Nat	Other	Total	Cons	Lib	Lab	Nat	Other	Total	Cons	Lib	Lab	Nat	Other	Total
Political	1.37	1.38	.13	.38	0.0	1.30	1.3	1.26	--	.36	0.0	1.24	1.49	1.61	.13	.39	---	1.39
Empire	.15	.11	0.00	.02	0.0	.12	.17	1.3	--	.04	0.0	.15	.13	.06	.00	.00	---	.09
Military	.18	.07	0.00	.00	0.0	.12	.18	.09	--	.01	0.0	.12	.17	.03	.00	.00	---	.09
Business	.03	.02	0.00	.01	0.0	.02	.03	.03	--	.01	0.0	.03	.03	.02	.00	.01	---	.02
Educational	.11	.10	.02	.00	0.0	.16	.12	.12	--	.00	0.0	.13	.10	.05	.02	.01	---	.07
Social	.24	.10	.02	.03	0.0	.18	.17	.09	--	.07	0.0	.13	.35	.12	.07	.03	---	.21
Literary	.20	.18	.07	.05	0.0	.14	.20	.21	--	.09	0.0	.15	.21	.13	.05	.15	---	.15
Regional	.22	.05	.05	.12	0.0	.10	.24	.06	--	.08	0.0		.21	.03	.05	.07	---	.13
Sports & Recreation	.14	.08	0.00	.06	0.0	.03	.05	.02	--	.03	0.0	.04	.28	.18	.00		---	.21
Unclassified	.02	.03	0.00	.02	0.0		.01	.03	--	.03	0.0	.02	.04	.03	.00	.01	---	.03
Total	2.60	2.11	.29	.69	0.0	2.27	2.47	2.04	--	.71	0.0	2.19	3.02	2.26	.29	.67	---	2.39

Dash (--) = No Data

Cons: Conservative   Lab: Labor
Lib: Liberal   Nat: Nationalist

10 *Imperium economicum –*
in retrospect

M. K. Gandhi, an unlikely imperialist, once wrote, "Though Empires have gone and fallen, this Empire perhaps may be an exception." That opinion was based on the conviction that the British Empire was "not founded on material but on spiritual foundations."[1] The future Mahatma was no more correct than the rhetoricians who saw the Empire as the expression of Britannia's divine mission. "Wherever her [Britain's] sovereignty has gone," one writer averred, "two blades of grass have grown where one grew before. Her flag wherever it has advanced has benefited the country over which it floats; and has carried with it civilization, the Christian religion, order, justice and prosperity."[2] Other observers were not so certain. In response to Betsy Prig's comment, " ... ain't it lovely to see 'ow Britannia improved her position, since Benjy picked up the dropt threads of England's imperial tradition." Clio, less sure, in an 1878 issue of *Punch* replied: "Fine phrases and flatulent figures (sez she) are the charlatan's tools."[3]

This book is essentially about the "flatulent figures" and the often eloquent message they carried. However difficult it may be to disentangle figures and messages, it is possible to measure one aspect of the Empire: its costs and its revenue. Even Disraeli, the great avatar of Britain's conquering might, in a brief incarnation as Chancellor of the Exchequer, referred to "Those wretched colonies..." as "a mill stone around our neck."[4] A few years later, Karl Marx, an observer of a different political stripe, filed a supportive brief in the *New York Daily Tribune* in which he wondered whether "this dominion [India] does not threaten to cost quite as much as it can ever be expected to come to."[5]

For whatever reason, Empire to many Britons seemed not only politically desirable but hypnotically alluring. Disraeli, despite his earlier reservations, thundered: " ... no Minister in this country will do his duty who neglects the opportunity of reconstructing as much as possible of our colonial empire. ... "[6] So potent was the message that the ordinarily archliberal Gladstone was forced to dissemble and to protest: " ... Gentlemen, while we are opposed to imperialism we are devoted to empire."[7] While he proclaimed that "nothing will induce me to submit to these colonial annexations," he nevertheless ordered the bombardment of Alexandria and the virtual annexation of Egypt.[8] To conclude that Disraeli had suddenly discovered that Empire was costless is wrong. He merely felt that other considerations were of greater importance than cost effectiveness. Even in the Crystal Palace Speech, he admitted that: " . . . It has been proved to us that we have lost money on our colonies. It has been shown with precise, with mathematical demonstration, that there never was a jewel in the Crown of England that was so costly as the possession of India."[9]

Although not alone, Joseph Chamberlain stands out as a latter-day prophet who actually espoused the principle that the Empire should be a source of monetary profit to the home country. Not only did he believe in imperial reciprocity between Britain and the Dominions, but he urged that "we should maintain firmly and resolutely our hold over the territories we have already acquired, and we should offer freely our protection to those friendly chiefs and people who are stretching out their hands to us."[10] A decade later a cynic might have inquired which chiefs in the Transvaal and Orange Free State were "stretching out their hands."

The move toward closer colonial association and imperial federation found support on both sides of the political spectrum. Not unexpectedly, on the one side were Salisbury, Balfour, and Hicks-Beach, joined later by Joseph Chamberlain. Across the aisle they found allies not only among the Roseberys, the Milners, and the "rad imps" (the latter group included not only Gladstonian free traders of the like of Harcourt and Campbell-Bannerman but the young intellectuals – G. K. Chesterton, G. M. Trevelyan, and Gilbert Murray to cite only three), but even some "rad libs" like Asquith, Edward Grey, and Haldane. Support was widespread, but because of the intransigence of the Dominions it was never possible to discover if the idea had any substance at all.

No one can sanely argue that there were not British politicians dedicated to maintaining and expanding the Empire, nor that there were not businessmen who recognized that such policies might redound to their profit. It may well have been that both groups increased in size after the mid-1880s as increasing political and economic competition from the continental powers and the United States exacerbated the rising protectionist sentiment both in the newly competitive nations and in the Dominions. Chamberlain, himself, bought Canadian Pacific Railroad bonds and lost £50,000 in an ill-fated attempt to grow sisal in the Bahamas.[11] Nevertheless, Lenin went too far when he concluded that, "leading British bourgeois politicians fully appreciated the connection between what might be called purely economic and the political–social roots of imperialism."[12]

Few of the nineteenth-century proponents and critics of Empire thought that the enterprise was without expense. Adderley had railed against the colonies' refusal to pay their just share of expenses; and Marx doubted that the Empire would ever carry its own financial weight. Disraeli, even as he proposed further imperial expansions, acknowledged that the Empire was costly and that India was a particularly expensive undertaking. Chamberlain, although he looked at imperial expenditures as potentially profitable investments, admitted that they required money; and Hicks-Beach at the Treasury had threatened his resignation when presented with the estimated expenses of one of the Colonial Secretary's development schemes. For those, like Chamberlain, who argued that the Empire was good business for the British, imperial costs had still to be offset against private profits in any calculation of social gain: a point Marx had recognized as early as 1858. Even if the claim was only that the Empire was good for a few but not for the many, the question still remains: How much did it cost the many to enrich the few?

Both Marx and Adderley emphasized the major, but not the only, element in the British subsidy to the imperial investor. The former, in reference to India, had pointed to "the military and naval expenses made by the people of England on Indian account," and the latter, speaking of a British colony, to the exemption "in purse and person from the cost of its own defense."[13] Despite the widespread recognition of the absurdity of the situation – an appreciation that had already in 1861 led to the creation of a Parliamentary select committee – there is no evidence that circumstances were significantly better in 1914 than they had been in that earlier year. The same Canadians who, in 1862 with an American invasion army poised on their borders, had said, "the best defense for Canada is no defense at all," in 1911 argued that the Canadian Fisheries Protection Service with its one (soon to be two) armed gunboat(s) on the Great Lakes was a sufficient contribution to imperial naval defense.[14]

The failure of a long succession of governments to distribute the defense burden between home and Empire in some more equitable fashion lay rooted in history, in the law, in the bureaucratic mire, and in the pressing nature of defense requirements. The colonies with responsible government argued that they did not have to contribute, the dependent Empire said that it could not afford to pay, and hence who but the British taxpayer was left to redress the balance? An attempt to ameliorate the situation had cost Britain the thirteen American colonies, and Yorktown can never have been far from the politicians' minds. In the dependent colonies the appointed representatives of the Crown often appeared to side more with the local taxpayers than with their nominal masters in Whitehall. Even in India – a dependency that probably assumed a greater fraction of the cost of its own defense than any other – a succession of Governors General strenuously resisted London's pressure to increase the subcontinent's commitment; " . . . it is my bounden duty," Ripon wrote, "to resist to the utmost of my power the imposition of any fresh burden. . . ."[15]

Nor was the peculiar inequity in the distribution of the burden a figment in the minds of British politicians. The expenditure figures suggest that, if anything, the magnitude of the problem was understated. On average, in the late nineteenth and early twentieth centuries, the cost of British defense was about two and a half times as great as that borne by the citizens of a typical developed country and almost twice that of the French and Germans. The denizens of the colonies with responsible government meanwhile assumed a fiscal responsibility only a quarter that of the resident of a foreign developed country; and in the dependent colonies, the impost was less than one-quarter of that demanded from inhabitants of underdeveloped nations. India paid relatively more, but even its figures do not appear high if the comparison is made not with the Empire but with the rest of the world. Indian per capita expenditures were substantially more than those of either the dependent colonies or the Indian Princely States, and they were only slightly less than the levels of expenditure maintained by the colonies with responsible government. At the same time, per capita defense costs were only about half as much as those of the foreign underdeveloped countries, and by the end of the period only a third. During a comparable period, Siam, for example, paid three times as much.

The evidence indicates that Britain actually maintained two defense establishments: one for the home islands and a second for the Empire. If the British burden is allocated between home and Empire on the basis of ships and men on station, domestic expenditures are about equal to those of Germany and France, and Empire ones slightly more than those of a typical developed country. If the British had been somewhat more exploitative – so coercive that they could have forced British subjects in the Empire to assume a burden *equal* to what they would have paid had they been independent – cost reduction would have been greater than £1 per person each year – more than two percent of income and a full one-fifth of per capita savings.

Although defense was the largest single component in the total imperial subsidy, it was by no means the only one. De facto and de jure guarantees made it possible for Empire governments to borrow at rates much below those available to non–Empire nations. The gains were not spread evenly over the Empire but, given the actual level of borrowing, the differentials meant that the residents of the colonies with responsible government saved about 10 percent of their tax bill and those of the dependent Empire about one-half that amount.

The British government also provided regular administrative subsidies to the dependent colonies and a substantial additional amount of direct support on an irregular basis. At times, those latter awards were relatively small. (Newfoundland, for example, received a grant of £260 in 1906 to help offset the effects of a severe depression in the fishing industry.) At other times, however, they were not. The Gold Coast received more than £400,000 in 1900, and the Ugandan railroad cost the British taxpayer almost £9 million between 1896 and 1914.

The fact that the sun never set on the Empire may well have provided vicarious pleasure to many inhabitants of the home islands; however, the global dispersion of Dominions and colonies did present serious problems of administration and control. To help provide the links necessary to hold the Empire together, the government found it necessary to subsidize both telegraphs and steamship lines. The British, for example, paid a quarter of a million pounds to help finance a cable connection between Australia and Canada; and, even in the 1860s, Empire shipping subsidies were running over a million pounds a year.

Finally, the British government founded and underwrote the operations of the Crown Agents. This organization acted as the marketing agency for the sale of colonial securities and as the purchasing agent for colonial supplies. Acting as an effective monopolist in the market for colonial issues and as an monopsonist in the market for the supplies bought by those colonial governments, the Agents obtained very fortuitous marketing arrangements for bond issues and equally favorable prices for the goods and services destined for their colonial customers.

It is difficult to measure precisely the total cost to the British of the nondefense component of the imperial subsidy, but it appears unlikely to have been less than one-fifth of the defense subsidy and it may have been twice that. Although the actual amount of Empire investment is unknown, the best estimates indicate that it amounted on average to about £17–8 per capita in prices of 1913.[16] As has been noted, the defense subsidy alone amounted to at least 10 shillings and 10 pence per year for every British man, woman, and child and it could have been as high as 12 shillings and 10 pence, more than 20 percent of national savings. The minimum figure suggests that private Empire returns would have to have been reduced by more than 3 percent to provide a true estimate of the social returns, even if the nondefense components of the subsidy were zero. At the other extreme, assuming the larger defense figure and a very generous £.20 for the nondefense component, the adjustment would be almost 5 percent. Even the lower charge is sufficient to reduce Empire returns below levels that could have been earned at home or in the foreign sector after the mid-1880s.

The British as a whole certainly did not benefit economically from the Empire. On the other hand, individual investors did. In the Empire itself, the level of benefits depended upon whom one asked and how one calculated. For the colonies of white settlement the answer is unambiguous: They paid for little and received a great deal. In the dependent Empire the white settlers, such as there were, almost certainly gained as well. As far as the indigenous population was concerned, while they received a market basket of government commodities at truly wholesale prices, there is no evidence to suggest that, had they been given a free choice, they would have bought the particular commodities offered, even at the bargain-basement rates.

It is clear that imperial exactions placed on the British taxpayer enabled the colonists and residents of the Dominions and the dependent Empire to pay fewer taxes and to devote a substantial proportion of the taxes they did pay to a variety of projects that did not include defense. The Empire was a political system, and it should have been possible to align the pattern of colonial expenditures so as to increase the level of support for business and to guarantee that the revenues required to command those resources were charged not to those businesses but to the taxpayers at large.

The potential for government subsidization is vast, and such subsidies can take as many forms as Joseph's coat had colors. Some, involving nothing but the manipulation of political decisions, are difficult to discover even at the time and probably impossible to uncover a century later. Many subsidies, however, involve government expenditures, and for those, the government budget provides a paper trail that can be followed. It is possible to measure the impact of government policy on expenditures on law and justice (costs incurred in part at least to maintain property rights and enforce contracts), public works (the real capital component of social overhead investment), science and human capital (the nontraditional component), and direct business support.

Whether it is the total package or its individual components that is analyzed, the pattern is the same. Great Britain spent somewhat more than other developed countries, but hardly more than that nation's advanced state of development would suggest. The same is not true for the colonies whether dependent or blessed with responsible government. On average the latter group of colonies spent at levels about twice those prevailing in Britain. The former spent at rates not much different from those at home; but that figure is remarkable given the fraction of a colony's total expenditures that were involved, the relative state of development of the colonies in question, and the amounts spent by countries in the underdeveloped world.

In India, however, the record was different. The decision to finance a railroad network aside, there were few policies designed to provide support for business; and at times even the railroad expenditures appear to have been made more because of considerations of famine relief or military necessity than a desire to increase the earnings of the business sector. Not only were expenditures on all levels of business support much below those observed in the underdeveloped world, but if railroads are excluded, they were below those of the Indian Princely States as well.

In general, the colonial Empire provides strong evidence for the belief that government was attuned to the interest of business and willing to divert resources to ends that the business community would have found profitable. That behavior is, however, not necessarily evidence that the British used the political process to distort the allocation of governmental resources. Expenditures that benefited business were greatest in the colonies with responsible government, where even the British government, let alone British businessmen, had almost no influence. They were next highest in the dependent colonies, where the British did have a very substantial voice in policy making but not a total monopoly. Moreover, within that set, expenditures tended to be larger in those colonies with some local participation in political decision making and smaller in those with little or no consultation. Finally, expenditures were lowest in

India, where British influence was strongest and where there were no representative institutions at the national level.

Perhaps the explanation for this ordering lies not with the British but with the local business community. Those merchants and manufacturers may have been quite willing and able to bend the structure of government expenditures to their own benefit. If that is correct, except in India, where financial crisis and the threat of famine overrode all other considerations, they appear to have been successful. It cannot be denied, however, that the policies adopted, perhaps under local business pressure, served the interest of the British investor as well as his colonial cousin.

In the late nineteenth century the London capital market acted as a conduit for the greatest international movement of private capital in the history of the world. Nevertheless, most of the flow of funds that passed through the stock exchange was not destined for the Empire. Of the almost £5-billion total, less than 70 percent passed out of Britain and almost two-thirds of that amount went to Europe and other parts of the world not pledging fealty to the House of Hanover. The largest single recipient was the United States, but a not-insubstantial portion (more than a quarter) was directed to the underdeveloped but politically independent countries of South America. In fact these Latin countries received substantially more than all the funds destined for the dependent Empire. Although the Empire as a whole absorbed nearly a quarter of the total, two-thirds of that amount went to the colonies of white settlement; and those colonies were, at least in matters economic, not likely objects for British exploitation. They were colonies that, since the middle of the nineteenth century, had begun pursuing a strongly protectionist policy – one aimed explicitly at British manufacturers and traders.

If Britain itself absorbed 30 percent of the total, if the nations over which the British exercised no political control drew an additional 45, and if the colonies over which its control was, at best, limited took an additional 16: Less than £1 in 10 remained for all of India and for colonies such as St. Kitts, the Bahamas, the Falklands, the Gold Coast, Malta, and Hong Kong, which had few representative institutions. Certainly, the amount of finance that was directed to the dependent Empire was substantial enough (it averaged more than £8 million per year) to ensure that some Englishmen could have become rich, but it appears doubtful (unless the "exploitative" profit rate was higher than even Lenin dreamed) that the total was sufficient – even if there were no offsetting social costs – to make the "average" British subject substantially better off.

Perhaps profits were very high, or possibly the dependent Empire was good business for the few but not for the many. In either case, financial flows were not evenly distributed across the world or across the industrial map. Of the £415 million received by India and the colonies of the dependent Empire, Asia received 65 percent (India alone, 56) and Africa an additional 19 percent. In India that investment was largely associated with railroads and, to a lesser extent, government finance. In the dependent colonies the relative concentrations of British investment were in the agriculture and extractive industries, in finance (the financial, land, and development companies) and in government. Just how profitable were these investments?

Although the measure of "the" rate of return is only approximate, the general outlines confirm the individual industry comparisons. Questions of timing and level are still open, but it would take a massive reversal of the evidence to alter the general conclusions. If the standard is domestic earnings, it appears that in the years before 1885 Empire returns were substantially higher. While some of the observed differences may reflect the small size of the sample and the mix of firms included in the study, it would be very difficult to argue that colonial profits were any less than domestic, and they were almost certainly substantially higher. In the case of the returns on manufacturing and commercial investments, for example, Empire returns through 1880 were one and one-quarter of domestic – and that measure is the most favorable for the home economy. Over time, the advantage eroded, and for the last half of the period Empire returns were substantially below those available at home. There was, however, some recovery in Empire earnings after the turn of the century, and in the last decade before the War they may well have equaled domestic.

As Marx had predicted, profits were falling; however, they were declining more rapidly in the Empire than in the foreign sector and faster there than in the domestic. It is, of course, not the trend but the home–Empire differential that is important for the Hobson–Lenin argument. In the same way that it is difficult to deny that the Empire was *relatively* very profitable in the earlier years, it is even more difficult to conclude that profits in the colonies were substantially above those at home in the later ones.

The explanation of the trends in relative returns can in large measure be traced to two phenomena. First, early entrants into new markets and regions had distinct advantages. To the extent that property rights were well defined and enforced they may have been able to acquire the potentially most profitable lands at bargain prices. Secondly, they frequently had an initial monopoly position that allowed them to exploit those new opportunities until, in Schumpeter's terms, the "herd like movement" of the imitative entrepreneurs undercut their profits. Evidence of these initial advantages can be found in the history of colonial agriculture and mines and even among the trading companies operating in the African wilderness. The Assam Tea Company, for example, had, because of the location of its plantations, a long, fairly profitable history despite growing world competition. Similarly, the records of the African traders are full of references to attempts to reestablish their earlier monopoly through the negotiation of an almost endless series of formal cartels. Their success was never great, and each new attempt was launched with a lament for the "good old days" before increased competition had blunted the position of the original traders. The Board of Directors of the African Association bemoaned the lack of cooperation between traders and asserted "the powers granted to the Royal Niger Co. will give them a virtual monopoly" at the expense of British enterprise in east Africa; but the company nonetheless continued its efforts to induce collaboration.[17] A few years later, however, the directors were able to report that, "In cooperation with other firms, efforts have been made, attended with partial success, to induce those interested in the trade of the Niger Protectorate District to unite in measures for placing prices of produce upon a profitable basis."[18]

Nor was initial advantage and later erosion limited to the Empire. The Liebig Extract of Meat Company found its profits falling because of competition from George Johnston's Bovril. In the United Kingdom, Peek-Frean learned that, although they could produce an acceptable chocolate biscuit before their competitors and although they were very adept at discovering how to tap the new mass consumer market, other firms could imitate their recipes and repeat their organizational innovations. While profits rooted in property rights could last as long as the political structure was undisturbed, the record indicates that in the absence of some legally enforced institutional arrangement, a firm could expect less than a decade of extra profits from its initial monopolistic advantage.

The relative trends can in part be explained by the surprising energy displayed by the domestic economy; a vigor many historians have overlooked. Kuznets long ago pointed out that no single industry can continue to grow indefinitely; and, if the British economy had remained wedded to traditional lines, it probably would have declined as rapidly as its critics charge it did. Instead, however, new industries emerged, and the post–1880s prosperity was led by firms serving the mass consumer market in Britain. They included Peek-Frean in the domestic sector, Liebig's in the foreign, and the Assam Tea Company in the Empire. Of course there were more of these firms at home than abroad.

If domestic performance is the yardstick, and the comparison focused on the years for which comparable data is available, the most profitable Empire activities were financial trusts, the agricultural and extractive industries, and waterworks. If the focus is narrowed to the present century, that list is modified by the addition of trams and omnibuses and gas and light companies and by the disappearance of financial trusts – they had become hardly more profitable than their domestic competitors.

The contrast between the initial profits of Empire public utilities and those observed later may have been associated with problems inherent in establishing a new service – it takes time to dig gas mains and lay tram tracks.[19] However, relative Empire profits rose in large measure because of increasing regulation and mounting intertechnological competition at home. In the Empire, home electricity arrived still later than in England, and even at the end of the period trams still faced little competition from subways or gasoline-powered omnibuses.

No matter what time period is chosen, after the mid-1880s, high Empire returns, to the extent that they existed at all, tended to be concentrated in the agricultural and extractive and in the public utility sectors. The great surprise is the relatively poor performance of colonial railroads. It may be that in the Empire – as in the United States – expansion into underdeveloped regions meant a long period of low profits. It has been argued that the American railroad network went bankrupt three times in the nineteenth century; and, even if that is something of an overstatement, it was a long time before those roads began to show regular profits.[20] In the Empire, railroad earnings had, by the present century, almost equaled the profits earned at home; however, both were still well below those available abroad.

Still, railroads aside – and for some Indian railroads the government did guarantee returns to their bond, if not their equity holders – the pattern of Empire profits is intriguing. Commercial and industrial returns were high in absolute terms, but after the mid-1880s, no higher than domestic. The most profitable Empire activities were those that depended, at least to some extent, on the political structure. In the case of the agricultural and extractive sector, profits were rooted in well-defined and enforced property rights; and British firms operating in the foreign sector frequently found those rights to be less than secure. The president of the Lautaro Nitrate Company, for example, voiced a common complaint when he said:

> Our lawsuits . . . are again the subject of a part of the Report. . . .
> I regret to say that our last year's expectation have proved correct,
> viz. during the year there has been no abatement in the tax against
> the Company. Incited . . . by the increased value of the nitrate
> grounds . . . persons of influence in the country, tempted by the
> profits to be realised on shares of new undertakings, have thrown
> themselves in with the parties who tried to upset our titles. . . . [21]

The experience of Antony Gibbs and numerous other companies operating in South America was similar. In the case of public utilities, firms that were natural or quasinatural monopolies, it was their skill in acquiring and retaining charters on favorable terms that made it possible to earn any profits at all. That ability was, again, not totally divorced from the vagaries of local politics. It is only necessary to glance at the history of the Rosario Gas Company to understand how difficult it must have been to maintain that quasimonopoly position in countries with a non–British legal and political environment.

While some stockholders clearly benefited from the imperial connection, the evidence indicates that probably at no time, and certainly not after the 1870s, were Empire profits sufficient to underwrite *British* prosperity. However, for the shareholders in the agricultural and extractive and the public utility sectors (and perhaps others as well), where competition was blunted or enforced property rights pushed potential competitors onto inferior lands, the Empire was important, and it was profitable. One can readily conclude that there should have been some economic imperialists. How many and who they were is a different matter.

In 1892 Edward Weatherley, meat merchant and poulter and master of the London Fishmongers and Poulters' Company, died. At his death his estate was valued at a £156,000. The estate inventory indicated that he owned, in addition to the usual real and personal property and £98,000 in British consols, bonds of New Zealand in the Empire, and Argentina, Brazil, Chile, China, Egypt, Greece, Hungary, the Ottoman Empire, Russia, Spain, and Uruguay outside. In addition, it listed issues of British local authorities in Billingsborough, Hounslow, Chingford, and Birchington, of Quebec City and Ottawa in Canada, of Wellington and New Plymouth in New Zealand, and of Santa Fe in Argentina. Also included were railroad securities from the Cordoba Central, the Great Indian Penninsula, the Quebec Latre de John, the Royal Trans Africa, the Russian Consolidated, the Scinde Punjab and Delhi, and the Temiscanta. There were also shares of the Brentford Gas, the London General Omnibus, the London & Provincial and the London Joint Stock Banks, and the Scottish Widows' Fund in Britain, and the Daira Sanieh Corporation, the Oceania and Transvaal Land Companies, and the East India Tramway, overseas.

It is difficult to determine how typical a middle-class investor Weatherley was. Suffice to say, by the turn of the century the habit of investing in symbolic capital had become deeply rooted in both the upper and middle classes, and, in response to this potential demand, paper securities streamed forth from firms and governments eager for finance. The opportunities, or at least the alternatives, were enormous. A saver could choose between shipbuilding in Glasgow, coal mining in Wales, aluminum manufacture in Canada, diamond mining in the Cape, oil exploration in California, railroad transport in China, the ground-nuts trade in West Africa, or cotton spinning in Russia. Those shares might have ended up in the hands of a small poultry merchant, a great London trader, a railroad contractor, or a cousin to the Queen. They could have been held in rural Rutland, in Aberdeen, in Manchester, in the City, or in Chelsea. Wentworth Blackett Beaumont, first Baron Beaumont, was in background and social status significantly removed from the world of Edward Weatherley. He died leaving an estate worth £3,189,144, yet the diversity of his holdings was less than Weatherly's, although his portfolio included the Union Pacific Railway, the Atchison Topeka and Santa Fe, the Bank of England, the Great Western Railroad, the Cordoba Central Railway, and the Southern Pacific Railway. The question still remains, however: Did members of various occupational and social classes and the residents of different parts of the United Kingdom display similar tastes for home, foreign, and Empire? What can be said about the demonstrated investment proclivity of those groups that together composed the British investing public?

A separation of investors into businessmen and elites (peers, gentlemen, financiers, and the like) indicates that, place of residence aside, businessmen were less likely to invest in foreign securities than were their elite counterparts. Moreover, they were *far* less inclined to invest in Empire than foreign enterprise; and among all businessmen, only merchants displayed any significant willingness to invest beyond the seas. In the Empire the elites were most willing to invest in commercial banks; in financial, land, and development companies; in iron, coal, and steel firms; and in the public utilities. To the extent that they entrusted their resources to the Empire at all, businessmen tended to put their funds to work in the private sector – competitive and less in need of government charters or licenses – industries, in short, much less dependent on political control.

The geographic distribution of shareholder "tastes" indicates that there were two very different groups of investors: those who lived in London, and others, who made their homes in the provinces. A typical Londoner's portfolio was composed of about one-quarter domestic, one-third foreign, and two-fifths Empire shares. Outside the metropolis, the portfolio was more than one-half domestic and contained less than one-quarter each of foreign and Empire shares. Within London, those who gave the City as their address preferred Empire to domestic securities, but much preferred foreign to Empire. Beyond the Wall, however, London investors appeared largely indifferent between home and foreign issues, but displayed a very strong preference for Empire over both. The London connection was particularly well illustrated in the case of South African gold mines, and even Rhodes turned to metropolitan investors when he needed further capital.[22]

Further exploration of the "two-England" hypothesis indicates that Empire investors in London were drawn from a different socioeconomic background than were the Empire investors who lived outside the capital. While London elites do not appear to have behaved substantially differently than their provincial counterparts, London businessmen acted very differently than their confreres residing elsewhere. London merchants, manufacturers, professionals, and managers all invested far less frequently in home and far more frequently in Empire activities. On average, London businessmen were only one-fifth as likely to invest in domestic securities as those businessmen who lived in places like Sheffield or Manchester, but they were half again as inclined to put their resources to work in the Empire.

Overall, Empire investors tended to be drawn from two groups: elites, wherever they lived, and businessmen (particularly, in terms of numbers, merchants) who resided in London. The attractiveness of the Empire seemed to decline almost exponentially the farther one traveled north from the City. In terms of the socioeconomic background of its participants, the British capital market was clearly two markets, and it is from one of those segments, the segment populated by elites and London businessmen, that the most strident Empire support could have been expected to come.

Finally, to the extent that the Empire investments were less profitable than home and foreign alternatives, it would have been expected that the elites, while continuing to rally political support for the Empire, would gradually have attempted to divest themselves of those securities and to reinvest their assets in other more viable enterprises. Although the data do not permit an exact test of this hypothesis, they do allow a less precise examination. If the firm sample is split at 1890 and the two parts compared, the ratio of elite to business investors is substantially lower in the second period. The decline, however, is not related to a rise in business holdings (in fact, they fell as well), but to an increase in the Other owners – including women, children, and retirees.

Both Gladstone and Disraeli had served an apprenticeship at the Treasury, and both recognized the "power of the purse" and, more importantly, the dependence of the exchequer on the state's power to tax. For a government to be effective, it must command resources and those resources must in large measure be derived from taxes. Very early in his tenure as chancellor, Disraeli had noted: " . . . we cannot distinguish Indian from English finance ultimately: we cannot permit the Indian government to go bankrupt. I need not point out the ultimate consequence on our exchequer."[23] Later, as the leader of the Conservative opposition and faced with looming demands for increases in defense and social expenditures, he fought hard and successfully against Gladstone's plans for abolishing the income tax.[24] Gladstone also required the powers inherent in the government's ability to tax, but as a true nineteenth-century Liberal he fought to hold taxes down. "All taxation operated in the restraint of trade, and, therefore, in order to reduce prices, in order to secure full employment, it was necessary to keep taxation and public expenditure at a minimum."[25] The income tax was, he argued, particularly pernicious since, "it tempted statesmen to expansion, it tempted taxpayers to fraudulent evasions."[26] In the last decade of his life these views put him in violent opposition to Joseph Chamberlain and the others who saw in the state's power to tax the solution to the problem of financing both imperial expansion *and* increased social legislation.[27]

Despite Gladstone's protestations, England had been and continued to be the most heavily taxed nation in the world. In 1776, a large part of Britain's Empire had exploded into war over the home government's attempt to increase slightly the tax burden on the

American colonists – settlers who must have been almost the most lightly taxed group in the civilized world. In the words of one historian: "The British Americans enjoyed a lighter tax burden than any [other] people in the western world except Poland and one knows what happened to Poland."[28] The cost and outcome of the American war appears to have remained fresh in the minds of British policy makers, for there is little evidence that they ever seriously attempted to make their "new" dependent Empire pay its own way.

At home, taxes at the national level averaged just less than £2–10–0 per person, and if local imposts are added, the total reaches nearly £3–10–0. The former figure contrasts with an average of less than £1 for a typical developed country. In the Empire the colonies with responsible government (particularly those in Oceania) tended to emulate the home country. Depending on how one counts, the average tax level in those colonies lay somewhere between £1–12–10 and £2–7–7. Even the lesser figure was almost twice the level prevailing in the foreign developed sector. Moreover, three-quarters of those taxes were raised through tariffs; and while they were paid by the colonists, they were taxes aimed in the main at British manufacturers and merchants. Taxes in the dependent Empire were some 20 to 40 percent less than in the underdeveloped world, and in India they were even lower than those levied in the Princely States. In the dependent colonies the greatest proportion of tax revenue was again raised by tariffs; however, in India the Lancashire textile manufacturers were successful in minimizing, if not eliminating, those trade barriers.

If the residents of the dependent Empire spent little on taxes, the British, as we have already seen, spent a great deal. Even the citizens of the colonies with responsible government, who chose to tax themselves more heavily than they might have, were largely freed of defense costs and thus able to devote the vast bulk of their resources to more directly productive ends. In the United Kingdom, however, the real tax level increased by about two-thirds over the half-century in question, and as a fraction of per capita national income it rose by about one-sixth.[29] In England the tax structure historically had depended very heavily on consumption taxes, and it was certainly regressive. As the second half of the century wore on, however, regressivity declined as customs and excises were replaced by increases in the income and inheritance taxes. The latter sources together had produced only about one-quarter of the total when Disraeli first became prime minister but had risen to account for more than £2 in 5 by the election of 1911. Over the same period, consumption taxes had declined from more than three-fifths to less than one-half of the all imposts. Over Gladstone's protests, the income tax had "lost its terrifying character" and by the mid-1890s, again despite Gladstone's reservations, death duties had begun to bite.

Even with the very regressive tax structure of the 1860s, between three-fifths and two-thirds of British taxes were paid by the middle and upper classes. Given the increasing reliance on income and inheritance taxes, it seems reasonable to conclude that this proportion did not decline and may have risen as the century wore on. Of more direct interest, the fraction that fell on the middle class was probably close to two and a half times the amount paid by the upper class. It is hardly surprising that the Gladstonian Liberals opposed higher taxes while the upper classes found that, if the resources gained by tax increases could be used for "productive purposes," they would not only countenance but support such levies. The middle class bore far more than its share of the imperial subsidy and, as is so apparent in an enumeration of their investments, they did not share equally in its benefits. The profits of Empire accrued largely to the upper class.

When it came to the formulation and execution of official policy toward the Empire, the responsibility, of course, rested fundamentally with Parliament and particularly the House of Commons. It was a quintessentially patrician legislative body, dominated by the elite classes, business, and the professions. The members had attended the ancient universities and the major public schools and they were "club men" with a vengeance. It is this homogeneity that makes it difficult to explain individual political behavior. In general, on imperial issues Liberals deviated more from established party positions than Conservatives and university-educated Liberals were particularly anti-imperial. The safeness of a member's seat, his club memberships, his profession, his level of education, and the district from which he was elected seem to provide very little help in explaining his voting behavior. On the fundamental question of the degree to which economic self-interest affected a House member's voting behavior on imperial issues, no intimate connection appears to exist between the two, although further research may prove otherwise.

Parliament, much as any other democratic legislative body, was subject to considerable outside pressure. Individual companies, the chambers of commerce, the trade associations, and a fluctuating array of usually short-lived commercial coalitions all tried to influence the course of events. Although not usually successful in the foreign arena, in the colonies with responsible government, and in the dependent colonies, because of long-established British disinclination to interfere on behalf of private businessmen, they were more effective in the case of India – the cotton tariffs being a case in point. Tariffs in the self-governing colonies attracted considerable attention from the various pressure groups, but constitutional inhibitions and lack of Parliamentary sympathy precluded the implementation of the desired policy. Even in the dependent colonies, the Crown Agents actively sought foreign bids when they felt domestic ones were excessive.

Much, no doubt, remains to be said concerning the relationship between Empire and economics. But perhaps, when all is said and done, Cecil Rhodes came closest to summing the whole thing up when he said, not totally in jest, that imperialism was nothing more than philanthropy plus 5 percent! But philanthropy for whom? It appears that imperialism can best be viewed as a mechanism for transferring income from the middle to the upper classes. Because of the technology of the imperial machine, the process involved some transfer of those resources to the colonies; however, it is not obvious that either India or the dependent colonies would have chosen to accept that imperial subsidy had they been given the opportunity to object. The Elites and the colonies with responsible government were clear winners; the middle class, certainly, and the dependent Empire, probably, were losers. A strange kind of philanthropy – socialism for the rich, capitalism for the poor.

Notes

Chapter 1

1 See J. S. Galbraith, "The Turbulent Frontier," as a factor in British Expansion," *Comparative Studies in Society and History*, II, 2, January 1960.

2 R. Robinson and J. Gallagher, "The Imperialism of Free Trade," *Economic History Review* (Second Series, VI, No.1, 1953), 1–15.

3 Joseph M. Schumpeter (Ed.), *Imperialism, Social Classes: Two Essays* (New York: Meridian Books, 1955), 72, and David Landes, "Some thoughts on the Nature of Economic Imperialism," *Journal of Economic History* (December, 1961), 511.

4 Ronald Robinson and John Gallagher, *Africa and the Victorians* (London, 1961).

5 John A. Hobson, *Imperialism – A Study* (London, 1954), 59.

6 V. I. Lenin, *Imperialism, the Highest State of Capitalism* (New York, 1934), 30.

7 Bernard Shaw, *Plays Pleasant and Unpleasant* (New York, 1898), Vol. II, "The Man of Destiny," 334–6.

8 H. M. Stanley, *The Autobiography of Sir Henry Morton Stanley, G. C. B.* (London, 1909), 237.

9 Jack Simmons, *Livingstone and Africa* (London, 1955), 79.

10 Bentinck Papers (Nottingham University), William Astall to Bentinck, January 20, 1828.

11 The Report of the Inter-Imperial Relations Committee, Imperial Conference, 1926, cited in A. B. Keith, *Speeches and Documents on the British Dominions 1918–1931* (London, 1948), 160.

12 *Hansard*, 3rd series, Volume 176, 536–48 (February 21, 1865).

13 *Parliamentary Papers*, 1865, Volume 412.

14 *Hansard*, 3rd series, Volume 181, 194–5 (February 8, 1866).

15 Disraeli's speech at the Crystal Palace, June 24, 1872, cited in George Bennett, *The Concept of Empire, Burke to Atlee 1774–1947* (London, 1953), 258.

16 Acquired during Disraeli's governments: Basutoland, Fiji, Perak, Selangor, Sungei-Ujong, Cyprus. New territories added to the Empire under Gladstone: North Borneo Co. Territory, Egypt, British New Guinea, Somali Coast Protectorate, Niger Coast Protectorate, Northern Nigeria, Bechuanaland, British Solomon Islands, Northern and Northwestern Rhodesia, Uganda.

17 The taxonomy adopted in this book divides the Empire into four parts:

(1) Britain itself, (2) colonies with responsible government, (3) all other colonial possessions regardless of the state of constitutional development, and (4) India. The last two are sometimes referred to collectively as the dependent Empire.

18 Cited in Robert A. Huttenback, *The British Imperial Experience* (New York, 1966), 20.

19 Lord Durham's Report on the Affairs of British North America, cited in A. B. Keith, *Speeches and Documents on Colonial Policy 1763–1917* (London, 1953), 137–8.

20 Richard Kesner tells us that while virtually all the senior officials of the Treasury had attended public schools less than half of their Colonial Office counterparts had done so. On the other hand, nearly all, as was the case with the Treasury, had taken degrees at universities. In Chamberlain's time, for example, only two had not. Two had attended Woolwich Military Academy, two were from Scottish universities, thirty-one from Oxford, and thirteen from Cambridge. Richard M. Kesner, *Economic Control and Colonial Development* (Westport, CT, 1981), 64, 245, FN 41.

21 Cited in Ann M. Burton, "Treasury Control and Colonial Policy in the Late Nineteenth Century," *Public Administration*, Volume 44 (Summer, 1966), 170.

22 Robert V. Kubicek, *The Administration of Imperialism: Joseph Chamberlain at the Colonial Office* (Durham, 1963), 70.

23 Burton, "Treasury Control," 189.

24 Ibid., 191.

25 T 7/23, 3587/85, Treasury to Colonial Office, March 2, 1885.

26 T 7/23, 2374/86, Treasury to Colonial Office, February 12, 1886.

27 T 7/26, 2768/89, Treasury to Colonial Office, March 27, 1889.

28 T 7/23, 11002/89, Treasury to Colonial Office, July 14, 1889.

29 T 7/27, 15971/93, Treasury to Colonial Office, November 11, 1893.

30 T 7/23, 18236/86, Treasury to Colonial Office, December 7, 1886.

31 T 7/26, 20183/88, Treasury to Colonial Office, January 20, 1888.

32 T 7/26, 30738/88, Treasury to Colonial Office, March 2, 1888.

33 Charles Lucas to Sir Robert Herbert, 1891, cited in Brian L. Blakely, *The Colonial Office 1868–1892* (Durham, 1972), 135.

Chapter 2

1 J. A. Schumpeter, *Business Cycles: A Theoretical and Statistical Analysis of the Capitalist Process* (New York, 1939) 2 vols., Vol. I, 398, 430–1.

2 Ibid., 430–1.

3 J. S. Mill, *Principles of Political Economy* (London, Longmans Green, 1907), 739.

4 Karl Marx, *Capital: A Critique of Political Economy* (Chicago, 1909), 3 vols., Vol. III, 278–9, 300.

5 Ibid.

6 Alfred Marshall, *Memorials* (London: 1890), 415–16.
7 J. A. Hobson, *Imperialism: A Study* (Ann Arbor: 1967), 40.
8 F. Engels, *Engels on Capital* (New York, International Publishers, 1937), 117. Rosa Luxemburg, quoted in K. J. Tarbaum, *The Accumulation of Capital – An Anti-Critique*; and Nicolai Burkharin, *Imperialism and the Accumulation of Capital* (New York, 1972), 253. V. I. Lenin, *Imperialism, the Highest State of Capitalism* (New York, 1972), 253.
9 V. I. Lenin, *Imperialism, the Highest State of Capitalism* (New York, 1959), 64.
10 Lenin, *Imperialism*, 78.
11 Joseph Chamberlain, speech to the Birmingham jewelers and silversmiths quoted in *The Times*, April 1, 1895.
12 R. V. Kubicek, *Administration*, 68–91.
13 C. K. Hobson, *The Export of Capital* (London, 1919). The marchers in that parade include Alexander Cairncross, Herbert Feis, Leland Jenks, Harvey Segal, and Mathew Simon. In the late nineteenth and early twentieth centuries the "financial press" meant the *Investor's Monthly Manual*, the *Stock Exchange Official Yearbook*, and *Burdett's Official Intelligence*.
14 A 1913 pound was worth $58.35 as of January 1, 1986.
15 D. C. M. Platt contends that the figure for total British investment abroad, placed by Imlah and Paish at 46 billion pounds, is about 35 percent too high. D.C.M. Platt, *Britain's Investment Overseas on the Eve of the First World War* (London, 1986) 1.
16 Peter J. Buckley and Brian R. Roberts, *European Direct Investment in the USA before World War I* (New York: 1982), 12–13.
17 M. Edelstein, *Overseas Investment in the Age of High Imperialism* (New York, 1982), 270–87.
18 It is very difficult to determine what fraction of these loans was actually financed by the British. C. K. Hobson, for example, reports that in the case of the indemnity loan of 1872 the amount was "covered five times over by the French capitalists and seven times over by foreign subscriptions, principally from England and Germany" (*The Export of Capital* [London, 1919, 138]). Simon claims his adjustments are more accurate, but does not explain how they were made. For the entire period the ratio of intermediate to minimum, and maximum to minimum, was as follows:

	I/M	M/M
U.K.	123	123
Foreign	126	153*
Empire	121	123
RG	119	120
DG	136	146
India	119	120

*122 without 1865–74.

19 C. Lewis, "British Railway Companies and the Argentine Govern-
    ment," in D. C. M. Platt (ed.), *Business Imperialism* (Oxford, 1977), 412.
20 Carnarvon Papers, PRO 30/6, Vol. 17(6), No. 21, Carnarvon to W. H.
    Smith, March 25, 1877.
21 A correction for that political revision would raise the share of the
    foreign sector to something well in excess of one-half.
22 Lenin, *Imperialism*, 78.
23 Kimberley Papers, British Library, Add. MSS., 44224, F.137, Kimberley
    to Gladstone, May 22, 1871.
24 As noted: Many of the private issues had government guarantees. The
    history of the government guarantees of the railroads in India is well
    known; however, there was hardly a foreign railroad outside the United
    States that was not recipient of some government guarantee or subsidy.
    Some lines even within the United States were assisted in this way.
    These arrangements were not always honored; however, the perva-
    siveness of these guarantees is suggested by the fact that as late as
    1903, of the 121 non–U.S. foreign railways whose issues traded on the
    London exchange, 74 still had some official support.
25 Cited in Clark C. Spense, *British Investments and the American Mining
    Frontier 1860–1901* (Ithaca: 1958), 86. The firm was the Cassels Gold
    Extracting Company.
26 Cited in W. Turrentine Jackson, *The Enterprising Scot* (Edinburgh, 1968),
    154.
27 Ibid., 137.
28 Ibid., 154.
29 Of the total foreign railroad investment, North America accounted for
    44 percent, and South America for an additional 20 percent.
30 Typescript manuscript, "The Forty Years of the Peruvian Corporation,
    1896–1936," deposited with the records of the Peruvian Corporation at
    University College, London.
31 Ibid., 21–2.
32 That surge was attributable to the activities of Canadian telephone and
    electric utilities.

Chapter 3

1 Sir John Clapham, *An Economic History of Great Britain* (Cambridge,
   1952), II, 1.
2 Ibid., II, 39.
3 Ibid., III, 202–3.
4 Michael Edelstein, "Foreign Investment and Empire, 1860–1914," in
   McCloskey, D., and Floud, R. (eds.), *The New Economic History of Britain,
   Since 1700* (Cambridge, 1981), V2, 72–3. A. K. Cairncross, *Home and
   Foreign Investment 1870–1913* (London, 1953), 179–81. Albert Imlah, *Economic Elements in the Pax Britanica* (Cambridge, Mass., 1958).

5   Bernard Shaw and H. M. Stanley. Refer to discussion in Chapter 1.
6   D.C.M. Platt contends that the figure for total British investment abroad placed at £4 billion by Imlah and Paish is about 35 percent too high. Platt, *Britain's Investment*. If he is correct, the required return would have had to have been more than 40 percent.
7   The averages are unweighted – that is, all firms (no matter what their size) are given equal weight. A number of alternative profit measures were calculated, but differences in rates of return do not appear to have been related to the location (i.e., home, foreign, or Empire) of the firm. Adjustments to accounting assets include the exclusion of "goodwill" and a recalculation of the value of fixed investment in plant and equipment so that all balance-sheet items are expressed in the same current (as opposed to historic) values as the other balance sheet, income, and cost items.
8   The reports of these 241 firms are on deposit in the Guild Hall Library of the City of London.
9   The exchange required that firms listed provide annual information on profits and on assets and liabilities. Most firms filed the required report, although it appears that in years of particularly poor profits they tended at times to "forget." There is, however, no evidence that failure to report was associated with their location.
10 In addition, the complete records of twelve firms in the stockholder sample were also utilized. For these we have *both* sets of records (reported and actual).
11 These documents include correspondence, minute books, original ledgers, journals, and published reports.
12 Seven British railroads were included.
13 Records of the Metropolitan Tower Construction Company, Board of Directors Meeting, August 1906.
14 Annual Report for 1911 of Peek–Frean Biscuit Co.
15 Tarkwa Trading Co., General Meeting of May 7, 1908.
16 Ibid.
17 Prospectus, Liebig Extract of Meat Co., 1867.
18 Liebig Co., Annual General Meeting, 1900.
19 Ibid., Annual Meeting of 1909.
20 Antony Gibbs and Sons Records, 11041, Antony Gibbs and Co. to the Japanese Ambassador in London, November 3, 1911.
21 Ibid., E. Yamaza, Japanese Chargé D'Affairs, to Gibbs and Co., London, November 7, 1911.
22 Donald McCloskey, "Did Victorian Britain Fail?", *Economic History Review*, 2nd Series, Vol. XXIII, No. 3, December 1970.
23 The Cunard Company, Annual Meeting of the Board of Directors, 1902.
24 Ibid.
25 The Cunard Co. Annual Meeting of the Board of Directors, 1904.
26 Leslie Hannah, *Electricity Before Nationalization* (Baltimore, 1979), 177.

27 Linda and Charles Jones and Robert Greenhill, "Public Utility Companies" in D. C. M. Platt (Ed.), *Business Imperialism 1840–1930* (Oxford, 1977), 86–7.
28 It would be much preferable if each industry in the general measure were weighted by some index of its importance. While it might be possible to produce some representative set of weights for the British economy, almost nothing is known of the economic structure of the foreign and Empire sectors.

Chapter 4

1 In determining the numbers which are reported, a population-weighted figure which weighs each colony or country by its population is used throughout the book:

$$\text{PW average} = \frac{\Sigma \ (\text{Budget Item} \times \text{Population})}{\Sigma \ \text{Population}}$$

2 Because of the wide spectrum of the public–private mix in railroad ownership and the range of maturities of loans, all figures are reported net of the capital and working expenses of railroads and of debt repayment.
3 The latter category was included partly for convenience – it is sometimes very difficult to separate educational from religious expenditures – and in part because policy makers often viewed religious instruction as an integral part of the investment in human capital.
4 Per capita GNP in Australia in 1901–3 was about £53.
5 Iddesleigh Papers, Northcote to Disraeli, November 17, 1866.
6 Ibid.
7 Charles Holt, *The Role of State Government in the 19th-Century American Economy: 1820–1902* (New York, 1977), 107–11, 268–71, and 311–12. John Legler, *Regional Distribution of Federal Receipts and Expenditures in the 19th Century: A Quantitative Study*, Ph.D. Dissertation, Purdue University, 1967, 86.
8 Milner Papers, Milner to Viscount Churchill, September 8, 1902.
9 John Holt Papers, December 18, 1902.
10 John Lawrence Papers, F.90, vol. 30, no. 62, Lawrence to Wood, October 19, 1865.
11 Ibid., Lawrence to Northcote, January 18, 1868.
12 Ibid., vol. 31, no. 31, Lawrence to Cranbrook, August 31, 1866.
13 Iddesleigh Papers, 50048, Northcote to Sir A. Cotton, January 18, 1868.
14 Bulwer-Lytton Papers, E 218/3/3, Lytton to Cranbrook, June 2, 1878.
15 Devonshire Papers, Devonshire to Ripon, January 14, 1881.
16 Ripon Papers, no. 43575, viceregal minutes, July 4, 1881.
17 Curzon Papers, F.111/158, no. 2–21, Curzon to Hamilton, February 16, 1899.
18 This fact is almost certainly a reflection of the nature of the sample –

because there was some railway construction in the Princely States. In the early years, the government of India had been cool to their desires to build railways, but later, for political reasons, it in some cases actively encouraged it. Hyderabad, for example, was urged to build a state railway and to do so with British support. Even in this sample, Cochin, Rampur, and Mysore all devoted some funds to state owned railroads.

19   The U.S. statistics are from *Historical Statistics of the United States: Colonial Times to 1870* (Washington, D.C., 1975), Part II, Series Y752, 1131; and Y821, 1134. Prussian figures are from *The Stateman's Yearbook, 1913* (London, 1913), 920.

20   For early evidence of this, see John Lawrence Papers, F.90, vol. 25, no. 55, Wood to Lawrence, October 15, 1864; Mayo Papers, vol. 37, no. 289, Mayo to C. Saunders, October 10, 1869.

21   Mayo Papers, vol. 44, no. 199, Mayo to Argyll, September 1, 1871.

22   Gladstone Papers, vol. 44286, no. 253, Ripon to Gladstone, October 22, 1881. A similar opinion was expressed in Devonshire Papers, 794, Devonshire to Ripon, July 1, 1881.

23   Randolph Churchill Papers, no. 1011, memorandum of October 1885.

24   Crewe Papers, Hardinge to Crewe, February 9, 1911.

25   Davidson Papers, Davidson to Colonial Office, November 3, 1908.

26   Ripon Papers, 43567, memorandum of August 4, 1882.

27   Morley Papers, D.573–17, Folio 41, Minto to Morley, June 17, 1908.

Chapter 5

1   L. Davis and R. Huttenback, "The Cost of Empire," in R. Ransom and R. Sutch (eds.), *Explorations in the New Economic History: Essays in Honor of Douglas North* (New York: Academic Press, 1982), 44.

2   Ebenezer Devotion, "The Examiner Examined: A Letter from a Gentleman in Connecticut to his friend in London, In Answer to a Letter from a Gentleman in London to his Friend in America" (New London, CT, 1766). *Evans Collection* #10280.

3   *Hansard*, May 31, 1860. Other similar debates were held on June 28, 1860, March 5, 1861, March 4, 1862, June 27, 1864, July 25, 1864, February 21, 1865.

4   Donald C. Gordon, *The Dominion Partnership and Imperial Defense, 1870–1914* (Baltimore, 1965), 14.

5   *Hansard*, March 4, 1862.

6   Onslow Papers 173–79, Statement by the Rt. Hon. Richard Seddon on the defences of the colony, 1900.

7   CO 48/513, Treasury cutting, Cape 9123, Treasury to Colonial Office, May 27, 1886.

8   CO 48/520, Minuting by Meade addressed to Edward Wingfield, October 27, 1886.

9   Clarendon Papers, Cardwell to Granville, No. GO-C500, received 1/69.

10 CO 129/243, Treasury to Colonial Office, September 26, 1889.
11 Gregory to Colonial Office, 1891, cited in J. K. Chapman, *The Career of Arthur Hamilton Gordon, First Lord Stanmore* (Toronto, 1964), 310.
12 CO 273/163, Colonial Office to Treasury, September 18, 1889.
13 Ibid., Minuting August 17, 1889.
14 By 1900 the Chest made £700,000 available annually at 17 sites: Kesner, 167.
15 CO 267/456, War Office to Treasury, December 3, 1900.
16 CO 267/509, War Office to Colonial Office, May 27, 1908; CO 267/514, War Office to Colonial Office; CO 267/514, War Office to Colonial Office, October 25, 1909.
17 Sanderson Papers, FP 800, Salisbury to Sanderson, no date, probably sometime in 1897.
18 Ibid., Minute of September 21, 1897.
19 T.7/11, Treasury to Colonial Office, March 22, 1862.
20 Ibid., Treasury to Colonial Office, April 26, 1862.
21 Hicks-Beach Papers, Hicks-Beach to Frere, December 25, 1878.
22 Hicks-Beach Papers, Wolseley to Hicks-Beach, February 2, 1880.
23 T.7/20, Treasury to Colonial Office, September 27, 1880. T.7/21, Treasury to colonial Office, January 23, 1882.
24 Hicks-Beach Papers, Frere to Hicks-Beach, February 3, 1879.
25 Ibid., Frere to Hicks-Beach, August 26, 1879.
26 T.7/21, Treasury to Colonial Office, January 23, 1882.
27 T.7/20, Treasury to Colonial Office, January 22, 1881.
28 T.7/27, Treasury to Colonial Office, March 20, 1891.
29 CO. 48/599, Treasury to Colonial Office, January 8, 1908.
30 Lowe to Gladstone, cited in C. P. Stacey, *Canada and the British Army, 1846–1871* (New York, 1936), 125.
31 Gladstone Papers, Lyttelton to Gladstone, No. 95, July 27, 1865.
32 Newcastle Papers, Newcastle to Sir Charles Monk, Governor General of Canada, June 30, 1863.
33 Stacey, 128–9.
34 Gladstone Papers 44142, Derby to Gladstone, July 7, 1883.
35 A British presence continued at Esquimalt and Halifax, two "imperial fortresses", until Haldane's reforms of 1906–7.
36 *Hansard*, June 13, 1866.
37 T.7/20, Treasury to Colonial Office, November 30, 1880.
38 T.7/27, Treasury to Colonial Office, May 11, 1894.
39 Hicks-Beach Papers, D. 2455/PCC 8/5 Hicks-Beach to Wolseley, November 11, 1879, quoting Wolseley.
40 Ibid.
41 Selborne Papers MS 1868, 192–4, Selborne to Gladstone, April 22, 1883.
42 R. Churchill Papers, No. 2046, Stanhope to Churchill, November 22, 1886.
43 CO 209/235, Normanby to Carnarvon, April 27, 1876.

44 Gladstone Papers, 44142, No. 122, Derby to Gladstone, April 1, 1885.
45 *Hansard*, November 28, 1864, moved by Sir Stafford Northcote and passed.
46 John Lawrence Papers, Lawrence to Northcote, November 4, 1867.
47 Ibid., Lawrence to Northcote, January 2, 1868.
48 Iddesleigh Papers, Lawrence to Northcote, January 20, 1868.
49 *Hansard* (Lords), July 25, 1882, and Northbrooke Papers, C.144/2, Ripon to Hartington, July 26, 1882.
50 Northbrooke Papers, C.144/2, 43513, Gladstone to Ripon, November 21, 1881.
51 Ibid., 143523, Kimberley to Ripon, January 11, 1883.
52 Curzon Papers, Hamilton to Curzon, February 27, 1903.
53 E. A. Benians, et al., *Cambridge History of the British Empire* (Cambridge, 1959), III, 239.
54 *Hansard* (Lords), July 30, 1907. The increase took effect in 1902. Of the £240,000, Australia was to contribute £200,000 and New Zealand £40,000. The First Lord of the Admiralty, Lord Tweedmouth, placed the annual cost of the squadron at the low figure of £581,954.
55 CAB 5 (Cabinet Papers), Colonial Defence, 1909.
56 *Hansard*, February 29, 1904.
57 *Hansard* (Lords), July 30, 1907, Lord Tweedmouth.
58 CO 201/590, Jervois to Mead, December 1, 1879.
59 Chamberlain Papers, JC 9/2/1k/4, Minto to Laurier, June 19, 1899. Ibid., JC 9/2/1k/5, Laurier to Minto, July 30, 1899.
60 Ibid., Chamberlain to Fielding, April 2, 1903.
61 Ibid., Hicks-Beach to Chamberlain, no date but some time in 1901–2.
62 Hicks-Beach Papers, D. 2455/PCC/34, Hicks-Beach to Salisbury, September 13, 1901.
63 Richard Jebb, *The Imperial Conference* (London, 1911), II. 160.
64 *Hansard* (Lords), July 30, 1907, Lord Tweedmouth. Background material in cabinet S/1, Committee on Imperial Defense, Vol. I, Colonial Defence, May 1903.
65 The cost of a capital ship was £1,700,000 or more.
66 The increase occurred in 1897 for Mauritius, 1898 for the Straits, and 1900 for Hong Kong, CO 273/208, Treasury to Colonial Office and June 14, 1895, CO 129,303, Treasury to Colonial Office, T 381, Treasury to Colonial Office, March 11, 1911.
67 CO 273/391, Straits 1420, Treasury to Colonial Office, January 31, 1912.
68 K. Marx, *The New York Daily Tribune*, No. 5123, September 21, 1857; reprinted in K. Marx and F. Engels, *The First Indian War of Independence 1857–1859* (London, 1960), 86–90.
69 There were, no doubt, some economies of scale vis-à-vis, particularly, India. It probably costs less than twice as much to defend a country of two million people than it does one of half that number.
70 The estimate allocates the Mediterranean fleet to home defense but

changing it to an Empire designation does not alter the results substantially. Because of changes in naval organization, the naval allocation for the period 1893–1912 is made on the basis of the distribution in 1893.

71 Some problems are raised by the experience of World War I. This study stops in 1912. One might, therefore, argue that the colonies always recognized a finite probability that they would be called upon to contribute to a major campaign, and that the dating of the study (encompassing as it does the period when benefits were high but excluding the period of very high costs) badly distorts the cost/benefit calculation. Certainly the real costs of the First World War were substantial. Of the 867,000 Empire military dead, 726,000 were from the United Kingdom, 119,000 from the colonies with responsible government, and 22,000 from India. Still, the evidence suggests that the argument is probably not correct. In the first place there was never any direct coercion by the British in raising resources (human and otherwise) from the Empire. Moreover, although there was a military draft in the United Kingdom after 1915, the Empire troops (with the exception of a few engendered by an archaic Canadian conscription bill passed toward the end of that year) were volunteers throughout. In the second place, although Britain had the power to commit the Empire to war in 1914, the speed at which the colonies with responsible government entered the Second World War – at a time when Britain had lost that power – was no less than it had been in 1914. It was clearly the close cultural rather than the political relations that brought about entry in 1914 and 1939 rather than (as with the United States) 1917 and 1941. Samuel Dumas and Ko Vedel-Petersen, *Losses of Life Caused by War* (London: Oxford Press, 1923), 135–9.

Chapter 6

1 Regarding the Sudan loan see Edward Grey Papers, FO 800/48, 88. On the Newfoundland loan see Gladstone Papers, 44227, no. 175, Kimberley to Gladstone, June 12, 1882; 44545, no. 151, Kimberley to Gladstone, June 14, 1882. With reference to Barbados, Carnarvon Papers, PRO 30/6, vol. 7(3), no. 78, Carnarvon to Northcote, July 4, 1876. Vis-à-vis Jamaica, see CO143 Colonial Office to Governor, February 16, 1893.

2 Carnarvon Papers, PRO 30/6, vol. 7(3), no. 79, Northcote to Carnarvon, July 6, 1876.

3 *Hansard*, August 15, 1907.

4 CO 137/606, Treasury to Colonial Office, August 21, 1899.

5 CO 137/660, Treasury to Colonial Office, May 7, 1901.

6 Harcourt Papers, Box 483, no. 2, Harcourt to Sir Percy Girouard, Governor of the East African Protectorate, March 9, 1911.

7 Milner Papers, Box 169 (deposit 46), vol. 44, Colonial Office to Treasury, 1901.

8 Crown Agents Records, CA (17) 60, cited in Kesner, 86.

9 *Statistical Abstract for the Several Colonies and Possessions of the United Kingdom*, cited in E A. Benians, et al., *The Cambridge History of the British Empire* (Cambridge, 1959), III, 197.

10 Carnarvon Papers, PRO 30/6, vol. 7(3), no. 43, Northcote to Carnarvon, February 9, 1875.

11 A comparison of Indian and colonial issues with rates paid by U.K. local authorities indicate that there was no significant difference between the Indian and U.K. rates after 1900, but there was before that date. In the case of dependent colonies there was a significant difference before 1900 and probably one thereafter. For those colonies with responsible government there was a significant difference both before and after. In no case, however, were the differences large. They amounted in the most extreme cases to about 7/10 of 1 percent, but most were smaller. In each case responsible governments paid more than the dependent colonies, and after 1900 that difference appears to have been significant. However, the differences were about 1/7 of 1 percent in the years before 1900 and about 1/5 of 1 percent thereafter. As compared with foreign developed countries, however, the differences ran the other way and may have been as much as 3 percent before 1900 and probably about 1 percent thereafter.

12 Carnarvon Papers PRO 30/6, vol. 17(6), no. 21, Carnarvon to W. H. Smith, March 25, 1875.

13 Ibid., vol. 7(4), no. 98, Carnarvon to Northcote, January 8, 1877.

14 It should be noted that the issue date of the shares does not always conform to the date of acceptance on the Official List. In general, acceptance took a few months so that it was normal for shares issued in the last three or four months of the year to appear on the list for the following year. In the case of some foreign issues, however, the delay could be as much as a decade or more, although this was rare.

15 The levels of significance on those differences are not great in any case, but the latter may be marginally significant at levels researchers are likely to quote. It is a somewhat surprising result in light of the supposed effects of the new Colonial Stock Act, but it probably reflects the growing esteem that investors felt for the issues of Canada, Oceania, and South Africa, and underlines the importance of the act, if the dependent colonies were to retain their previous position.

16 Although it is not directly related to the question at hand it is of some interest that: (1) the consol rate was important to Empire issues, but much less so to foreign ones, (2) that rates were lower for larger than they were for smaller issues, and (3) that rates were lower for issues of longer maturities than they were for ones with shorter durations.

17 Local units appear to have had to pay more than "national" units, but the difference seems to be independent of the Empire connection.

18 Karl Marx, *New York Daily Tribune* #5243, February 9, 1858. Reprinted in *The First Indian War of Independence 1857–1859*, 124–8.

19 Calculations of the interest subsidy: (1) The amount of loans outstanding was calculated for each government class for each year by summing the issues for a number of previous years (34 for colonies with responsible government, 31 for dependent colonies, and 30 for India). Those numbers are the average maturities for the new issues on the London market 1882–1912. For the years before 1865 Indian debt was assumed to be zero. For the colonies, borrowing 1850 to 1864 was assumed to have been at the average level 1865–9. For the years before 1850 it was assumed to have been zero. (2) The rate subsidy was calculated by subtracting the implied rate differential between Empire and foreign borrowing from the regression estimates for maximum maturities. For India the subtraction was foreign underdeveloped (4.26) less India (.64); for the dependent colonies it was foreign underdeveloped (4.26) less dependent (.85); and for the colonies with responsible government it was foreign developed (2.04) less responsible (1.14). The implied rate subsidies are then: responsible government, .90; dependent colonies, 3.41; and India, 3.62 percent. (If the rate differentials implied by the average instead of the maximum maturities had been used, the figures would have been: responsible government, 3.66; dependent colonies, 4.59; and India, 2.45. This alternative would have increased the subsidies accruing to the colonies with responsible government and the dependent colonies, but reduced the Indian subsidy. Overall, the total estimate would have increased substantially – from £210,091 to £464,483 or from £.02 to £.04 per capita. (3) For each year the rate subsidy was multiplied by the estimate of the volume of loans outstanding.

20 Kesner, 34–43.

21 Gladstone Papers, 4427, Kimberley to Gladstone, June 22, 1882.

22 Kesner, 51–2.

23 Howard Robinson, *Carrying British Mail Overseas* (New York, 1964), 234–5.

24 Kesner, 122–6.

25 Ibid., 142–5.

26 Ibid., 136.

27 It should be remembered that these totals do not include implicit interest payments on capital advances nor do they reflect any payment to India or the colonies with responsible government.

28 Kesner, 34–43.

29 Sir Andrew Cohen, *British Policy in Changing Africa* (Evanston, 1959), 12.

30 Kesner, 51–2.
31 C.3073, Papers Explanatory of the Functions of the Crown Agents for the Colonies, August 1881, no. 6, Colonial Office to the Treasury, November 26, 1880.
32 C. 4473, February 1909, Report of the Committee of Enquiry into the Organization of the Crown Agents' Office, V.
33 Kesner, 61.
34 Ibid., 57.
35 House of Commons Papers, 194, June 1904, "Return showing how many Firms were invited by the Crown Agents to Tender for the Supply of each of the following Articles, etc."
36 Ibid.
37 The figures were £2,541,936 for 1904; £2,455,066 for 1909; £2,104,104 for 1910; £2,216,787 for 1911; and £2,536,844 for 1912. Parliamentary Papers (194 of 1904; Cd 5391 of 1909; Cd5774 of 1910; Cd 6279 of 1911, and Cd 6862 of 1912).
38 A. W. Abbott, *A Short History of the Crown Agents and Their Office* (London, 1952), 1–2.
39 A. W. Abbott, "The Crown Agents as an Issuing House" (unpublished), Chapter 1, 8.
40 Blakely, 94–5.
41 Milner Papers, Milner to Lyttelton, September 3, 1904.
42 Kesner, 85–6.
43 New Zealand marketed £21 million; the Cape, £13 million; Natal, £9 million; and Western Australia, more than £1 million.
44 The last issues handled by the Crown Agents were, for example, 1881 for the Cape, 1883 for New Zealand, and 1902 for Natal. See Crown Agents' Papers.
45 F. Lavington, *The English Capital Market* (London: 1921), 197.
46 Ibid., 199.
47 Records of the Crown Agents, File 42A, Malaya, 1906–7.
48 Records of the Crown Agents, File A.6.
49 Ibid., File A.67, Anderson to Crewe, October 18, 1910.
50 Ibid., Crown Agents to Colonial Office, December 23, 1910.
51 Records of the Crown Agents, File A–50, Blake to Sir Matthew Nathan, February 9, 1906.
52 Ibid., A. W. Abbott, File 60, "The Crown Agents as an Issuing House."
53 Records of the Crown Agents, File A.100, 1891.
54 Ibid., Abbott, "Issuing House," File 60.
55 Ibid., Records of the Crown Agents, File A.100, 1903.
56 Cd. 4473, 1909, App. III.
57 Kesner, 85–6.
58 Figures are drawn from Parliamentary Papers LXX (1867–80), LXVIII (1870), LXXIV (1885–7), Cd. 7241, 1914 (1910–12), and CO. 442.

Chapter 7

1 Companies were placed in one of the three sectors on the basis of information in that chronicle, the original prospectuses, and the financial press. Firms were classified by industry on the basis of the classifications made by the editors of the *SEAOB*. The industries were the same as those used by the editors in the year 1903 except that no insurance firms were included. The industries are (1) commercial banks; (2) breweries and distilleries; (3) canals and docks; (4) commercial and industrial; (5) financial, land, and development; (6) financial trusts; (7) gas and light; (8) iron, coal, and steel; (9) mines; (10) railroads; (11) shipping; (12) tea and coffee; (13) telephone and telegraphs; (14) tramways and omnibuses; and (15) waterworks. The Stock Exchange lists, however, include only Empire tea and coffee companies and none but foreign and Empire telephone and telegraph companies and waterworks. Moreover, no United Kingdom (domestic) railroads were included in the sample.

2 Initially all stockholders were classified into thirty-three occupational categories. The thirty-three were divided into twelve "superoccupations," and the twelve were again subdivided into the general categories business, elites, and others. In the case of multiple occupations, any occupation took precedence over deceased or retired; all but deceased and retired took precedence over "woman"; all but those three took precedence over "peers and gents"; and all but those four took precedence over MP. Thus, a baronet who was also retired and a shipbuilder was included as a shipbuilder (manufacturer). Anyone who was listed as an MP had no other classification except, perhaps, deceased, retired, or peers and gents; however, a separate listing includes the holdings of all MPs regardless of their occupations. For other joint occupations, the first listed was given precedence, but dividing the shares between occupations does not affect the results. Shares held jointly by several persons were divided equally between the occupations of the joint holders.

3 The phrase "and another" is easy, but that classification is significant only in the case of railroads.

4 Nominee holders were less common than on the Continent, and when they did exist they tended to be most often used by peers and gents, and shareholders in Empire and foreign firms.

5 In this context, the value and total value refer to the amount actually raised not the face value of the security. For each firm the percentage is calculated and then those percentages are averaged across all firms in an industry–location. Thus each firm no matter what its size carries equal weight.

6 The income (dividends plus capital gains) from a class of securities

received by an occupational group or that income as compared with the total income of the group are examples of such alternative measures. Since the focus of this study is on the effects of stock ownership on economic and political behavior, ideally one would want a measure of the importance of each class of securities to each group of holders (e.g., the amount of income [dividends plus capital gains] on Empire investments as compared with the total income earned by members of the group in question).

7   R. Dudley Baxter, *The Taxation of the United Kingdom* (London, 1869), 114.

8   A further breakdown of those figures indicates that of the total, 11 percent were from engineering and iron and steel, 12 percent from brewing and distilling, 12 percent from textile manufacturing, and 20 percent from commercial and merchant banking. D. Rubenstein, *Men of Property* (London, 1981), 61–70.

9   Rubenstein, 103.

10 The data are constructed by first calculating the home, foreign and Empire distribution of the "average stockholder." Second, the holdings of each occupational group were expressed as a fraction of that "typical" percentage; and finally, the foreign and Empire figures were compared with domestic.

$$\frac{\%\ \text{Industry–Elite}}{\%\ \text{in ''All'' Industry–Elite}} \bigg/ \frac{\%\ \text{in Industry–Business}}{\%\ \text{in ''All'' Industry–Business}}$$

11 Joseph Schumpeter, *Imperialism, Social Classes: Two Essays* (New York: Noon Day Press, 1955), 74–77.

12

$$\frac{\dfrac{\text{Value Held by Non–London Merchants in U.K.}}{\text{Total Value Held by Non–London Merchants in U.K., Foreign, and Empire}}}{\dfrac{\text{Value Held by London Merchants in U.K.}}{\text{Total Value Held by All London Merchants in U.K., Foreign and Empire}}}$$

Chapter 8

1   Although the term "middle class" has not been precisely defined in all contexts it is used here in much the same context as it is used by Hobsbawn in *Labouring Men*. While public officials and the clergy have been assigned to the elite category, the middle class includes shopkeepers, billposters, printers, bookmakers, boardinghouse keepers, insur-

ance agents, commercial travelers, and clerks. See E. J. Hobsbawn, *Labouring Men* (New York: Anchor Books, 1967), 316–17.

2 Unless otherwise noted, the data are drawn from the same sources used to analyze the composition of public expenditures (Chapter 4). The reader should approach this work with the same caveats regarding the size of the political unit.

3 The increase was from £.85 to £2.15, and from .46 to .64 of the British average.

4 Gladstone Papers, 4424, 137, Kimberley to Gladstone, May 22, 1871.

5 The Commonwealth broadened its revenue sources and the rates declined to about 62 percent.

6 Hicks-Beach Papers, D2455, PCC/3/4, Frere to Hicks-Beach, January 17, 1880.

7 Carnarvon Papers, PRO 30/6/7, 164, Carnarvon to the Chancellor of the Exchequer, October 27, 1874.

8 Milner Papers, Milner to Browne, September 18, 1904.

9 Carnarvon Papers, PRO 36/6/38 (18), 375, Wolseley to Carnarvon, August 27, 1875.

10 Gladstone Papers, 44320, 112, Hamilton Gordon to Gladstone, May 3, 1871.

11 Carnarvon Papers, PRO 30/6/41 (19), 73, W. Robinson to Carnarvon, February 14, 1875.

12 John Lawrence Papers, F.90/32A, 7, Lawrence to Cranborne, January 21, 1867.

13 Kilbracken Papers, F102/1, 95, Dawkins to Kilbracken, December 7, 1879.

14 Bulwer-Lytton Papers, (3) E.218/3/2, pp. 1034–5, Sales to Lytton, November 23, 1877.

15 Mayo Papers, 42, Mayo to Argyll, March 22, 1871.

16 John Lawrence Papers, 42, Lawrence to Northcote, July 16, 1867.

17 Bulwer-Lytton Papers, (8) E.218/3/4, pp. 394–5, Lytton to Cranbrook, September 18, 1877.

18 Randolph Churchill Papers, memo 1011, October 28, 1885.

19 Curzon Papers, F.111/162, 2–269–70, Curzon to St. John Brodrick, October 28, 1903.

20 John Lawrence Papers, F.90/31, no. 13, p. 3., Lawrence to Lord De Grey, March 20, 1860.

21 Ibid., F.90/31, Letter no. 60, Lawrence to Cranborne, December 22, 1866.

22 Gladstone Papers, 44229, 92, Kimberley to Gladstone, June 11, 1893.

23 Kilbracken Papers, F.102/5, 74, Northbrook to Kilbracken, August 19, 1894.

24 Bulwer-Lytton Papers, (2–2) E.218/514/4, p. 347, Lytton to Cranbrook, May 12, 1879.

25 Ibid., (4) E.218/3/3, p. 635, Lytton to Stanhope, September 8, 1878.

26   Iddesleigh Papers, 50023, 37, Lawrence to Northcote, March 25, 1867.
27   Mayo Papers, 34, Mayo to Argyle, February 21, 1869.
28   Bulwer-Lytton Papers, (2–1) E.218/518/1, p. 312, Lytton to Salisbury, July 22, 1876.
29   Ibid., (3) E.218/3/2, pp. 1042–3, Lytton to Sir Louis Mallet, November 30, 1877.
30   Randolph Churchill Papers, 1010, Reay to Churchill, October 29, 1885.
31   Crewe Papers, C/17, 59, Hardinge to Crewe, September 14, 1911.
32   For the rest of this chapter the specific information on tax rates is drawn from either John Noble, *The Queen's Taxes: an Inquiry into the Amount, Incidence & Economic Results, of the Taxation of the United Kingdom, Direct and Indirect* (London, 1870) or from W.M.J. Williams, *The King's Revenue being a Handbook to the Public Revenue* (London, 1908).
33   Between 1860 and 1880 there were no specific excises on beer, but there was an excise duty on malt and, given contemporary brewing methods, the tax worked out to 5 shillings, 5 pence, a 36-gallon barrel. R. Dudley Baxter, *National Income: The United Kingdom* (London: 1869), 32.
34   Figures from the Committee on National Debt and Taxation indicate that in 1913–14 the per capita consumption of beer was eight times as high for a family with an income of £50 a year than it was for a family earning £2,000. *Report of the Committee on National Debt and Taxation*, Cmd. 2800 1927, 90–2.
35   Sir Robert Peel speech of March 27, 1846; cited in John Noble, *The Queen's Taxes*, 221.
36   Iddesleigh Papers, 50016, 158, Northcote to Disraeli, January 25, 1874.
37   In 1902, the tax rate varied from a low of 2 pence to a high of 15 pence per pound.
38   This figure compares with 1,190,000 in 1913–14 and 1,262,000 in 1868 (when the exemption was only £100 as opposed to the £160 in the later years). Of those reporting, income averaged £770. J. C. Stamp, *British Incomes and Property: The Application of Official Statistics to Economic Problems* (London, 1916), 432 and 449.
39   The reader should be reminded that over the period 1860–1914 national income per head (in prices of 1900) rose from £19.4 to £43.7 [B. R. Mitchell and Phyllis Dean, *Abstract of British Historical Statistics* (Cambridge, 1962), 367–8].
40   Cromer Papers, FO 633/18, 11, Bernard Mallet to Cromer, December 10, 1907.
41   Asquith Papers, 11, 1624, Haldane to Asquith, August 9, 1908.
42   The profiles for 1903–4 can be taken as "correct" in the sense that they come from official sources. The profiles for 1863–4 and 1883–4 are produced by applying the parameters from 1903–4 to tax data for those earlier years. They are certainly less reliable, but they do appear to provide some useful insights.

43 The secondary peak occurred at an income level of £200 in 1863–4, £500 in 1883–4, and £1,000 in 1903–4.

44 The only exception to the pattern of continually declining rates beyond the secondary peak can be observed in the 1903–4 profile for half-earned, half-property income. In that instance, after some continued decline for incomes between £1,000 and £2,000, the rates edged gradually upward, and the burden on incomes over £5,000 actually exceeded that of the middle-income class.

45 Baxter, 119.

46 Leone Levi, *Wages and Earnings of the Working Class* (Shannon, Ireland, 1971) (First Edition, London, 1888), 63–5.

47 Twelve separate studies (including Baxter's) place the working class's share of income between .36 and .43 with an average value of .395. That compares very closely to Baxter's .39 estimate. The latest study (1908) puts the share at .38. See Stamp, 427.

48 Baxter, for example, divides his nonworking classes into "middle" (97 percent) and "upper" (3 percent), but his definition is income, not occupation or social standing.

49 Of the thirty-three largest British fortunes probated between 1860 and 1912, twenty-eight were businessmen. While this preponderance largely reflects the inheritance laws, it does suggest that there were many rich businessmen. W. D. Rubenstein, "The Victorian Middle Classes: Wealth, Occupation and Geography," *Economic History Review*, 2nd series, Vol. XXX, No. 4, November 1977.

50 Baxter, 36; Leon Levi, 48; and Williams, 186–7.

51 The lower figure includes only direct out-of-pocket costs (defense and imperial subsidies), the higher one encompasses estimates of the interest subsidy and the Crown Agents' contributions as well.

Chapter 9

1 Minutes of the Meetings of the Directors of the Sunderland and South Shields Water Co., February 15 and March 17, 1899.

2 Minutes of the Meetings of the Directors of Samuel Fox and Co., Ltd., August, 1896.

3 Minutes of the Annual Meetings of Shotts Iron Co., November, 1880.

4 Minutes of the Meetings of the Directors of Stavely Coal and Iron Co., April 27, 1912.

5 Minutes of the Meetings of the Directors of the Barclay Perkins Brewery, April 23, 1903.

6 Minutes of the Meetings of the Proprietors of the City and West End Properties Co., May 11, 1906.

7 Records of Antony Gibbs and Co., no. 11039, Alban Gibbs to Balfour, July 2, 1905.

8   Ibid., Hunsdon to Asquith, February 21, 1909.
9   Ibid., 1041/2, Herbert Gibbs to Steel-Maitland, October 26, 1911.
10 Ibid., 1042/1, Herbert Gibbs to Lomax, August 8, 1913.
11 Clapham, II, 145.
12 Minutes of the Meetings of the Associated Chambers of Commerce of the United Kingdom, February 21, 1877.
13 Minutes of the Meetings of the Glasgow Chamber of Commerce, December 22, 1885.
14 Minutes of the Meetings of the Liverpool Chamber of Commerce, October 31, 1903.
15 Ibid.
16 Minutes of the meetings of the Glasgow Chamber of Commerce, May 12, 1872.
17 Minutes of the meetings of the London Chamber of Commerce, May 8, 1900. Minutes of meetings of the the the Birmingham Chamber of Commerce, May 20, 1891 and October 16, 1907.
18 Lytton Papers, E.218/517/1, no. 201(a), Morley to Lytton, April 20, 1876.
19 Ibid., (5) E.218/516/4, no. 8, Cranbrook to Lytton, February 4, 1879.
20 Ibid., (6) E.218/516/4, no. 14, Cranbrook to Lytton, February 23, 1879.
21 Kilbracken Papers, F.107, Kilbracken to Brodrick, October 23, 1903.
22 Curzon Papers, F.111/161, no. 272, Hamilton to Curzon, August 13, 1902.
23 Elgin Papers, F.84/299, no. 12, Godley to Elgin, March 2, 1894.
24 Cross Papers, E.243/19, p. 64, Cross to Lansdowne, March 22, 1889.
25 Hardinge of Penshurst Papers, V, 927/Vc5, no. 291, Hardinge to Chirol, February 16, 1911.
26 Winfried Baumgart, *Imperialism* (New York, 1982), 130, citing Morier to Rosebery, April 22, 1886.
27 John S. Galbraith, *MacKinnon and East Africa 1878–1895* (Cambridge, 1972), 161.
28 Platt, *Business Imperialism*, 1–14.
29 Ripon Papers, Meade to Ripon, December 31, 1894.
30 Records of Antony Gibbs and Sons, Herbert Gibbs to Mallet, 1041, December 23, 1907.
31 Minutes of the Meetings of the Board of Directors of the Peruvian Corporation, December 1, 1898.
32 Ibid.
33 Cited in D. C. M. Platt, "The Imperialism of Free Trade: Some Reservations," *Economic History Review*, 2nd series, vol. XXI, no. 2, 1888.
34 D. P. M. McCarthy, "The British in the Atacama Desert," *Journal of Economic History*, vol. 35, no. 1, March 1975, 122.
35 Peter Winn, "British Informal Empire in Uruguay in the Nineteenth Century," *Past and Present*, vol. 73, November 1976, 115.
36 D. C. M. Platt, *Latin America and British Trade 1800–1914* (London, 1972), 163.

37 Nathan A. Pelcovits, *Old China Hands and the Foreign Office* (New York, 1948), *vii*.

38 Dean Britten, "British Informal Empire: The Case of China," *The Journal of Commonwealth and Comparative Politics*, vol. XIV, no. 1, March 1976.

39 David McLean, "Commerce, Finance and British Diplomatic Support in China, 1885–1886," *Economic History Review*, vol. 26, no. 3, August 1973, 464.

40 James C. Ingram, *Economic Change in Thailand, 1850–1970* (Stanford, 1971), 2.

41 Gladstone Papers, 44290, no. 176, Rosebery to Gladstone, August 26, 1893, quoted in Ian Brown, "British Financial Advisors in Siam in the Reign of King Chulalonghorn," *Modern Asian Studies*, vol. 12, no. 1, February 1978, 200.

42 Minutes of the Meetings of the Directors of the Bathurst Trading Co., June 3, 1904.

43 Records of the British Imperial East Africa Co., MacKinnon to Salisbury, December 17, 1898.

44 Ibid., Mackenzie to Smith, September 10, 1892.

45 Cited in R. Robinson and J. Gallagher, *Africa and the Victorians* (London, 1961), 221.

46 Because political control did not change and the second session was so brief, the fifth and sixth parliaments were combined for the remainder of this analysis. Although not strictly accurate, the term "session" is synonymous with "Parliament" in this chapter.

47 It must be remembered that many Parliamentary decisions were made without a division. Moreover, it was next to impossible to discover all the imperial issues hidden in supply and ways and means votes.

48 The sources used include, among others, M. Stenton (and for volumes II and III, S. Lees) *Who's Who of British Members of Parliament* (London: 1976, 1978, 1979); *Who's Who* (London, 1959–); *Who Was Who* (London, 1897–); *The Dictionary of National Biography* (Oxford, 1926); *Burke's Genealogical and Heraldic History of the Landed Gentry* (London, 1892–); *Burke's Genealogical and Heraldic History of the Peerage, Baronetage and Knightage* (London, 1907–).

49 J. E. T. Rogers, *The Economic Interpretation of History, Lectures delivered at Worcester College Hall, Oxford, 1887–8* (London, 1888), 380.

50 J. E. Cairnes, "Colonization and Colonial Government," reprinted in *Essays in Political Economy Theoretical and Applied* (London, 1873).

51 Rogers, 378–439, cited in John C. Wood, *British Economists and Empire* (New York, 1983), 59.

Chapter 10

1 M. K. Gandhi, *The Collected Works of Mahatma Gandhi* (Delhi, 1958), XII, 505.

2   David Wells, "Great Britain and the United States: Their True Relations," *North American Review*, CLXII, April, 1896.

3   *Punch*, August 17, 1878, cited in Koebner and Schmidt, *Imperialism* (Cambridge, 1965), 148.

4   Letter to Lord Malmesbury, August 13, 1852, cited in W. F. Moneypenny and G. E. Buckle, *The Life of Benjamin Disraeli, Earl of Beaconsfield* (London, 1914), IV (1868–1876), 385.

5   K. Marx and F. Engels, *The First Indian War of Independence 1857–1859* (London, 1960), 86–90, New York Daily Tribune, No. 5123, September 21, 1857.

6   Speech to the National Union, June 24, 1872, cited in Buckle, V (1868–1876), 195.

7   P. Magnus, *Gladstone, A Biography* (London, 1954), 237.

8   Ibid., 287.

9   Buckle, *Disraeli*, V, 195.

10 Speech to London Chamber of Commerce, May 14, 1888, cited in James L. Garvin, *The Life of Joseph Chamberlain* (London: 1933), II (1885–1895), 465.

11 Kubicek, 11–12.

12 V. I. Lenin, *Imperialism, the Highest Stage of Capitalism*, 78.

13 Marx and Engels, *The First Indian War*, 86–90, *New York Daily Tribune*, #5123, September 21, 1887. C. Adderley, *Hansard*, May 31, 1860.

14 Newcastle Papers, Newcastle to Sir Charles Monk, June 30, 1863 and Jebb, II, 160.

15 *Hansard (Lords)*, July 25, 1882, and Northbrooke Papers, C144/2, Ripon to Hartington, July 26, 1882.

16 The overseas capital estimates are from C. H. Feinstein, *National Income Expenditure and Output of the United Kingdom 1855–1965* (Cambridge, 1972), Table T 50. The Empire proportion is estimated by summing the Empire component of overseas finance and dividing that figure by the accumulated total of all overseas finance.

17 The African Association, Minutes of the Board of Directors, June 22, 1892.

18 Ibid., September 30, 1897.

19 The Calcutta Electric Supply Company, for example, had revenues of only £600 its first year of operation, and £2,000 the second.

20 The history of American railroads is captured in the bankruptcy statistics of the late nineteenth century. In 1872, the list included the Erie, the Kansas Pacific, the Northern Pacific, and several lesser roads; in the 1890s it involved railroads controlling 30 percent of the nation's mileage (the Burlington, the Norfolk and Western, the Santa Fe, the Frisco, the Union Pacific, the Northern Pacific, and the Georgia Central); and in the first decade of the twentieth century, the Pere Marquette, the Chicago and Eastern Illinois, the Rock Island, the Missouri Pacific,

the Kansas, Missouri and Texas, and the Frisco all sought the protection of the federal bankruptcy laws.

21 Lautaro Nitrate Co., Minutes of the Board of Directors, July 1907.
22 See Kubicek, 125.
23 Disraeli to Derby, August 31, 1852, in Moneypenny and Buckle, III (1846–53), 397–8.
24 G. E. Buckle, V (1868–1876), 272, 306–7, the election of 1874 was fought largely on that issue.
25 Magnus, 149–50
26 Ibid., 112–13.
27 Michael Barker, *Gladstone and Radicalism: The Reconstruction of Liberal Policy in Britain 1885–1914* (New York: 1975), 50, 250–1.
28 Robert R. Palmer, *The Age of Democratic Revolution: A Political History of Europe and America 1760–1800* (Princeton, 1959), 156.
29 National income figures are from Feinstein, *National Income*, Table 17.

Index